The Essential Guide to

Language, Writing, & Literature

Red Level

Editorial Director	Julie A. Schumacher
Consulting Editor	Terry Ofner
Senior Editor	Gay Russell-Dempsey
Writers	Cynthia Clampitt
	Larkin Page-Jacobs
	Carol Skinner
Photo Research	Anjanette Miner
Design	Herman | Adler
	Evanston, Illinois

2 3 4 5 6 7 RRD 13 12 11 10 09 08

Softcover ISBN 13: 978-0-7891-7080-4

Softcover ISBN 10: 0-7891-7080-9

Hardbound ISBN 13: 978-0-7569-7106-9

Hardbound ISBN 10: 0-7569-7106-3

The Essential Guide to

Language, Writing, & Literature

Red Level

Critical Readers

Lisa A. Avram
Senior Compositon
Rockford High School
Rockford, Michigan

John Cadwell
English Department Chair
New Trier High School
Winnetka, Illinois

Scott Eggerding
English Department Chair
Lyons Township High School
La Grange, Illinois

Jean B. Ellerhoff
Central Academy
Des Moines, Iowa

Victor Jaccarino
Herricks Public Schools
New Hyde Park, New York

Tunde Robinson
Plantation High School
Plantation, Florida

Anna J. Small Roseboro
Grand Valley State University
Grand Rapids, Michigan

Edie Weinthal
Pascack Valley Regional
High School
Hillsdale, New Jersey

Contents

Grammar, Usage, and Mechanics

Grammar

Chapter 1   The Parts of a Sentence 2
- The Sentence 3
- Subjects and Predicates 3
- Kinds of Sentences 9

Chapter 2   Nouns and Pronouns 10
- Nouns 11
- Pronouns and Antecendents 12
- Kinds of Pronouns 14

Chapter 3   Verbs 18
- Verbs 19
- Action Verbs 19
- Transitive and Intransitive Verbs 20
- Linking Verbs 21
- Helping Verbs 23

Chapter 4   Adjectives and Adverbs 24
- Adjectives 25
- Adverbs 29

Chapter 5   Prepositions, Conjunctions, & Interjections 32
- Prepositions 33
- Conjunctions 35
- Interjections 37

Chapter 6   Complements 38

Complements 39
Direct Objects 39
Indirect Objects 40
Predicate Nominatives 42
Predicate Adjectives 43

Chapter 7   Phrases 44

Prepositional Phrases 45
Appositives and Appositive Phrases 48

Chapter 8   Verbals and Verbal Phrases 50

Verbals 51
Participles and Participial Phrases 51
Gerunds and Gerund Phrases 55
Infinitives and Infinitive Phrases 56

Chapter 9   Clauses 58

Clauses 59
Independent Clauses 59
Subordinate Clauses 60
Sentence Structure 66

Chapter 10   Sentence Fragments and Run-ons ... 68

Sentence Fragments 69
Run-on Sentences 71

Usage

Chapter 11   Using Verbs 72

Parts of Verbs 73
Tenses of Verbs 79
Verb Conjugations 82
Active and Passive Voice 86

Chapter 12   Using Pronouns 88
The Cases of Personal Pronouns 89
Pronouns and Their Antecedents 98

Chapter 13   Subject & Verb Agreement 102
Subject and Verb Agreement 103
Common Agreement Problems 105

Chapter 14   Using Adjectives and Adverbs 114
Comparison of Adjectives and Adverbs 115
Problems with Modifiers 118

A Writer's Glossary of Usage 120

Mechanics

Chapter 15   Capitalization 130
Basic Rules of Capitalization 131
Other Uses of Capital Letters 139

Chapter 16   End Marks and Commas 142
End Marks 143
Frequently Used Commas 146
Commas That Separate 148
Commas That Enclose 151

Chapter 17   Italics and Quotation Marks 154
Italics and Underlining 155
Quotation Marks 157

Chapter 18   Other Punctuation 162
Apostrophes 163
Semicolons 168
Colons 170
Hyphens 171

Six Traits and the Writing Process

Chapter 19 Introduction to the Writing Process .. 174
Using the Writing Process 175
Prewriting 176
Drafting 185
Revising 188
Editing 191
Publishing 193

Chapter 20 The Six Traits of Good Writing 196
Ideas 197
Organization 200
Voice 203
Word Choice 204
Sentence Fluency 204
Conventions 205

Chapter 21 Developing Your Writing Style 206
Choosing Vivid Words 207
Sentence Combining 211
Creating Sentence Variety 213
Writing Concise Sentences 216

Chapter 22 Writing Well-Structured Paragraphs . 218
Paragraph Writing 219
Building Your Paragraph 221
Developing and Polishing Your Paragraph 225

Chapter 23 Writing Effective Compositions 228
Writing an Effective Composition 229
Prewriting 231
Drafting 234
Revising 237
Editing and Publishing 239

Chapter 24   Personal Writing 240

The Personal Narrative 241
Prewriting 243
Drafting 244
Revising and Editing 246

Chapter 25   Using Description 248

Writing to Describe 249
Prewriting 252
Drafting 256
Revising 257
Editing and Publishing 259

Chapter 26   Writing to Inform and Explain 260

Informative Writing 261
Prewriting 262
Drafting 271
Revising 274
Editing and Publishing 275

Chapter 27   Writing to Persuade 276

Persuasive Writing 277
Prewriting 280
Drafting 285
Revising and Editing 288

Chapter 28   Creative Writing 290

The Creative Work 291
Writing a Short Story 291
Prewriting 297
Drafting 302
Revising 303
Editing and Publishing 304
Writing a Scene for a Play 305
Writing a Poem 309

Chapter 29   Writing About Literature 312
The Literary Essay 313
Prewriting 320
Drafting 327
Revising 328
Editing and Publishing 329

Chapter 30   Writing Research Reports 330
Report Writing 331
Prewriting 332
Drafting 340
Revising 350
Editing and Publishing 351

Chapter 31   Written Communication 352
The Purpose of Written Communication 353
Writing Informal Letters 353
Writing Business Letters 357
Writing E-mail 365

Skill Building

Chapter 32   Critical Thinking 370
Thinking Skills 371
Propaganda 378

Chapter 33   Critical Reading 380
Creating Meaning 381
Before You Read 382
Skills to Use While You Read 386
Strategies to Use While You Read 394
After You Read 398

Chapter 34   Study and Test-Taking Skills 400
Learning Study Skills 401
Taking Standardized Tests 405
Taking Essay Tests 411

Chapter 35   Vocabulary Development 416

Varieties of English 417
Words That Communicate 418
Determining Word Meaning 420
Dictionary Skills 424

Chapter 36   Spelling Strategies 436

Learning Spelling Strategies 437
Spelling Patterns 438
Plurals 440
Prefixes and Suffixes 445
Words to Master 449

Chapter 37   Speaking and Listening 450

Developing Your Speaking Skills 451
Preparing Your Speech 453
Practicing Your Speech 455
Delivering Your Speech 456
Developing Your Listening Skills 456

Literature

A Guide to Literature 460

All About Authors 461
Good Reading for Young Adults 481
Famous Characters from Literature 492
Characters, Places, and Creatures from Mythology 502
Characters and Creatures from Folklore 513
A Guide to Literary Genres 517
A Glossary of Literary Terms 522

Glossary of Grammar, Composition, and Thinking Terms 527

Index 534

The Parts of a Sentence

QuickGuide

The Sentence page 3	A **sentence** expresses a complete thought, but a sentence fragment does not.
Subjects and Predicates pages 3–8	The **subject** names the person, place, thing, or idea that the sentence is about. The **predicate** tells something about the subject.
Kinds of Sentences page 9	There are four kinds of sentences: **declarative, interrogative, imperative,** and **exclamatory.**

The Sentence

A *sentence* is a group of words that expresses a complete thought. It has a subject and a predicate.

To express a complete thought, a sentence must have a subject and a predicate.

I went shopping downtown yesterday.

Kerri and I want to see that concert.

My friend Mustafa visited Egypt last summer.

A group of words that does not expresses an complete thought is called a **sentence fragment.**

went shopping downtown yesterday

want to see that concert

visited Egypt last summer

You will learn more about fragments in chapter 10.

Subjects and Predicates

The *subject* of a sentence names the person, place, thing, or idea that the sentence is about.

The *predicate* of a sentence tells something about the subject.

	Subject	Predicate
Person	Pat	swims faster than anyone else in the entire state.
Place	The park	is my favorite place in the world.
Thing	My shoes	fell off while I was riding the Ferris wheel.
Idea	Fairness	requires that we give you another chance at bat.

Complete Subjects

A **complete subject** includes all words used to identify the person, place, thing, or idea that the sentence is about.

> ## As You Write
>
> To find a complete subject, ask yourself one of these questions: *Who or what is doing something? About whom or what is the statement being made?*
>
> The birds in our backyard built a nest from my old sweater.
>
> (*Who* or *what* did something in this sentence? *The birds in our backyard* is the complete subject.)

Simple Subjects

The **simple subject** is the main word (or words) of the complete subject.

The birds in our backyard built a nest from my old sweater. (What is the main word in the complete subject? The simple subject is *birds*.)

Grant's Second Chance is a great place to buy used sports equipment. (*Grant's Second Chance* is the simple subject. All three words form the name of one place.)

Katharine is writing a complete novel in her journal. (A complete subject and a simple subject can be the same.)

Throughout the rest of this book, the simple subject will be called *the subject*.

Understood Subjects

When the subject of a sentence is not stated, the subject (you) is said to be *understood*. The subject *you* is not stated in a command or a request.

(you) Watch out for that cord on the floor! (command)

(you) Please get me a drink of water. (request)

Complete Predicates

A **complete predicate** includes all the words that tell about the subject or what the subject is doing.

Simple Predicates, or Verbs

The **simple predicate** is the main word or phrase in the complete predicate. The simple predicate is often referred to as the **verb**.

My older brother <u>takes</u> terrific still photographs. (What is the main word in the complete predicate? What does the subject do? The simple predicate is *takes*.)

Marisa <u>dreamed</u> about returning to the ruins at Machu Pichu. (What did the subject do? The simple predicate is *dreamed*.)

A complete predicate and a simple predicate can be the same.

The computer <u>froze</u>.

Throughout the rest of this book, the simple predicate will be called the *verb*.

Verb Phrases

A *verb phrase* includes the main verb plus any helping, or auxiliary, verbs.

Rhanna <u>will be circulating</u> her petition today in the cafeteria.

Helping verb are often forms of the verbs *be, have, do, may, can,* and *shall.* Look at the chart below.

Helping Verbs	
be	am, is, are, was, were, be, being, been
have	has, have, had
do	do, does, did
other verbs	may, might, must, can, could, shall, should, will, would

You can learn more about verbs and verb phrases in chapters 3 and 8.

Interrupted Verb Phrases A verb phrase is often interrupted by one or more words. Negative words such as *not, never,* and the contraction *n't* are not part of the verb phrase.

Some schools will not allow students to wear T-shirts with words on them. (*Will allow* is the verb phrase—interrupted by the word *not.*)

He should never have tried to take that three-foot drop on skates. (*Should have tried* is the verb phrase—interrupted by the word *never.*)

I didn't want to criticize the way you threw the ball. (*Did want to criticize* is the verb phrase—interrupted by the contraction *n't)*

Different Positions of Subjects

A sentence is in **natural order** when the subject comes before the verb.

Our camping trip lasted from Friday evening until Sunday afternoon.

The dog scratched at the door until no one could stand it anymore.

When the verb or part of the verb phrase comes before the subject, the sentence is in **inverted order**.

Never would I have believed it.

Roaring out of the dark night is a bullet train destined for New York.

As You Write

Inverted sentences are often questions or sentences that start with *there* or *here*. To find the subject in an inverted sentence, turn the sentence around to its natural order.

Inverted Order	Only once have I broken my vow never to share chewed gum.
Natural Order	I have broken my vow to share chewed gum only once.
Inverted Order	Is it silly for us to wear costumes to that film?
Natural Order	It is silly for us to wear costumes to that film.
Inverted Order	A place to dig up dinosaur fossils is in South Dakota.
Natural Order	You can dig up dinosaur fossils at a place in South Dakota. (Sometimes *there* must be dropped for the sentence to make sense.)

Compound Subjects and Predicates

A **compound subject** is made of two or more subjects in one sentence that have the same verb and are joined by a word such as *and* or *or*.

One Subject	Solar panels can harness the energy of the sun.
Compound Subject	Both Solar panels and wind turbines are sources of renewable energy.

Wind turbines in California

A **compound predicate** is two or more verbs that have the same subject and are joined by a word such as *and* or *or*.

Simple Predicate	The glaciers at the North and South Poles are melting. (The predicate has only one verb—*are melting.*)
Compound Predicate	The glaciers at the North and South Poles are melting and breaking apart in large chunks. (The predicate has two verbs—*are melting and (are) breaking.*)

A sentence can include both a compound subject and a compound verb.

Compound Subject and Compound Predicate	George Washington and Abraham Lincoln served our country and became great heroes.
	Jack and Sally set up the lighting and the sound equipment and began filming.

Kinds of Sentences

All sentences can be grouped according to their purpose. A sentence can make a statement, ask a question, give a command, or express strong feeling. The punctuation mark that belongs at the end of a sentence is determined by its purpose.

A *declarative sentence* makes a statement or expresses an opinion and ends with a period.

> Leonardo da Vinci designed a workable airplane long before anyone could build one. (statement)

> Hot, humid weather is worse than the most severe cold wave. (opinion)

An *interrogative sentence* asks a question and ends with a question mark.

> How can I convince you I'm mature enough to see that movie?

> Can you pat your head and rub your stomach at the same time?

An *imperative sentence* makes a request or gives a command and ends with either a period or an exclamation point.

> Go straight for three blocks and then turn left on Elm Street. (This imperative sentence ends with a period because it is a mild request.)

> Don't touch that computer! (This sentence ends with an exclamation point because it is a strong command.)

An *exclamatory sentence* expresses strong feelings and ends with an exclamation point.

> What an awesome band they are!

> They are coming back to play another set!

CHAPTER 2

Nouns and Pronouns

QuickGuide

Nouns pages 11–12	A **noun** names a person, place, thing, or idea. There are several kinds of nouns, including **concrete** and **abstract** nouns, **compound** and **collective** nouns, and **common** and **proper** nouns.
Pronouns and Antecedents pages 12–13	A **pronoun** takes the place of one or more nouns; an **antecedent** is a noun or pronoun to which a pronoun refers.
Kinds of Pronouns pages 14–17	There are several kinds of pronouns, including **personal**, **possessive**, **reflexive** and **intensive**, **indefinite**, **demonstrative**, and **interrogative**.

Nouns

A *noun* is a word that names a person, place, thing, or idea.

There are several kinds of nouns.

Concrete and Abstract Nouns

Nouns that name things that can be seen or touched are called **concrete nouns**.

Concrete Nouns	
People	girl, men, scientist, Dr. Taylor, singer, friend, Ms. Brown
Places	library, Mars, Dallas, Atlantic Ocean, Baltimore, Elm Street
Things	rain, wind, trees, cotton, clouds, shoes, devices

Nouns that name ideas, qualities, or characteristics are called **abstract nouns**.

Abstract Nouns	
Ideas	love, friendship, kindness, thoughtfulness, grief
Qualities	courage, patriotism, hope, ideals, ambition

Compound and Collective Nouns

A **compound noun** is made up of more than one word.

As You Write

Compound nouns may be written as a single word (baseball), two words (home run), or with a hyphen (T-shirt). Always use a dictionary to check the spelling of an unfamiliar compound word.

One Word	football, dugout, sideline
Two Words	first base, Super Bowl, jump ball
Hyphenated Words	runner-up, warm-up, half-sister

Collective nouns name a group of people or things.

Collective Nouns			
band	congregation	flock	orchestra
class	crew	group	swarm
colony	crowd	herd	team
committee	family	league	tribe

Common and Proper Nouns

A **common noun** names any person, place, or thing. A **proper noun** names a particular person, place, or thing. Proper nouns always begin with a capital letter.

Common Nouns	Proper Nouns
girl	Amy Clark
country	United States
book	*Hatchet*

As you can see from the chart, some proper nouns may be more than one word. Even though *United States* is two words, it names only one place.

Pronouns and Antecedents

A *pronoun* is a word that takes the place of one or more nouns.

Look at each pair of sentences below. Notice how pronouns save the second sentence of each pair from being boring, repetitious, and even silly.

Adam bought a large pizza and ate the pizza in one sitting.

Adam bought a large pizza and ate **it** in one sitting.

When Franklin Roosevelt was President, Franklin Roosevelt broadcast Franklin Roosevelt's famous "fireside chats" over the radio.

When Franklin Roosevelt was President, **he** broadcast **his** famous "fireside chats" over the radio.

The word or group of words that a pronoun replaces is called its *antecedent*.

An antecedent comes before the pronoun. It may be in the same sentence as the pronoun or in another sentence. In the following examples, arrows point from the pronouns to their antecedents.

Daronna stopped at the pet store and bought some angelfish. **They** were beautiful! (The antecedent *angelfish* is in the preceding sentence.)

After I got obedience training for the dog, **he** behaved pretty well. (The antecedent *dog* is in the same sentence.)

A pronoun can have more than one antecedent. And more than one pronoun can refer to same antecedent.

The songwriter and the composer were pleased with **their** new material.

The karate master took **his** best students on retreat with **him**.

Kinds of Pronouns

Pronouns come in many forms and serve different functions in a sentence. Following are the various forms.

Personal and Possessive Pronouns

Of all the different kinds of pronouns, **personal pronouns** are used most often. **Possessive pronouns** are personal pronouns that show possession. Personal pronouns are categorized as being in the first person, second person, or third person. In the chart below, the possessive pronouns are in red.

	Singular	Plural
First Person (speaker)	I, me, my, mine	we, us, our, ours
Second Person (person spoken to)	you, your, yours	you, your, yours
Third Person (person or thing spoken about)	he, him, his, she, her, hers, it, its	they, them, their, theirs

Here are some examples of personal pronouns used in sentences.

Examples	
First-Person Pronouns	**I** must have left **my** script at the audition.
	Come with **me** to the gym. **We** have to sign up for **our** tryouts.
Second-Person Pronouns	**You** shouldn't ride a bike without **your** helmet.
	You left **your** new jerseys behind, so **you** will have to wear **your** old ones.
Third-Person Pronouns	**He** thought the books were **his**, so **he** took **them** home.
	She grabbed **her** sister's coat and tore **its** sleeve.
	They took **their** computer with **them** on **their** vacation.

Reflexive and Intensive Pronouns

You can add *–self* or *–selves* to some personal pronouns to add emphasis or to refer back to a noun. These are called **reflexive** and **intensive pronouns**.

Reflexive and Intensive Pronouns	
Singular	myself, yourself, himself, herself, itself
Plural	ourselves, yourselves, themselves

Robert kept telling **himself** that the situation was temporary. (The reflexive pronoun *himself* refers to *Robert.*)

We worried about how to protect wild birds, but the falcons **themselves** found a way to survive in big cities. (The intensive pronoun *themselves* emphasizes who came up with the survival strategy. Intensive pronouns often come immediately after the antecedent.

As You Write

Reflexive and intensive pronouns must always have an antecedent. Never use them alone. They must always refer to a noun or pronoun already in the sentence.

Incorrect	Mark joined Arnetta and myself at the art fair. (The reflexive pronoun *myself* has no antecedent in this sentence.)
Correct	Mark joined Arnetta and me at the art fair.

Indefinite Pronouns

Indefinite pronouns usually refer to unnamed people or things. Unlike personal pronouns, indefinite pronouns do not have a definite antecedent.

Common Indefinite Pronouns			
all	both	few	nothing
another	each	many	one
any	either	most	several
anybody	everybody	neither	some
anyone	everyone	none	someone
anything	everything	no one	something

Did **anyone** notice **something** strange about the end of the movie?

No one knew **anything** about the film.

Can **anybody** here talk to the manager?

Demonstrative Pronouns

Demonstrative pronouns do what their name suggests. They demonstrate, or point out, people or things.

Demonstrative Pronouns			
this	that	these	those

As You Write

This and *these* point to people or things that are near in space or time. *That* and *those* point to people or things that are farther away in space or time.

Near	**This** is my best drawing.
Farther Away	**Those** are my early attempts.

Note that demonstrative pronouns stand alone. When pronouns modify nouns, they are called *demonstrative adjectives*.

Demonstrative Pronoun	**Those** were awesome.
Demonstrative Adjective	**Those** skateboards were awesome.

Interrogative Pronouns

In the last chapter, you learned that interrogative sentences ask questions. **Interrogative pronouns** also ask questions.

Interrogative Pronouns				
what	which	who	whom	whose

What did you want with a bag of water balloons?

Which of these backpacks is mine and **which** is yours?

Who wants to ride in the school van with the principal?

To **whom** did Luke give his new CD?

Whose is this?

Verbs

QuickGuide

Verbs page 19	A **verb** is a word or phrase that tells about an action or a state of being.
Action Verbs page 19	An **action verb** tells what action a subject is performing.
Transitive & Intransitive Verbs page 20	A **transitive verb** is an action verb that expresses action directed at a person or thing. An **intransitive verb** is an action verb whose action is not directed at a person or thing. A transitive verb has a **direct object**; an intransitive verb does not.
Linking Verbs pages 21–22	A **linking verb** links the subject to another word in the predicate. The other word either renames or describes the subject.
Helping Verbs page 23	A **helping verb** is used with a main verb to form a **verb phrase**.

Verbs

A *verb* is a word or phrase that tells about an action or a state of being.

> The singer **walked** onto the stage. (The action verb *walked* tells what action the subject performed.)

> People **were** in their seats an hour before the show. (The state-of-being verb *were* tells that the subject *is* or *exists* in a certain place.)

Action Verbs

An **action verb** tells what action a subject is performing. Action verbs can show physical action, mental action, or ownership.

To find an action verb, find the subject of the sentence and ask yourself, *What is the subject doing?*

Physical Action	The Olympians **ran** to condition their bodies. (The subject is *Olympians.* What did the Olympians do? *Ran* is the action verb.)
	They **trounced** their opponents in the semi-finals. (*They* is the subject. What did they do? *Trounced* is the action verb.)
Mental Action	I **forgot** the dancer's name. (The subject is *I. Forgot* shows mental action.)
	Clark **knows** the steps to that dance. (The subject is *Clark. Knows* shows mental action.)
Ownership	Jeffrey **has** two bikes. (The subject is *Jeffrey. Has* shows ownership.)
	The bikes once **belonged** to his older brothers. (The subject is *bikes. Belonged* shows ownership.)

Transitive and Intransitive Verbs

An action verb that has an object is *transitive*. An action verb that does not have an object is *intransitive*.

Action verbs are **transitive** when the action they express is directed at a person or thing. In other words, transitive verbs have direct objects. Other action verbs are **intransitive**. The action they express is not directed at anyone or anything. Transitive verbs do not have direct objects.

As You Write

To decide whether an action verb is transitive or intransitive, first find the verb. Then, ask yourself *who or what experienced or received the action of the verb.* If the question cannot be answered because there is no object, it means that the verb is intransitive. Notice that some verbs can be transitive in one sentence and intransitive in another.

Transitive	Marie **put** special food in the dogs' bowls. (Marie put what? *Food* is the object. Therefore, *put* is a transitive verb.)
Intransitive	She **works** at the animal shelter on weekends. (She works what or whom? There is no way to answer this question. Therefore, *works* is an intransitive verb.)
Transitive	The rock star **wrote** a song for the girl who left him. (The rock star wrote what? *Song* is the object, so *wrote* is transitive.)
Intransitive	He **wrote** about the girl who left him. (He wrote *what* or *whom*? There is no object in this sentence.)

Linking Verbs

A linking verb links the subject to another word in the predicate.

Mason and Sharon **were** slower than the rest of the contestants.
(The linking verb *were* connects the subject *Mason and Sharon* to the word *slower* in the predicate.)

The children **grew** bored with the clown's silly antics.

Most linking verbs are **state-of-being verbs** (forms of the verb *to be*). Other verbs can also link parts of a sentence. They express a condition.

Linking Verbs			
Forms of the Verb *To Be*			
be	shall be	have been	
is	will be	has been	
am	can be	had been	
are	could be	could have been	
was	should be	should have been	
were	would be	may have been	
may be	might have been		
might be	must have been		
Verbs That Express a Condition			
appear	grow	seem	stay
become	look	smell	taste
feel	remain	sound	turn

When a linking verb links the subject with another word in the predicate, the other word either describes or renames the subject.

Describing   The sweater **looked** handmade. (*Looked* links *sweater* with *handmade. Handmade* describes the sweater— *the handmade sweater.*)

Renaming   Believe it or not, Lewis's

favorite food **is** sushi. (*Is* links *food* with *sushi. Sushi* renames the subject.)

Linking Verb or Action Verb?   To tell whether a verb is a linking verb or an action verb, ask yourself this question: *What is the verb doing in the sentence?* If the verb links a subject to a word that renames or describes it, the verb is a linking verb. If the verb is used to show action, it is an action verb.

Linking Verb   The man in the train **looked** anxious. (*Looked* links *man* and *anxious. Anxious* describes the subject, *man.*)

Action Verb   He **looked** desperately for his missing wallet. (*Looked* shows action. It tells what the subject is doing. Also, there is no word in the sentence that renames or describes the subject.)

Helping Verbs

Helping verbs "help" other verbs express meaning. A main verb plus any helping verbs make up a **verb phrase**. Notice that a helping verb may be part of a contraction.

> I **am trying** to figure out why I ever wanted to learn archery. (*Am* is a helping verb that tells more about the main verb *trying*.)

> Jamalia **might go** to the dance if you invite her. (*Might* is a helping verb that tells more about the main verb *go*.)

> I'**m finishing** this milk shake because I **do**n't **like** to see food go to waste. (*Am* is part of the contraction *I'm*, and *do* is part of the contraction *don't*.)

A verb phrase may have more than one helping verb.

> We **have been gathering** recyclables at the riverfront all day. (*Have been gathering* is a verb phrase. *Have* and *been* are helping verbs.)

One or more words may interrupt a verb phrase. Note that *not* and its contraction *n't* are not part of the verb.

> We **have** just **received** word that the shuttle **has** almost **landed**. (The verbs are *have received* and *has landed*.)

> He **should**n't **try** that move without a spotter. (The verb is *should try*.)

Common Helping Verbs	
be	am, is, was, were, are, be, being, been
have	has, have, had
do	do, does, did
other verbs	may, must, might, can, could, shall, should, will, would

CHAPTER 4

Adjectives and Adverbs

QuickGuide

Adjectives pages 25–28	An **adjective** modifies a noun or a pronoun. There are several kinds adjectives including **articles** and **proper adjectives.**
Adverbs pages 29–31	An **adverb** modifies a verb, an adjective, or another adverb. Many adverbs end in *–ly.*

Adjectives

An *adjective* is a word that modifies a noun or a pronoun.

Our language would be dull indeed if the only parts of speech we had to use were nouns and verbs. Fortunately, we have lots of **modifiers**—words that can change or add meaning to other words. Modifiers describe other words. They add color and exactness to a sentence. One kind of modifier is the **adjective.** An adjective answers the following questions about nouns and pronouns:

What kind?   How much?

Which one?   How many?

In the following examples, an arrow points from the adjective to the noun or pronoun it modifies.

What Kind?   **Rough** seas upset the **ship's** passengers.

Which One?   **This** ship is more stable than **that** one.

How Much?   **More** space in the cabin would be a **great** relief.

How Many?   **Few** people liked the size of the **two** ships.

Different Positions of Adjectives Usually an adjective comes right before the noun or pronoun it modifies. Sometimes, though, an adjective follows that word. An adjective can also follow a linking verb.

Before a Noun   The **brave, adventurous** diver explored the cave.

After a Noun   The diver, **brave** and **adventurous**, explored the cave.

After a Linking Verb   The diver was **brave** and **adventurous** to explore the cave.

As You Write

When two or more adjectives are used to modify one noun and they are not connected by the words *and* or *or,* you may have to put a comma between them. To decide whether to use a comma, read the adjectives with the word *and* in between. If the phrase makes sense with the word *and,* you should use a comma.

Incorrect	A **young enthusiastic** environmentalist addressed our ecology group. (The environmentalist is young *and* enthusiastic. A comma is needed.)
Correct	A **young, enthusiastic** environmentalist addressed our ecology group.
Incorrect	The auto show featured **several, incredible, hybrid** vehicles. ("Several *and* incredible *and* hybrid vehicles" does not read well. Leave the commas out.)
Correct	The auto show featured **several incredible hybrid** vehicles.

Usually no comma is needed after a number or after an adjective that refers to size, shape, or age.

> That **skinny old** fellow can play tennis almost as well as I can.

Articles

A, an, and *the* form a special group of adjectives called **articles**. There are two kinds of articles, **definite** and **indefinite**. The definite article (*the*) is used to point out a specific noun; the indefinite articles (*a* and *an*) are used to refer to any member of a group. Use the article *a* before words that begin with a consonant sound; use the article *an* before words that begin with a vowel sound.

Definite   **The** girl led **the** artist to **the** stage.

Indefinite   **A** girl led **an** artist to **a** stage.

Proper Adjectives

Proper adjectives are related to proper nouns. Like proper nouns, they are capitalized.

> For tomorrow's picnic, let's make sandwiches with **French** bread. (*French* is a proper adjective formed from the proper noun *France*.)

Proper Noun	Proper Adjective
Europe	European
America	American
Sudan	Sudanese
Spain	Spanish

Adjective or Noun?

A word's part of speech depends on how it is used in a sentence. Nouns can often serve as adjectives.

Noun	The **street** was crowded.
Adjective	**Street** theatre is so colorful.
Noun	**Water** conducts electricity.
Adjective	I work in a **water** park.

Adjective or Pronoun?

A word can be a pronoun in one sentence and an adjective in another. For example, the word *this* is a pronoun if it stands alone and takes the place of a noun. The word *this* is an adjective if it modifies a noun or a pronoun.

Adjective	**This** number is a prime number. (*This* modifies the noun *number*.)
Pronoun	**This** is a prime number. (*This* replaces the noun *number*.)
Adjective	**Which** problem did you solve? (*Which* modifies the noun *problem*.)
Pronoun	**Which** did you solve? (*Which* replaces the noun.)

The words below are often used as both pronouns and adjectives.

Words Used as Pronouns or Adjectives		
Demonstrative Pronouns	**Interrogative Pronouns**	**Indefinite Pronouns**
this	what	all · many
these	which	another · more
that	whose	any · most
those		both · neither
		each · other
		either · several
		few · some

Adverbs

An *adverb* modifies a verb, an adjective, or another adverb.

Many adverbs are formed by adding –*ly* to adjectives.

Hold the rope **tightly** and **slowly** lower the bucket. (The adverb *tightly* modifies the verb *hold*. The adverb *slowly* modifies the verb *lower*.)

These old wells are **terribly** dangerous. (The adverb *terribly* modifies the predicate adjective *dangerous*.)

The common adverbs below do not end in –*ly*.

Common Adverbs		
afterward	here	slow
again	instead	so
almost	just	sometimes
already	late	soon
also	long	still
always	more	then
back	near	there
down	never	today
even	next	tomorrow
ever	not (n't)	very
far	now	well
fast	often	yet
forth	quite	
hard	rather	

Adverbs That Modify Verbs

Most adverbs modify verbs. To find these adverbs, identify the verb and ask yourself, *Where? When? How?* or *To what extent?* A word that answers one of these questions is an adverb.

Usually, when an adverb modifies a verb, it can be placed anywhere in the sentence.

Where? Last spring, everyone gathered **outside** to watch the solar eclipse.

When? **Sometimes** I wonder if I'll **ever** see one.

How? We gathered **expectantly** to watch.

To What Extent? Clouds **completely** obscured our view of the eclipse.

More than one adverb can modify the same verb.

Ray **never** ran **fast**, but he **always** ran **well**.

When there are helping verbs in addition to the main verb, an adverb modifies the entire verb phrase.

You should accept a compliment **graciously**. (*Graciously* modifies the verb phrase *should accept*.)

An adverb sometimes interrupts a verb phrase in a statement or a question.

Statement I have **always** enjoyed helping out at the nature center. (The adverb *always* interrupts the verb phrase *have enjoyed*.)

Question Did**n't** she know her competitors would see her posters? (*Did know* is the verb phrase interrupted by the adverb *not* (*n't*).)

Adverbs That Modify Adjectives and Other Adverbs

Almost all adverbs modify verbs. However, occasionally an adverb, such as *quite*, *rather*, *so*, *somewhat*, and *very*, modifies an adjective or another adverb. Such an adverb usually comes immediately before the word it modifies.

Modifying an Adjective   Inventors are **very** creative. (*Creative* is an adjective. *Very* is an adverb that modifies *creative*. It tells how creative inventors are.)

Modifying an Adverb   The inventor worked **especially** fast. (*Fast* is an adverb. *Especially* is an adverb that modifies *fast*. It tells how fast the inventor worked.)

As You Write

When you write, you convey your ideas better when you use specific adverbs. Try to avoid repeating adverbs or using abstract adjectives.

Vague	Pedro is a **very, very good** inventor
	Meghan is **really** a **very sweet** person.
Specific	Pedro is a **creative** and **extremely intelligent** inventor.
	Meghan is a **thoughtful** and **generous** person.

You can learn more about using adjectives and adverbs in Chapter 14.

CHAPTER 5

Prepositions, Conjunctions, & Interjections

QuickGuide

Prepositions pages 33–35	A **preposition** shows the relationship between a noun or a pronoun and another word in the sentence. A **prepositional phrase** is a group of words made up of a preposition, its object, and any words that modify the object.
Conjunctions pages 35–36	A **conjunction** connects words or groups of words. There are three kinds of conjunctions: **coordinating, correlative,** and **subordinating.**
Interjections page 37	An **interjection** is used to express surprise or strong feeling.

Prepositions

A *preposition* shows the relationship between a noun or a pronoun and another word in the sentence.

If someone gives you directions, a preposition such as *beside, on,* or *under* could make all the difference.

First I looked **on** the desk.

Then I remembered that the money was hidden **under** the desk.

The following is a list of common prepositions. Notice that some prepositions can be made up of more than one word.

Common Prepositions			
about	below	inside	to
above	beneath	into	toward
according to	beside	like	under
across	between	near	underneath
after	beyond	of	until
against	by	off	up
along	down	on	upon
among	during	out of	up to
around	except	over	with
at	for	past	within
before	from	since	without
because of	in	through	
behind	in front of	throughout	

Prepositional Phrases

A preposition is usually part of a group of words called a **prepositional phrase**. A prepositional phrase is a group of words made up of a preposition, its object, and any words that modify the object.

> Look **under the kitchen table.** (*Under* is the preposition and *table* is the object. *Kitchen* modifies the object.)

> We are **among friends, young and old.** (*Among* is the preposition and *friends* is the object. *Young* and *old* modify the object.)

Prepositional phrases are common in both subjects and predicates of sentences.

> The largest remaining rainforest **in Mexico** is endangered. (The prepositional phrase is in the subject.)

> I was afraid **of your pitch** last year. (The prepositional phrase is in the predicate.)

A sentence can have more than one prepositional phrase.

> The players **on that team** are old friends **of mine**.

Compound Objects A prepositional phrase can have more than one object. Such an object is called a **compound object of a preposition**.

> We packed boxes **of clothes, toiletries, and canned goods** for the hurricane survivors.

Preposition or Adverb? Some words can be a preposition in one sentence and an adverb in another sentence. *Around*, for example, is a preposition when it is part of a prepositional phrase. *Around* is an adverb, however, when it stands alone.

Preposition	The designer moved the cursor **around the computer screen**. (*Around the computer screen* is a prepositional phrase.)
Adverb	Alana and I were just hanging **around**. (*Around* is an adverb that tells where Alana and I were "hanging.")

Conjunctions

A *conjunction* connects words or groups of words.

There are three kinds of conjunctions: coordinating, correlative, and subordinating. Here we will learn about two of these: coordinating conjunctions and correlative conjunctions. You will learn about subordinating conjunctions in Chapter 9.

Coordinating Conjunctions A **coordinating conjunction** is a single connecting word. The coordinating conjunctions in the sentences on the next page connect both single words and groups of words.

Coordinating Conjunctions			
and	but	or	yet

Bill **and** *Melinda Gates* give away some of their fortune each year. (The coordinating conjunction *and* connects two proper nouns.)

You may have *soup* **or** *salad* with your grilled cheese. (The coordinating conjunction *or* connects two common nouns.)

The students *saw* **and** *reviewed* the latest animated feature. (The coordinating conjunction *and* connects two verbs.)

Lina's comedy routine was *funny* **but** *long*. (The coordinating conjunction *but* connects two adjectives.)

He climbed *slowly* **yet** *purposefully* over the mountain for help. (The coordinating conjunction *yet* connects two adverbs.)

Jay wove the bandage *over his ankle* **and** *around his foot*. (The coordinating conjunction *and* connects prepositional phrases.)

He began *taking off his coat* **and** *explaining why he was late*. (The coordinating conjunction *and* connects complete predicates.)

Marisa likes water with her meals, **but** *Joseph likes milk better.* (The coordinating conjunction *but* connects sentences.)

Correlative Conjunctions are always used in pairs. Like coordinating conjunctions, **correlative conjunctions** connect words or groups of words.

Correlative Conjunctions		
both/and	either/or	neither/nor

No ball game is complete without **both** *peanuts* **and** *Cracker Jack*. (The correlative conjunction *both/and* connects nouns.)

My opponent's remark was **neither** *honest* **nor** *accurate*. (The correlative conjunction *neither/nor* connects adjectives.)

My homework is **either** *in the car* **or** *on the shelf*. (The correlative conjunction *either/or* connects prepositional phrases.

Either *pay me now*, **or** *buy your ticket at the door*. (The correlative conjunction *either/or* connects sentences.)

Interjections

An *interjection* is used to express surprise or strong feeling.

Words such as *ugh, whew,* and *wow* are **interjections**. An interjection usually comes at the beginning of a sentence. It is followed by an exclamation point or a comma.

Common Interjections			
aha	oh	ugh	yes
goodness	oops	well	yikes
hooray	ouch	wow	yippee

Ouch! That antiseptic lotion stings.

Oh, I just remembered I have something for you.

Suprise! We didn't forget your birthday after all.

As You Write

Use interjections and exclamation points sparingly. When they are overused, interjections lose their power. Try to save them for truly strong emotions so they will have a greater impact on your reader.

Overdone	**Wow!** Did you see that! I don't think I will ever forget it!
Better	**Wow!** Did you see that double play?

Complements

QuickGuide

Complements page 39	A **complement** completes the meaning of a sentence. There are four main kinds of complements: **direct objects, indirect objects, predicate nominatives,** and **predicate adjectives.**
Direct Objects pages 39–40	A **direct object** is a noun or pronoun that receives the action of a verb. It tells *whom* or *what* an action is about.
Indirect Objects pages 40–41	An **indirect object** is a noun or pronoun that tells *to whom, for whom, to what,* or *for what* an action is done.
Predicate Nominatives page 42	A **predicate nominative** is a noun or a pronoun that follows a linking verb and identifies, renames, or explains the subject.
Predicate Adjectives page 43	A **predicate adjective** is an adjective that follows a linking verb and modifies or describes the subject.

Complements

A *complement* is a word or phrase that follows the verb and completes its meaning.

While it is possible to have a complete sentence with only a subject and a verb, other words are usually needed to complete the meaning. These words are called **complements**.

There are four main kinds of complements. **Direct objects** and **indirect objects** always follow action verbs. **Predicate nominatives** and **predicate adjectives** always follow linking verbs and are called **subject complements** because they refer back to the subject.

Direct Objects

A *direct object* is always a noun or a pronoun that follows an action verb. A direct object answers the questions *Whom?* or *What?*

To find a direct object, first find the subject and the action verb in the sentence. Then ask yourself *whom?* or *what?* receives the action of the verb. The answer to either question will be a direct object.

> ┌—d.o.—┐
> Carrie <u>invited</u> **everyone** to a party at the museum. (Carrie invited *whom?*
> *Everyone* is the direct object.)

> ┌—d.o.—┐
> Mark <u>will exhibit</u> a **painting** in the art show at school. (Mark will exhibit
> *what? Painting* is the direct object.)

To find the direct object in a question, change the question into a statement.

Question   When you went to the Louvre, <u>did</u> <u>you</u> <u>see</u> the *Mona Lisa?*

                                                         ┌—d.o.—┐

Statement   When you went to the Louvre, <u>you</u> <u>did see</u> the ***Mona Lisa***.

                       (You did see *what? The Mona Lisa* is the direct object.)

Compound Direct Object A compound direct object consists of two or more direct objects following the same verb.

                    ┌─d.o.─┐   ┌─d.o.─┐
Chagall <u>used</u> bright **colors** and **fantasy** in his paintings. (Chagall used *what*? *Colors* and *fantasy* make up the compound direct object.)

Indirect Objects

An *indirect object* is a noun or pronoun that tells *to* or *for whom* or *what* something is done.

An indirect object provides more information about the direct object. To have an indirect object, therefore, a sentence *must* have a direct object.

Like a direct object, an indirect object follows an action verb. It always comes before the direct object. To find an indirect object, first find the direct object. Then ask yourself the following questions.

To whom?	For whom?
To what?	For what?

                      i.o. ┌─d.o.─┐
The guest <u>speaker</u> <u>showed</u> **us** a video of an Iditarod sled race. (*Video* is the direct object. The guest speaker showed the video *to whom*? The speaker showed it to us. *Us* is the indirect object.)

                              ┌──i.o. ──┐   ┌─d.o.─┐
The <u>lady</u> on TV <u>gave</u> her disgusting **casserole** a fancy name. (*Name* is the direct object. The lady gave a name *to what*? She gave it to the casserole. *Casserole* is the indirect object.

Indirect Object or Object of a Preposition? When a noun follows a preposition, it is the **object of the preposition**, not an indirect object.

Indirect Object	I gave **Jake** the extra sandwich because he is always hungry. (*Sandwich* is the direct object. *Jake* is the indirect object.)
Object of Preposition	I gave the extra sandwich to **Jake** because he is always hungry. (*To Jake* is a prepositional phrase that comes after the object. *Jake* is the object of the preposition.)

Compound Indirect Object A compound indirect object consists of two or more indirect objects that follow the same verb.

I brought **Tony** and **Mona** games to make baby-sitting easier. (I brought games *for whom*? *Tony and Mona* make up the compound indirect object.)

As You Write

When you write, you can combine sentences by using direct and indirect objects. The combined sentences will have action verbs and will allow you to say more in fewer words and sentences. See how the twelve words in the first two sentences below can be combined to make one sentence of seven words.

I bought a gift of apples. I gave the apples to Mary.

I bought Mary a gift of apples.

Predicate Nominatives

A *predicate nominative* is a noun or pronoun that follows a linking verb and identifies, renames, or explains the subject.

To find a **predicate nominative**, locate the subject and the linking verb. Then find the noun or the pronoun that follows the verb and relates to the subject. This word will be a predicate nominative.

Remember that the most common linking verbs are forms of *to be* (*be, is am, are, was, were*). See chapter 3 to review linking verbs.

┌ p.n. ┐
He was Atlanta's **actor** of the year in 2006. (*Actor* is the predicate nominative that renames the subject *he.*)

┌ p.n. ┐
She might be a famous **actress**. *(Actress renames the subject she.)*

Compound Predicate Nominative A compound predicate nominative consists of two or more predicate nominatives following the same verb.

┌ p.n. ┐ ┌ p.n. ┐
The earliest television comediennes were **Lucille Ball** and **Imogene Coca**. (*Lucille Ball and Imogene Coca* is the compound predicate nominative that renames the subject *comediennes.*)

Like other parts of speech, predicate nominatives appear in questions as well as sentences. To find the predicate nominative, change the question into a statement.

Question   Was that you in the documentary about young activists?

┌ p.n. ┐
Statement   That was **you** in the documentary about young activists.
(*That* is the subject. *You* renames *that.*)

Predicate Adjectives

A *predicate adjective* is an adjective that follows a linking verb and modifies the subject.

To find a **predicate adjective**, first find the subject and the linking verb. Then find an adjective that follows the verb and describes the subject. This will be the predicate adjective.

┌─p.a.─┐
Pigs are basically **clean** and prefer cool water to mud. (*Clean* is the predicate adjective that describes the subject, *pigs.*)

┌─p.a.─┐
Did the new student seem **anxious** about introducing himself? (*Anxious* is the predicate adjective that describes the subject, *student.*)

Compound Predicate Adjective Two or more predicate adjectives that follow the same verb are called compound predicate adjectives.

┌─p.a.─┐   ┌─p.a.─┐
The auditorium was **clean** and **comfortable**. (Both *clean* and *comfortable* describe the subject, *auditorium.*)

7 Phrases

QuickGuide

Prepositional Phrases pages 45–48	A **prepositional phrase** is a group of words that begins with a preposition and ends with a noun or pronoun.
Appositives and Appositive Phrases pages 48–49	An **appositive** is a noun or a pronoun that identifies or explains another noun or pronoun. An **appositive phrase** consists of an appositive and its modifiers.

Prepositional Phrases

A **phrase** is a group of words that acts like a single part of speech. One kind of phrase is the prepositional phrase.

A *prepositional phrase* begins with a preposition and ends with a noun or a pronoun.

There are two kinds of prepositional phrases: **adjective phrases** and **adverb phrases**.

Adjective Phrase	The girl **with the pink hair** is a calculus expert. (The prepositional phrase *with the pink hair* is used as an adjective modifying *girl*.)
Adverb Phrase	The hero leaped **over the blockade**. (The prepositional phrase *over the blockade* is used as an adverb modifying *leaped*.)

You learned about prepositions in Chapter 5. Revisit the chart on page 33 for a list of commonly-used prepositions.

Adjective Phrases

An *adjective phrase* is a prepositional phrase that is used like a single adjective.

Adjective	Buddy Guy is a **popular** musician.
Adjective Phrase	Buddy Guy is a musician **with a loyal following**.

An adjective phrase answers the question *Which one?* or *What kind?* just as a single adjectives does.

Which One?	The CD **without a label** is my copy.
What Kind?	Mom bought a car **with an MP3 player**.

A sentence can have more than one adjective phrase.

People **from three states** came to the benefit concert **for the flood victims**.

Sometimes an adjective phrase may modify a noun or a pronoun in another phrase.

I want to see that show **about music of the punk era**.

The section **on the early roots of the style** should be interesting.

As You Write

When an adjective phrase is too far away from the word or words it modifies, it is called a **misplaced modifier.** A misplaced modifier can confuse the meaning of a sentence or make the sentence sound silly.

The teacher gave the microscopes to the students without batteries. (The modifier *without batteries* is misplaced. Is it the students or the microscopes that are without batteries?)

In the glass jar, Li studied the cockroaches. (Because of this misplaced modifier, Li seems to be in the glass jar.)

To correct a misplaced modifier, place the adjective phrase as close as possible to the word it modifies. If necessary, change the phrase to clarify it.

The teacher gave the students the microscopes, but no batteries.

Li studied the cockroaches in the glass jar.

Adverb Phrases

An *adverb phrase* is a prepositional phrase that is used to modify a verb or an adverb.

Adverb	Unsure of his English, the artist spoke **softly**.
Adverb Phrase	Unsure of his English, the artist spoke **in a whisper**.

Like single adverbs, adverb phrases usually answer one of the following questions:

Where?   The potter moved **into a new studio.**

When?   **On Friday**, he began to throw a new series of vases.

How?   The potter works **on a precise schedule.**

Why?   He built a new kiln **for his larger pots.**

Two adverb phrases can modify the same verb. Also notice that adverb phrases may appear anywhere in a sentence.

After Friday but **before Sunday**, he should complete the set of plates.

The potter had waited **for clay** **for five days.**

Appositives and Appositive Phrases

An *appositive* is a noun or pronoun that explains or identifies another noun or pronoun in the sentence.

> We talked about our common interest, **music**. (The appositive *music* explains *our common interest*.)

When an appositive has modifiers, it is called an **appositive phrase**.

> Dr. Spin, **the new disc jockey**, chooses great music. (The appositive phrase *the new disc jockey* identifies *Dr. Spin*.)

As You Write

If the information in an appositive phrase is essential, no commas are needed. Information is essential if it identifies a person, place, or thing in the sentence and is necessary for understanding the meaning of the sentence.

If the information in the phrase is not essential, it must be set off from the sentence by commas. Information is not essential if it can be removed without changing the meaning of the sentence.

Essential	The poem "Mother to Son" was written by Langston Hughes. (If *Mother to Son* were dropped, the sentence would lose much of its informational value. Thus, the appositive phrase is essential.)
Not Essential	"Mother to Son," a poem by Langston Hughes, is one of my teacher's favorite poems. (If the appositive phrase were dropped, the sentence would still make sense. Therefore, the appositive phrase is not essential and needs to be set off by commas.)

Langston Hughes, Winold Reiss, 1925

Verbals and Verbal Phrases

QuickGuide

Verbals **page 51**	A **verbal** is a verb form that functions like another part of speech. There are three kinds of verbals: **infinitives, gerunds,** and **participles**.
Participles and Participial Phrases **pages 51–54**	A **participle** is a verb form that is used as an adjective. A **participial phrase** is a participle with modifiers and complements all working together as an adjective.
Gerunds and Gerund Phrases **pages 55–56**	A **gerund** is a verb form that is used as a noun. Gerunds usually end in *–ing*. A **gerund phrase** is a gerund with modifiers and complements all working together as a noun.
Infinitives and Infinitive Phrases **pages 56–57**	An **infinitive** is a verb form that can be used as a noun, an adjective, or an adverb. An **infinitive phrase** is an infinitive with modifiers and complements all working together as a noun, an adjective, or an adverb. Infinitives and infinitive phrases usually begin with the word *to*.

Verbals

A *verbal* is a verb form that functions like another part of speech.

A verbal looks like a verb, but it acts like an adjective, an adverb, or a noun. There are three kinds of verbals: **infinitives, gerunds,** and **participles.** Look at the following examples.

> We heard the **crying** child. (*Crying* is a participle used as adjective.)

> **Hiking** is great exercise. (*Hiking* is a gerund used as noun.)

> We drove home **to wait**. (*To wait* is an infinitive used as an adverb.)

Often verbals are linked with related words to form phrases. These may be participial phrases, gerund phrases, or infinitive phrases.

> **Listening carefully**, we heard the cry. (*Listening carefully* is a participial phrase modifying *we*.)

> **Hiking in the wild** is fun. (*Hiking in the wild* is a gerund phrase used as the subject of the sentence.)

> We drove home **to wait for Al**. (*To wait for Al* is an infinitive phrase used as an adverb modifying *drove*.)

Participles and Participial Phrases

A *participle* is a verb form that is used as an adjective.

Like an adjective, a participle modifies a noun or a pronoun. Participles answer the following questions:

> **Which One?** The **humming** computer has started to emit wisps of smoke. (*Humming* answers the question *Which One?*)

> **What Kind?** The **ruined** shipment must be replaced before the day of the auction. (*Ruined* answers the question *What Kind?*)

The two forms of participles are: **present participles** and **past participles**. Present participles always end in *–ing*. Past participles usually end in *–ed* or *–d*. Some, however, have irregular endings, such as *–n, –t,* or *–en.*

Verb	Present Participle	Past Participle
fade	fading	faded
freeze	freezing	frozen
grow	growing	grown
look	looking	looked
make	making	made
send	sending	sent
speak	speaking	spoken
talk	talking	talked
tear	tearing	torn

Present Participle	The **standing** passenger lost her balance on the bus. (*Standing* is a present participle that modifies *passenger*.)
Past Participle	All **broken** bottles belong in the recycling container. (*Broken* is a past participle that modifies *bottles*.)

Participle or Verb? A participle is formed from a verb, but it cannot be used alone as a verb. To act as a verb, a participle needs to be combined with a helping verb.

Participle	Everyone clapped for the **prancing** horses.
Verb	The horses **were prancing** across the ring.
Participle	The **banging** door broke my concentration.
Verb	The door **was banging** the entire day.

Because a participle is a verb form, it has some of the features of a verb. It can have one or more complements. In addition, it can be modified by an adverb or an adverb phrase. A participle and any modifiers or complements form a **participial phrase**.

Participle with a Complement	**Risking life and limb**, he set out on his journey to a new land. (*Risking* modifies *he. Life and limb* are complements.)
Participle with an Adverb	That **unbelievably daring** move won Boris the chess match! (The adverb *unbelievably* modifies *daring*.)
Participle with a Prepositional Phrase	Concertgoers, **hoping for a glimpse of the band**, arrived early. (The prepositional phrase *for a glimpse* modifies *hoping*.

As You Write

A participial phrase that comes at the beginning of a sentence is always followed by a comma.

Listening carefully, the colonists learned from the Indians.

Participial phrases in the middle or at the end of a sentence may or may not need commas. If the information in the phrase is **essential** to the meaning of the sentence, no commas are needed. If the information in the phrase is **not essential,** it should be set off from the sentence by commas.

Essential	The corn crop **growing in the back field** is ready to be harvested. (The participial phrase *growing in the back field* is needed to identify which corn crop must be harvested, therefore no commas are necessary.)
Nonessential	The corn crop, **growing much too slowly**, could be ruined by an early frost. (The participial phrase *growing much too slowly* could be removed from the sentence without changing the meaning, therefore commas are needed.)

Misplaced Participial Phrases Like other adjective phrases, a participial phrase must be placed near the noun it modifies. If it is placed nearer to another noun, it can cause confusion.

Misplaced Modifier	**Hanging on the wall of the old house,** Ben saw a beautiful but mysterious painting. (This sentence suggests that Ben was hanging on the wall, not the painting.)
Corrected	Ben saw a beautiful but mysterious painting **hanging on the wall of the old house.**
Misplaced Modifier	The travel agent called the innkeeper **searching for a hotel in Williamsburg.** (The participial phrase *searching for a hotel* is placed too far from the noun it modifies— *travel agent*. A reader might think that the innkeeper is looking for a hotel.)
Corrected	The travel agent, **searching for a hotel in Williamsburg,** called the innkeeper.

The town square in Williamsburg, Virginia

Gerunds and Gerund Phrases

A *gerund* is a verb form that ends in *–ing* and is used as a noun.

Like a noun, a gerund can function as a subject, a direct object, an indirect object, an object of a preposition, a predicate nominative, or an appositive.

Gerund as Subject	**Hiking** is exercise disguised as adventure. (*Hiking* tells what the sentence is about.)
Gerund as Direct Object	My family enjoys **hiking**. (What does my family enjoy? *Hiking* is the direct object.)
Gerund as Indirect Object	If I could, I'd give **hiking** all my free time. (I'd give *what*? *Free time* is the direct object. I have to give attention *to what*? *Hiking* is the indirect object.)
Gerund as Object of a Preposition	The hardest part of **hiking** is a steep, rocky trail. (*Hiking* is the object of the preposition *of*.)
Gerund as Predicate Nominative	My brother's favorite sport is **hiking**. (*Hiking* renames the subject *sport*.)
Gerund as Appositive	Rick has a new hobby, **hiking**. (*Hiking* identifies Rick's new hobby.)

Gerund or Participle? Gerunds and participles both end in *–ing*, but gerunds are used as nouns, and participles are used as adjectives.

Gerund	Jessica's **writing** is quite good. (*Writing* is used as a noun, the subject of the sentence.)
Participle	The **writing** lessons were fantastic. (*Writing* is an adjective that tells what kind of lessons.)

A **gerund phrase** is made up of a gerund with its modifiers and complements all working together as a noun. The examples that follow show how a gerund phrase can be made up of several different groups of words.

Gerund with an Adjective	Jon's **colorful painting** won him many awards.
Gerund with an Adverb	**Painting expressively** creates superb results.
Gerund with a Prepositional Phrase	I always enjoy **painting during summer vacations**.
Gerund with a Complement	**Painting portraits** is difficult for me.

Infinitives and Infinitive Phrases

An *infinitive* is a verb form that can be used as a noun, an adjective, or an adverb. An infinitive usually begins with the word *to*.

Infinitive as Noun	**To wait** was the only choice during the gasoline shortage. (*To wait* is the subject. It tells what the sentence is about.)
Infinitive as Adjective	Do you have a good reason **to wait**? (*To wait* modifies reason.)
Infinitive as Adverb	Jordan went to the end of the line **to wait**. (*To wait* modifies *went*; it tells why Jordan went to the end of the line.)

An **infinitive phrase** consists of an infinitive with its modifiers and complements all working together as a noun, an adjective, or an adverb. An infinitive phrase can be made up of several different combinations of words.

Infinitive Phrase with an Adverb	Her heartfelt questions made us want **to reply thoughtfully**.
Infinitive Phrase with a Prepositional Phrase	When the next Harry Potter book is released, I plan **to read around the clock**.
Infinitive Phrase with a Complement	They say the house is haunted, but I still want **to open the door.**

Infinitive or Prepositional Phrase? Sometimes infinitives are confused with prepositional phrases that begin with *to*. Remember, an infinitive phrase is the word *to* plus a verb form. The prepositional phrase is the word *to* plus a noun or a pronoun.

Infinitive	The interactive game you bought me is fun **to play**. (The phrase *to play* includes the verb *play*.)
Prepositional Phrase	For the party, we can each bring our favorite CD **to music class**. (The prepositional phrase *to music class* includes the noun *class*.)

9 Clauses

QuickGuide

Clauses page 59	A **clause** is a group of words that has a subject and a verb.
Independent Clauses page 59	An **independent (main) clause** expresses a complete thought. It can stand alone as a sentence.
Subordinate Clauses pages 60–65	A **subordinate (dependent) clause** does not express a complete thought. It cannot stand alone. There are several types of subordinate clauses, including **adjective clauses, adverb clauses,** and **noun clauses.**
Sentence Structure pages 66–67	Sentences can be classified as **simple, compound,** or **complex**, depending upon the number and types of clauses they contain.

Clauses

A *clause* is a group of words that has a subject and a verb.

In Chapter 8 you learned about groups of words called phrases that can be used as adjectives, adverbs, or nouns.

Clauses are also groups of words that can be used in the same ways, but there is one important difference. A clause has a subject and a verb. A phrase does not.

Phrase	I wrote a letter **after dinner.** (*After dinner* is a prepositional phrase that modifies the verb *wrote*.)
Clause	I wrote a letter **after dinner was finished.** (*Dinner* is the subject of the clause; *was finished* is the verb.)

There are two kinds of clauses: independent and subordinate.

Independent Clauses

An *independent (main) clause* can stand alone as a sentence because it expresses a complete thought.

When an independent clause stands by itself, it is called a sentence. It is called an independent clause when it appears in a sentence with another clause. In the following example, the two independent clauses are joined with a comma and a conjunction. The subject in each clause is underlined once; the verbs are underlined twice.

┌──────────Independent Clause──────────┐   ┌──Independent Clause──┐
Alicia decorated the hall for the party, **and** Shelly prepared the music.

Both of these clauses can stand alone as single sentences.

┌─────────── Sentence ───────────┐┌─────── Sentence ───────┐
Alicia decorated the hall for the party. Shelly prepared the music.

Subordinate Clauses

A *subordinate (dependent) clause* cannot stand alone. It does not express a complete thought.

Even though the subordinate clauses below have subjects and verbs, they cannot stand alone. They need another clause to complete their meaning.

Subordinate Clause	Complete Sentence
after the game ended	**After the game ended,** the players left the field.
wherever children play	The environment should be safe **wherever children play**.

Like phrases, subordinate clauses can be used as adjectives, adverbs, and nouns.

Adjective Clauses

An *adjective clause* is a subordinate clause that is used like an adjective to modify a noun or a pronoun.

Single Adjective
Synthesizers are **versatile** instruments.

Adjective Phrase
Synthesizers are instruments **of great versatility.**

Adjective Clause
Synthesizers are instruments **that enable musicians to make many different sounds.**

Adjective clauses answer the questions *Which one?* and *What kind?*

Which One?
Ken's bike, **which is blue and white**, is new.

What Kind?
Kate wishes she lived in a house **that was closer to the park**.

Relative Pronouns Most adjective clauses begin with a relative pronoun. A **relative pronoun** connects an adjective clause to the noun or the pronoun it modifies.

Relative Pronouns				
who	whom	whose	which	that

I just met the girl **who lives in the yellow house on the corner**.

George, **whose house caught fire last week**, is staying with us.

Functions of a Relative Pronoun In addition to introducing an adjective clause, a relative pronoun has another function. It can serve as a subject, a direct object, or an object of a preposition within the adjective clause. It can also show possession.

Subject	The Great Depression, **which began in 1929,** was a bleak time in American history. (*Which* is the subject of *began*.)
Direct Object	The economic confidence **that most Americans enjoyed** was shattered. (*That* is the direct object of *enjoyed*.)
Object of a Preposition	The time period **about which I am writing** lasted for eleven years. (*Which* is the object of the preposition *about*.)
Possession	Few were the Americans **whose lives were unaffected**. (*Whose* shows possession of *lives*.)

Sometimes the relative pronoun *that* is omitted from an adjective clause. Nevertheless, it still has its function.

The Grapes of Wrath is a novel **John Steinbeck wrote about the Depression.** (*That John Steinbeck wrote about the Depression* is the adjective clause. *That* [understood] is the direct object within the adjective clause.)

As You Write

If the information in an adjective clause is **essential**, no commas are needed to set it off from the rest of the sentence. Information is essential if it identifies a person, place, or thing and is necessary for understanding the meaning of the sentence.

If the information in an adjective clause is **not essential**, it must be set off from the sentence by commas. Information is not essential if it can be removed without changing the meaning of the sentence.

Essential	A vaccine *that* **will prevent the disease** was discovered in the laboratory. (The adjective clause is needed to identify which vaccine was discovered, therefore no commas are necessary.)
Nonessential	The mad scientist, *who* **also works in the laboratory**, conducted a secret experiment. (The adjective clause could be removed from the sentence without changing the meaning, therefore commas are necessary.)

Eccentric junk collector Bruce Lacey known as the "Mad Professor"

***That* or *Which*?** In formal writing it is customary to use the relative pronoun *that* with essential clauses and the relative pronoun *which* with nonessential clauses.

Misplaced Adjective Clauses An adjective clause must be placed near the word it modifies. If it is too far away, it may cause confusion.

Misplaced Adjective Clause	Mandy donated the centerpiece *who* **runs the garden shop.** (The adjective phrase *who runs the garden shop* is too far away from *Mandy*. The centerpiece did not run the garden shop.)
Corrected	Mandy, *who* **runs the garden shop**, donated the centerpiece.

Adverb Clauses

An *adverb clause* is a subordinate clause that is used like an adverb to modify a verb, an adjective, or another adverb.

Single Adverb   Let's meet **there**.

Adverb Phrase   Let's meet **at the corner**.

Adverb Clause   Let's meet **where we met before**.

Like an adverb, an adverb clause answers the questions *How? When? Where? How much?, To what extent, Why?* and *Under what condition?*

How?   Adam described the piano **as if he had seen it before**.

When?   **When he saw the harpsichord**, his mouth dropped open.

Where?   We will go **wherever we get our next gig**.

Why?   We missed the train **because Antonio's watch stopped**.

Under What Condition?   **If you want to hear a good band**, go to that concert.

Subordinating Conjunctions An adverb clause begins with a **subordinating conjunction**. A few of the subordinating conjunctions listed in the chart below—such as *after, as, before,* and *until*—can also be used as prepositions. Remember that these words are subordinating conjunctions only if they are followed by a group of words with a subject and a verb.

Common Subordinating Conjunctions			
after	as soon as	in order that	until
although	as though	since	when
as	because	so that	whenever
as far as	before	than	where
as if	even though	though	wherever
as long as	if	unless	while

As You Write

Always place a comma after an adverb clause that comes at the beginning of a sentence.

Before we toured Ireland, we visited London.

If our flight is late, the tour bus will wait for us.

Sometimes an adverb clause will interrupt an independent clause. If it does, place a comma before and after the adverb clause.

Our schedule, **as far as I can tell,** seems reasonable.

When an adverb clause follows an independent clause, no comma is needed.

We will drive **so that we can see the countryside.**

Noun Clauses

A *noun clause* is a subordinate clause that is used as a noun.

Single Noun   Show us the **poem**.

┌─Noun Clause─┐
Noun Clause   Show us **what you read**.

Like a noun, a noun clause can serve as a subject, an object, or a predicate nominative.

Subject	**Whatever poem you choose to read** is bound to be a hit. (*Whatever poem you choose to read* is the subject.)
Direct Object	We'll rent **whatever movie is your favorite**. (*Whatever movie is your favorite* is the direct object.)
Indirect Object	Give **whoever comes to class** a copy of the reading list. (*Whoever comes to class* is the indirect object. The direct object is *copy.*)
Object of a Preposition	Matt was confused by **what the umpire shouted**. (*What the umpire shouted* is the object of the preposition *by.*)
Predicate Nominative	My vacation was exactly **what I was hoping for**. (*What I was hoping for* renames the subject, *vacation.*)

Noun clauses often begin with words such as those listed in the following table.

Common Introductory Words for Noun Clauses		
how	where	whom
if	wherever	whomever
that	whether	whose
what	which	why
whatever	who	
when	whoever	

Do not rely on introductory words alone to identify a noun clause. Instead, figure out how the clause is being used in a sentence.

Sentence Structure

Sentences are classified as either **simple, compound,** or **complex**. You can determine a sentence's structure by looking at the number and kind of clauses it contains.

Simple Sentences

A *simple sentence* consists of one independent clause.

> Theirry <u>caught</u> several fish.

> Thierry <u>caught</u> several fish in the mountain stream.

Sometimes a simple sentence contains a compound subject.

> <u>Whitney</u> and <u>Rob</u> <u>gave</u> away all their old toys.

Sometimes a simple sentence contains a compound verb.

> The <u>sailor</u> <u>untied</u> the lines and <u>jumped</u> onto the ship.

Compound Sentences

A *compound sentence* contains two or more independent clauses.

Each independent clause in a compound sentence can stand alone as a separate sentence. Compound sentences are usually joined by a coordinating conjunction such as *and, or, but,* or *yet.*

> ┌──────Independent Clause──────┐   ┌──Independent Clause──┐
> We'll <u>play</u> our jazz piece during halftime, **and** the <u>pep squad</u> <u>will dance</u>.

> ┌──Independent Clause──┐   ┌─Independent Clause─┐
> The fishing <u>party</u> <u>is</u> ready, **but** the <u>guide</u> <u>is</u> not here.

The independent clauses of a compound sentence can also be joined by adding a semicolon. The semicolon replaces the conjunction.

> ┌Independent Clause┐ ┌──────Independent Clause──────┐
> The <u>fish</u> <u>were</u> biting; <u>everyone</u> on the boat <u>caught</u> something.

Complex Sentences

A *complex sentence* contains one or more independent clauses and one or more subordinate clauses.

┌────Subordinate Clause────┐ ┌Independent Clause┐
Although she was nervous, Alicia hit a home run.

┌────Subordinate Clause────┐ ┌Independent Clause┐ ┌Independent Clause┐
Although she was nervous, Alicia hit a home run, and the crowd cheered.

┌Independent Clause┐ ┌────────Subordinate Clause────────┐
Alicia hit a home run, although she had never played baseball before.

As You Write

When you write, think about your audience as you choose the kinds of sentences you use. Simple sentences are most appropriate for a young audience. Compound and complex sentences are more difficult to understand, but they show the relationship between ideas.

The electric car was new. We did not have to recharge the battery.

The electric car was new, and we did not have to recharge the battery.

Because the electric car was new, we did not have to recharge the battery.

Inventor Jonathan Tennyson in his solar-electric vehicle

10

Sentence Fragments and Run-ons

QuickGuide

Sentence Fragments pages 69–71	A **sentence fragment** is a group of words that does not express a complete thought.
Run-on Sentences page 71	Two or more independent clauses that are joined without adequate punctuation form a **run-on sentence**.

Sentence Fragments

A *sentence fragment* is a group of words that does not express a complete thought.

A sentence fragment may lack a subject or a verb or both.

No Subject	Wrote the editorial about the bubble gum problem. (Who wrote the editorial? There is no subject.)
Sentence	**Tolley** wrote the editorial about the bubble gum problem.
No Verb	The new members of the student council. (What did the new members do? There is no verb.)
Sentence	The new members of the student council **sponsored** a dance.
No Subject or Verb	Across the dance floor. (Who did what across the dance floor? There is no subject or verb.)
Sentence	**Maria and Dave waltzed** across the dance floor.

Phrase Fragments

When phrases are not joined to independent clauses, they result in **phrase fragments**.

A phrase fragment can be corrected by adding a subject and verb to the phrase or by attaching the phrase to an independent clause. The phrase fragments that follow are in **bold type**.

Prepositional Phrase Fragment	I delivered the newspaper. **Onto the Engs' front porch**.
Corrected	I delivered the newspaper. It flew onto the Engs' front porch. (Add a subject and predicate.)
	I delivered the newspaper onto the Engs' front porch. (Attach the fragment to the independent clause.)

Appositive Phrase Fragment	For breakfast I drink chocolate milk. **My favorite food**.
Corrected	For breakfast I drink chocolate milk. It is my favorite food. (Add a subject and predicate.)
	For breakfast I drink chocolate milk, my favorite food. (Attach the fragment to the independent clause.)
Participial Phrase Fragment	**Sitting on the steps.** I waited for my friends to show up.
Corrected	I was sitting on the steps. I waited for my friends to show up. (Add a subject and predicate.)
	Sitting on the steps, I waited for my friends to show up. (Attach the fragment to the independent clause.)
Infinitive Phrase Fragment	Heidi bought a new camera. **To take on her trip**.
Corrected	Heidi bought a new camera. She will take it on her trip.
	(Add a subject and predicate.)
	Heidi bought a new camera to take on her trip. (Attach the fragment to the independent clause.)

Clause Fragments

As you have learned, a subordinate clause does not express a complete thought, even though it has a subject and a verb. If it is not attached to a sentence, it is called a **clause fragment.**

A clause fragment can be corrected by revising it to create independent clauses or by attaching it to an independent clause. The clause fragments on the next page are in **bold type.**

Adverb Clause	**When I design a product.** I list materials it will require.
Corrected	When I design a product, I list materials it will require. (Replace the period with a comma to attach the fragment to the independent clause.)
Adjective Clause	I suggest a protest. **In which we make our point peacefully.**
Corrected	I suggest a protest in which we make our point peacefully. (Remove the period to attach the fragment to the independent clause.)

As You Write

Fragments are often used in dialogue or by professional writers who wish to achieve a specific tone or effect in their writing. However, fragments are rarely, if ever, appropriate for use in school assignments.

Run-on Sentences

Two or more independent clauses that are joined without adequate punctuation form a **run-on sentence**. To correct a run-on sentence, simply add appropriate punctuation, revise existing punctuation, or revise the sentence.

Run-on	The concert is beginning, it will be over by lunchtime.
Corrected	The concert is beginning. It will be over by lunchtime. (The revision contains two separate sentences.)
	The concert is beginning; it will be over by lunchtime. (The revision contains two independent clauses joined by a semicolon.)
	The concert is beginning, and it will be over by lunchtime. (The revision contains two independent clauses joined by a comma and a coordinating conjunction.)

CHAPTER

11 Using Verbs

QuickGuide

Parts of Verbs pages 73–79	A verb has four principal parts: the **present**, the **present participle**, the **past**, and the **past participle**.
Tenses of Verbs pages 79–81	The time expressed by a verb is called its **tense**. The six verb tenses are **present, present perfect, past, past perfect, future,** and **future perfect**.
Verb Conjugations pages 82–86	A **conjugation** lists all the singular and plural forms of a verb in its six tenses.
Active Voice and Passive Voice pages 86–87	**Active voice** indicates that the subject is performing the action. **Passive voice** indicates that the action of the verb is being performed on the subject.

Parts of Verbs

A verb has four *principal parts*: present, present participle, past, and past participle.

A verb shows action or tells something about its subject. A verb also tells when something happened (or is happening).

The principal parts of the verb *jog* are used in the following examples. Notice that the present participle and the past participle include helping verbs.

Present	I **jog** two miles every day.
Present Participle	I *am* **jogging** to the lake and back.
Past	Yesterday I **jogged** to the park.
Past Participle	I *have* **jogged** every day this week.

Regular Verbs

A **regular verb** forms its past and past participle by adding *–ed* or *-d* to the present form of the verb.

Present	Present Participle	Past	Past Participle
lift	(is) lifting	lifted	(have) lifted
wonder	(is) wondering	wondered	(have) wondered
hire	(is) hiring	hired	(have) hired
skip	(is) skipping	skipped	(have) skipped
cry	(is) crying	cried	(have) cried

Notice that when you add *–ed* or *–ing* to some verbs, the spelling changes slightly, as in *hire*, *skip*, and *cry*.

Irregular Verbs

An **irregular verb** does not form the past and past participle by adding *-ed* or *-d* to the present. Look at the following verb groups.

Group 1 These irregular verbs have the same form for the present, the past, and the past participle.

Present, Past, and Past Particle Use the Same Form			
Present	**Present Participle**	**Past**	**Past Participle**
burst	(is) bursting	burst	(have) burst
cost	(is) costing	cost	(have) cost
hit	(is) hitting	hit	(have) hit
let	(is) letting	let	(have) let
put	(is) putting	put	(have) put

Group 2 Some irregular verbs change entirely to form the past tense but have the same form for the past and the past participle.

Past and Past Participle Use the Same Form			
Present	**Present Participle**	**Past**	**Past Participle**
bring	(is) bringing	brought	(have) brought
buy	(is) buying	bought	(have) bought
catch	(is) catching	caught	(have) caught
leave	(is) leaving	left	(have) left
lose	(is) losing	lost	(have) lost
make	(is) making	made	(have) made
say	(is) saying	said	(have) said
teach	(is) teaching	taught	(have) taught

Group 3 These irregular verbs form their past participle by adding *-n* to past tense.

Past Participle Formed by Adding *-n* to the Past Tense			
Present	**Present Participle**	**Past**	**Past Participle**
break	(is) breaking	broke	(have) broken
choose	(is) choosing	chose	(have) chosen
freeze	(is) freezing	froze	(have) frozen
speak	(is) speaking	spoke	(have) spoken
steal	(is) stealing	stole	(have) stolen
tear	(is) tearing	tore	(have) torn

Group 4 These verbs form their past participle by adding *-n* to the present tense.

Past Participle Formed by Adding *-n* to the Present Tense			
Present	**Present Participle**	**Past**	**Past Participle**
blow	(is) blowing	blew	(have) blown
draw	(is) drawing	drew	(have) drawn
drive	(is) driving	drove	(have) driven
give	(is) giving	gave	(have) given
grow	(is) growing	grew	(have) grown
know	(is) knowing	knew	(have) known
see	(is) seeing	saw	(have) seen
take	(is) taking	took	(have) taken
throw	(is) throwing	threw	(have) thrown

Group 5 These irregular verbs form their past and past participle by changing a vowel. In these verbs the *i* in the present changes to an *a* in the past and to a *u* in the past participle.

Past and Past Participle Formed by Changing a Vowel			
Present	Present Participle	Past	Past Participle
begin	(is) beginning	began	(have) begun
drink	(is) drinking	drank	(have) drunk
ring	(is) ringing	rang	(have) rung
sing	(is) singing	sang	(have) sung
sink	(is) sinking	sank	(have) sunk
swim	(is) swimming	swam	(have) swum

Group 6 These irregular verbs form the past and the past participle in other ways.

Past and Past Participle Formed in Other Ways			
Present	Present Participle	Past	Past Participle
come	(is) coming	came	(have) come
do	(is) doing	did	(have) done
eat	(is) eating	ate	(have) eaten
fall	(is) falling	fell	(have) fallen
go	(is) going	went	(have) gone
ride	(is) riding	rode	(have) ridden
run	(is) running	ran	(have) run
write	(is) writing	wrote	(have) written

Six Problem Verbs

The following common verbs are often misused.

Bring and Take

Bring indicates motion toward the speaker. *Take* indicates motion away from the speaker.

Present	Present Participle	Past	Past Participle
bring	(is) bringing	brought	(have) brought
take	(is) taking	took	(have) taken

Bring
Our dog **brings** us the newspaper every morning.

Grandma **is bringing** us her famous lemon shortbread.

Dan **brought** a friend from college home with him.

That tourist **must have brought** his entire wardrobe with him!

Take
Take this misdirected mail to the Smith family.

Ryan **is taking** his sister across town to visit her best friend.

"**Take** me with you," I begged.

Sometimes I think I**'ve taken** every stray in town to the shelter.

Learn and Teach

Learn means "to gain knowledge." *Teach* means "to instruct" or to "show how."

Present	Present Participle	Past	Past Participle
learn	(is) learning	learned	(have) learned
teach	(is) teaching	taught	(have) taught

Learn	I **learn** best on a full stomach.
	He **is learning** to toss a bone in the air and catch it in his jaws.
	I **learned** never to fall asleep with bubble gum in my mouth.
	I **have** already **learned** the six most basic guitar chords.
Teach	**Teach** me to play the new song you wrote.
	He's an old dog, but I**'m teaching** him new tricks anyway.
	I **taught** my baby sister to put her foot in her mouth.
	I**'ve taught** this technique to klutzier people than you!

Leave and Let

Leave means "to depart" or "to go away." *Let* means "to allow" or "to permit."

Present	Present Participle	Past	Past Participle
leave	(is) leaving	left	(have) left
let	(is) letting	let	(have) let

Leave	You**'d** better **leave** now before it starts raining.
	We**'re leaving** for the theater in five minutes.
	Shaq **left** his watch in the locker room .
	Emily **had** never **left** for school so early before.

Let	Let the dog out before you leave for the day.
	I'm **letting** you borrow this shirt because you're my best friend.
	Let me concentrate on this putt.
	She **has let** me borrow her car every Friday since the year began.

Tenses of Verbs

The time expressed by a verb is called its *tense*.

There are six verb tenses: **present, present perfect, past, past perfect, future,** and **future perfect.** The following examples show how the verb *walk* is used in all six tenses.

Present	Every day I **walk** five miles.
Past	I **walked** five miles yesterday.
Future	I **will walk** again tomorrow.
Present Perfect	For one year I **have walked** every morning.
Past Perfect	I **had** not **walked** much before that.
Future Perfect	I **will have walked** eight hundred miles by May.

Uses of the Tenses

All six verb tenses can be formed from the principal parts of verbs—along with the helping verbs *have, has, had, will,* and *shall.*

Present Tense is used to express an action that is going on now. To form the present tense, use the present form (the first principal part of the verb) or add *-s* or *-es* to the present form.

Present Tense	Michele **gives** tours.
	I **paint** pictures.

Past Tense expresses an action that already took place or was completed in the past. To form the past tense of a regular verb, add *-ed* or *-d* to the present form. To form the past of an irregular verb, check a dictionary for the past form.

Past Tense	Michele **gave** a tour last night.
	I **painted** a picture last night.

Future tense is used to express an action that will take place in the future. To form the future tense, use the helping verb *will* or *shall* with the present form.

Future Tense	Michele **will give** a tour at noon tomorrow.
	I **shall paint** another picture tomorrow.

You can learn more about the correct use of shall *and* will *on page 127.*

Present Perfect Tense expresses an action that was completed at some indefinite time in the past. It also expresses an action that started in the past and is still ongoing. To form the present perfect tense, add *has* or *have* to the past participle.

Present Perfect Tense	Michele **has given** tours for a long time.
	I **have painted** portraits of my family members.

Past Perfect Tense expresses an action that took place before some other action. To form the past perfect tense, add *had* to the past participle.

| Past Perfect Tense | Michele took a break after she **had given** the tour. |
| | I **had painted** landscapes before I painted portraits. |

Future Perfect Tense expresses an action that will take place before another future action or time. To form the future perfect tense, add *shall have* or *will have* to the past participle.

| Future Perfect Tense | Michele **will have given** one hundred tours before her summer job ends. |
| | I **shall have painted** more than three new pictures by the end of the month. |

Verb Conjugations

A *conjugation* lists all the singular and plural forms of a verb in its six tenses.

Regular and irregular verbs are conjugated differently. The following is a conjugation of the regular verb *fix*.

Present	
Singular	**Plural**
I fix	we fix
you fix	you fix
he, she, it fixes	they fix
Past	
I fixed	we fixed
you fixed	you fixed
he, she, it fixed	they fixed
Future	
I shall/will fix	we shall/will fix
you will fix	you will fix
he, she, it will fix	they will fix
Present Perfect	
I have fixed	we have fixed
you have fixed	you have fixed
he, she, it has fixed	they have fixed
Past Perfect	
I had fixed	we had fixed
you had fixed	you had fixed
he, she, it had fixed	they had fixed

Future Perfect	
I will/shall have fixed	we will/shall have fixed
you will have fixed	you will have fixed
he, she, it will have fixed	they will have fixed

Here is a conjugation of the irregular verb *give*, whose four principle parts are *give, giving, gave,* and *given.*

Present	
Singular	**Plural**
I give	we give
you give	you give
he, she, it gives	they give
Past	
I gave	we gave
you gave	you gave
he, she, it gave	they gave
Future	
I shall/will give	we shall/will give
you will give	you will give
he, she, it will give	they will give
Present Perfect	
I have given	we have given
you have given	you have given
he, she, it has given	they have given
Past Perfect	
I had given	we had given
you had given	you had given
he, she, it had given	they had given

Future Perfect	
I will/shall have given	we will/shall have given
you will have given	you will have given
he, she, it will have given	they will have given

As You Write

Most folk literature is written in the past tense, as is this excerpt from "Hansel and Gretel."

> Hard by a great forest dwelt a poor wood-cutter with his wife and his two children. The boy was called Hansel and the girl Gretel. He had little to bite and to break, and once when great dearth fell on the land, he could no longer procure even daily bread.
>
> —Grimm Brothers, "Hansel and Gretel"

When you write about the literature you read, however, it is proper to write about it in the present tense. For example, if you were to write about the passage above, you might say:

> The story of "Hansel and Gretel" opens with a description of the sad state of the children's family. Hansel and Gretel live with their father and his wife in a great forest. They barely ever have enough food, and it soon becomes impossible for the wood-cutter to get any food at all to feed his family.

Progressive Verb Forms

Each of the six tenses has a **progressive form**. These forms are used to express continuing or ongoing action. The progressive forms add a special meaning to verbs that the regular tenses do not. Notice the differences in meaning in the following examples.

Present	She **runs**. (*Runs* shows that she can or does run.)
Present Progressive	She **is running**. (*Is running* shows that she is running right now.)
Past Progressive	She **was running**. (*Was running* shows an ongoing action that took place in the past.)

The use of progressive forms of verbs often brings a sense of excitement because something is happening right then and there. That is why sports announcers and radio commentators often use the progressive form when they describe something that is going on.

To form the progressive, add a form of the verb *be* to the present participle. Notice in the following examples that all of the progressive forms end in *-ing*.

Progressive Forms	
Present Progressive	I am giving
Past Progressive	I was giving.
Future Progressive	I will (shall) be giving.
Present Perfect Progressive	I have been giving
Past Perfect Progressive	I had been giving.
Future Perfect Progressive	I will (shall) have been giving.

When you read a story, you quickly learn when it took place by noting the tense of the verbs. When you write, you pass on that same kind of information to your readers. Keep your tenses consistent as you write. For example, if you are telling a story that took place in the past, use the past tense of verbs. If you suddenly shift to the present, you probably will confuse your readers.

Avoid unnecessary shifts in tense within a sentence or within related sentences.

Inconsistent	past present After I **laid** the blanket on the beach, the sun **goes** behind a cloud.
Consistent	past past After I **laid** my blanket on the beach, the sun **went** behind a cloud.
Inconsistent	present future I **wear** my shirt and I **won't burn**.
Consistent	future future I **will wear** my shirt and I **won't burn**.

Active and Passive Voice

In addition to a tense, a verb is said to be in the *active* or the *passive voice*.

The **active voice** indicates that the subject is performing the action. The **passive voice** indicates that the action of the verb is being performed on the subject.

Active Voice	Mr. Takamoto **placed** the round stones in the garden.
Passive Voice	The round stones **were placed** in the garden by Mr. Takamoto.

Active Voice	The wind **rattles** the tall stalks of bamboo.
Passive Voice	The tall stalks of bamboo **are rattled** by the wind.

A verb in the passive voice consists of a form of the verb *be* plus a past participle. The forms of *be* used for the passive voice are *is, are, was, were, has been, have been,* and *had been.* Study the following examples.

Active Voice	The wind **blew** over the small pine on the hill. (*The wind* is performing the action.)
Passive Voice	The small pine on the hill **was blown** over by the wind. (*The pine* is receiving the action of the verb. *Was* is a form of the verb *be,* and *blown* is the past participle of *blow.*)

As You Write

When you write, use the active voice as much as possible. The active voice is more forceful and adds life to your writing. The only time the passive voice is more appropriate is when the doer of the action is unknown or unimportant.

Passive Voice	Irises **were planted** beside the stream.

Vase with Irises, Henri Matisse, 1912

CHAPTER 12

Using Pronouns

QuickGuide

The Cases of Personal Pronouns pages 89–98	**Case** is the form of a noun or pronoun that indicates its use in a sentence. There are three cases: The **nominative case** is used for subjects and predicate nominatives. The **objective case** is used for direct objects, indirect objects, and objects of prepositions. The **possessive case** is used to show ownership or possession.
Pronouns and Their Antecedents pages 98–101	A pronoun must agree in **number** and **gender** with its **antecedent**. Every personal pronoun must clearly refer to a specific antecedent.

The Cases of Personal Pronouns

Case is the form of a noun or pronoun that indicates its use in a sentence.

Personal pronouns have different forms, called cases, depending on whether they are subjects, objects, or possessives in a sentence.

She helped him.

Rob helped **his** aunt.

In English, there are three cases: the **nominative case**, the **objective case**, and the **possessive case.**

Nominative Case (used for subjects and predicate nominatives)		
	Singular	**Plural**
First Person	I	we
Second Person	you	you
Third Person	he, she, it	they

Objective Case (used for direct objects, indirect objects, and objects of prepositions)		
	Singular	**Plural**
First Person	me	us
Second Person	you	you
Third Person	him, her, it	them

Possessive Case (used to show ownership or possession)		
	Singular	**Plural**
First Person	my, mine	our, ours
Second Person	your, yours	your, yours
Third Person	his, her, hers, its	their, theirs

The Nominative Case

The *nominative case* is used for subjects and predicate nominatives.

The personal pronouns in the following chart are in the nominative case.

Nominative Case Pronouns		
	Singular	**Plural**
First Person	I	we
Second Person	you	you
Third Person	he, she, it	they

Pronouns in the nominative case are used as subjects and as predicate nominatives.

Subject   **She** rescued the dog.

Predicate   The man in the blue suit is **he**.
Nominative

You can learn more about personal pronouns on page 14.

Pronouns Used as Subjects   A **subject** names the person, place, or thing the sentence is about. Because the pronouns in the sentences below are used as subjects, the nominative case is used.

Subjects   I decorated my room.

Do **they** live in that apartment? (Turn a question into a statement: *They do live in that apartment.* Then it is easy to see that *they* is the subject.)

When a sentence has only one subject, choosing the correct pronoun is usually not a problem. If a sentence has a compound subject, however, it is easy to make a mistake.

Compound   Mom and (I, me) painted the fence.
Subject

To find the correct pronoun, say the sentence as if each pronoun stood alone.

Correct   **I** painted the fence.

Incorrect   **Me** painted the fence.

By separating the choices, you can see and hear which pronoun is correct. The nominative case *I* is the correct form to use.

Correct   Mom and **I** painted the fence.

You can learn more about finding the subject of a sentence on pages 4–7.

Pronouns Used as Predicate Nominatives   A **predicate nominative** is a word that follows a linking verb—verbs such as *is, were,* or *has been*—and identifies or renames the subject. A pronoun used as a predicate nominative is in the nominative case.

Predicate   The best dancer is **he**.
Nominatives

Are the two in costumes **they**? (Turn a question into a statement: *The two in costumes are they.* Then, it is easy to see that *they* renames the subject.)

Check for the correct case of a pronoun in a compound predicate nominative by turning the sentence around to make the predicate nominative the subject. Then say each pronoun separately to learn which is correct.

Predicate Nominative	The musicians will be Brett and (she, her).
	Brett and (she, her) will be the musicians.
Correct	**She** will be a musician.
Incorrect	**Her** will be a musician.
Correct	The musicians will be Brett and **she**.

Sometimes sentences with pronouns used as predicate nominatives sound wrong even though they are technically correct. When you write, you can avoid these awkward-sounding sentences by reversing them. Turn the predicate nominatives into the subjects.

Awkward	The best dancer is **he**.
Better	**He** is the best dancer.
Awkward	The two in costumes are **they**.
Better	**They** are the two in costumes.
Awkward	The musicians will be Brett and **she**.
Better	**She** and Brett will be the musicians.

As You Write

Expressions like *It's me* or *That's her* are acceptable in informal speech. When you write, however, the required expressions are *It is I* and *That is she* because *I* and *she* are predicate nominatives.

You can learn more about predicate nominatives on page 42.
You can learn more about linking verbs on pages 21–22.

The Objective Case

The *objective case* is used for direct objects, indirect objects, and objects of prepositions.

The following personal pronouns are in the objective case.

Objective Case Pronouns		
	Singular	**Plural**
First Person	me	us
Second Person	you	you
Third Person	him, her, it	them

Direct Object	The Web site interested **us**.
Indirect Object	Mom gave **us** directions to the site.
Object of a Preposition	She always shares interesting sites with **us**.

Pronouns Used as Direct and Indirect Objects A **direct object** follows an action verb and answers the question *Whom?* or *What?*

Direct Object	The Walkers invited **us** to their slumber party. (Invited whom? *Us* is the direct object.)
	Did you see **them**? (Turn a question into a statement: *You did see them.* You did see whom? *Them* is the direct object.)

An **indirect object** comes before a direct object and answers the question
To or for whom? or *To or for what?*

Indirect Object	i.o. ⌐——d.o.——⌐ Ms. Green gave **us** the assignment. (Ms. Green gave what? *Assignment* is the direct object. She gave the assignment to whom? *Us* is the indirect object.)
	i.o. ⌐d.o.⌐ Did you give **her** the tickets? (Turn a question into a statement: *You did give what? Tickets* is the direct object. Give the tickets to whom? *Her* is the indirect object.)

Check for the correct case of a compound object in the same way you check for the correct case of a compound subject. Say the nominative and objective case pronouns separately.

Direct Object	Did Miguel thank Chris and (he, him)?
Incorrect	Miguel did thank **he**.
Correct	Miguel did thank **him**.
Correct	Did Miguel thank Chris and **him**?
Indirect Object	Mom handed Kim and (I, me) a gift.
Incorrect	Mom handed **I** a gift.
Correct	Mom handed **me** a gift.
Correct	Mom handed Kim and **me** a gift.

You can learn more about direct objects and indirect objects on pages 39–41.

Pronouns Used as Objects of Prepositions A **prepositional phrase** begins with a preposition, such as *with, to, by,* or *for*. A prepositional phrase ends with the **object of a preposition**. A pronoun used as an object of a preposition is in the objective case.

Objects of Prepositions	Did David talk **to *them***? (*To them* is the prepositional phrase.)
	Nicole mailed the tickets **to *us***. (*To us* is the prepositional phrase.)

You can find a list of prepositions on page 33.

As You Write

People sometimes make a common mistake when they use the preposition *between*. In an attempt to sound formal or correct, people often use nominative case pronouns after *between*. However, all pronouns used as objects of prepositions must be in the objective case. In this instance, what sounds more natural is correct.

Incorrect	The argument was between **he** and **I**.
Correct	The argument was between **him** and **me**.

The Possessive Case

The *possessive case* is used to show ownership or possession.

The following personal pronouns are in the possessive case.

Possessive Case Pronouns		
	Singular	**Plural**
First Person	my, mine	our, ours
Second Person	your, yours	your, yours
Third Person	his, her, hers, its	their, theirs

Possessive pronouns can be divided into two groups: (1) those that are used like adjectives to modify nouns and (2) those that are used alone.

Uses of Possessive Pronouns	
Used Like Adjectives	my, your, his, her, its, our, their
Used Alone	mine, yours, his, hers, its, ours, theirs

Pronouns used as adjectives are sometimes called **possessive adjectives**.

My hat is here, but **yours** is over there.

Her sweater is yellow, and **mine** is green.

Apostrophes are used with possessive nouns, but they are never used with possessive forms of personal pronouns.

Possessive Noun	Is this **Jessica's** coat?
Possessive Pronoun	Is this coat **hers**? (not *her's*)

Possessive Pronoun or Contraction? Sometimes some contractions are confused with personal pronouns because they sound alike.

Possessive Pronouns and Contractions	
Possessive Pronouns	its, your, their, theirs
Contractions	it's (it is), you're (you are), they're (they are), there's (there is)

The best way to separate these words in your mind is to say the two words that a contraction stands for.

Possessive Pronoun or Contraction?	Is (you're, your) coat here?
Incorrect	Is **you are** coat here?
Correct	Is **your** coat here?

As You Write

When you speak, some contractions and possessive pronouns sound the same. When you write, you have to know which one to use. One of the most frequent mistakes is writing *it's* for *its*. Remember that no possessive pronoun has an apostrophe. When you aren't sure whether to write *it's* or *its*, mentally substitute the word *his*. If *his* makes sense, then write *its*.

Because the door to **its** cage was left open, the hamster escaped.

Because the door to **his** cage was left open, the hamster escaped

The dog knocked over **its** dish.

The dog knocked over **his** dish.

Pronoun Problem: *Who* or *Whom*?

Who and *whom* can be used as interrogative pronouns. Like personal pronouns, these pronouns also have case.

Who is in the nominative case and can be the subject.

Subject	**Who** decorated the classroom for the party?

Whom is in the objective case and can be used as a direct object or as an object of a preposition.

Direct Object	**Whom** did you see during the school trip? (Turn a question into a statement. *You did see whom during the school trip. Whom* is the direct object.)
Object of a Preposition	From **whom** did you receive those magazines? (*From whom* is a prepositional phrase.)

Whose can also be used as an interrogative pronoun. It always shows possession.

Whose is this backpack on the floor? (*Whose* modifies *backpack.*)

Looking at all the backpacks, we didn't know **whose** were **whose**! (*Whose* is used as a subject and then as a predicate nominative.)

Pronouns and Their Antecedents

A pronoun must agree in *number* and *gender* with its *antecedent*.

The word or group of words that a pronoun refers to or replaces is called the pronoun's **antecedent**. In the following sentences, *Maria* is the antecedent of *her*, and *Waltons* is the antecedent of *they*.

Pronouns and Antecedents	**Maria** raised **her** hand and volunteered.
	The **Waltons** are our neighbors. **They** are planning a garage sale.

Because a pronoun and its antecedent both refer to the same person, place, or thing, they must be in agreement.

Number is the term used to indicate whether a noun or pronoun is singular (one) or plural (more than one). A pronoun must be singular if its antecedent is singular. It must be plural if its antecedent is plural.

Singular   **Luis** is preparing **his** presentation for the meeting.

Plural   The **teachers** have turned in **their** grades for the semester.

The personal pronouns *you, your,* and *yours* can be either singular or plural.

Gender tells whether a noun or a personal pronoun is masculine, feminine, or neuter. A personal pronoun must also agree with its antecedent in gender. The chart below lists personal pronouns according to their gender.

Gender of Personal Pronouns	
Masculine	he, him, his
Feminine	she, her, hers
Neuter	it, its

Things and places are neuter in gender. Unless animals are given proper names, they are usually also considered neuter.

Masculine   **Brian** forgot **his** sneakers.

Feminine   **Amy** gave **her** cat a bath.

Neuter   Wash the **car** and wax **it**.

The plural pronouns *them* and *their* have no gender. They can have masculine, feminine, or neuter antecedents. Their antecedents may also be combinations of masculine and feminine.

The three **women** presented **their** report to the board.

The **men** and **women** on the board compared **their** notes.

Indefinite Pronouns as Antecedents

An **indefinite pronoun** can be the antecedent of a personal pronoun. Some indefinite pronouns are singular, and others are plural. Still other indefinite pronouns may be either singular or plural.

When one of the following indefinite pronouns is the antecedent of a personal pronoun, the personal pronoun must be singular.

Singular Indefinite Pronouns			
anybody	either	neither	one
anyone	everybody	nobody	somebody
each	everyone	no one	someone

Singular   **One** of the boys can't open **his** locker.

Someone in the girls' chorus forgot **her** music.

Sometimes the gender of a singular indefinite pronoun is not indicated in the sentence. Standard English solves this problem by using the phrase *his or her*.

Everyone must finish **his or her** homework.

Although sentences like the previous one are correct, some may sound awkward. You can often eliminate awkwardness by rewriting a sentence in the plural form.

All **students** must finish **their** homework.

When one of the following indefinite pronouns is the antecedent of a personal pronoun, the personal pronoun is plural.

Plural Indefinite Pronouns			
both	few	many	several

Plural   **Several** of the women offered **their** help.

Both of my brothers lost **their** keys.

When one of the following indefinite pronouns is the antecedent of a personal pronoun, that pronoun can be either singular or plural.

Singular or Plural Indefinite Pronouns				
all	any	most	none	some

A personal pronoun used with one of these indefinite antecedents agrees in number and gender with the object of the preposition that follows it.

Singular All of the **art** was returned to **its** owner. (The pronoun *its* agrees with the object of the preposition *art*.)

Plural Some of the **players** wore **their** uniforms. (The pronoun *their* agrees with the object of the preposition *players*.)

As You Write

Unclear or Missing Antecedents The meaning of your writing and speaking can become confusing if the pronouns you use do not have clear antecedents. Remember this rule:

Every personal pronoun should clearly refer to a specific antecedent.

Unclear	Nicholas told Scott **he** could get the tickets. (Who could get the tickets—Nicholas or Scott? The pronoun *he* has two possible antecedents.)
Clear	Nicholas agreed that **Scott** could get the tickets. Nicholas was reassured that **Scott** could get the tickets.
Missing	My brother is a musician, but I know nothing about **it**. (What does *it* refer to? The antecedent is missing.)
Clear	My brother is a musician, but I know nothing about **music**.

CHAPTER 13

Subject & Verb Agreement

QuickGuide

Subject and Verb Agreement **pages 103–104**	A verb must agree with its subject in **number**. A singular subject takes a singular verb; a plural subject takes a plural verb.
Common Agreement Problems **pages 105–113**	The following situations can present agreement problems for writers. • Verb Phrases • Contractions • Interrupting Words • Subjects in Inverted Order • Compound Subjects • Collective Nouns • *You* and *I* as Subjects • Indefinite Pronouns • Words Expressing Amounts and Time • Singular Nouns That Have Plural Forms • Titles

Subject and Verb Agreement

The subject and verb in a sentence must agree in *number*.

Number

As you may recall, **number** is the term used to indicate whether a word is singular—meaning "one"—or plural—meaning "more than one." Nouns, pronouns, and verbs all have number.

The Number of Nouns and Pronouns The plural of most nouns is formed by adding *-s* or *-es* to the singular form. A few nouns, however, form their plurals in other ways. A dictionary always lists irregular plurals.

Nouns				
Singular	monkey	church	mouse	child
Plural	monkey**s**	church**es**	**mice**	child**ren**

Pronouns also have number. For example, *I, he, she,* and *it* are singular, and *we* and *they* are plural. *You* can be singular or plural.

The Number of Verbs Most verbs in the present tense add *-s* or *-es* to form the singular. Plural forms of verbs in the present tense drop the *-s* or *-es*.

Singular

The forward { dribbl**es.**

pivot**s.**

pass**es.**

Plural

The forwards { dribble.

pivot.

pass.

Be, *have*, and *do* have special singular and plural forms in the present tense. *Be* also has special forms in the past tense. Look at the following chart.

Forms of *Be*, *Have*, and *Do*		
	Singular	**Plural**
be	is (present) was (past)	are (present) were (past)
have	has	have
do	does	do

Singular and Plural Subjects

A singular subject takes a singular verb; a plural subject takes a plural verb.

To make a verb agree with its subject, ask two questions: *What is the subject?* and *Is the subject singular or plural?* Then choose the correct form.

Singular   That man coaches a softball team each Saturday.

               She was on the team.

Plural   Those men coach a softball team each Saturday.

               They were on the team.

As You Write

Keeping in mind the rules you just studied will help you remember how to make subjects and verbs agree. One question that you can ask to clear up your own confusion is this: What do you do when the subject and predicate nominative are joined by a linking verb? You know the answer: Make the verb agree with the subject.

The solution is longer study halls. (*Is* agrees with *solution*, not *halls*.)

Longer study halls are the solution. (*Are* agrees with *halls*, not *solution*.)

Common Agreement Problems

Some subjects and verbs present agreement problems for writers. The following are some of the most common.

Verb Phrases

If a sentence has a verb phrase, the first helping verb must agree in number with the subject.

Remember, a verb phrase is a main verb plus one or more helping verbs. In the examples below, subjects are underlined once, verbs are underlined twice, and the first helping verb is in bold type.

Singular   Victoria **is** collecting batteries for the recycling drive.

            (*Victoria* and the helping verb *is* are both singular.)

Plural   We **have** been planning to recycle old telephones.

            (*We* and the first helping verb *have* are both plural.)

The following table shows the singular and plural forms of common helping verbs.

Common Helping Verbs	
Singular	am, is, was, has, does
Plural	are, were, have, do

Contractions

The verb part of a contraction must agree in number with the subject.

When contractions are used, agreement with a subject can be confusing. When you write a contraction, always say the individual words that make up the contraction. Then check for agreement with the subject.

Incorrect	This piece **do**n't fit into the puzzle we're trying to solve. (*Do* is a plural verb form that does not agree with the singular subject *piece*.)
Correct	This piece **does**n't fit into the puzzle we're trying to solve. (*Does* is a singular verb form, which agrees with *piece*.)
Incorrect	They **does**n't appreciate being talked to in that manner. (*Does* is a singular verb form.)
Correct	They **do**n't appreciate being talked to in that manner. (*Do* is a plural verb form, which agrees with *they*.)

The following table shows the singular and plural forms of common contractions.

Contractions	
Singular	doesn't, isn't, wasn't, hasn't
Plural	don't, aren't, weren't, haven't

Interrupting Words

The agreement of a verb with its subject is not changed by interrupting words.

Words, such as prepositional phrases, can come between a subject and its verb. When this happens, a mistake in agreement is easy to make. Sometimes the verb is mistakenly made to agree with a word that is closer to it, rather than with the subject.

In the following examples, notice that each subject and verb agree in number—despite the words that come between them. The best way to find the correct agreement in these sentences is to mentally take out all of the prepositional phrases. Then it is easy to see the remaining subject and verb.

Singular	The juice from these oranges is sour. (*Is* agrees with the subject *juice*, not with the object of the preposition *oranges*—even though *oranges* is closer to the verb.)
Plural	The fruits in this beverage are oranges and raspberries. (*Are* agrees with the subject *fruits*, not with the object of the preposition *beverage*.)

Compound prepositions, such as *in addition to, as well as,* and *along with,* often begin interrupting phrases. Make sure the verb always agrees with the subject, not the object of the preposition.

Blackberry pie, as well as several other desserts, was on the menu. (*Was* agrees with the subject *pie*—not with *desserts*, the object of the compound preposition *as well as*.)

Cinnamon and mocha ice cream flavors, in addition to vanilla, were available. (*Were* agrees with the subject *flavors*—not with *vanilla*.)

Subjects in Inverted Order

A verb must agree in number with the subject, whether the subject comes before or after the verb.

In a sentence's natural order, the subject comes before the verb. However, in a sentence with **inverted order,** the verb or part of the verb phrase comes before the subject. A verb always agrees with its subject, whether the sentence is in natural order or in inverted order.

To find the subject of an inverted sentence, turn the sentence around to its natural order.

Inverted Order	On the glacier were two penguins.
Natural Order	Two penguins were on the glacier.
Question	Can these large birds fly?
Natural Order	These large birds can fly.
Sentence Beginning with _Here_	Here is the penguins' nesting colony.
Natural Order	The penguins' nesting colony is here.
Sentence Beginning with _There_	There were no babies in the nest.
Natural Order	No babies were in the nest. (Sometimes _here_ or _there_ must be dropped to make a sentence sound right.)

Remember that the words _here_ and _there_ are never the subject of a sentence.

Compound Subjects

Agreement between a verb and a compound subject can sometimes be confusing. The following rules will help you avoid agreement errors.

When subjects are joined by *and* or *both/and*, they require a plural verb.

Plural Verb	Jordan **and** Hannah **are** filming the poor conditions on the playground.
	Both the camera **and** the computer belong to Hannah.

When a compound subject is joined by *or, either/or,* or *neither/nor,* the verb agrees with the subject that is closer.

Singular	**Either** Whitney **or** Sonny **is** going to drag the furniture onstage. (The verb is singular because *Sonny*, the subject closer to it, is singular.)
Plural Verb	**Neither** the twigs **nor** sticks are dry enough to be kindling. (The verb is plural because *sticks*, the subject closer to it, is plural.)

This rule is especially important to keep in mind when one subject is singular and the other is plural.

> **Either** chicken wings **or** a hamburger is the special today. (The verb is singular because *hamburger*, the subject closer to it, is singular.)

Collective Nouns

In Chapter 2 you learned that a **collective noun** names a group of people or things.

Common Collective Nouns			
band	congregation	flock	orchestra
class	crew	group	swarm
colony	crowd	herd	team
committee	family	league	tribe

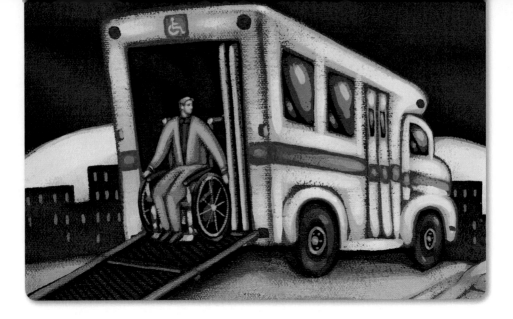

How a collective noun is used determines its agreement with the verb.

Use a singular verb with a collective noun that is perceived as a unit. Use a plural verb with a collective noun that is perceived as more than one individual unit.

> The group **is** going together on the bus. (*Group* is a single unit and takes a singular verb.)

> The group are paying for their tickets individually. (The group members are acting separately, so the verb is plural.)

To make the second sentence clearer—and less awkward—you could reword it.

> Each member of the group will purchase a ticket.

You and *I* as Subjects

The pronouns *you* and *I* do not follow the ordinary rules for subject-verb agreement.

Use a plural verb with *you*—whether *you* refers to one person or more than one person.

Plural Verbs	Martina, you are an excellent poet and performer.
	Students, you have shown amazing calm in this disaster.

Use a plural verb with *I* except with the verbs *am* and *was*.

| Plural Verbs | I help out at the food pantry every Tuesday night. |
| | I have a burning desire to see the Grand Canyon this year. |

| Singular Verbs | I am a pianist, a violinist, and a soprano. |
| | I was standing there behind that plant when you walked in. |

Use a plural verb with compound subjects that contain the pronoun *I*.

Jordan **and** I are poets.

Miriam **and** I were the readers for the poetry slam.

Indefinite Pronouns

When an indefinite pronoun is the subject of a sentence, the verb must agree with the indefinite pronoun.

Some indefinite pronouns are singular, some are plural, and some can be either singular or plural.

The following table shows some common indefinite pronouns.

Common Indefinite Pronouns	
Singular	anybody, anyone, each, either, everybody, everyone, neither, nobody, no one, one, somebody, someone
Plural	both, few, many, several
Singular/ Plural	all, any, most, none, some

| Singular | Someone **has** been calling you all afternoon. (*Has* agrees with the singular indefinite pronoun *someone*.) |
| | Neither of the twins is crazy about pepperoni. (*Is* agrees with the singular indefinite pronoun *neither*, not with the object of the preposition, *twins*.) |

Plural   Few of us <u>want</u> winter to be colder and longer. (*Want* agrees with the plural indefinite pronoun *few*.)

Both of the fans **are** <u>planning</u> to dress in team colors for the first game. (*Are* agrees with the plural indefinite pronoun *both*.)

All, any, most, none, and *some* can be either singular or plural. The number of each of these pronouns is determined by the object of the preposition that follows it.

Singular   All of the **money** <u>goes</u> to researching the prairie ecosystem. (*Money* is singular, so *goes* is also singular.)

Plural   When the ecologist arrives, <u>most</u> of the **prairie dogs** <u>hide</u>. (*Prairie dogs* is plural, so *hide* is also plural.)

Words Expressing Amounts and Times

A subject that expresses an amount, a measurement, a weight, or a time is usually considered singular and takes a singular verb.

Subjects expressing amounts can be confusing because they are sometimes plural in form.

Amount   Five dollars is the price of admission to the dance.

                 (*Five dollars* is one sum of money.)

Time   Nine-tenths of Adriana's spare time **has** been spent

                 planning the dance. (*Nine-tenths* is one part of the time.)

Some amounts are thought of as individual parts. When this happens, a plural verb must be used.

Three quarters **were** left in the cash box.

Singular Nouns That Have Plural Forms

Use a singular verb with certain subjects that are plural in form but singular in meaning.

Words like *measles, mathematics, economics,* and *news* each end in –*s*, but they name single things, such as one disease or one area of knowledge.

In middle school, mathematics was Felicia's best subject.

The news is that she now likes English better.

Titles

A title takes a singular verb.

Titles may have many words, and some of those words may be plural. Nevertheless, a title is the name of only one book or work of art.

Wuthering Heights by Emily Brontë is Andrea's favorite Victorian novel.

Van Gogh's *Irises* hangs next to the bookshelf in Georgia's living room.

CHAPTER 14

Using Adjectives and Adverbs

QuickGuide

Comparison of Adjectives and Adverbs **pages 115–117**	Most adjectives and adverbs have three degrees of comparison: the **positive**, the **comparative**, and the **superlative**.
Problems with Modifiers **pages 118–119**	Watch for these common problem areas when using modifiers. • *Other* or *Else*? • Double Comparisons • Double Negatives • *Good* or *Well*?

Comparison of Adjectives and Adverbs

Writers often compare one thing with another. Adjectives and adverbs generally have three forms that are used for comparisons. These forms are called **degrees of comparison**.

Most adjectives and adverbs have three degrees of comparison: the *positive*, the *comparative*, and the *superlative*.

The positive degree is used when no comparison is being made.

Adjective	The new hotel downtown is **big**.
Adverb	The bicycle messenger moves **swiftly** through the traffic.

The comparative degree is used when two people, things, or actions are being compared.

Adjective	That hotel is **bigger** than the one where we are staying.
Adverb	The bicycle messenger moves **more swiftly** than the taxis.

The superlative degree is used when more than two people, things, or actions are being compared.

Adjective	The **biggest** hotel faces Lake Michigan.
Adverb	The police officer on horseback moves **most swiftly**.

Regular Comparison

Most adjectives and adverbs form the comparative and superlative degrees in a regular manner. The form often depends on the number of syllables in the modifier.

Add -er to form the comparative degree and -est to form the superlative degree of one-syllable modifiers.

Some One-Syllable Modifiers			
	Positive	**Comparative**	**Superlative**
Adjective	bright	brighter	brightest
	sad	sadder	saddest
Adverb	soon	sooner	soonest

A spelling change sometimes occurs when -er or -est is added to certain modifiers. For example, *sad* becomes *sadder* and *saddest*. Check a dictionary if you are not sure how to spell a modifier with a comparative or superlative ending.

Many two-syllable modifiers are formed exactly like one-syllable modifiers. A few, however, would be difficult to pronounce if -er or -est was added. "Usefuler" and "usefulest," for instance, sound awkward. For such two-syllable modifiers, *more* and *most* are used to form the comparative and superlative forms. Also, *more* and *most* are usually used with adverbs ending in -ly.

Use -er or more to form the comparative degree and -est or most to form the superlative degree of two-syllable modifiers.

Two-Syllable Modifiers			
	Positive	**Comparative**	**Superlative**
Adjective	funny	funnier	funniest
	cheerful	more cheerful	most cheerful
Adverb	early	earlier	earliest
	quickly	more quickly	most quickly

When a modifier ends in *y*, the *y* changes to *i*: *funniest, easiest*.

All modifiers with three or more syllables use *more* to form the comparative degree and *most* to form the superlative degree.

Three-Syllable Modifiers			
	Positive	**Comparative**	**Superlative**
Adjective	difficult	more difficult	most difficult
Adverb	frequently	more frequently	most frequently

Irregular Comparison

A few adjectives and adverbs are compared in an irregular manner.

Irregular Modifiers		
Positive	**Comparative**	**Superlative**
bad/badly	worse	worst
good/well	better	best
little	less	least
much/many	more	most

Positive	He knows **little** about American football.
Comparative	He knows even **less** about basketball.
Superlative	The sport he knows the **least** about is lacrosse.

Do not add regular comparison endings to the comparative and superlative degrees of these irregular modifiers. For example, *worse* is the comparative form of *bad*. You should never use "worser."

There are no degrees of comparison for some adjectives—such as *unique, universal, perfect, infinite*—and their adverb forms. The words themselves describe a quality of being complete or perfect.

Problems with Modifiers

Once you know how to form the comparative and superlative forms of modifiers, there are a few problems you should avoid.

Other or *Else*?

Add *other* or *else* when comparing one member of a group with the rest of the group.

Incorrect	Dan is taller than any student in the eighth grade. (This sounds as though Dan is not in the eighth grade.)
Correct	Dan is taller than any **other** student in the eighth grade.
Incorrect	Beth runs faster than anyone in that class.
Correct	Beth runs faster than anyone **else** in that class.

Double Comparisons

Do not use both *-er* and *more* to form the comparative degree, or both *-est* and *most* to form the superlative degree.

Use only one method to form the comparative or the superlative of a modifier. Using *-er* and *more* together, for example, produces a double comparison, which is incorrect.

Double Comparison	Can you stuff the tissues in the chicken wire **more quicklier**?
Correct	Can you stuff the tissues in the chicken wire **more quickly**?
Double Comparison	This project is the **most hardest** we've been assigned.
Correct	This project is the **hardest** we've been assigned.

Double Negatives

Avoid using double negatives.

When two negative words are used together to express the same idea, the result is a **double negative.**

Common Negatives			
no	nobody	nothing	never
not (-n't)	no one	none	hardly

Double Negative	We did drills, but we did**n't** swim **no** laps today.
Correct	We did drills, but we did**n't** swim any laps today.
	We did drills, but we swam **no** laps today.
Double Negative	Carmen did**n't hardly** touch her dessert last night.
Correct	Carmen **hardly** touched her dessert last night.

Good or *Well*?

Good is always an adjective. *Well* is usually an adverb that follows an action verb. However, when *well* means "in good health" or "satisfactory," it is used as an adjective. Remember that adjectives can follow linking verbs.

Adjective That bend in the river was a **good** spot for trout fishing. (*Good* modifies the noun *spot.*)

The fishing was **good** today. (*Good* is a predicate adjective that describes *fishing.*)

I haven't felt **well** since I ate that day-old sushi. (In this sentence *well* is a predicate adjective that means "in good health.")

Adverb Michael read the story **well**. (*Well* is an adverb that tells how Michael read.)

A Writer's Glossary of Usage

In the last four chapters, you covered the fundamental elements of usage. A Writer's Glossary of Usage presents some specific areas that might give you difficulty. Before you use the glossary, though, there are some terms that you should know.

You will notice references in the glossary to various levels of language. Two of these levels of language are standard English and nonstandard English. **Standard English** refers to the rules and the conventions of usage that are accepted and used most widely by English-speaking people throughout the world. **Nonstandard English** has many variations because it is influenced by regional differences and dialects, as well as by current slang. Remember that nonstandard does not mean that the language is wrong but that the language may be inappropriate in certain situations. Because nonstandard English lacks uniformity, you should use standard English when you write.

You will also notice references to formal and informal English. **Formal English** is used for written work because it follows the conventional rules of grammar, usage, and mechanics. Examples of the use of formal English can usually be found in business letters, technical reports, and well-written compositions. **Informal English,** on the other hand, follows the conventions of standard English but might include words and phrases that would seem out of place in a formal piece of writing. Informal English is often used in magazine articles, newspaper stories, and fiction writing.

The items in this glossary have been arranged alphabetically so that you can use this section as a reference tool.

a, an Use *a* before words beginning with consonant sounds and *an* before words beginning with vowel sounds.

> Did you buy **a** new CD?

> No, it was given to me as **an** early birthday gift.

accept, except *Accept* is a verb that means "to receive with consent." *Except* is usually a preposition that means "but" or "other than."

> Everyone **except** Bernie **accepted** the news calmly.

advice, advise *Advice* is a noun that means "a recommendation." *Advise* is a verb that means "to recommend."

> I usually follow my doctor's **advice.**

> He **advised** me to exercise more often.

affect, effect *Affect* is a verb that means "to influence" or "to act upon." *Effect* is usually a noun that means "a result" or "an influence." As a verb, *effect* means "to accomplish" or "to produce."

> Does the weather **affect** your mood?

> No, it has no **effect** on me.

> The medicine **effected** a change in my disposition.

ain't This contraction is nonstandard English. Avoid it in your writing.

Nonstandard	Ken **ain't** here yet.
Standard	Ken **isn't** here yet.

all ready, already *All ready* means "completely ready." *Already* means "previously."

> We were **all ready** to go by seven o'clock.

> I had **already** told my parents that we were going to the movies.

all together, altogether *All together* means "in a group." *Altogether* means "wholly" or "thoroughly."

> Let's try to sing **all together** for a change.

> The traditional song will sound **altogether** different if we do.

a lot People very often write these two words incorrectly as one. There is no such word as "alot." *A lot,* however, even when it is written as two words, should be avoided in formal writing.

Informal	Famous movie stars receive **a lot** of fan mail.
Formal	Famous movie stars usually receive **a large quantity** of fan mail.

among, between These words are both prepositions. *Among* is used when referring to three or more people or things. *Between* is used when referring to two people or things.

> Put your present **among** the others.

> Then come and sit **between** Judith and me.

amount, number *Amount* refers to things in bulk or mass that cannot be counted, whereas *number* refers to things that can be counted.

> Although there were a **number** of rainy days this month, the total **amount** of rain was less than usual.

> I was surprised at the **amount** of coffee he drank. (Coffee cannot be counted.)

> He put a large **number** of coffee beans into the machine. (Coffee beans can be counted.)

anywhere, everywhere, nowhere, somewhere Do not add *–s* to any of these words.

> I looked **everywhere** but could not find my keys.

at Do not use *at* after *where.*

Nonstandard	Do you know **where** we're **at?**
Standard	Do you know **where** we are?

a while, awhile *A while* is made up of an article and a noun; together, they are mainly used after a preposition. *Awhile* is an adverb that stands alone and means "for a short period of time."

We can stay on the job for **a while.**

After we work **awhile,** we can take a break.

bad, badly *Bad* is an adjective and often follows a linking verb. *Badly* is used as an adverb. In the first two examples, *felt* is a linking verb.

Nonstandard	Luke felt **badly** all day.
Standard	Luke felt **bad** all day.
Standard	Luke **badly** needs a haircut.

bring, take *Bring* indicates motion toward the speaker. *Take* indicates motion away from the speaker.

Bring me the stamps.

Now, please **take** this letter to the post office.

can, may *Can* expresses ability. *May* expresses possibility or permission.

I **can** baby-sit for you tonight.

May I watch TV after Kenny is asleep?

doesn't, don't *Doesn't* is singular and must agree with a singular subject. *Don't* is plural and must agree with a plural subject, except when used with the singular pronouns *I* and *you.*

This article **doesn't** make sense to me. (singular subject)

These articles **don't** make sense to me. (plural subject)

double negative Words such as *barely, but* (when it means "only"), *hardly, never, no, none, no one, barely, nobody, not* (and its contraction *n't*), *nothing, nowhere, only,* and *scarcely* are all negatives. Do not use two negatives to express one negative meaning.

Nonstandard	I **hardly never** see you anymore.
Standard	I **hardly see** you anymore.
Standard	I **never see** you anymore.

etc. *Etc.* is an abbreviation for the Latin phrase *et cetera,* which means "and other things." Never use the word *and* with *etc.* If you do, what you are really saying is "and and other things." You should not use this abbreviation at all in formal writing.

| Informal | Before moving, we had to pack our clothes, books, records, **etc.** |
| Formal | Before moving, we had to pack our clothes, books, records, **and other belongings.** |

fewer, less *Fewer* is plural and refers to things that can be counted. *Less* is singular and refers to quantities and qualities that cannot be counted.

There seem to be **fewer** hours in the day.

I seem to have **less** time to get my homework done.

good, well *Good* is an adjective and often follows a linking verb. *Well* is an adverb and often follows an action verb. However, when *well* means "in good health" or "satisfactory," it is used as an adjective.

The biscuits smell **good.** (adjective)

Janice cooks **well.** (adverb)

I feel quite **well** after eating the chicken soup. (adjective meaning "in good health")

have, of Never substitute *of* for the verb *have*. When speaking, many people make a contraction of *have*. For example, they might say, "We should've gone." Because *'ve* may sound like *of, of* is often mistakenly substituted for *have* in writing.

Nonstandard	We should **of** started earlier.
Standard	We should **have** started earlier.

hear, here *Hear* is a verb that means "to perceive by listening." *Here* is an adverb that means "in this place."

I can't **hear** the music from **here**.

hole, whole A *hole* is an opening. *Whole* means "complete" or "entire."

Have you noticed the **hole** in your coat?

Did you leave your coat on for the **whole** movie?

in, into Use *in* when you are referring to a stationary place. Use *into* when you want to express motion from one place to another.

Is the money **in** your coat pocket?

Why don't you transfer it **into** your wallet?

its, it's *Its* is a possessive pronoun and means "belonging to it." *It's* is a contraction for *it is*.

The dog returned home to **its** owner.

It's fun to watch **its** happy expression.

knew, new *Knew*, the past tense of the verb *know*, means "was acquainted with." *New* is an adjective that means "recently made" or "just found."

Michael's sneakers looked so clean and white that I **knew** they were **new**.

learn, teach *Learn* means "to gain knowledge." *Teach* means "to instruct" or "to show how."

> I just **learned** how to use that computer program that Mom bought for us.
>
> Now I can **teach** you how to use it.

leave, let *Leave* means "to depart" or "to go away from." *Let* means "to allow" or "to permit."

Nonstandard	**Leave** me help you carry those packages into the house.
Standard	**Let** me help you carry those packages into the house.
Standard	Don't **leave** before you help me carry in my packages.

lie, lay *Lie* means "to rest or recline." *Lie* is never followed by a direct object. Its principal parts are *lie, lying, lay,* and *lain. Lay* means "to put or set (something) down." *Lay* is usually followed by a direct object. Its principal parts are *lay, laying, laid,* and *laid.*

Lie	Our kittens always **lie** on the sofa.
	They are **lying** there now.
	They **lay** there all morning.
	They have **lain** there for a long time.
Lay	**Lay** their food dish on the floor. (Dish is the direct object.)
	Jill is **laying** the dish on the floor.
	Molly **laid** the dish on the floor yesterday.
	Until recently Gary always has **laid** the dish on the floor.

like, as *Like* is a preposition that introduces a prepositional phrase. *As* is usually a subordinating conjunction that introduces an adverb clause.

Standard	Betty should read stories **like** these. (prepositional phrase)
Nonstandard	Betty usually does **like** she is told. (clause)
Standard	Betty usually does **as** she is told.

rise, raise *Rise* means "to move upward" or "to get up." *Rise* is never followed by a direct object. Its principal parts are *rise, rising, rose,* and *risen. Raise* means "to lift (something) up," "to increase," or "to grow something." *Raise* is usually followed by a direct object. Its principal parts are *raise, raising, raised,* and *raised.*

> Dad will **rise** at 7:00 A.M.
>
> At that time, he will **raise** the shades. (*Shades* is the direct object.)

shall, will In formal English *shall* is used with first-person pronouns and *will* is used with second- and third-person pronouns. Today, *shall* and *will* are used interchangeably with *I* and *we,* except that *shall* should be used with *I* and *we* for questions.

> **Shall** I invite her to join the club?
>
> I **will** ask her tonight.

sit, set *Sit* means "to rest in an upright position." *Sit* is never followed by a direct object. Its principal parts are *sit, sitting, sat,* and *sat. Set* means "to put or place (something)." *Set* is usually followed by a direct object. Its principal parts are *set, setting, set,* and *set.*

> After Mom has **set** the timer, we will **sit** and wait thirty minutes for dinner. (*Timer* is the direct object of *set.*)

than, then *Than* is a subordinating conjunction and is used for comparisons. *Then* is an adverb and means "at that time" or "next."

> **Nonstandard** Jupiter is much larger **then** Saturn.
>
> **Standard** After learning that Jupiter is much larger **than** Saturn, we **then** learned other facts about our solar system.

that, which, who All three words are relative pronouns. *That* refers to people, animals, or things; *which* refers to animals or things; and *who* refers to people.

> The airline tickets **that** I bought for the trip were expensive.
>
> From the air we saw the cows, **which** looked like little dots.
>
> The flight attendant **who** was on our plane gave instructions.

their, there, they're *Their* is a possessive pronoun. *There* is usually an adverb, but sometimes it begins an inverted sentence. *They're* is a contraction for *they are.*

> Tell them to take **their** time.
>
> **There** will be many reporters gathered in the hall.
>
> **They're** meeting at seven o'clock for the press conference.

theirs, there's *Theirs* is a possessive pronoun. *There's* is a contraction for *there is.*

> These messages are ours; those messages are **theirs.**
>
> **There's** a message for you in the office.

them, those Never use *them* as a subject or as an adjective.

Nonstandard	**Them** are freshly picked tomatoes. (subject)
Standard	**Those** are freshly picked tomatoes.
Nonstandard	Did you like **them** tomatoes? (adjective)
Standard	Did you like **those** tomatoes?

this here, that there Avoid using *here* or *there* in addition to *this* or *that.*

Nonstandard	**That there** chair is very comfortable.
Standard	**That** chair is very comfortable.
Nonstandard	**This here** sofa matches your chair.
Standard	**This** sofa matches your chair.

threw, through *Threw* is the past tense of the verb *throw. Through* is a preposition that means "in one side and out the other."

> Denny **threw** the ball over the fence.
>
> He's lucky that it didn't go **through** the window of the house.

to, too, two *To* is a preposition. *To* also begins an infinitive. *Too* is an adverb that modifies a verb, an adjective, or another adverb. *Two* is a number.

Keith went **to** the gym **to** practice.

Two members of the team arrived **too** late.

Only one was asked **to** play in the game, but the other played **too**.

when, where Do not use *when* or *where* directly after a linking verb in a definition.

Nonstandard	A presbyope is **when** a person is farsighted.
Standard	A presbyope is a farsighted person.
Nonstandard	A domicile is **where** people live.
Standard	A domicile is a place **where** people live.

where Do not substitute *where* for *that*.

| Nonstandard | I heard **where** crime rates are going down. |
| Standard | I heard **that** crime rates are going down. |

who, whom *Who*, a pronoun in the nominative case, is used as either a subject or a predicate nominative. *Whom*, a pronoun in the objective case, is used as a direct object, an indirect object, or an object of a preposition.

Who is coming to your party? (subject)

Whom did you choose? (direct object)

whose, who's *Whose* is a possessive pronoun. *Who's* is a contraction for *who is*.

Whose is the bicycle that you borrowed?

Who's going to ride with you?

your, you're *Your* is a possessive pronoun. *You're* is a contraction for *you are*.

Are these **your** campaign posters?

You're the one we want for president of the class.

Capitalization

QuickGuide

Basic Rules of Capitalization pages 131–138	Follow these rules of capitalization for **first words**, the **pronoun *I***, and **proper nouns**.
Other Uses of Capital Letters pages 139–141	Follow these rules of capitalization for **proper adjectives** and **titles**.

Basic Rules of Capitalization

Capital letters can be as important to writing as the words themselves. The correct use of capital letters makes your writing easier to understand.

First Words

A capital letter clearly marks the beginning of a new idea—whether that idea is in a sentence, a line of poetry, a letter, or an outline.

Sentences and Poetry A capital letter always tells readers that a new sentence or a new line of poetry has begun.

Capitalize the first word of a sentence and the first word of a line of poetry.

Sentence	There are about twenty-five species of apples.
Lines of Poetry	Of Jonathan Chapman Two things are known, That he loved apples, That he walked alone.

> — Stephen Vincent Benét, "Johnny Appleseed"

Some modern poets purposely misuse capital letters or do not use any capitals at all in their poetry. When you quote such a poem, copy it exactly as the poet wrote it.

Parts of Letters Certain parts of a letter stand out because they begin with a capital letter.

Capitalize the first word in the salutation of a letter and the first word in the closing of a letter.

Greetings and Closings	
Salutation	Dear Mr. Chapman:
Closing	Sincerely yours,

Outlines Capital letters make parts of an outline stand out.

Capitalize the first word of each item in an outline as well as the letters that begin major subsections of the outline.

I. Apple production in the U. S.

II. How apple trees and apples are used

    A. Foods and beverages prepared from apples

    B. The uses of apple wood

        1. Uses in manufacturing

        2. Used for smoking meats

    C. Ornamental uses of apple trees

The Pronoun *I* The pronoun *I* is always capitalized.

Capitalize the pronoun *I*, both alone and in contractions.

Alone	Yesterday I bought a pound of apples.
Contraction	Today I'm going to make a pie.

Proper Nouns

A **proper noun** is the name of a particular person, place, thing, or idea. A proper noun begins with a capital letter.

Common and Proper Nouns	
Common Nouns	boy, park, cat
Proper Nouns	Daniel Lopez, Big Bend National Park, Smoky

Capitalize proper nouns and their abbreviations.

Study the rules for capitalizing proper nouns on page 133. Then refer to them when you edit your writing.

Names of persons and animals should be capitalized. Also capitalize the initials that stand for people's names.

Names of Persons and Animals	
Persons	Kayla; V. H. Tang; James R. Ricco, Jr.
Animals	Max, Ginger, Meatloaf, Miss Kitty

Geographical names, which name particular places and bodies of water, are capitalized. Do not capitalize prepositions, articles, or the conjunction *and* in geographical names or other proper nouns.

Geographical Names	
Streets and Highways	Avery Road (Rd.), Ohio Turnpike (Tpk.), Route (Rt.) 128, Fifty-sixth Street (St.) (The second part of a hyphenated numbered street is not capitalized.)
Cities and States	Los Angeles, California (CA); Plano, Texas (TX)
Counties and Parishes	Medina County (Co.), Acadia Parish
Countries	United States of America, Czech Republic, Egypt, Brazil
Continents	North America, Africa, Antarctica
World Regions	Western Hemisphere, Pacific Rim, North Pole
Islands	South Padre Island, Long Island
Mountains	Rocky Mountains, Mount (Mt.) Hood
Forests and Parks	Superior National Forest, Great Basin National Park
Bodies of Water	Mississippi River, Lake Ontario, Pacific Ocean, Gulf of Mexico
Sections of the Country	the South, the West Coast, New England (Simple compass directions are not capitalized. *Go south on Main Street.*)

Words such as *street, lake, ocean,* and *mountain* are capitalized only when they are part of a proper noun.

> We live near some mountains, but they are small compared to the **R**ocky **M**ountains.

As You Write

In geography class you might say a sentence like this:

> The **I**sthmus of **P**anama lies between the **A**tlantic **O**cean and the **P**acific **O**cean.

You can shorten the sentence by changing it to the following:

> The **I**sthmus of **P**anama lies between the **A**tlantic and the **P**acific oceans.

Notice that in the second sentence the word *oceans* is not capitalized because it is no longer a part of a proper name. You're saying that the isthmus lies between the two oceans known as the Atlantic and the Pacific.

The Isthmus of Panama as seen from space

Nouns of historical importance should be capitalized. Capitalize the names of historical events, periods, and documents.

Historic Names	
Events	the French Revolution, the Battle of Hastings, World War II (WWII)
Periods of Time	the Victorian Era, the Space Age, the Dark Ages
Documents	the Declaration of Independence, the Articles of Confederation, the Mayflower Compact

Do not capitalize prepositions such as *of* in the names of events and documents.

Names of groups and businesses begin with capital letters. These include the names of organizations, businesses, institutions, teams, and government bodies and agencies.

Names of Groups	
Organizations	Little League, the National Organization for Women (NOW), American Medical Association (AMA)
Businesses	Casper's Market, F. Rosenberg & Company (Co.), the Westward Corporation (Corp.)
Institutions	Glover Memorial Hospital, Wayne Middle School, the University of California at Los Angeles (UCLA)
Teams	the Dallas Cowboys, the Bayside Tigers, the Minnesota Twins
Government Bodies and Agencies	the Senate, Congress, the Federal Trade Commission (FTC)
Political Parties	Democratic Party, a Republican, a Democrat

Specific time periods and events begin with capital letters.
Capitalize the days of the week, the months of the year, civil and religious
holidays, and special events. Also capitalize the abbreviations used in giving
dates and the time of day.

Time Periods and Events	
Days, Months	Monday (Mon.), Tuesday (Tues.), February (Feb.), March (Mar.)
Holidays	Martin Luther King Day, Presidents' Day, the Fourth of July
Special Events	the New York Marathon, the Festival of Roses
Time Abbreviations	A.D. 466, 100 B.C., 6:30 A.M., 9:00 P.M.

Do not capitalize the seasons of the year unless they are part of a specific name.

Each summer the library runs a special reading program.

Here is a flyer about the library's Summer Festival of Books.

Names of nationalities and ethnic groups should be capitalized.

Nationalities and Ethnic Groups	
Nationalities	a Nigerian, a Seminole, a Canadian
Ethnic Groups	Caucasian, Hispanic

Religions, religious references, and religious holidays and holy
days begin with capital letters.

Religious Names	
Religions	Catholicism, Buddhism, Judaism, Islam
Religious Holidays and Holy Days	Hanukkah, Christmas, Ramadan, Epiphany, Yom Kippur, St. Michael's Day
Religious References	God, the Almighty, the Old Testament, the Talmud, the Koran, the Vedas

The word *god* is not capitalized when it refers to polytheistic gods. Their proper names, however, are capitalized.

> The Greek god who gave fire to mortals was **P**rometheus.

Prometheus Carrying Fire, Jan Cossiers

Names of planets, moons, stars, and constellations are capitalized. Do not capitalize the words *sun* and *moon*.

Astronomical Names	
Planets and Moons	Mercury, Uranus, Neptune, Ganymede
Stars	the North Star, Sirus, Canopus
Constellations	Big Dipper, Orion, Ursa Major

Do not capitalize the word *earth* unless it appears in the sentence with other astronomical names that are capitalized.

Capital	Is Venus larger or smaller than Earth?
No Capital	Six billion people live on earth.

Languages and specific school courses followed by a number are capitalized.

Languages and School Courses	
Languages	English, Turkish, Russian, Spanish, French
Computer Languages	Java, Cobol, Visual Basic
Numbered Courses	Art II, Algebra I, Biology II

Course names such as *history, math, science,* and *physical education* are not capitalized.

Other proper nouns should also begin with capital letters.

Other Proper Nouns	
Awards	Nobel Peace Prize, World Cup, Grammy Award
Brand Names	Ultrasheen shampoo, Sunrise orange juice, Roadrunner vans (The product itself—such as *shampoo, orange juice,* and *vans*—is not capitalized.)
Bridges and Buildings	Brooklyn Bridge, Empire State Building, World Trade Center, Windsor Castle
Internet Terms	the Internet, the Web, World Wide Web, Web page, E-mail
Monuments and Memorials	Gateway Arch, Pearl Harbor Memorial, Washington Monument
Vehicles	the *Queen Mary, Apollo V, Air Force One*

In writing, the names of vehicles should be italicized or underlined.

Other Uses of Capital Letters

There are other uses for capital letters in addition to the ones you have already learned. Some proper adjectives are capitalized. The titles of certain people and works of art are also capitalized.

Proper Adjectives

Like proper nouns, most proper adjectives begin with a capital letter.

Proper Nouns and Adjectives	
Proper Nouns	**Proper Adjectives**
Asia	Asian art
Canada	Canadian provinces
Rome	Roman baths
Copernicus	Copernican theory
South America	South American rivers
Florida	Florida oranges

As You Write

A cookbook may refer to both *French food* and *french fries*. Some words or phrases from proper nouns become so common that they are written entirely in lowercase letters. Some examples are *brussels sprouts*, *dutch oven*, *india ink*, *manila envelope*, *plaster of paris*, and *venetian blinds*. When you use words like these, check a dictionary to see whether you should use a capital letter or not.

Titles

Capital letters are used in the titles of people, written works, and other works of art.

Titles Used with Names of Persons Capitalize a title showing office, rank, or profession when it comes before a person's name. The same title is usually not capitalized when it follows a name.

Before a Name	That woman is Colonel Hanks.
After a Name	When was Ann promoted to colonel?

Titles Used in Direct Address A noun of direct address is used to call someone by name. Capitalize a title used alone, instead of a name, in direct address.

Direct Address	What is your opinion, Professor?
	What, Senator, do you think about a possible tax increase?

You can learn more about commas with titles used in direct address on page 151.

Titles Showing Family Relationships Capitalize titles showing family relationships when the titles come before people's names. Capitalize the titles, also, when they are used instead of names or used in direct address.

Used Before a Name	Is Uncle David staying for dinner?
Used as a Name	Yesterday Dad helped me with my homework.
Used In Direct Address	Thanks for the ride, Mom.

When a possessive noun or pronoun comes before a title showing a family relationship, do not capitalize the title—unless it is considered part of the person's name.

No Capital   My aunt is talking to Linda's uncle.

Capital   Is your **A**unt Harriet from Arizona visiting?

You can learn about the use of possessive nouns with apostrophes on pages 163–164 and about the use of possessive pronouns on pages 95–97 and page 164.

Titles of Written Works and Other Works of Art Capitalize the first word, the last word, and all important words in the titles of books, newspapers, magazines, stories, poems, movies, plays, musical compositions, and other works of art. Do not capitalize a short preposition, a coordinating conjunction, or an article unless it is the first or last word in a title.

Titles of Written Works and Other Works of Art	
Books and Chapter Titles	I am reading the chapter "**P**eople and **L**and" in our textbook *The Geography of the World.*
Short Stories	Have you read Arthur Conan Doyle's story "**T**he **H**ound of the **B**askervilles"?
Poems	Edgar Allan Poe wrote a poem called "**T**o **M**y **M**other."
Magazines and Magazine Articles	He found the facts in an article called "**A**re **C**ats **S**mart?" in *Discover* magazine.
Newspapers and Newspaper Articles	My sister wrote "**N**ew **D**igs for **D**inosaur **B**ones" for the *Valley Banner.* (The word *the* is not usually capitalized before the title of a newspaper.)
Television Series	She tapes the *Wild World* programs to watch later.
Musical Compositions	Have you heard Beethoven's *Fifth Symphony*?
Movies	Most people are surprised by the ending of *Citizen Kane.*

End Marks
and Commas

QuickGuide

End Marks pages 143–146	Follow these rules when using **periods** (.), **question marks** (?), and **exclamation points** (!).
Frequently Used Commas pages 146–147	Commas are used in **dates, addresses,** and **letters.**
Commas That Separate pages 148–150	Follow rules for commas when writing **items in a series, multiple adjectives before a noun, compound sentences,** and **introductory elements.**
Commas That Enclose pages 151–153	Follow rules for commas when writing **direct addresses, parenthetical expressions, appositives,** and **essential** and **nonessential elements.**

End Marks

The purpose of a sentence determines its end mark.

Place a period after a statement, after an opinion, and after a command or request made in a normal tone of voice.

Period	I want to study forest management from a conservationist point of view. (statement)
	Prairies look peaceful, but they are full of conflict and stress. (opinion)
	Sign up for the career workshop. (command)

Place a question mark after a sentence that asks a question.

Question Mark	Would you rather work outdoors or indoors at a desk?

Place an exclamation point after a sentence that expresses strong feeling or after a command or request that expresses great excitement.

Exclamation Point	The fire has jumped the firebreak and is headed toward the town!
	If you hear a roaring sound, head for the basement!

You can learn more about kinds of sentences in Chapter 1.

Other Uses of Periods

Periods are used in other places besides the ends of sentences. For example, they are used with most abbreviations.

With Abbreviations **Abbreviations** are brief ways of writing words. They are handy shortcuts when you are writing messages or taking notes in class. Most abbreviations, however, should not be used in formal writing such as letters, stories, or reports.

The following is a list of common abbreviations. For the spelling and punctuation of other abbreviations, look in a dictionary. Most dictionaries include a section that lists abbreviations.

Common Abbreviations	
Days	Sun. Mon. Tues. Wed. Thurs. Fri. Sat.
Months	Jan. Feb. Mar. Apr. Aug. Sept. Oct. Nov. Dec. (*May, June,* and *July* should not be abbreviated.)
Addresses	Ave. Blvd. Dr. Hwy. Pl. Rd. Rt. St. Apt.
Titles with Names	Mr. Mrs. Ms. Dr. Rev. Gen. Sgt. Lt. Jr. Sr. Pres.
Initials for Names	R. L. Rosen, Kenneth A. Brevik, L. Ana Page
Companies	Assn. Co. Corp. Dept. Inc. Ltd.
Times with Numbers	6:45 A.M. (*ante meridiem*—before noon) 9:00 P.M. (*post meridiem*—after noon) 4 B.C. (before Christ) or 4 B.C.E. (before the common era) A.D. 650 (*anno Domini*—in the year of the Lord) or 650 C.E. (common era)

Some organizations are known by abbreviations that stand for their full names. The majority of these abbreviations do not use periods. In addition, a few other common abbreviations do not include periods. Always check a dictionary if you are not sure whether an abbreviation needs periods.

Abbreviations Without Periods	
ATM = automated teller machine	FAX = facsimile
CD = compact disc	km = kilometer
CIA = Central Intelligence Agency	l = liter
IQ = Intelligence Quotient	UN = United Nations

Today almost everyone uses the post office's two-letter state abbreviations. These abbreviations do not include periods. A list of these state abbreviations usually can be found in the front of a telephone book. Here are a few examples.

State Abbreviations		
AL = Alabama	MD = Maryland	OH = Ohio
AK = Alaska	MI = Michigan	TX = Texas
HI = Hawaii	MN = Minnesota	UT = Utah
IL = Illinois	MO = Missouri	VT = Vermont
IA = Iowa	MT = Montana	VA = Virginia
KY = Kentucky	NV= Nevada	WA = Washington
ME = Maine	NY= New York	WV = West Virginia

Map, Jasper Johns, 1961

With Outlines In an outline, periods set apart the letters and numbers from the text that follows.

Use a period after each number or letter that shows a division in an outline.

I. Routes to Oregon in the early 1800s

    A. Oregon Trail

        1. Steamship from St. Louis to Independence

        2. Covered wagons to plains and Rockies

    B. The journey around Cape Horn

II. New routes to California

As You Write

When a sentence ends with an abbreviation that uses a period, use only one period. It serves as both the period for the abbreviation and the end mark for the sentence.

The man in the brown suit is Michael Alvarez, Jr.

Frequently Used Commas

You will use some commas more often than others. On the following pages are some examples of the most frequently used commas.

With Dates and Addresses

Use commas to separate elements in dates and addresses. When a date or an address comes within a sentence, use another comma to separate the date from the rest of the sentence.

On Tuesday, December 7, 2006, our voyage began. (No comma is used between the month and the day.)

We arrived home in January 2007. (No comma is used between the month and the year if no day is given.)

Write to us in care of Anna Melon, 791 Reata Lane, Arizona City, Arizona 85223, until March 4. (No comma is used between the state and the ZIP Code, but a comma is used after the ZIP code to separate the address from the rest of the sentence.

A preposition can take the place of a comma between parts of an address.

We live at 18 Elgin Street **in** Boston, Massachusetts.

In Letters

Commas are used to set off parts of a letter. Use a comma after the salutation of a friendly letter and after the closing of all letters.

Salutations	Dear Aunt Chris,
	Dear Dad,
Closings	Yours truly,
	Sincerely yours,

Still Life with Letter to Denis Gale, William Michael Harnett, 1879

Commas That Separate

Commas keep similar items from running into each other and prevent misunderstanding by the reader.

Items in a Series

A **series** is three or more similar words or groups of words listed one after another.

Use commas to separate items in a series.

Words	We saw crabs, pelicans, and sandpipers. (simple nouns)
	We found seashells, starfish, and seaweed. (compound nouns)
Groups of Words	We will pack a lunch, walk to the dunes, and look for shells. (complete predicates)
	Paul is either on the beach, in the bait shop, or on his way to the pier. (prepositional phrases)

If a conjunction such as *and* or *or* connects all the items in a series, no commas are needed.

> Swimming and boating and hiking are fun beach activities.

Adjectives Before a Noun

If you list only two adjectives before a noun, you may or may not need a comma.

A comma is needed between two adjectives if it is replacing the word *and*.

> I read new, unusual facts about Juana Briones de Miranda. (The facts were new *and* unusual.)

A comma is not needed if the two adjectives sound better without the word *and* between them.

> She was a strong pioneer woman like her mother and grandmother before her. (Since a *strong and pioneer* woman sounds awkward, no comma is used.)

Usually, no comma is used after a number or after an adjective that refers to size, shape, or age.

> He received six E-mail messages in response to the ad.

> They were all about his young black kitten.

Compound Sentences

A comma and a conjunction often separate the independent clauses in a compound sentence. *And, but, or, nor,* and *yet* are commonly used conjunctions.

Use a comma to separate the independent clauses of a compound sentence if the clauses are joined by a conjunction.

> Many animals are plant eaters, and a few plants are animal eaters.

> Most soils nourish plants, but the soil in bogs may lack nitrogen.

Keep in mind the difference between a compound sentence and a simple sentence that has a compound verb. No comma is needed to join the two parts of a compound verb.

Compound Sentence	Bog plants attract insects, and the insects provide necessary nutrients. (A comma is needed because there are two sets of subjects and verbs.)
Compound Verb	Bog plants attract insects and get nutrients from them. (No comma is needed with a compound verb.)

Using a comma and a conjunction together is one way to correct a run-on sentence.

Run-on Sentence	Carnivorous plants can survive without insects, they grow better with insects in their diet.
Corrected Compound Sentence	Carnivorous plants can survive without insects, **but** they grow better with insects in their diet.

You can learn more about compound sentences in Chapter 9. You can learn about other ways to correct run-on sentences in Chapter 10.

Introductory Elements

Use a comma after certain introductory elements.

Interjections A comma sometimes separates an interjection from the rest of a sentence. Words like *no, now, oh, well, why,* and *yes* can be used as interjections.

> Yes, I really do enjoy hiking.

> Well, my last hike was a real disaster!

An interjection can also be followed by an exclamation point.

> Oh! I almost forgot my compass.

Prepositional Phrases A comma follows an introductory prepositional phrase that has four or more words. Also place a comma after two or more prepositional phrases that come at the beginning of a sentence.

> **Inside the dense forest,** the trail forked in two directions.
> (one prepositional phrase with four words)

> **With my lucky pencil in hand,** I walked into the testing center.
> (two prepositional phrases)

You can learn more about prepositional phrases in Chapter 3.

Participial and Infinitive Phrases A comma follows a participial or infinitive phrase that comes at the beginning of a sentence.

> **Bubbling and murmuring,** the stream rushed down the hillside.
> (participial phrase)

> **To get to my destination,** I'll have to take a bus and a train and walk five blocks. (infinitive phrase.)

You can learn more about participial and infinitive phrases in Chapter 8.

Adverb Clauses A comma follows an adverb clause when it comes at the beginning of a sentence.

> **If I can save enough money for tickets,** I'll ask Gayle to the concert.

You can learn more about adverb clauses in Chapter 9.

Commas That Enclose

Commas are used to enclose some expressions that interrupt the main idea of a sentence. When you read a sentence aloud, you naturally pause before and after an interrupting expression. Commas are placed where these pauses would occur. If you take interrupters enclosed by commas out of a sentence, the sentence will still make sense.

Direct Address

In conversation people are often addressed by name. This kind of interrupter is called a **noun of direct address.** Since nouns of direct address interrupt the flow of a sentence, they should be set off by commas.

> The community picnic, **Brian,** will start at 11:00 A.M. (The noun of direct address, *Brian,* could be removed.)

> Please, **Dana and James,** help me get this dog back in the yard. (More than one noun can be included in direct address. *Dana and James* could be removed.)

> Dim the lights, **kids,** and I'll tell you the scariest story ever. (Direct address might include a noun that is not a proper noun.)

In the following examples, only one comma is needed because the noun of direct address comes at the beginning or at the end of the sentence.

> Mom, where is the bicycle pump I bought last year?

> May we borrow your phone for a minute, Kiera?

Parenthetical Expressions

One type of interrupter is called a **parenthetical expression**. The following parenthetical expressions should be enclosed by commas.

Common Parenthetical Expressions		
after all	however	of course
at any rate	I believe (guess, hope)	on the contrary
by the way	in fact	on the other hand
consequently	in my opinion	simply stated
for example (instance)	moreover	to tell the truth
generally speaking	nevertheless	

Use commas to set off parenthetical expressions.

> Soccer**, in fact,** is preferred to baseball in many countries. (*In fact,* could be removed without affecting the meaning of the sentence.)

In the following examples, only one comma is needed because the parenthetical expression comes at the beginning or at the end of the sentence.

> **In my opinion,** that sculpture is a big waste of money.

> I would go to your show if it were on a weekend night**, of course.**

Appositives

An **appositive** renames, or explains, a noun or pronoun in the sentence. Usually an appositive comes immediately after that noun or pronoun and is written with modifiers. Because they interrupt the sentence, appositives should be set off by commas.

> Texas**, my home state,** has an interesting history.

In the following example, only one comma is needed because the appositive comes at the end of the sentence.

> La Salle established Fort St. Louis**, the first French settlement here.**

Do not use commas to set off an appositive if it is necessary to clarify or name one or more items in a broader category.

> The street I live on was named after the writer **Goethe.** (*Goethe* is not the only writer that exists. The appositive clarifies, rather than defines, the noun.)

Essential and Nonessential Elements

Like parenthetical expressions, entire phrases and clauses can interrupt a sentence. When they are necessary to complete the meaning of the sentence, they do not require commas. If a phrase or clause is not essential, or necessary, to the meaning of the sentence, it requires one or more commas to set it off from the sentence.

Essential	Games **played in the ancient world** were often taken seriously. (The phrase *played in the ancient world* is essential to the meaning of the sentence. No commas should be used.)
Nonessential	Outdoor games**, played in most cultures,** are enjoyed by old and young alike. (*Played in most cultures* is not essential to the meaning of the sentence. It is set off from the sentence by two commas.)

Italics and Quotation Marks

QuickGuide

Italics and Underlining

pages 155–156

Follow these rules for Italics (or underlining) when—

- writing the titles of **long written or musical works.**

- writing the **titles of paintings and sculptures.**

- writing **letters, numbers, and words** if they are used to represent themselves.

- writing **foreign words or phrases.**

- writing the names of **vehicles.**

Quotation Marks

pages 157–161

Follow these rules for using quotation marks when—

- writing **titles of chapters, articles, stories, one-act plays, short poems, and songs.**

- writing a **person's exact words.**

- using **dialogue.**

- quoting a **passage of more than one paragraph.**

- writing **indirect quotations.**

- writing **quotations within quotations.**

Italics and Underlining

When certain titles, letters, numbers, and words appear in a book, they are printed in italics. *Italic print, a special kind that slants to the right, is the kind used in this sentence.*

When you use a computer, highlight the words you want to italicize. Then use the command for italics.

When you are writing by hand, underline an item to indicate that it should be italicized.

Italics	Have you ever read the book *Dragonwings* by Laurence Yep?
Underlining	Have you ever read the book <u>Dragonwings</u> by Laurence Yep?

The titles of longer works should be italicized (or underlined).

Titles Requiring Italics	
Written Works	**Other Media**
books, and magazines	CD and album titles
newspapers	ballets and dance performances
full-length plays	operas
long poems	radio series
movies	symphonies
pamphlets	television series
	Web sites, browsers, and software programs
	paintings and sculptures

Books	After I have finished reading *Robinson Crusoe,* I'm going to read *Treasure Island.* (Punctuation immediately following an italicized item should also be italicized.)

Magazines	I used *National Geographic* magazine for my research. (Designations that describe a title, such as *magazine*, are not italicized unless they are part of the actual title.)
Newspapers	The *Chicago Tribune* is delivered to our house every day. (The word *the* is not usually considered part of a newspaper or magazine title.)
Plays and Movies	*Cats* is one of America's longest-running Broadway musicals.
TV Series	*Survivor* is a popular reality television show.
Works of Art	Edward Hopper painted *Railroad Sunset* and other works of modern realism.

You can learn about the capitalization of titles in Chapter 15.

Letters, numbers, and words should be italicized (or underlined) when they are used to represent themselves.

Letters	His *I* looks like an *L*.
Numbers	Does your telephone number have a *3* in it?
Words	The word *paint* can be a noun, adjective, or verb.

Foreign words and phrases that have not become part of the English language should be italicized (or underlined).

Of course I will go to the dance with you, *mi amor.*

They served us *sopas* and tortilla chips.

The proper names of vehicles should be italicized (or underlined).

The *Titanic* was considered unsinkable until it took its maiden voyage. (The word *the* is not considered a part of the name of the vehicle.)

Quotation Marks

Quotation marks (" ") always come in pairs. They are used to enclose certain titles. Quotation marks also are used to enclose a person's exact words, whether in print or in dialogue. Without quotation marks, a conversation between people in a story would be difficult to identify.

Quotation Marks with Titles

Long works, which are italicized (or underlined), often contain smaller parts. A book, for example, might contain short stories, poems, or titled chapters. The titles of these smaller parts are enclosed in quotation marks.

Titles Requiring Quotation Marks	
Written Works	**Other Media**
chapters of books	individual songs
magazine articles	individual dances
newspaper articles	operatic arias
one-act plays	radio shows
short poems	symphony movements
shorts in a long movie	television episodes
speeches	Web articles within a Web site

Chapters in Books	Our assignment is to read the chapter "A Disappearing Frontier" in our history book, *The American Experience*.
Article in Magazines and Newspapers	The lead story in this week's *Newsweek* is "DNA Solves Crimes."
	The *Sunday Salem News* had a feature called "Garbage Gardening."
Short Stories in Books and Magazines	Of all Shirley Jackson's stories, my favorite is "The Lottery."

Short Poems	For the citywide competition, I memorized "The Raven," a poem by Edgar Allan Poe.
Songs	Aretha Franklin's "Respect" is an old song, but it still has power.

Quotation Marks with Direct Quotations

Quotation marks are used to enclose a **direct quotation**—the exact words of a person in dialogue or in print.

> Scott said, "I rowed across the entire harbor."

> "The sea was very calm," he added.

Quotation marks do not enclose an **indirect quotation**—a rephrasing of a person's exact words.

> Scott said he rowed across the entire harbor.

> He added that the sea was very calm.

Use only one set of quotation marks to set off two or more sentences in a direct quotation, as long as the sentences are not interrupted by a **speaker tag.** A speaker tag is a phrase that tells who is speaking.

> Clark said, "The tide tonight comes in at six. The ship will sail then. Will you be there?" (Quotation marks surround the quote as a whole.)

The Boatman, Winslow Homer

Capital Letters with Direct Quotations

Begin each sentence of a direct quotation with a capital letter. Do not capitalize the middle of a quoted sentence.

> "Last summer we vacationed at a lake in Minnesota," she said.
>
> She said, "Last summer we vacationed at a lake in Minnesota."
>
> "Last summer," she said, "we vacationed at a lake in Minnesota."
> (Do not capitalize *we* because it is the middle of the speaker's sentence.)

Punctuating Direct Quotations

Use a comma to separate a direct quotation from a speaker tag. Place the comma immediately after the last word of a quotation if the quotation comes first in the sentence. Place the comma immediately after the speaker tag if the speaker tag comes first. Be sure to place the comma at the end of a quotation within the quotation marks.

> "A penny saved is a penny earned," said Ben Franklin.
>
> Ben Franklin said, "A penny saved is a penny earned."
>
> "A penny saved," said Ben Franklin," is a penny earned."

Place periods that end quotations within the quotation marks. Question marks and exclamation points go inside the closing quotation marks when they are part of the quotation.

> Raul commented, "This model is in extremely good condition for its age."
>
> Alex shouted, "Don't touch that live wire!"
>
> Seema asked, "Why do you want to go to the dance with me?"

When a statement comes just before a speaker tag, use a comma to separate the statement from the speaker tag. Place it inside the closing quotation marks.

> "This model is in extremely good condition for its age," Raul commented.

When a question or exclamation comes just before a speaker tag, place it inside the closing quotation marks. Then add the speaker tag.

> "Don't touch that live wire!" Alex shouted.
>
> "Why do you want to go to the dance with me?" Seema asked.

When a quotation appears in a sentence that is a question or exclamation, the end punctuation comes after the quotation marks.

Do you know why Ajax said, "Anya is no longer my friend"?

I couldn't believe how calmly he said, "There is a fire in the hallway"!

Writing Dialogue

A **dialogue** is a conversation between two or more persons. The way that it is written shows who is speaking. When writing dialogue, begin a new paragraph each time the speaker changes.

"How long have you been helping at the computer club?" Miguel asked.

"I started last year," Lisa answered.

"I'm thinking of joining the club, but I don't know if I should," he told her.

Lisa answered, "Oh, I think you should. It's fun!"

Quoting Passages

When you write a report, you may want to support a point with quotations from a work of literature or from experts in the field you are studying. These quotations follow the same rules as other quotations.

Introduce or identify short quotations with a tag.

In his book *The Revenge of Anguished English,* Richard Lederer asserts, "A perpetual lack of power is the bane of every child's life."

"A perpetual lack of power is the bane of every child's life," according to Richard Lederer in his book *The Revenge of Anguished English.*

Richard Lederer thinks that powerlessness is "the bane of every child's life." (If a partial quotation is used to complete a sentence, it need not begin with a capital letter.)

When quoting a passage of more than one paragraph, place beginning quotation marks at the start of each paragraph—but at the end of *only* the last paragraph. This will remind your readers that they are reading quoted material.

"Charles Dickens wrote some of the most popular books of the nineteenth century. He was one author who enjoyed as much fame during his lifetime as after his death. (no closing quotation marks)

"The characters created by Dickens still resonate with modern readers of all ages. From the rags-to-riches-to-rags Pip of *Great Expectations* to the tragic Sydney Carton in *A Tale of Two Cities,* Dickens wrote remarkable accounts of the human condition." (closing quotation marks)

Block Quotations Another way to quote a long passage is to set it off from the rest of the text by indenting both left and right margins. When you use the "block method," as it is called, no quotation marks are needed.

> Charles Dickens wrote some of the most popular books of the nineteenth century. He was one author who enjoyed as much fame during his lifetime as after his death.
>
> The characters created by Dickens still resonate with modern readers of all ages. From the rags-to-riches-to-rags Pip of *Great Expectations* to the tragic Sydney Carton in *A Tale of Two Cities,* Dickens wrote remarkable accounts of the human condition.

Quotation with a Quotation A quotation within a quotation follows the rules covered previously in this chapter. To avoid confusion, however, use single quotation marks to enclose the inside quotation.

"The song 'Food, Glorious Food' from the musical *Oliver* is by Lionel Bart."

Mr. Sanders said, "The most famous of Oliver Twist's lines in Dickens's book and Bart's musical is 'Please, Sir, I want some more.'"

Notice in the second example above that the closing single quotation mark and the closing double quotation marks come together.

Other Punctuation

QuickGuide

Apostrophes Pages 163–167	Use **apostrophes** to create possessive nouns, in contractions to show where one or more letters have been omitted, and to form certain plurals.
Semicolons Pages 168–170	Use **semicolons** between the clauses of some compound sentences and in a series of items that contains commas.
Colons Pages 170–171	Use **colons** to write hours and minutes, in Biblical chapters and verses, and after the salutations of business letters.
Hyphens Pages 171–173	Use **hyphens** to divide a word at the end of a line, to spell some compound words, when spelling out certain numbers, and when writing fractions used as adjectives.

Apostrophes

An *apostrophe* (**'**) is used to show possession and to form a contraction.

Apostrophes to Show Possession

You see apostrophes used most often to show that a person owns something or that a thing has something.

Paolo**'s** shirt = a shirt that belongs to Paolo

the shirt**'s** buttons = the buttons that the shirt has

Add 's to form the possessive of a singular noun.

Nick + **'s** = Nick**'s**   Is that Nick**'s** green backpack?

backpack + **'s** = backpack**'s**   The backpack**'s** zipper is broken.

teacher + **'s** = teacher**'s**   That notebook is the teacher**'s**.

class + **'s** = class**'s**   The class**'s** assignment is on the board.

box + **'s** = box**'s**   The box**'s** flaps were torn.

There are two rules to follow when forming the possessive of plural nouns.

When a plural noun ends in *s*, form the possessive by adding only an apostrophe.

boys + **'** = boys**'**   The two boys**'** pets are dogs.

dogs + **'** = dogs**'**   The dogs**'** tails are bushy.

When a plural noun does not end in *s*, form the possessive by adding 's.

men + **'s** = men**'s**   The men**'s** cars are red.

sheep + **'s** = sheep**'s**   The sheep**'s** coats are wool.

Deciding which rule to follow is easy if you take two steps. First, write the plural of the noun—as it is. Second, look at the ending of the word. If the word ends in an *s,* add only an apostrophe; otherwise, add an apostrophe and an *s.*

Forming the Possessive of Plural Nouns			
Plural	**Ending**	**Add**	**Possessive**
lions	*s*	'	lions' roars
cats	*s*	'	cats' whiskers
mice	no *s*	's	mice's tails
deer	no *s*	's	deer's antlers

The Possessive Forms of Pronouns

Personal pronouns do not use an apostrophe to show possession the way nouns do. Instead, they change their form.

His skateboarding skills are Olympic in caliber.

Its fur was matted and filthy from its visit to the dump.

Possessive Personal Pronouns	
Singular	my, mine, your, yours, his, her, hers, its (whose)
Plural	our, ours, your, yours, their, theirs (whose)

Add **'s** to form the possessive of an indefinite singular pronoun.

She always asks everyone**'s** opinion before she makes a decision.

I found someone**'s** unsigned homework on the floor of the bus.

Common Indefinite Pronouns	
Singular	anybody, anyone, each, either, everybody, everyone, neither, nobody, no one, one, somebody, someone
Plural	both, few, many, several

Apostrophes with Contractions

Besides showing possession, an apostrophe is used in **contractions**. Two or more words are combined to form a contraction. The apostrophe replaces one or more of the missing letters.

Use an *apostrophe* in a contraction to show where one or more letters have been omitted.

Contractions	
is n~~o~~t = isn**'**t	let ~~u~~s = let**'**s
who ~~i~~s = who**'**s	there ~~i~~s = there**'**s
I ~~am~~ = I**'**m	~~of the~~ clock = o**'**clock
he ~~i~~s or ~~has~~ = he**'**s	she ~~had~~ or ~~would~~ = she**'**d

Do not confuse contractions with possessive pronouns, which have no apostrophe. When you are wondering whether to use an apostrophe, it can be helpful to say the individual words of a contraction.

Contractions	
it**'**s = it is	**It's** the other way around. I live here; my family lives in England.
you**'**re = you are / you were	**You're** going to visit them in England soon, right?
they**'**re = they are / they were	No, **they're** going to visit me.
there**'**s = there is / there has (been)	**There's** been a change of plans.
who**'**s = who is / who has (been)	**Who's** going to let them know?

Apostrophes with Certain Plurals

To prevent misreading, certain items form their plurals by adding *'s*.

Add *'s* to form the plural of lowercase letters, some capital letters, and some words used as words that might otherwise be misread.

Lowercase Letters	My *u***'s** and *i***'s** look too much alike. (Without the apostrophe, *u*'s would look like *us* and *i*'s would look like *is*.)
Capital Letters	How many *A***'s** did you write on your paper? (Without the apostrophe, *A*'s would look like *As*.)
Words Used as Words	Our *hi***'s** echoed down the hallway. (Without the apostrophe, *hi*'s would look like *his*.)

Numbers, letters, symbols, and words used as words are italicized (underlined), but the apostrophe and the *s* are not.

The plurals of most capital letters, symbols, numerals, and words used as words can be formed by adding just an *s*.

Capital Letters	How many *T***s** did you have in the first part of the survey?
Symbols	I used ***s** to mark the important information.
Numerals	There are three *2***s** in her phone number.
Words Used as Words	Don't use too many *and***s** in your sentences. (Words used as words are italicized [or underlined]. The *s* that forms the plural is not.)

Apostrophes in Certain Dates

Use an *apostrophe* to show that numbers have been left out of a date.

My grandmother marched for civil rights back in '65. (1965)

The hurricane of '05 was a terrible disaster. (2005)

To form the plural of years in a decade, add an *s* after the date. Remember to use an apostrophe for any missing digits in a date.

Sometimes my father likes to listen to music from the '60s.

I listen to some old bands from the 1980s.

Semicolons

A **semicolon** (;) usually signals a pause between clauses in a compound sentence.

Semicolons with Compound Sentences

A **compound sentence** has two or more independent clauses. These clauses can be joined by a comma and a coordinating conjunction or by a semicolon.

Use a *semicolon* between the clauses of a compound sentence that are not joined by a coordinating conjunction. Coordinating conjunctions include *and, but, or,* and *yet*.

Comma and Coordinating Conjunction	Jane wants to cut down the buckthorn shrubs in the forest, **but** I'd rather encourage these native plants.
Semicolon	Jane wants to cut down the buckthorn shrubs in the forest; I'd rather encourage these native plants.
Comma and Coordinating Conjunction	My father's ancestors came from Ireland, **and** my mother's ancestors were Swedish.
Semicolon	My father's ancestors came from Ireland; my mother's ancestors were Swedish.

You can learn more about compound sentences in Chapter 9.

You can use a semicolon to correct a run-on sentence.

Run-on	Everyone in my family is tall, my brother, for example, is six feet tall.
Correct	Everyone in my family is tall; my brother, for example, is six feet tall.

You can learn more about run-on sentences in Chapter 10.

Semicolons with Conjunctive Adverbs and Transitional Words

Use a *semicolon* between clauses in a compound sentence that are joined by certain conjunctive adverbs or transitional words.

When a compound sentence contains a **conjunctive adverb** or **transitional phrase,** place a semicolon between the two clauses. Then place a comma after the conjunctive adverb as you would after any other parenthetical expression.

Kim practiced repeatedly; **therefore,** she played well at the recital.

She had worried about stage fright; **in fact,** she performed calmly.

Common Conjunctive Adverbs		
accordingly	furthermore	otherwise
also	hence	similarly
besides	however	still
consequently	instead	therefore
finally	nevertheless	thus
Common Transitional Phrases		
as a result	in addition	in other words
for example	in fact	on the other hand

As You Write

Some of the adverbs and transitional words shown in the chart above can also be used as parenthetical expressions within a single clause. In this case, use commas—not a semicolon and a comma—to set them off.

Joining Clauses   I play the guitar; **however,** I have never performed in public.

Within a Clause   My brother, **however,** has played in several concerts.

Semicolons in a Series

Use a *semicolon* instead of a comma between the items in a series if the items themselves contain commas.

> For the picnic, Jeri made individual packets of bacon, lettuce, and tomato; ketchup, mustard, and relish; and sour cream with dill.

> They stayed in Jacksonville, Florida; Albany, Georgia; and Mobile, Alabama. (In ordinary usage, place a comma after both the city and state in a sentence.)

Colons

A *colon* (:) is used most often to introduce a list of items.

> I want do one of three things this summer: sail, scuba dive, or hike in the wilderness.

> The exhibit will present the following periods: the Jurassic, the Triassic, and the Permian.

> My aunt jokes that kids believe in four food groups: chips, candy, ice cream, and pop.

A colon is not needed between a verb and its complement.

Incorrect	The earth's four main layers include: the inner core, outer core, mantle, and crust.
Correct	The earth's four main layers include the inner core, outer core, mantle, and crust.

A colon is not needed directly after a preposition.

Incorrect	The earth's mantle consists mainly of: silicon dioxide, magnesium oxide, and iron oxide.
Correct	The earth's mantle consists mainly of silicon dioxide, magnesium oxide, and iron oxide.

Additional Uses for Colons

Use a colon when writing hours and minutes, Biblical chapters and verses, and salutations in business letters.

> Even on Saturdays, I set my alarm for 6:30 A.M.

> The sad man sitting next to me on the train was reading Job 28:18.

> Dear Sir:
> Please consider publishing my poem in your magazine.

Hyphens

A *hyphen* (-) is used to join some words, including numbers, fractions, and compound nouns. Hyphens may also be used to divide words at the end of a line.

Hyphens with Compound Nouns

A **compound noun** is a noun that is made up of two or more words. Some compound nouns are composed of two separate words, some are written as one word, and others are made of two words joined by a hyphen. If you are not sure how to write a compound word, look it up in a dictionary.

Compound Words	
One word	birdlike, worldwide, crossroads, supermarket
Two words	comic book, grocery store, dump truck, sports car
Hyphenated	first-class, cross-examine, great-grandmother

Hyphens with Numbers

Use a hyphen when writing out the numbers *twenty-one* through *ninety-nine*.

Wait until you read the surprise ending on page ninety-six!

If a number is the first word of a sentence, spell it out. Do not add the coordinating conjunction *and* to the numbers you spell out.

One hundred sixty-four students attended the rally last month. (Do not write one hundred *and* sixty-four.)

Hyphens with Fractions

When a fraction is used as a noun, it does not require a hyphen. When it is used as an adjective, it does require a hyphen.

No Hyphen   Three fourths of the members were present. (**Three fourths** is a noun used as the subject.)

Hyphen   A three-fourths majority is needed to pass the amendment. (*Three-fourths* is an adjective that describes *majority*.)

Hyphens with Divided Words

Occasionally it is necessary to divide a word at the end of a line to keep the right margin even. You can use a hyphen to divide a word at the end of a line and indicate that it continues on the following line.

The following chart lists guidelines for dividing a word at the end of a line.

Guidelines For Dividing Words

1. Divide words only between syllables.

pro•duc•tion   pro-duction or produc-tion

2. Never divide a one-syllable word.

Do Not Break   dine   cheap   strength

3. Do not divide a word after the first letter.

Do Not Break   omit   able   enough

4. Divide hyphenated words only after the hyphens.

Divide After Hyphen   sister-in-law   maid-of-honor   side-by-side

If you are not certain about the location of syllable breaks in a word, look up the word in a dictionary.

Introduction to the Writing Process

QuickGuide

Using the Writing Process pages 175–176	Writing is a process. You move back and forth among the five steps of the process — prewriting, drafting, revising, editing, and publishing—to achieve your purpose.
Prewriting pages 176–185	**Prewriting** includes all of the thinking, imagining, and planning you do before starting your first draft.
Drafting pages 185–187	In **drafting**, you use all your prewriting ideas and plans and start writing
Revising pages 188–190	In **revising**, you look at your writing with fresh eyes to see how you can improve your work.
Editing pages 191–192	In **editing**, you polish your writing to prepare it for publishing.
Publishing pages 193–195	In **publishing**, you share your work with others.

Using the Writing Process

Your **writing process** is the series of stages that you go through when developing your ideas and discovering the best way to express them.

Writing is a creative process. As a writer you can shift from one stage to another or change the order of the stages you follow. For example, you may choose to revise your writing as you draft it, or edit your writing as you revise it. Each stage has its own distinct characteristics.

You will notice this feature throughout the writing chapters of this book. It will help you to focus on the Six Traits of Good Writing. The Six Traits are an integral part of the writing process. You will learn more about them in Chapter 20.

The Process of Writing

Here are the five stages of the writing process. Remember that you can go back to any stage at any point until you are satisfied with your writing.

Prewriting includes the planning you do before writing your first draft. During prewriting you find and develop a subject, determine your purpose, and think about your audience. You also collect ideas and details and make a basic plan for presenting them.

Drafting is expressing your ideas in sentences and paragraphs following your plan. It also includes incorporating new ideas you discover while writing. During drafting, you develop your content. Don't worry about spelling or punctuation at this point. You can catch this kind of error later. For now, just get your ideas down on paper.

Revising means rethinking what you have written and working to improve it. At this stage you will focus on organization to make sure your writing is logical and complete. You will also work on refining your voice, word choice, and sentence fluency, so that your ideas come through clearly.

Editing involves looking for and correcting errors of convention—grammar, usage, spelling, and mechanics—and proofreading your final version before making it public.

Publishing is sharing your work in a way that is appropriate for both the ideas and the audience.

Prewriting

Prewriting **includes all the thinking, imagining, and planning you do before starting your first draft.**

Some event, idea, or problem usually triggers the act of writing: your teacher gives you an assignment, your cousin sends you an urgent E-mail, or you have a great idea for a science fiction story. Once you decide to write something, you set in motion a writing process. Where do you begin? The answer is almost always with prewriting. **Prewriting** is all of the planning and thinking that takes place from the moment you decide to write, up to the time you begin the first draft.

Strategies for Finding Subjects

Finding a good subject—one that will truly interest you and your readers—is your first task. You may discover good ideas through your own experiences, through reading or watching movies, through talking with others, in a class, or while listening to the radio. The strategies on the next two pages will help you discover ideas for writing.

Take an Interest Inventory Much of the writing you do will grow out of your own interests, experiences, and knowledge. One way to find a writing subject is to concentrate on topics that are familiar to you. Use the following phrases to take a personal interest inventory. Write as many items as you can to complete each phrase.

1. My favorite subjects in school are . . .
2. My friends and I like to . . .
3. I could teach someone how to . . .
4. My favorite places are . . .
5. I often dream of . . .
6. I would like to know more about . . .
7. I wish . . .
8. I enjoy reading (or watching) . . .
9. I often see . . .
10. I sometimes hear . . .

Expand Your Horizons Get out and discover what is going on around you. Join clubs. Get involved in community projects. Talk to family members and neighbors. Visit museums, parks, gardens, libraries, businesses, and so on. The more you see and do, the more ideas you will have for writing.

Read and Research Talk to the librarian to find out what new books he or she recommends. Ask people about interesting Web sites you could check out. There is nothing like reading and researching to trigger ideas for more reading and researching—and writing.

Freewrite Another strategy for discovering possible subjects is freewriting. Just as the word implies, **freewriting** means writing freely on whatever comes to mind, without stopping and without worrying about making mistakes. If you get stuck, look around you at an object or person and write about that. The example on the next page shows how potential subjects come to the surface through freewriting.

> It's raining outside and I think my feet are getting colder and colder. Why didn't I wear my boots? I'm wondering what to write about. I can't think of anything. My mind feels blank. Sometimes I let my mind go blank, like when I'm trying to relax before a game. Then I let my muscles go, and I stare up at the sky. I don't try to remember anything about what the coach said for a few minutes. Then I go over plays in my head. We have a great team but I don't get to play too much.

As the student wrote, several thoughts—enjoying sports and preparing for a game—started to emerge. Freewriting can result in different ideas that can be related to one another or lead to totally different subjects or ideas.

Keep a Journal An excellent way to explore your thoughts and discover subjects is through journal writing. A **journal** is a notebook in which you record your thoughts, feelings, ideas, and observations about life, people, or the world around you. Your teacher might ask you to keep a writing journal of responses to stories, poems, and other literature. You may also want to keep a personal journal. Because both journals contain what is important to you, your entries can be a good source of ideas for writing.

Keep a Learning Log A **Learning Log** is a section of your journal that can be used to write ideas and information on subjects that interest you. The Learning Log can help you organize your thoughts, discover new topics of interest, or inspire you to look at a subject differently. A Learning Log entry might look like this.

> A new photography exhibit opened at the museum. I saw an exhibit on antique furniture last week, and one on sculpture the week before. I wonder what it would be like to work at a museum. Seems like you have to keep your mind open to different kinds of artworks. What kind of art would I need to study? What experience would I need to work in a museum? Maybe the museum curator could give me some advice, or I can search the Internet.

Choose and Limit a Subject

Choosing a Subject Making an inventory of your interests, freewriting, exploring the Internet, and reading literature are all activities that can be helpful in generating new writing ideas. Here are some guidelines to help you choose a subject.

Guidelines for Choosing a Subject
- Choose a subject that genuinely interests you.
- Choose a subject that you think will interest your readers.
- Choose a subject that you know something about.

Limiting a Subject The subject you choose may be very broad. Subjects such as "music" or "school" are too general to cover completely in a single composition. To limit your subject, use the strategies listed below.

Strategies for Limiting a Subject
- Focus on one example that represents the subject.
- Limit your subject to a specific time or place.
- Focus on a particular event or person.
- Choose one effect or one purpose of your subject.

Targeting the Six Traits: Ideas

Good writing needs good ideas. The better the idea, the better the writing. For example, you might decide that peanuts would make a good topic. But *peanuts* is too broad a topic. To focus your thinking, start a list of questions such as the ones below.

Where did peanuts come from?

Where are peanuts grown?

Are peanuts good for you?

What is the nutritional value of a peanut?

Can you do anything with peanuts besides eat them?

Consider Your Purpose, Occasion, and Audience

Your purpose is the reason you have for writing. You may think the only reason you are writing is because you have an assignment for a class, but that is not what is meant. Generally, you will have one or more of the following purposes for writing: **to inform, to entertain, to persuade**, or **to express yourself.** It is important that you decide what your purpose is before you write, because your purpose may affect the type of writing you choose. For example, if your purpose is to entertain, you might write a short story or play. A poem or journal might be a good outlet for self-expression. Of course, you can have more than one purpose, such as a very funny and entertaining essay that also persuades people to do something.

The occasion for writing can also affect the way you write. If you have to give a speech about fire safety in front of the class, you would write differently than if you were explaining how to play a game.

Your audience is the reader to whom you are writing. You want to think about your audience so you can decide on the best way to get your ideas across. Are you writing to a friend or a newspaper editor? These are two very different audiences, and would require different writing styles. The same is true if your audience is much younger than you or your same age.

Audience Profile Questions
- Who will be reading my work?
- How old is my reader?
- Do I need to define words or explain ideas to my reader?
- What do I think will interest my reader?
- What do I want readers to know about the subject I've chosen?
- What will they already know about my subject?

Developing Your Voice

Voice in writing is the particular sound and rhythm of the language a particular writer uses. Voice is an important part of your writing that has to do with word choice.

Targeting the Six Traits: Voice

The voice you use when writing is what helps establish what you are like and how you will relate to your audience. If you are writing to friends, your voice may be playful. If you are writing to a company about a product you bought, your voice may be business-like. If you are writing about a sick relative, your voice may be very serious. The most important thing to remember is that, whatever the *mood* or *tone* of your voice in your writing, you want it to be clear and easily understood.

Reading your work aloud will help you hear whether your writing voice sounds the way you intended. An oral reading can detect things that a silent reading can not.

Strategies for Developing Your Subject

After you have chosen and limited your subject—and you have considered your occasion, audience, and purpose—you should collect specific details that will help you develop your writing. **Main ideas** are the points you want to get across. **Supporting details** are the facts, examples, incidents, reasons, or other specific points that back up your main ideas. Following are some prewriting strategies for gathering information.

Researching Once you have determined your subject, you can begin looking for details and information to support your main idea. This is called **researching**. Depending on your topic or main idea, this may take the form of reading, watching films or television programs, looking up facts on the Internet, or interviewing people.

Observing Observation is an important tool for collecting information and for developing your own view and interpretation of a subject. **Observing** involves using your senses to take in the sights, sounds, smells, tastes, and feelings associated with your subject. The techniques at the top of the next page will help you improve your powers of observation.

Techniques for Observing

- Be aware of why you are observing. Keep your purpose in mind as you decide what and how to observe.
- Depending on what you are observing, try to use all your senses. As appropriate, look, listen, smell, touch, and taste.
- Observe from different viewpoints. Look at your subject from all angles: near and far, above and below, and inside and out.
- Sketch your subject. Make a drawing of what you observe.

Brainstorming for Details **Brainstorming** is the process of writing everything that comes to mind when thinking about a particular subject. Once you have chosen and limited a subject, brainstorming can help you discover supporting details. Although it is possible to brainstorm with yourself, this strategy is most effective when done in a group.

Guidelines for Brainstorming

- Set a time limit, such as 15 minutes.
- Assign one group member to record ideas.
- Brainstorm for details—facts, examples, reasons, and connections.
- Build on the ideas of other group members.
- Keep your mind open and avoid criticizing others.

When you have finished brainstorming, you should get a copy of all the supporting details from the group recorder. Select details that support your subject or use the details to generate new ideas.

Look at this list on how a sports player prepares.

> Preparing for a Game
> — Practice long and hard ahead of time
> — Remember to bring a bottle of water!
> — Visualize the big play
> — End-around; fake pass; defense-heavy formation; study other special plays
> — Team meetings

Clustering Another strategy for developing your subject is clustering. Clustering is a visual form of brainstorming in which you not only jot down details as you think of them, but also make connections among those details. Often, writers use clustering to help organize their thoughts.

A cluster can look like a wheel. At the hub, or center, is your subject. Each idea that supports or explains your subject is connected to the hub by a line, like a spoke in a wheel. Sometimes supporting ideas become hubs of their own, with new spokes coming out of them.

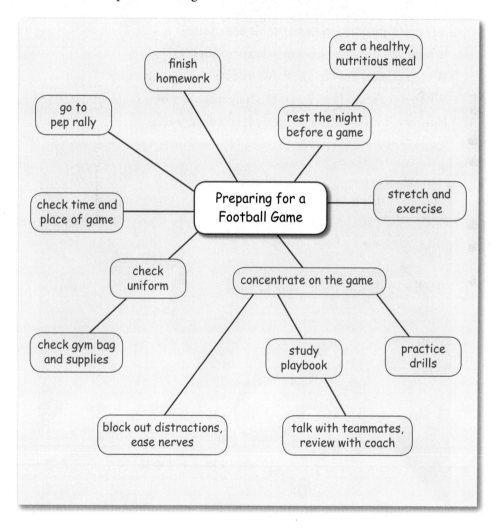

Inquiring Another strategy for exploring a subject is to ask yourself questions concerning that subject. *Who, what, where, when, why,* and *how* questions can provide answers and generate ideas that are helpful in developing the details for a composition. Suppose, for example, that you are asked to write a report on studying insects. You might start with the following questions.

Who are some of the experts in the field of insect study?

What specific details do people look for when they study different insects, and **what** tools are used?

Where are the best places to look for insects?

Why is gaining knowledge about insects useful to people?

When did people first begin to study insects?

How are insects captured, named, and observed?

Strategies for Organizing Details

Prewriting strategies such as freewriting, brainstorming, researching, inquiring, observing, and clustering help you search for subjects and details for your writing. Once you have collected details, you need to organize them. Arranging them in a logical order will not only support your subject, but will also help you achieve your purpose and make sense to your readers. Study the chart below to determine the types of order and kinds of writing that work well together.

Ways to Organize Details		
Types of Order	**Definition**	**Examples**
Chronological	The order in which events occur	story, explanation, history, biography, drama
Spatial	Location or physical arrangement	description (top to bottom, near to far, left to right, etc.)
Order of Importance	Degree of importance, size, or interest	persuasive writing, description, explanation
Logical	Logical progression, one detail leads to another	classifications, definitions, comparison and contrast

Choose the type of order most appropriate to your writing purpose. For example, if you were writing to persuade, you might choose to use order of importance, whereas if you were to write about a past vacation or trip, you might choose to use chronological order.

Drafting

Drafting is the stage in writing where all your ideas from prewriting are put into sentences and paragraphs. Your first draft is just a rough sketch that allows you to see how your details and ideas fit on paper. You will probably have to write several complete drafts. The strategies on the next page will help you prepare a first draft.

Strategies for Drafting

- Try drafting an introduction that will capture the reader's interest and express your main idea.
- Use your organized prewriting notes as a guide while you write. Depart from those notes, however, when a good idea occurs to you.
- Write fairly quickly without worrying about spelling or phrasing. You will have the opportunity to go back and fix your writing when you revise.
- Stop frequently and read aloud what you have written. This practice will help you move logically from one thought to the next.
- Return to the prewriting stage whenever you need to clarify your thinking. You can always stop and freewrite, brainstorm, or cluster for more ideas.
- Write a conclusion that drives home the main point of the composition.

Drafting an Introduction The introduction is where you state your main idea. You need to make it as clear as possible to your audience. This is where you "hook" the readers, and invite them to read the details that support your main idea.

If you are having trouble creating an introduction, simply write your main idea down, and then work on the body of the draft. It is often easier to go back and create a good introduction later in the process.

Drafting the Body This is where you support your main idea. The body should be organized so that the details, ideas, information that you have gathered, or points you want to make flow logically from your main idea to your conclusion. Each paragraph should have a topic sentence that clearly relates to the main idea and details that support the topic sentence.

Drafting a Conclusion The conclusion should summarize the information you presented in your writing. It may simply be a restatement of the main idea. It may be a surprise, like the punch line of a joke. However you end your work, the conclusion should leave the reader with a memorable idea or image, something that sums up all the details and drives home your point.

The draft on the next page was written from the brainstorming and clustering notes about preparing for a football game. Notice that the writer did not take the time to fix mistakes. The errors will be corrected later.

What goes into preparing for a big game. It takes a lot of time getting ready for the important games. We players have to do a lot to get ready.

One thing is having team meetings, these help build team spirit and make you want to do good for all the other players. The fans are also counting on you. I always hope we will have good weather. It also helps to concentrate only on the game and the game plan. If you let your mind wander, you can forget or make a mistake on a important play. Team meetings also help you get all the plays straight. Even more important, though, is the long, hard practice you put in all season long. nothing can take the place of practice. Practice makes perfect. Maybe the most important thing is visualizing, or picturing, victory or a big play.

Lots of practice and believing in ourselves. That's how we prepare for a big game.

Drafting a Title When you have written a complete draft of your composition, take some time to come up with a good title for it. Choose one that captures your reader's interest and suggests the main idea of your composition.

Revising

Revising challenges you as a writer to look at the style and content of your work.

When asked if he ever rewrote his stories, writer Frank O'Connor replied, "Endlessly, endlessly, endlessly." In some ways, writing is never completely finished. It can always be improved just a little bit more. When you revise, you rework your draft as often as needed until it is as good as you can make it.

Strategies for Revising

Before you revise your writing, set it aside for a while. When you come back to it, you will be able to see both its strengths and its weaknesses with fresh eyes. You can then use the following strategies to improve your work.

Add Details and Information If your composition seems weak and empty, ask yourself whether more information is needed. Brainstorm, cluster, or do additional research to come up with more details. Add whatever seems to be missing.

Delete Unnecessary Words or Ideas If you find that you have included details that stray from your subject, cross them out. Also delete repetition that does not serve a useful purpose.

Substitute Words and Sentences Read your writing aloud. Are there places where you have used a weak, vague word instead of a strong, specific one? Are there any places where your sentences sound monotonous? Substitute more lively words and more varied sentences.

Rearrange Look carefully at the organization of your words, sentences, and ideas. Are any out of place? Rearrange any part of your draft that is out of order.

Use the Six Traits and Evaluation Checklists Revising challenges you to look at the style and content of your work. Using a checklist will help you evaluate your writing to see whether your latest draft includes the features of a good composition. You will learn more about the Six Traits of Good Writing in Chapter 20. For now, study the chart and checklist on the next page.

Six Traits Checklist	
1. Ideas	Be sure your main idea is clear and that your details support your main idea.
2. Organization	Your writing must be organized in such a way that details logically support your main idea. Can the reader follow your points easily?
3. Word Choice	Use specific, descriptive words that help the reader "see" what you are describing or that emphasize your ideas.
4. Voice	Let your personality be evident in your writing. Readers must believe you care about what you have written.
5. Sentence Fluency	The language you use, its patterns and rhythm, must have a natural flow that makes your work easy to read. Varying sentence type and length helps create a natural flow.
6. Conventions	Your writing must be correct grammatically and in terms of usage, spelling, and punctuation. (You will concentrate on this trait more at the editing stage.)

The checklist below will help identify any changes you need to make.

Evaluation Checklist for Revising

✓ Did you clearly state your main idea?

✓ Does your composition have a strong introduction and conclusion?

✓ Does the body support your main idea with enough details?

✓ Did you present your ideas in logical order?

✓ Do any of your sentences stray from the main idea?

✓ Are your words specific?

✓ Are any words or ideas repeated unnecessarily?

✓ Are your sentences varied and smoothly connected?

✓ Is the purpose of your composition clear?

✓ Is your writing suited to your audience?

Conferencing

When you are fairly pleased with the changes you have made, you may wish to conference. **Conferencing** means sharing your writing with a "test reader" to see if there are any other ways you could improve your work. Listen carefully to what your conference partner has to say. Keep in mind, however, that your partner's comments are suggestions only. You are the final judge.

Peer Conferencing

One way to conference is to form a group with several other students and exchange drafts. Then take turns reading and discussing each person's written work. During this time, offer praise, constructive criticism, and suggestions for improvement. The following guidelines will help you get the most out of conferencing as a revising technique.

Guidelines for the Writer

- List some questions for your classmates. What aspects of your writing most concern you?
- Try to be grateful for your critic's honesty rather than being upset or defensive. Keep in mind that the criticism you are getting is well-intended.

Guidelines for the Reader

- Read your partner's work carefully. What is the writer's purpose?
- Point out strengths as well as weaknesses.
- Be specific. Refer to a specific word, sentence, or section of the compostion when you comment.
- Be sensitive to your partner's feelings. Phrase your criticisms as questions. You might say, "Do you think your details might be stronger if . . . ?"

Editing

Using an Editing Checklist

When you edit you should go over your work at least three times, each time looking for a different kind of problem. For example, the focus of one reading might be misspellings. During another reading, focus on usage errors, such as subject-verb agreement. The last reading can be reserved for identifying and fixing errors in punctuation or capitalization.

Editing Checklist

✓ Are sentences free of errors in grammar and usage?

✓ Did you punctuate each sentence correctly?

✓ Did you spell each word correctly?

✓ Did you use capital letters where needed?

Creating a Personalized Editing Checklist A **Personalized Editing Checklist** is a section of your journal where you can catalog errors that you make frequently, such as commonly misspelled words or grammar rules you sometimes forget. Write the following headings on every other page: *Grammar Problems, Usage Problems, Spelling Problems,* and *Mechanical Problems.* Use these pages to record your errors.

Proofreading You may become so familiar with your work during the revising stage that you skip over mistakes. Proofreading during the editing stage may help you see mistakes that you missed earlier. **Proofreading** is the process of carefully rereading one's work and marking corrections in grammar, usage, spelling, and mechanics. The following techniques may help.

Proofreading Techniques

- Focus on one line at a time.
- Exchange your work with a partner and check each other's work.
- Read your composition backward, word by word. By changing the way you read your work, you will find errors you may have otherwise missed.
- Read your writing aloud, very slowly.
- Use a dictionary and a handbook to check spelling, grammar, usage, and mechanics.

Proofreading symbols are convenient shorthand notations that writers frequently use during the editing stage. The most commonly used proofreading symbols are shown below.

Proofreading Symbols

Symbol	Meaning	Example
∧	insert	We completed an journey. *(went on / eventful)*
⌃	insert comma	Meg enjoys hiking, skiing and skating.
⊙	insert period	Dr Chan told me to call.
ℯ	delete	Refer back to your notes.
¶	new paragraph	¶ Before dawn the fog had lifted . . .
...	let it stand	I appreciated her sincere honesty.
#	add space	Jack hit a homerun.
⌣	close up	I'll do it my self.
∼	transpose	They only have two dollars left.
≡	capital letter	The party is on saturday.
/	lowercase	Where is the highest Mountain?
(SP)	spell out	I ate 2 oranges.
"" ""	insert quotes	I hope you can join us, said my brother.
⌐	insert hyphen	I attended a school related event.
⌄	insert apostrophe	The ravenous dog ate the cats food.
♂	move copy	I usually on Fridays go to the movies.

Publishing

Most of the writing you do is meant to be shared with others. **Publishing**, the final stage of the writing process, involves presenting your completed work in a final form to an audience.

Ways to Publish Your Writing

In School

- Read your work aloud to a small group in your class.
- Display your final draft on a bulletin board in your classroom or school library.
- Read your work aloud to your class or present it in the form of a radio program or video.
- Create a class library and media center to which you submit your work. The class media center could be a collection of folders or files devoted to different types of student writing and media presentations.
- Create a class anthology to which every student contributes. Share your anthology with other classes.
- Submit your work to your school literary magazine, newspaper, or yearbook.

Outside School

- Submit your written work to a newspaper or magazine.
- Share your work with an interested professional.
- Present your work to an appropriate community group.
- Send a video based on your written work to a local cable television station.
- Enter your work in a local, state, or national writing contest.

Using Standard Manuscript Form

The appearance of your composition may be almost as important as its content. A marked-up paper with inconsistent margins is difficult to read. A neat, legible paper, on the other hand, makes a positive impression on your reader. Use the guidelines for standard manuscript form on the next page to help you prepare your final draft. The model on page 195 shows how the writer used these guidelines to prepare his final draft.

Standard Manuscript Form

- Use standard-sized 8½-by-11-inch white paper. Use one side of the paper only.
- If handwriting, use black or blue ink. If using a word-processing program, use black ink and double-space the lines.
- Leave a 1.25-inch margin at the left and right. The left margin must be even. The right margin should be as even as possible.
- Put your name, the course title, the name of your teacher, and the date in the upper right-hand corner of the first page. Follow your teacher's specific guidelines for headings and margins.
- Center the title of your composition two lines below the date. Do not underline or put quotation marks around your title.
- If using a word-processing program, skip four lines between the title and the first paragraph. If handwriting, skip two lines.
- If using a word-processing program, indent the first line of each paragraph five spaces. If handwriting, indent the first line of each paragraph one inch.
- Leave a 1-inch margin at the bottom of all pages.
- Starting on page 2, number each page in the upper right-hand corner. Begin the first line 1 inch from the top. Word-processing programs allow you to insert page numbers.

Omar Byrne
English: Ms. Weymouth
September 18, 2007

The Name of the Game

You might be surprised to learn how much goes into preparing for a big game. Players spend a lot of time and effort to get ready for an important event.

1.25 inches ⟷

One key part of preparing is having team meetings. These build team spirit and make you want to do your best for all your teammates. Team meetings also help you get the plays straight in your mind and let you concentrate on the game and the game plan. If you let your mind wander, you can make a mistake on an important play.

1.25 inches ⟷

Even more important are the long hours of hard practice you put in all season. Nothing can take the place of practice for making sure that each player knows exactly what to do on each play. Maybe the most important thing of all, though, is visualizing, or picturing, victory or a big play. You have to see yourself making an interception or tackling a runner or else you won't succeed.

Teamwork, lots of practice, and believing in each other: that is how we prepare for a big game.

1 inch

CHAPTER 20 The Six Traits of Good Writing

QuickGuide

Ideas pages 197–199	People write about **ideas** that interest them and use **details** that help explain their ideas.
Organization pages 200–203	Good writing has an evident **organization,** with a clear beginning, middle, and ending.
Voice page 203	**Voice** is the quality in writing that makes writing sound natural, as if a real person is behind the words.
Word Choice page 204	Good writers use verbs that are strong and full of action. Their nouns are precise and their modifiers are vivid.
Sentence Fluency pages 204–205	Good writers vary the length and structure of their sentences and weave their ideas together with transitions.
Conventions page 205	Good writers follow the rules of grammar, usage, and mechanics, including correct spelling, capitalization, and punctuation.

Ideas

You can hunt for ideas through brainstorming, freewriting, clustering, or keeping a journal. Here is how one student used freewriting to chase down an idea when the teacher suggested writing about summer vacation.

> I'm supposed to write about my summer vacation, but I didn't go anywhere. I didn't do anything exciting. I'm trying to think of something interesting to write about, but nothing really happened. I saw a few movies with my friends. I watched some television but it was all reruns. It was pretty boring. Watching that nest outside our window was actually more fun than all those reruns. I could write about the birds, I guess. My whole family got into watching that nest from our window.

Narrowing and Focusing Your Idea Once you have a general idea, you need to limit it to a specific topic and decide on your purpose and audience. The student who explored the topic of birds decided that his purpose was to tell the story of the bird's nest. To meet that purpose, he narrowed the rough idea of *the birds outside my window* to *what happened in the nest outside my window.*

Developing Your Idea **Details** are what bring any written composition to life. The kinds of details a writer uses to develop a subject vary with the writer's purpose.

Purpose	Kinds of Details
To Inform or Explain	Facts (statements that can be proved true), examples, reasons, statistics (facts using numbers), comparisons, contrasts, steps in a process
To Describe	sights, sounds, smells, tastes, feelings
To Tell a Story	Events, actions, character and setting descriptions
To Persuade	Facts, examples, reasons, statistics, appeals to feelings

Some of the same strategies you use for thinking of ideas are also good for discovering supporting details. Here's how the student brainstormed to think of details to support his main idea: the story of the birds in the nest. He let his writing purpose—to tell a story—help him think of all the events and descriptions he wanted to use to bring the story to life.

- nest in vine outside window
- saw eggs
- saw tiny birds with heads up waiting to be fed
- mother sat on eggs to hatch them
- father would feed hungry birds
- father attacked his reflection in the window
- babies looked pink and bare
- father would stuff food down their mouths

Staying Focused In the process of thinking of lively details, you let your mind run free. That is a very good way to think of supporting ideas. Sometimes in that process, though, you also think of things that don't relate very directly to your main idea.

Read the following draft of a paragraph about a student's comic book collection. Can you see where she veered off the topic?

Because I am a pack rat, I may be a rich person someday. Five years ago my aunt gave me a subscription to The Fantastic Four. I once saw a Fantastic Four cartoon movie. Since I never throw anything away, I kept all the copies of the old comic books in a box in my closet. I keep my sports equipment there too. Just recently I learned that those old comic books are worth money. If I keep them for ten more years, they will be worth even more. Maybe I will sell them then!

If you thought the sentences about the cartoon movie and sports equipment were off topic, you were right. Those sentences are loosely tied to the topic, but they don't relate specifically to the worth of the old comic books. Good writing keeps the reader's attention focused on the main idea.

Avoiding the Obvious Another thing that can sidetrack readers is "filler"—words and sentences whose purpose is to take up space. Filler is often a problem at the beginnings and endings of compositions. In her first draft, the student who was writing about the value of her comic book collection started this way:

> Children all over the world like comic books. Comic books have lots of pictures that children like. Many children have spent countless hours enjoying comic books.

These sentences convey ideas that everyone knows already. When the writer reread her paragraph, she realized that her opening wasn't the best way to start. Those sentences drew the reader away from the main idea, which was the value of her comic books.

Organization

When you start writing, you may be "driving in the dark" at first until you have found your way to your idea. Once *you* know the way, however, you can help your reader understand it clearly by providing a strong organization. Good writing leads readers from one idea to the next. It presents details in a logical, easy-to-follow order and uses clear transitions to help readers connect ideas.

The Basic Structure

Well-organized writing has a clear **beginning, middle,** and **ending**.

A Good Beginning A strong beginning captures the attention of readers and makes them want to read more. It also sets the direction for the rest of the composition. Does the opening sentence below accomplish those purposes?

In this composition, I would like to tell you the story of the birds outside our window.

If you are like most readers, you would probably say that it sets the direction for the composition. You might think, however, that it does not do a very good job of capturing your attention. See what you think about his second draft.

> By mid-summer I was bored. I had already seen all the movies I wanted to. The only shows on television were reruns. Most of my friends were out of town. How was I going to make it through the summer? Just when I thought I would be bored the rest of my life, something happened that made it interesting again. It happened right outside my window, too. There, before my eyes, a new family of birds came into being.

This opening makes the direction of the composition clear. It also manages to draw readers in and hold their attention.

A Clear Middle Good writing moves from idea to idea in a clear organizational pattern. It uses transitions to help readers follow the train of thought. Different kinds of writing often call for different patterns.

Purpose	Organizational Patterns	Common Transitions
To Inform	Order of Importance	first, next, most important
	Comparison/Contrast	similarly, in contrast, on the other hand
	Cause/Effect	as a result, for that reason, because
To Tell a Story	Chronological (Time) Order	first, yesterday, the next day, last year, next, until
To Describe	Spatial (Location) Order	at the top, near the middle, to the right, on the other side, next to, behind
To Persuade	Order of Importance	the most important, equally important, in addition, also, in fact

To match his purpose of telling a story, the student writing about the birds chose chronological order for the middle of his composition. The transitions he used are in blue type. They all relate to the passing of time.

It started **in early July, when** we heard noises outside the window. We all peered through the window and saw that a cardinal had made a nest in the honeysuckle vine. **Over the next several days** we kept checking the nest. **Before long** we discovered three speckled eggs. We could see them only when the brownish-colored mother cardinal left the nest.

As the days passed, the mother sat on the eggs, warming them with her body to help them hatch. **Every now and then** the bright red father cardinal would sit on the eggs instead. The father cardinal seemed very protective. **Once** it seemed like he was attacking our window. **Then** we realized he saw his reflection and thought it was another male trying to take over his territory.

Finally, twelve days later, the time came. **That morning** we saw three little birds with their heads tilted straight back and their beaks wide open, waiting for food. It was their father who came around to feed them, stuffing their hungry throats. He kept close watch over the baby birds **for ten days. By then** they were able to take care of themselves.

The Ending Good writing provides a strong finish to the composition. A strong ending gives the writing a completed feeling. It often reflects back to words or thoughts in the introduction as a way to tie things together. A strong ending also can make the readers think about ideas in new ways.

The summer definitely picked up **after that.** I actually lost interest in movies and television **for a while.** I felt like maybe I was missing too many things by watching other people's lives in movies or on TV. Right outside my window was an amazing story. I started looking around more, trying to see what else I might have been missing. **As soon as** I did that, the summer began to race by, and I didn't feel bored anymore.

In this ending, the writer returned to the idea of being bored that was in his introduction. He also presented a new understanding that the experience had given him.

Voice

Reading has been described as a conversation between the writer and the reader. When you read something well-written, you tend to "hear" a writer's voice. **Voice** is the quality in writing that makes it sound as if there is a real, live person behind the words. It reflects the writer's personality. "Listen" for the voice in the following passages.

> By mid-summer I was bored. I had already seen all the movies I wanted to.

> Hurricanes are tropical creatures that begin to stir off the coast of Africa after the summer sun has heated the ocean to the temperature of balmy bath water.
>
> —"Where a Hurricane Gets Its Force," *Time*

> Her name was Ann, and we met in the Port Authority Bus Terminal several Januarys ago. I was doing a story on homeless people.
>
> — "Homeless," from *Living Out Loud* by Anna Quindlen

Voice varies greatly from writer to writer. It must be authentic and must also suit the writer's audience and purpose. When you write about birds in your backyard, you can use a casual voice. Writing about hurricanes calls for less emphasis on the writer's personality and more emphasis on the subject, so the voice is more formal. Writing about homeless people calls for a serious voice.

Purpose	What the Writer's Voice Should Convey
To Explain and To Persuade	Honest interest in the subject, often telling why the subject is important to the writer and reader; respect for differing views; confidence without being conceited.
To Describe and To Tell a Story	A true-to-life, not phony, personality; honest personal statements and a sense of trust.

Word Choice

The words you choose make a big difference in how your message gets across to readers.

Specific Words

In strong writing, words are specific rather than general. Compare the following sentences.

General	Near the water stood a tree, some flowers, and a stone.
Specific	Near the waterfall stood a crooked birch, daffodils in bloom, and a boulder the size of a bear.

This chart shows some general and specific words.

	General	Specific
Nouns	road	path, avenue, lane, boulevard
Verbs	said	mumbled, boasted, muttered, demanded
Adjectives	big	lofty, bottomless, thick, towering
Adverbs	slowly	gradually, gently, cautiously, lazily

Good writing uses fresh comparisons to help readers picture something. In the specific sentence above, the writer compared the boulder to a bear to give a sense of the rock's size.

Sentence Fluency

Fluency means "the ability to flow." Sentences in strong writing seem to flow easily from one to the next. Writers create this flow with the help of transitions, repeated words, and words such as pronouns that refer back to an earlier word.

Varied Sentence Patterns Another way good writing achieves sentence fluency is by using a variety of sentence types and lengths.

You can change short, choppy sentences into longer and smoother sentences by combining details.

Choppy	The kite bobbed. The kite was huge. It bobbed gently. It bobbed in the wind.
Smooth	The huge kite bobbed gently in the wind.

Vary Sentence Beginnings Strong writing also has a variety of sentence starters. Here are some examples.

Sentence Starters	
Subject	The **raft** floated slowly down the river.
Adverb	**Slowly** the raft floated down the river.
Subject	A souvenir **banner** hung on the wall.
Prepositional Phrase	**On the wall** hung a souvenir banner.

Varying Sentence Type In addition to varying sentence beginnings, good writers also vary the types of sentences they use. You will learn more about sentence structure in Chapter 21.

Conventions

Writers must follow the rules of written conventions. Good writing does not detract from the main ideas with errors in spelling, capitalization, and punctuation. It lays out the ideas in well-arranged paragraphs, which in turn are built of solid, grammatical sentences. Every word seems to be carefully chosen to convey exactly what the writer wants. The writing chapters in this book will provide checklists to help you review your work. However, you may also want to keep a **Personalized Editing Checklist** of mistakes you have made more than once.

Developing Your Writing Style

QuickGuide

Choosing Vivid Words **pages 207–210**	Use specific and colorful nouns, verbs, adjectives, and adverbs to bring life and energy to your writing.
Sentence Combining **pages 211–213**	Learn to combine sentences to create paragraphs that flow naturally.
Creating Sentence Variety **pages 213–216**	Varying your sentence structure makes your writing easier to read—and livelier.
Writing Concise Sentences **pages 216–217**	You can lose your reader if you wander too much, whether the wandering is rambling sentences or phrases that don't add to your meaning.

Choosing Vivid Words

Your **writing style** is the distinctive way you express yourself through the words you choose and the way you shape your sentences.

The words you use can transmit a strong message or leave your reader guessing your meaning. Pick words that help the reader connect with your ideas and that breathe life into your work.

Specific Words

Read the following movie reviews. Which one gives you a better idea of the film?

> The movie was very good. The actors were good. The special effects were great. The story was interesting.

> *Star Base* is thrillingly entertaining. The young cast performed sensitively. The special effects were dazzling. The story throbbed with action and conflict and concluded with a surprise ending.

The first review uses only general words. Since general words can mean different things to different people, they do not communicate precisely. The second review replaces the general words with specific words that call precise images to mind.

The more specific your words are, the more likely it is that your reader will know what you are talking about.

Specific Nouns Don't say "dog" if you can say "collie," "poodle," or "German shepherd." Don't say "ball" if you can say "baseball," "basketball," or "ping-pong ball." Don't say "food" if you can say "steak," "broccoli," or "yogurt." There will be times you have to use non-specific nouns. It would be awkward to write "I walked back to my two-story apartment building" rather than "I walked back to my apartment," but on the whole, if you are trying to communicate with a reader, the more specific you can be the better. Remember, the reader can't see what you see unless you show it and can't know what you're thinking unless you write it.

Specific Verbs There are plenty of times when "says" and "looks" are just the right words to use, but you can communicate more if you use verbs that are specific to the situation. For example, instead of "says," perhaps the person *shouts, whispers, sighs, declares, announces,* or *mumbles.* Instead of "looks," perhaps a person *glances, stares, glares, glowers, inspects,* or *peeks.* Try to communicate emotion as well as action with the words you choose.

Specific Modifiers Adjectives should be specific too. If you use a non-specific word such as "beautiful" to describe a stretch of road, a nature-lover may imagine trees and flowers lining the road in question. A highway engineer, on the other hand, might imagine smooth, level concrete and clearly painted lines.

In general, don't say a dress is "cute" if you can say it is "dark blue with lace trim." Don't say a person is "nice" if you can say that the person is "friendly, upbeat, and always thinking of others." Adverbs can also help you be more specific. Saying that someone moves across the room "quickly and nervously" tells you more than just saying he moved across the room. Adverbs can also help enrich your adjectives. For example, if a green paint is really bright, you might write that it is vividly green, instead of just saying it's green.

Use some of the prewriting techniques you learned in Chapter 19 to come up with words that will help you describe an object, feeling, place, idea, person, or anything else you may write about in very specific terms. For example, you might use brainstorming or clustering to come up with words that can help you write more vividly.

What I'm describing: the big, old town hall

Specific words to use in description:
One hundred years old
Red brick with white columns
Three stories tall
A block wide
Covered in ivy
Lots of people work there and lots visit; always bustling

Once you've finished your brainstorming, you can write a much more specific description of the town hall. It's not just "big" and "old," it's a "hundred-year-old, red brick building that is a block wide and three stories tall."

Appealing to the Senses Most of the impressions you gather come to you through your five senses. Your experiences are based on what you see, hear, smell, taste, or touch. You can share these experiences in writing by using words that appeal to your readers' senses. Compare the following two sentences.

Josie felt very sad.

Josie **slumped** in the **overstuffed** chair, **moaning** and pressing her **fists** against her eyes to try to hold back the **tears**.

The first sentence *tells* a reader that Josie is sad. The second sentence *shows* the sadness. A reader can see Josie's posture and hear her moaning. These sensory details communicate much more clearly than the adjective *sad* in the first sentence.

When you are writing, take time during the prewriting stage to think of vivid sensory details you will be able to use in your composition. The techniques of clustering and brainstorming will help you come up with details that will appeal to your readers' senses. The following cluster shows a number of sensory words that could be used to describe a peach.

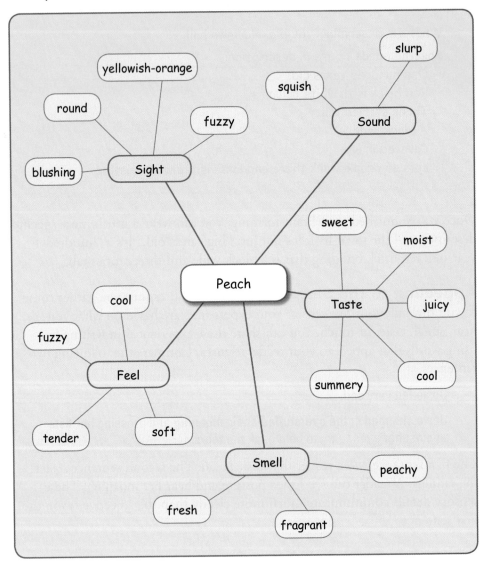

Sentence Combining

Like a bumpy road, writing that has nothing but short sentences makes the going rough. A good mix of sentence types and structures will make the flow of sentences smoother and will help keep your readers interested. **Sentence combining** is one way to vary the patterns of your sentences.

Combining with Specific Details One good strategy for creating sentence variety is to combine specific details from a number of short, choppy sentences into one interesting sentence.

Choppy Sentences The zoo has a tiger. It is a Siberian tiger. It is 500 pounds. The tiger paced to its den. Then it paced to the lake. It went to its den again.

Combined Sentence The zoo's 500-pound Siberian tiger paced back and forth between its den and the lake.

If your combined sentence contains two or more adjectives in a row, remember that you many need to separate the adjectives with commas.

Choppy Sentences The museum has a submarine. It is **rusting**. It is **German**.

Combined Sentence The museum has a **rusting**, **German** submarine.

German submarine U-505 gets a new home at The Museum of Science and Industry in Chicago, Illinois.

Combining by Coordinating You can also combine choppy sentences by **coordinating**, or linking, ideas of equal importance. Use the coordinating conjunctions *and, but, or,* and *yet* to combine subjects, to combine verbs, and to combine parts of sentences.

Choppy	Two huge tusks are one characteristic of the walrus. A mustached upper lip is another characteristic.
Combined Subjects	Two huge tusks **and** a mustached upper lip are characteristics of the walrus.
Choppy	Scientists have observed the walrus for many years. Scientists still have much to learn.
Combined Verbs	Scientists have observed the walrus for many years **but** still have much to learn.
Choppy	The walrus is a powerful member of the seal family. The walrus is timid.
Combined Parts of Sentences	The walrus is a powerful **yet** timid member of the seal family.

Combining by Subordinating If the ideas in two short sentences are of unequal importance, you can combine them by **subordinating.** This technique turns one of the sentences into a clause that becomes part of the combined sentence. The following are some **conjunctions** that can be used to combine by subordinating.

Conjunctions for Subordinating		
after	even if	that
although	even though	though
as	if	unless
as far as	inasmuch as	until
as if	in order that	when
as long as	lest	whenever
as much as	now that	where
as soon as	provided that	whereas
as though	since	wherever
because	so that	whether
before	than	while

Here are some examples.

Choppy	He was late. He had tried to get there on time.
Combined	**Even though** he had tried to get there on time, he was late.
Choppy	I go to the movies. I buy popcorn at the movies.
Combined	I buy popcorn **whenever** I go to the movies.

Creating Sentence Variety

Varying your sentences makes your writing easier to read—and livelier. You can add variety by varying the lengths of sentences or by varying the way you begin or construct your sentences.

Varying Sentence Length You have learned how to use sentence combining to create longer sentences out of short, choppy sentences. On occasion, you will want to make a sentence shorter. A long, rambling sentence that combines too many ideas can be difficult to follow. Also, an occasional punchy, short sentence helps you make a point.

Long Rambling Sentence	He thought about the red bicycle he wanted with the chrome wheels, which he knew he could only buy if he worked all summer.
Short Sentence for Emphasis	He thought about the red bicycle with the chrome wheels, which he knew he could only buy if he worked all summer. **He wanted it now.**

Varying Sentence Beginnings The most natural way to begin a sentence is with the subject. For variety, experiment with other sentence beginnings.

Subject	**Chi Cheng** was a very fast runner in her high school days.
Phrase	**In her high school days,** Chi Cheng was a very fast runner.

The following sentences show just a few of the ways you can begin your sentences.

Prepositional Phrase	**At the age of 16**, she represented Taiwan in the 1960 Olympics.
Adjective	**Steadfast,** she kept up her running even though she hurt her leg during the second Olympic match.
Adverb	**Altogether** Cheng broke or matched seven world records during the next five years.

Chi Cheng (center) at the 1968 Olympics in Mexico City

Varying Sentence Construction Using different types of sentences is another way to add variety to your writing. You might consider rewriting a statement as a question. You could also use quotations in place of statements.

Statement	Senator Smith told the crowd that she was not running for reelection.
Dialogue	"I am definitely not running for reelection," Senator Smith told the crowd.

Targeting the Six Traits: Sentence Fluency

Varied sentences sound more like natural conversation. The way you vary sentence structure will become an important element of your personal writing style. As you combine, break apart, and reconstruct your sentences, make sure you don't lose track of what is happening. It is easy to move a pronoun so far away from the antecedent noun that a reader is no longer certain what it refers to. Also make sure that you have added transitions that keep the text flowing smoothly. Think of a stream; you want little white-water rushes, short falls, and gentle turns that make it more interesting, but you don't want something to stop the water from running.

Writing Concise Sentences

When you shop, you want the most value for your dollar. When you write, you want the most value for each word you use. Avoid bulky writing. Be economical and concise. If you have worked on developing your ideas and have made good word choices, you don't want to have readers get bogged down with rambling sentences, repetition, or empty expressions. These simply weaken your writing.

Rambling Sentences   One cause of bulky writing is throwing too many ideas into one sentence. The result, called a rambling sentence, is hard to read and understand.

Rambling Sentence	About seven million people in the United States do not eat meat, but they find protein in other types of food, and they combine certain kinds of food, such as rice and beans, to make sure they eat complete proteins, or they sometimes eat such dairy products as cheese, milk, and yogurt.
Revised Sentences	About seven million people in the United States do not eat meat. Instead, they find protein in other types of food. They also combine certain foods, such as rice and beans, to make sure they eat complete proteins. Dairy products such as cheese, milk, and yogurt can also provide protein.

Repetition Sometimes without thinking you may repeat an idea unnecessarily.

Repetitive	I resolved to try again and not give up.
Concise	I resolved to try again.
Repetitive	Sam's face looked pale and colorless.
Concise	Sam's face looked pale.
Repetitive	The hungry guests were eager to eat.
Concise	The guests were eager to eat.

Empty Expressions Empty expressions are wasted words that add no real meaning to a sentence.

Empty	What I mean is, I learned a difficult lesson.
Concise	I learned a difficult lesson.
Empty	The Girl Scouts met their fund-raising goal due to the fact that cookie sales were high.
Concise	The Girl Scouts met their fund-raising goal because cookie sales were high.

The cleaner your writing is, the better it will be.

Avoid—	Use—
the reason why is that	because
in spite of the fact that	though or although
owing to the fact that	since or because
as a result of	because
on account of	because

Writing Well-Structured Paragraphs

QuickGuide

Paragraph Writing pages 219–221	A **paragraph** is a group of related sentences that present and develop one main idea.
Building Your Paragraph pages 221–224	The structure of a paragraph helps you present and support your ideas through appropriate use of topic, supporting, and concluding sentences.
Developing and Polishing Your Paragraph pages 225–227	Make certain your paragraph really says what you want it to say by— • checking for paragraph development • checking for unity and coherence • using the Six Traits of Good Writing.

Paragraph Writing

A *paragraph* is a group of related sentences that present and develop one main idea.

Developing Your Paragraph Writing Skills

A paragraph is a unit of thought. It can be part of a long composition, or it can stand alone as a short composition, complete within itself. However it is used, a paragraph always sticks to one main point or focus.

Each time you write a paragraph that stands alone, you will be going through the whole writing process—prewriting, drafting, and revising. The result— a well-structured paragraph with vivid words and smooth sentences—should be as satisfying to read as it is to write.

Paragraph Structure

Most paragraphs that stand alone consist of three main types of sentences. These are the topic sentence, the supporting sentences, and the concluding sentence. Each type of sentence performs a special function in a paragraph, as shown in the chart below.

Structure of a Paragraph	
Topic Sentence	states the main idea
Supporting Sentences	expand on the main idea with specific facts, examples, details, or reasons
Concluding Sentence	provides a strong ending

In the paragraph on the following page, all the other sentences relate directly to the main idea stated in the topic sentence. (Note that the topic and concluding sentences are in blue type.)

The Man Who Rode the Thunder

Topic Sentence Marine pilot William Rankin made history in 1959 when he survived a nine-mile fall from the sky. Over Norfolk, Virginia, Rankin had engine trouble and had to **Supporting Sentences** eject himself from his plane. After he had fallen for about eight minutes, his parachute opened perfectly. To his dismay, however, he found himself in the middle of a thunderstorm. The strong winds kept driving him up instead of down toward the earth. For forty minutes Rankin was tossed by fierce winds and surrounded by blasts of thunder and sheets of lightning. Finally he **Concluding Sentence** reached the ground, frostbitten and injured, but alive. Soon after, newspapers all around the world honored "the man who rode the thunder."

The main idea in this paragraph is that William Rankin survived a nine-mile fall. The rest of the paragraph backs up that main idea by providing the startling details.

Varied Paragraph Structures While the model paragraph on the previous page begins with a topic sentence and ends with a concluding sentence, you may construct a paragraph differently. For example, you may express your main idea in the middle of the paragraph or at the end. Your paragraph may not need a concluding sentence if you end with your topic sentence or if your paragraph is part of a longer composition. In a one-paragraph composition, however, you must make the main idea clear, no matter what paragraph structure you choose.

Guidelines for a One-Paragraph Composition

- Make your main idea clear.
- Develop your main idea fully.
- Provide a strong ending.

You may accomplish these three goals by including a clear topic sentence, a body of supporting sentences, and an effective concluding (or transition) sentence.

Building Your Paragraph

Even though a paragraph is a unit of thought, the three types of sentences that make it up need to be thought of separately.

Topic Sentence

No matter where in the paragraph you choose to put your topic sentence, it serves the same purpose—to focus the reader's attention on the main idea. The topic sentence is usually, but not always, more general than the other sentences in a paragraph.

Features of a Topic Sentence

A topic sentence—

- states the main idea.
- focuses the limited subject to one main point that can be adequately covered in the paragraph.
- is more general than the sentences that develop it.

The following paragraph begins with a very general sentence. The second sentence, which is the topic sentence, limits the broad subject to one specific aspect.

The Emperor's Feet

Topic Sentence

The bitterly cold climate of Antarctica is hostile to many forms of life. Even the emperor penguin, which thrives in the cold, has had to develop unusual behaviors to hatch a chick. If an egg were allowed to touch the frozen ground, the developing chick inside would not survive. To protect the chick, the male penguin carries the egg on his feet, tucking it under the feathers on his body. For two months, while the female penguin is away storing food in her belly, the male goes nowhere without the egg. Cuddled securely in the male's warmth, the chick can survive until hatching. At that time the mother returns and takes over the care of her newborn chick. Even then the down-covered chick needs its mother's feet and feathers to shield it from the frigid weather of Antarctica.

Supporting Sentences

Supporting sentences make up the body of a paragraph. Their purpose is to back up the main idea in the topic sentence with specific information. They explain or prove a topic sentence with specific details, facts, examples, or reasons.

Supporting sentences also provide answers to questions that readers might have. Read the following topic sentence. Think of questions that you would expect the supporting sentences to answer.

Topic Sentence   People who lived in pioneer days would never have believed that world news could be received as quickly as it is today.

Most readers would probably want to know how news traveled during pioneer days and how news travels today. Look at the paragraph on the next page. The supporting sentences answer these questions. They provide facts and examples that relate to the main idea.

From 1860 to 1861, the Pony Express was the fastest way to send mail across the country.

Changes in News Communication

Topic Sentence	People who lived in pioneer days would never have believed that world news could be received as quickly as it is today.
Supporting Sentences	In earlier times newspapers were often several months old by the time they reached a settlement. Letters were carried by travelers who happened to be going in the right direction and often were received months after they were written. Today by radio, television, newspapers, and the Internet, we get world news almost at once. Letters arrive in distant countries overnight.
Concluding Sentence	It is hard to believe that such changes have taken place in less than 100 years.

Concluding Sentence

Every good composition has a clear beginning, middle, and end. In a single paragraph, the concluding sentence serves as the ending.

Strategies for Ending a Paragraph

- Restate the main idea using different words.
- Summarize the paragraph.
- Add an insight about the main idea.
- Express how you feel about the subject.

Medic Alert Saves Lives

Topic Sentence	The Medic Alert bracelet was designed to help people with medical problems in emergency situations.
Supporting Sentences	If the wearer of the bracelet is unconscious or otherwise unable to talk, the bracelet can tell medical workers what they need to know about the patient. On the back of the Medic Alert bracelet are listed the patient's medical problem, an identification number, and an emergency number. By dialing this telephone number, the medical workers can find out about the patient's special condition from a computer.
Concluding Sentence	In an emergency, a Medic Alert bracelet can become a lifesaver.

Developing and Polishing Your Paragraph

A topic sentence is like a baseball score. It gives the general idea without the specifics of how the game developed. Readers, like sports fans, want more information. There are a variety of ways to develop the idea introduced in the topic sentence.

Strategies for Developing a Paragraph

- Give descriptive details.
- Give facts, examples, or reasons.
- Relate an incident.
- Make a comparison or draw a contrast.
- Give directions or explain the steps in a process.

Insufficiently developed writing makes readers quickly lose interest. Even an interesting idea loses merit if not backed up with sufficient information. With adequate development, the main idea is supported with specific details. These specific details can take the form of facts or examples, reasons, incidents, or descriptive images. Regardless of the form, supporting details must be numerous and specific enough to make the main idea clear, convincing, and interesting.

The following paragraph provides specific details that develop the subject.

Childhood Treasures

Aunt Sally's cabinet of art supplies was like a toy chest to me. The top shelf, beyond my reach, had an endless supply of paper. There was stiff, brilliant-white paper for watercolors, blank newsprint for charcoals, glossy paper, dull paper, and tracing paper. On the second shelf sat oozing tubes of bright-colored oil paints, bottles of the blackest ink, and cartons of chalk in sunrise shades of pastels. The third shelf—my favorite—held the damp lumps of gray clay, waiting to be shaped into creatures only my aunt and I would recognize. On the bottom shelves were brushes and rags for cleaning up. Despite the thorough cleanups Aunt Sally insisted on, that cabinet was a paradise of play for me on countless Sunday afternoons.

Unity A paragraph has **unity** when all of the supporting sentences relate directly to the main idea. Paragraphs without unity include unrelated ideas that distract readers from the main point. Suppose you are writing a paragraph about tricks your dog can do. In the process of writing, you can sometimes lose your focus. You may be led to include other details about your dog, such as where and when you got him, or what his favorite foods are. Although these relate to your dog generally, they probably do not belong in a paragraph about the tricks your dog can do.

Coherence **Coherence** in a paragraph is the quality that makes each sentence seem connected to all the others. One way to achieve coherence is to present ideas in a logical order. Another way is to use transitions. **Transitions** are words and phrases that show how ideas are related. The following chart shows some common types of logical order and the transitions often used with them.

Transitions for Different Types of Order		
Types of Order	**Definition**	**Transitions**
Chronological	The order in which events occur	first, second, third, before, after, next, on Tuesday, later, finally
Spatial	Location or physical arrangement	left, right, in front of, behind, next to, south of
Order of Importance	Degree of importance, size, or interest	first, finally, in addition, smallest, largest, more/most important
Compare/ Contrast	Similarity and/or differences between objects or ideas	similarly, in contrast, on the other hand

Chronological order is used with events or stories to tell what happened first, next, and so on. It is also used when giving directions or the steps in a process. **Spatial order** is used in descriptions to show how objects are related in location. **Order of importance** is often used in paragraphs that explain or persuade. **Compare/Contrast** is used in paragraphs that explain.

For more about transitions, review Chapter 20.

Using the Six Traits of Good Writing

Use the Six Traits of Good Writing checklist to revise your paragraph and ensure that your work is as good as you can make it.

Six Traits of Good Writing Checklist

Ideas

✓ Is the subject focused enough to be covered in one paragraph?

✓ Do your details demonstrate what you want to say?

✓ Did you present your ideas in logical order?

✓ Do any of your sentences stray from the main idea?

Organization

✓ Does your topic sentence introduce the subject and suggest your overall impression of it?

✓ Do your supporting sentences supply specific details and sensory words?

✓ Does your conclusion wrap up the ideas in your paragraph?

Voice

✓ Can a reader detect your interest in your subject while reading your paragraph?

✓ Is your personality reflected in your writing?

Word Choice

✓ Did you pick precise nouns and verbs to express your ideas?

✓ Will the adjectives you used help the reader understand your ideas?

Sentence Fluency

✓ Are your sentences varied in length and structure?

✓ Do you use adverbs to create smoother flowing sentences?

Conventions

✓ Are your sentences free of errors in grammar and usage?

✓ Did you spell each word correctly?

✓ Did you use capital letters where needed?

✓ Did you punctuate sentences correctly?

✓ Did you indent each paragraph?

CHAPTER 23

Writing Effective Compositions

QuickGuide

Writing an Effective Composition pages 229–230	A **composition** presents and develops one main idea in three or more paragraphs.
Prewriting pages 231–233	Select the main idea for your composition and begin to gather and organize details to support it.
Drafting pages 234–237	Begin to develop your main idea and supporting details.
Revising pages 237–238	Review and rework your composition until it communicates your ideas clearly and effectively.
Editing and Publishing page 239	Polish your work and present it to the intended audience.

Writing an Effective Composition

A *composition* presents and develops one main idea in three or more paragraphs.

Think of one of your favorite topics—science, sports, music, films, nature, hobbies—and imagine discussing it with someone who knows nothing about it. If it's something that really interests you, you probably cannot share everything you know about it in two or three sentences. Similarly, if you were to write about it, even the longest paragraph would probably be too short to contain all the information and points that you would want to make. A composition would be more suitable.

The Parts of a Composition

Compositions have three main parts: the **introduction,** the **body,** and the **conclusion.** The introduction captures the reader's attention and sets forth the main idea. The body presents supporting details. The conclusion adds a strong ending and may leave the reader with a thought-provoking concept or idea.

In the following example, the three main parts of a composition are labeled.

Messages into Space

Introduction
Captures reader's attention and provides main idea (in blue type) and background Information

Two space missions from recent years are carrying our messages into interstellar space. *Pioneer 10* is carrying a plaque with a drawing of a man and a woman plus some information about earth and its inhabitants. *Voyager* is carrying a "cosmic LP" a two-hour recording. Encoded on the record are photographs, diagrams, and drawings that represent life on this planet. It also contains greetings from earth spoken in 53 languages, musical selections, sounds of our animal life, the roar of the surf, the cry of a baby, and the soft thump of the human heartbeat.

Thirty-two thousand years will pass before *Pioneer 10* draws close to a star. After that approach a million years will go by before there is another close approach, and still another million years will elapse before a third occurs.

Body
Provides specific information

Because of the emptiness of interstellar space, the spacecraft's ancient hulk will probably never be seen by alien eyes. In fact, the messages aboard the *Pioneer* and *Voyager* spacecraft were composed with little hope that anyone would ever discover them. They were only bottles thrown in a cosmic ocean, a symbol of our deep desire to communicate with a civilization other than our own.

Conclusion
Adds a strong ending

Millions of years from now, those messages will still be journeying through the universe. They may never be found. They will, however, be a solid piece of evidence that a tiny inhabited planet exists, or once existed, in the suburbs of a small galaxy with the odd name Milky Way.

—Margaret Poynter and Michael J. Klein,
Cosmic Quest

Prewriting

Through *prewriting* you find and select the main idea of your composition and begin to gather the details to support it.

Choosing and Limiting a Subject

After exploring your interests, the next step is to choose one subject and refine it for development in a composition.

Determining Your Purpose As a first step, think about your purpose for writing. Ask yourself "Do I want to provide information? Do I want to give directions? Do I want to persuade my readers to do or think something?"

Determining Your Audience Once you have decided on a purpose, consider your audience. Develop an audience profile to help you understand your readers' knowledge, attitudes, and beliefs. You may want to refer to the Audience Profile Questions in Chapter 19 to help you focus on your audience.

Listing Focus Points As a final step, list several possible focus points. **Focus points** are specific aspects of your general subject. In the following writer's notes, the general subject of snorkeling is too large for a short composition. Any of the focus points, however, would be a suitably limited subject.

Subject	snorkeling (underwater exploring)
Purpose	to explain
Audience	people who do not know much about it
Focus Points	• what equipment is needed
	• how to control breathing and clear snorkel
	• what someone can do while snorkeling
	• how to make different kinds of surface dives

Listing Supporting Details

After narrowing your topic, you need to develop supporting details. The kinds of supporting details you use will depend on your purpose for writing.

Supporting Details	
Purpose	**Kinds of Details**
To Inform	details that relate causes and effects or likenesses and differences
To Explain	facts, examples, reasons
To Give Directions	steps in a process
To Persuade	reasons, based on fact, to support an opinion
To Create	details that develop characters and incidents

Brainstorming One way to find supporting details is to brainstorm with yourself. Write down everything that comes to mind about your subject.

Limited Subject	Things to Do While Snorkeling
Brainstorming Ideas	• collect shells
	• feed fish
	• master basic snorkeling techniques
	• shells are sometimes hidden in sea grasses
	• fish will eat bread or cheese
	• carry the food in a bag you can close
	• taking pictures
	• need waterproof camera equipment
	• some places, it is illegal to collect shells
	• know which sea creatures are dangerous

In addition to brainstorming, you could also use the strategies of freewriting and clustering to develop details. You can review these techniques in Chapter 19.

Arranging Details in Logical Order

After brainstorming, arrange your ideas in a logical order. The table below explains the types of logical order you might use to arrange your ideas.

Types of Order	
Chronological	Items are arranged in time order.
Spatial	Items are arranged in location order.
Importance or Degree	Items are arranged in order of least to most or most to least important.
Sequential	Steps in a process are arranged in their proper sequence.

As you group your ideas, you may find that some do not fit in neatly. Save these for possible use later. Notice the order of the notes about things to do while snorkeling.

Snorkeling Activites: Arranged by Difficulty Level	
Least Difficult	• feeding fish • fish will eat bread or cheese • carry the food in a bag you can close
Next in Difficulty	• collecting shells • shells are on the seafloor, sometimes hidden in sea grasses • some places, it is illegal to collect shells • know which sea creatures are dangerous
Most Difficult	• taking pictures • need waterproof camera equipment
Use Elsewhere?	• mastering basic snorkeling techniques

Drafting

In *drafting* you start writing your composition.

When your notes are organized, you are ready to begin the second stage of the writing process—drafting. Remember that your goal in drafting is to turn your prewriting notes into connected sentences and paragraphs.

Drafting the Introduction

The introduction to a composition has two main goals. The first is to arouse your reader's interest and make him or her want to read on. The second is to state clearly the main idea of the composition. In the following introduction on the subject of snorkeling, the sentence stating the main idea is in blue type.

Introduction	Imagine the feeling of suddenly having all of your weight lifted from you. You glide along almost without effort. You feel the coolness of water around you. You see the brilliant colors of fish swimming past you, and the sounds of the world outside are muffled. These are just a few of the pleasures of snorkeling. For those who have mastered the basic techniques, however, the
Main Idea	pleasures are even greater. Instead of simply gliding and observing, an experienced snorkeler can keep busy underwater with several interesting activities.

A strong introduction—

- captures the reader's attention with an interesting fact, detail, incident, or description.
- gives background information if needed.
- includes a sentence expressing the main idea.
- does not include empty expressions such as "In this composition I will . . ." or "This composition will be about . . . ."

Drafting the Body

As you write the body of your composition, keep your reader in mind. Try to make your message as clear as possible. Use your prewriting notes to write complete, varied sentences with vivid words. Use transitions to connect one idea to the next.

Compare the following composition body with the prewriting notes listed earlier. The transitions are printed in blue type. You will find lists of transitions on page 201 of Chapter 20 and page 226 of Chapter 22.

One of the easiest and most enjoyable underwater activities is feeding fish. Fish particularly like bread or cheese. If you want to feed fish, carry the food in a bag you can close. In that way you can keep hungry fish from swimming inside your food bag. Another activity, shell collecting, requires slightly more skill. A good shell collector must know where to look for shells that might be hidden in grasses on the seafloor. He or she must also recognize dangerous animals that might be hiding near the shells. A third activity, taking pictures underwater, requires the most skill and equipment. The camera and gear must all be designed for working underwater.

Drafting the Conclusion

A **conclusion** to a composition is like a farewell. It wraps up the ideas in the composition and provides a strong ending.

> Almost anything you do while snorkeling is a pleasure. The nearness to sea creatures, the beauty of a coral reef, and the feel of the water all add up to an unforgettable experience. When you actually interact with the life underwater by feeding fish, collecting empty shells, or taking action pictures, you will feel even more a part of the mysterious sea.

Use the guidelines below when writing a conclusion.

A strong concluding paragraph—

- emphasizes the main idea without restating it exactly.
- may refer to ideas in the introduction.
- does not introduce a completely new idea.
- does not use such empty expressions such as "I have just told you about . . ." or "Now you know about . . . ."

Targeting the Six Traits: Organization

The strength of any presentation, written or spoken, is in the organization of the information. If you give details before you give the main idea, a reader doesn't have any idea what you are talking about. The information seems irrelevant, and the reader stops reading. If the supporting details are not in logical order, your reader may not see your point or may not be convinced of the strength of your argument.

It may be helpful to you to create an outline of your topic before you start to write. If you don't see your supporting details fitting into an outline, they may not work well in your composition. If you work from an outline, you can move back and forth between the introduction, body, and conclusion, developing them as ideas occur to you. This is often easier than trying to finish your introduction before starting the body of your composition. Your outline will remind you where you are going in your writing and keep you on track.

Revising

In *revising,* you review your composition and rework it until it communicates your ideas clearly and effectively.

Once your ideas are down on paper, you can stand back and look at them to see how they can be improved. If possible, put your draft aside for a while before revising. That way you will approach the revision stage with "new eyes."

Using the Six Traits of Good Writing

The revision stage is where you put the Six Traits into practice. As you revise your composition, refer to the items listed under the first five traits on the following page. (You will work on the sixth trait, *conventions,* when you edit your paper.)

Six Traits of Good Writing Checklist

Ideas

✓ Are your ideas clear and interesting?

✓ Is your main idea well defined and focused?

✓ Have you identified or researched enough points to support your main idea?

Organization

✓ Do you have an interesting introduction that states the main idea of the composition?

✓ Do all your sentences relate to the main idea? In other words, does your composition have unity?

✓ Are your ideas arranged logically with transitions? In other words, is your composition coherent?

✓ Do you have a strong conclusion?

Voice

✓ Does the composition sound as though you wrote it?

✓ Does your writing show that you care about your subject?

✓ Can a reader recognize your writing style?

Word Choice

✓ Are your words fresh, vivid, and specific?

✓ Have you used strong verbs?

✓ Do your words create pictures for the reader or appeal to the reader's senses?

Sentence Fluency

✓ Did you eliminate short, choppy sentences by combining related sentences?

✓ Did you vary the length and beginnings of your sentences?

✓ Did you eliminate rambling sentences?

✓ Are your sentences free of repetition and empty expressions?

Editing and Publishing

Through *editing* you polish your work; through *publishing* you present it to the intended audience.

Editing

When you are satisfied with your ideas and organization, you are ready to check your composition carefully for errors.

Editing Conventions Checklist

✓ Are your sentences free of errors in grammar and usage?

✓ Did you spell each word correctly?

✓ Did you use capital letters where needed?

✓ Did you punctuate sentences correctly?

Targeting the Six Traits: Conventions

You may think that your ideas are so solid and your details so good that you don't need to worry about spelling and punctuation. You might be surprised, however, at how easy it would be to confuse your reader or fail to make a point if there are errors in your writing. Even if your reader understands your ideas, failing to follow the conventions may imply that you don't care about your subject—or your reader.

Publishing

The appearance of your composition is important. A neat paper makes a positive impression on your reader. Prepare your final copy. When you are satisfied with the results, share your composition with others.

Personal Writing

QuickGuide

The Personal Narrative pages 241–242	**Personal writing** can lead to a deeper understanding of events and ideas, as well as more insight into issues and greater knowledge of yourself.
Prewriting page 243	A piece of personal writing begins and ends with the writer's own experience and ideas.
Drafting pages 244–245	Your ideas gain power and coherence when they are written down.
Revising and Editing pages 246–247	Find the right balance between vivid details and the overall impression you want to make.

The Personal Narrative

When you write about an event in your life and tell how it affected you, you are writing a **personal narrative.** The process of writing a personal narrative may require some reflection as you reconstruct what happened and determine the meaning it has for you.

A powerfully written personal narrative can touch your heart, stir up angry feelings in you, or motivate you to take action. It can also inspire you to write your own real-life story. In the following excerpt, Jamaica Kincaid recalls how she learned about her personal history.

> From time to time, my mother would fix on a certain place in our house and give it a good cleaning. If I was at home when she happened to do this, I was at her side, as usual. When she did this with the trunk, it was a tremendous pleasure, for after she had removed all the things from the trunk, and aired them out, and changed the camphor balls, and then refolded the things and put them back in their places in the trunk, as she held each thing in her hand she would tell me a story about myself. Sometimes I knew the story first hand, for I could remember the incident quite well; sometimes what she told me had happened when I was too young to know anything; and sometimes it happened before I was even born. Whichever way, I knew exactly what she would say, for I had heard it so many times before, but I never got tired of it.
>
> —Jamaica Kincaid, *Annie John*

Narrative Paragraph Structure The following list shows how each part of a personal narrative helps to tell a story.

Structure of a Personal Narrative

- The topic sentence introduces the story by making a general statement, setting the scene, or capturing the reader's attention.
- The supporting sentences tell the story, event by event, and answer the questions *Who? What? Where? Why? When?* and *How?*
- The concluding sentence ends the story by summarizing the events or making a point about the story.

The following narrative paragraph describes a woman's visit to the Serengeti, a large wildlife preserve in northern Tanzania. The writer begins with a topic sentence that makes a general statement. The concluding sentence summarizes the events. As you read the paragraph, notice how the story unfolds.

A Surprise Visitor

Topic Sentence

My nights in camp were often exciting. I could hear lions prowling around. I even came to recognize the voices of most of them. Once I awoke to hear

Supporting Sentences

lapping noises. Being half asleep, I listened for some time before I realized that a lioness was inside my tent drinking out of my basin. I shouted at her to go away, which finally she did. I reported this incident to the park warden. He told me that lions of the Serengeti were known occasionally to go into tents and take a look around to see what was going on. I

Concluding Sentence

shall never forget the night that nothing but a table stood between me and Africa.

—Joy Adamson, *Forever Free*

Joy Adamson in Africa, 1971

Prewriting

"Great thoughts come from the heart," wrote Luc de Clapiers, an eighteenth-century French writer. He might have been referring to the art of writing a personal narrative. When you write about experiences in your own life, your thoughts should come from the heart; that is, you should write about an experience that is meaningful to you.

Choose and Limit Your Subject During the prewriting stage, your mind should be free to wander as you search your memories for possible subjects. Use prewriting techniques such as brainstorming, clustering, and freewriting to help get ideas flowing.

You may also want to refer to your journal or learning log to remind yourself of things that have captured your attention before. Your calendar, souvenirs, a chat with a friend or family member, or even your assignment notebook might bring to mind good topics for a personal narrative. Make a list of topics, and then choose the one that interests you the most. However, be sure to focus your subject so that you can cover it in a short composition.

Chronological Order Most personal narratives are in chronological order. In **chronological order,** or time order, events are arranged in the order in which they happened. The following notes on one writer's first horse ride are arranged in time order.

> **Riding a horse for the first time**
> Always dreamed of riding a horse
> Finally got a chance
> Got on a beautiful gray horse
> Started slowly down the forest path
> Horses broke into a canter
> Then sped into a gallop
> Everything fine until we started to trot
> Bounced wildly for what seemed liked hours
> Lead horse finally headed back to stable at a slow walk
> Learned what it meant to be saddle sore

Drafting

Writing the first draft of your personal narrative is a matter of transforming your ideas first into sentences and then into paragraphs.

Because your purpose and intended audience will affect the voice you use and determine how formal the structure needs to be, don't forget to think about these issues as you begin the drafting process.

Targeting the Six Traits: Voice

With personal writing you should focus on your writing "voice." Imagine you are sharing your thoughts with a friend. Let your enthusiasm and natural energy flow into your writing. You can improve the word choice and polish the conventions later, but at the drafting stage, just relax and be yourself. Then, when you are through revising and editing, the voice that will shine through will be authentic. It will be polished, but it will still be your voice.

Transitions

Presenting your ideas in chronological order will help your readers follow the events in narrative writing. Use the transition words and phrases in the chart below to make sure that the order is clear.

Transitions for Chronological Order			
after	during	later	then
after a while	finally	meanwhile	the next day
afterward	first	next	until
at last	immediately	second	when
before	just as	suddenly	while

The following draft narrative is by the student who wrote notes about her first horse ride. Transitions appear in blue type.

Anything But Trotting

I had often dreamed of riding a horse, of sailing smoothly as if horse and rider were one. Today was my day. Here I was perched on top of a huge gray horse. At first everything was fine. The horses in my group were walking slowly down the forest path. Before long we came to a clearing and the horses broke into a canter, a smooth and easy-to-ride gait. Then the lead horse sped into a gallop, a thunderous gait that was surprisingly easy to ride. Everything went fine for the rest of the morning until the lead horse started to trot. With the first trot, my dream of horse and rider as one vanished. I was bouncing wildly and could hardly catch my breath. After minutes that seemed like hours, we finally headed back to the stable at a slow walk. By then I knew very well what it meant to be saddle sore. The only place I wanted to be for the next few days was in a very soft chair.

First Person and Third Person Narratives In personal narratives, the person telling the story is a character in the story. In this type of narrative, the first person pronouns *I, we, me, us, my,* and *our* are used. These narratives are called **first-person narratives.**

Mike and I were just packing away our gear after a successful day of fishing when the trouble began. As storm clouds started to gather, we headed for the shore. Suddenly . . . .

Some narratives do not involve the writer at all. Writers telling a story about other people will refer to them with the third person pronouns *he, she, they, his, her,* and *their.* These stories are called **third-person narratives.**

The boys were just packing away their gear after a successful day of fishing when the trouble began. As storm clouds started to gather, they headed for shore. Suddenly . . . .

Revising and Editing

Once you have turned your thoughts and reflections into a rough draft, you can start revising. Revising a personal narrative involves attention to three important points.

- Have you developed your personal narrative in enough detail?
- Have you made your ideas and feelings clear?
- Have you maintained a consistent voice?

Checking for Adequate Development Check to make sure you have included enough specific details to make your reader clearly see and hear what you want to share. The following strategies will help you do that.

Revising for Adequate Development	
Events	Visualize the experience you are writing about. Write down the details that you "see" in your mind's eye.
People	Visualize each person in your narrative. Think about their facial expressions and body movements. Write down details as you "see" them.
Places	Visualize the place you are describing from left to right, from top to bottom, and from foreground to background.
Feelings	Relive the experience, focusing on your thoughts and feelings.

Targeting the Six Traits: Word Choice

As you visualize the events, people, places, or feelings that are part of your narrative, make quick notes of what you are seeing or imagining. Write down details, colors, emotions, shapes, smells, tastes, weather, texture, sounds, and anything else that is part of your remembering or visualizing. This will not only help you uncover details, it will help you choose vivid, specific words. The more precisely you can communicate your details, the more your audience will share your experience.

Six Traits of Good Writing Checklist

As you revise your personal writing, refer to the elements in the checklist below.

Ideas

✓ Are your ideas clear and interesting?

✓ Do your ideas show your perspective?

✓ Do you include details that will capture a reader's interest?

Organization

✓ Does your introduction let the reader know what your subject is?

✓ Does your composition have unity?

✓ Are your ideas arranged logically with transitions?

✓ Do you have a strong conclusion?

Voice

✓ Does the composition sound as though you wrote it?

✓ Does your writing show that you care about your subject?

✓ Can a reader recognize your writing style?

Word Choice

✓ Are your words vivid and specific?

✓ Have you used sensory details that will help readers connect with your emotions and your experience?

✓ Do your words create pictures for the reader?

Sentence Fluency

✓ Did you vary the length and beginnings of your sentences?

✓ Are your sentences easy to read aloud?

✓ Are your sentences well constructed?

Conventions (Editing)

✓ Are your sentences free of errors in grammar and usage?

✓ Did you spell each word correctly?

✓ Did you use capital letters where needed?

✓ Did you punctuate sentences correctly?

✓ Did you indent each paragraph?

CHAPTER 25

Using Description

QuickGuide

Writing to Describe **pages 249–252**	When you write to describe, you use sensory words that express what you see, hear, smell, taste, or feel.
Prewriting **pages 252–256**	Details are the key to effective descriptive writing.
Drafting **pages 256–257**	Use the details you have gathered to build your composition.
Revising **pages 257–259**	Revise your paper to make the description more vivid.
Editing and Publishing **page 259**	Prepare to share your descriptive writing.

Writing to Describe

When you write to describe, you use sensory words that express what you see, hear, smell, taste, or feel. Vivid description makes the difference between writing that just sits on the page and writing that dances off the page straight into the reader's imagination.

Good descriptive writing employs all the senses: sight, sound, taste, touch, and smell. The words that you use must be precise and well organized to create as clear a picture as possible. Remember, as the writer you are responsible for pointing out all the details you want your reader to experience.

Elements of Descriptive Writing Descriptive writing has three main elements: the introduction, the body, and the conclusion.

- The introduction captures the reader's attention, introduces the subject, and often suggests an overall impression of the subject.
- The body presents details, especially sensory details, that bring the subject to life.
- The conclusion reinforces the overall impression and may present a final vivid image.

In the following descriptive paragraph, Joanna Greenfield describes a close encounter with an animal. As you read, notice that this encounter is both physical and emotional—a deadly flesh-and-blood bond.

Hyenas

Opening	Spotted hyenas are the sharks of the savanna, super-predators and astounding recyclers of garbage. They hunt in large, giggling groups, running alongside their prey
Supporting Details	and eating chunks of its flesh until it slows down through loss of blood, or shock, or sheer hopelessness, and then the hyenas grab for the stomach and pull the animal to a halt with its own entrails or let it stumble into the loops
Concluding Image	and whorls of its own body. They eat the prey whole and cough back, like owls, the indigestible parts, such as hair and hooves.

—Joanna Greenfield, *Hyena*

The opening sentence of the paragraph on the previous page draws the reader in through a startling image: that hyenas are "the sharks of the savanna." The supporting details of the paragraph show specific ways in which hyenas are like sharks. The concluding sentence leaves the reader with yet another strong image.

Specific Details and Sensory Words A **main impression** is at the core of good descriptive writing. This overall impression comes to life when you use your supporting details to *show* the subject rather than simply tell about it. When you show readers, chances are you are using strong specific details and words that appeal to the senses. You are making your readers see, hear, smell, and feel the impression you are creating.

Writer Barry Lopez is especially good at painting word pictures. In the following selection, he describes his impression of a wolf moving through the northern woods.

> He moves along now at the edge of a clearing. The wind coming down-valley surrounds him with a river of odors, as if he were a migrating salmon. He can smell ptarmigan and deer droppings. He can smell willow and spruce and the fading sweetness of fireweed. Above, he sees a hawk circling, and farther south, lower on the horizon, a flock of sharp-tailed sparrows going east. He senses through his pads with each step the dryness of the moss beneath his feet, and the ridges of old tracks, some his own. He hears the sound his feet make. He hears the occasional movement of deer mice and voles. Summer food.
>
> Toward dusk he is standing by a creek, lapping the cool water, when a wolf howls—a long wail that quickly reaches pitch and then tapers, with several harmonies, long moments to a tremolo. He recognizes his sister. He waits a few moments, then, throwing his head back and closing his eyes, he howls. The howl is shorter and it changes pitch twice in the beginning, very quickly. There is no answer.
>
> —Barry Lopez, *Of Wolves and Men*

Lopez's description of the wolf succeeds through the writer's generous use of specific details and sensory words.

Specific Sensory Details	
Sights	edge of a clearing, hawk circling, flock of sharp-tailed sparrows
Sounds	his own footsteps, occasional movement of deer mice and voles, howl of other wolf with its distinctive sound, his own shorter howl with its own distinctive changes of pitch
Smells	ptarmigan and deer droppings; willow, spruce, and fireweed
Taste	cool water
Feelings	wind, dryness of moss and ridges of old tracks through pads of his feet, throwing head back, closing eyes

Figurative Language Writers rely on imaginative comparisons to help pump life into their descriptions. These can be either similes or metaphors. A **simile** is a comparison between two unlike things using the word *like* or *as.* It says that one thing is *like* another. A **metaphor** makes a similar kind of comparison but without using *like* or *as.* It says that one thing *is* another.

Comparisons	
Simile	They eat the prey whole and cough back, like owls, the indigestible parts . . . . (Eating habits of hyenas are compared to those of owls.)
	. . . as if he [the wolf] were a migrating salmon. (The wolf is compared to a migrating salmon.)
Metaphor	Spotted hyenas are the sharks of the savanna. (Hyenas are compared to sharks.)
	The wind coming down-valley surrounds him with a river of odors. . . . (The wind is compared to a river.)

Prewriting

Some people think of writing as a product: a sentence, a paragraph, an essay. Yet writing is a process, a tool. Even though the term *prewriting* suggests an activity that takes place before writing starts, you should do this work in writing. Often you cannot really focus your thoughts until you put your ideas on paper.

Choosing a Subject

A good subject for a description does not have to be about one of life's mysteries, but it does have to have real meaning for you. First, choose a subject that you care about. Your interest will carry over to the reader. Also, choose a subject that you can develop with descriptive details such as sensory words and figurative language. Finally, the subject should be one you know well.

Developing a Description

With your topic in mind, you can begin to generate details you will use to develop your description.

Strategies for Developing a Description

- Use your memory and direct observation, if appropriate, to list the sights, sounds, smells, tastes, and feelings you associate with your subject. Making a graphic like the one below may help.
- Brainstorm for a list of imaginative comparisons that will help readers understand your description. These could be metaphors or similes or other types of comparisons.
- Gather any factual details and information you might need to provide background for your readers or to help set the stage for your overall impression.
- If you are describing a scene, draw a picture or a map so you can clearly see the relationship of one part of the subject to another.
- Apply your filter: remember to test each detail against your desired overall impression to make sure it adds rather than detracts.

Using a Sensory Diagram Once you have a topic, you might use a sensory diagram to help you develop specific details. Here are the ideas one writer generated about her main focus—a crowded swimming pool.

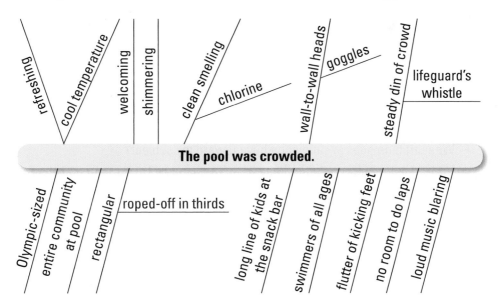

refreshing • cool temperature • welcoming • shimmering • clean smelling • chlorine • wall-to-wall heads • goggles • steady din of crowd • lifeguard's whistle

The pool was crowded.

Olympic-sized • entire community at pool • rectangular • roped-off in thirds • long line of kids at the snack bar • swimmers of all ages • flutter of kicking feet • no room to do laps • loud music blaring

Developing an Overall Impression If you tried to include every detail about your subject, the resulting writing would be a meaningless overload. Readers depend on writers to filter out the details they do not need. To know what is important, you need to remember the overall impression you want to convey. What is the general feeling you have about your subject? You need to have a clear sense of this in order to develop your work successfully and to decide on which details to include.

The writer who decided to write about a swimming pool generated a long list of strong sensory images. However, only a few actually addressed the "crowded pool" idea she wanted to convey. These are the details she chose to reinforce her overall impression.

> **The pool was crowded.**
> steady din of crowd
> entire community at pool
> wall-to-wall heads
> long line of kids at the snack bar
> no room to do laps

Identifying Your Audience A reader who does not know your school would need more background for a description of your campus than a fellow student would. It is always good to know your intended audience.

Questions for Analyzing an Audience

- What does my audience already know about my subject?
- What background information, if any, do I need to provide to make the description more meaningful?
- What attitude does my audience have toward my subject?
- Do I want to reinforce that attitude or try to change it?

Organizing Details Once you have details for your description, you should organize them in a logical order. One way is to organize details in a spatial order. **Spatial order** arranges details according to their location. You then use transition words or phrases to lead a reader's eye from spot to spot. The chart on the next page shows four directions commonly used with spatial order and the transitions associated with each one.

Spatial Order	Transitions
Near to Far (or reverse)	close by, beyond, around, farther, across, behind, in the distance
Top to Bottom (or reverse)	at the top, in the middle, lower, below, at the bottom, above, higher
Side to Side	at the left (right), in the middle, next to, at one end, to the west (east)
Inside to Outside (or reverse)	within, in the center, on the inside (outside), the next layer

In the following descriptive paragraph, the details are arranged in spatial order from top to bottom. The transitions are printed in blue type.

Yoda's Face

Every detail in the face of Yoda, the Jedi master in the *Star Wars* movies, suggests his wisdom and intelligence. His green body is dwarfed by his huge head. His high forehead gives the impression of a large, busy brain. Beneath his forehead his expressive eyes show both disappointment and hope at his young pupil's progress. His huge pointed ears that reach the same level as his eyes show his ability to take in sounds that others would miss. Below his eyes, a smallish nose twitches in response to events around him. At the bottom of his face, a mouth that knows how to stay shut reveals his ability to concentrate. At first sight, Yoda may appear ugly, but as you see his great intelligence at work, his face begins to show the wisdom of the Jedi masters.

Targeting the Six Traits: Organization

Spatial order is not always the right order for descriptive writing, but it is very useful for describing places, people, or things. Events or emotions might be described in **chronological order** or organized by **cause-and-effect**. Explanations or directions might be organized in **sequential order**.

Another way to order details is by **importance** or **prominence**. If, for example, someone has a dazzling smile, you might start with that, and then move on to other features.

There is no one right order for description, but the organization you choose should be logical. Your writing will be better if you have an organizational plan in mind and then follow that plan.

Drafting

If you have taken your prewriting work seriously, by now most of the hard work of writing your description is over. During the drafting stage, concentrate on the flow of your ideas, always thinking about your reader. Keep the following points in mind as you draft your description.

Tips for Drafting a Description

- Experiment with interest-catching introductions. (Review the selections in this chapter for ideas.)
- Suggest your overall impression early in your writing to frame your description for readers.
- Use fresh, vivid, descriptive words that appeal to the senses.
- Remember to use transitions appropriate to the type of order you have chosen. This will help your reader move smoothly from one point to the next.
- Look for a strong way to end your description and consider referring back to an idea in your introduction.

The student writing about the crowded pool created this rough draft.

Rough Draft: The Pool on a Hot Day

It was hot. The air conditioner was working overtime. I decided to ride my bike to the pool to do some laps. I knew I was in trouble when I saw the parking lot. It was full. Even the bike rack was full. The entire community must have been in the pool. Even so, I couldn't wait to dive into the cool blue water. But when I got to the pool, I couldn't even see the water. All I could see was wall-to-wall heads. It was free swim time, so the lap lanes were full of kids playing with beach balls and diving for pennies. Music was blaring and the lifeguard was blowing his whistle. I decided to wait until free swim was over, but I couldn't find a place to sit. I stepped into the water once, but I was hit in the head with a ball. "That's it," I said. I grabbed my towel, fought my way through the line of kids waiting at the snack bar, and left. Maybe it will be less crowded later--after the sun goes down.

Revising

"You always feel when you look it straight in the eye," wrote Canadian artist Emily Carr, "that you could have put more into it, could have let yourself go and dug harder." Look your description "straight in the eye" as you begin the revising stage. Where could you have "put more into it"? Where could you have "dug harder"?

Targeting the Six Traits:
Sentence Fluency

Writing a description is a little like weaving a spell. You want to draw your reader in, have them experience what you are writing. Sentence fluency can help with this. The rhythm of the sentences can underscore meaning. Just as your voice varies when you are excited or frightened or secretive or worried, the flow of your sentences should vary according to the mood.

Varying the length of words can add to sentence fluency as well. For example, you might use the word "crimson" if you are seeking a poetic and fluid feel. The word "red," on the other hand, is punchier and more direct. You might use it in an action-oriented piece. Each of these words changes the flow of a sentence, contributing both to fluency and impact.

Read your descriptions aloud and listen to the flow. Does it create the impression you are seeking?

Using the Six Traits of Writing

Use the Six Traits of Writing Checklist that follows to revise your description. When you are reasonably satisfied that you can answer "yes" to all the questions on the checklist, divide into small groups and share your paper with a classmate.

Ideas
✓ Is your reason for writing evident early on?
✓ Are you providing all the background information your audience may need?
✓ Did you give your audience all the information necessary to convey your main idea?
✓ Are all your details clear and well supported?

Organization
✓ Does the paper present your ideas in logical order?
✓ Are transitions clear and smooth?
✓ Does your paper have a beginning, a middle, and a conclusion?
✓ Have you referred back to an idea or image presented in the introduction?

Voice

✓ Is your energy and enthusiasm for your subject apparent?

✓ Does your personality shine through?

Word Choice

✓ Did you choose words that "show" rather that "tell" the audience?

✓ Does your writing use vivid, accurate descriptions?

✓ Is your vocabulary appropriate to the audience?

✓ Did you choose sensory words and details?

✓ Did you use comparisons and figurative language to enhance details?

Sentence Fluency

✓ Are your sentences varied in length and structure?

✓ Do the sentences flow naturally one to the next?

✓ Do your sentences proceed in logical order?

✓ Do your words and sentences support the overall impression or idea?

Editing and Publishing

Editing After you have put your revised draft away for a short time, reread it to check for the conventions of language. Use the checklist below to make sure your grammar, punctuation, and spelling are correct.

Editing for Conventions Checklist

✓ Does your grammar conform to conventions?

✓ Does every sentence end with correct punctuation?

✓ Do transition words signal the sequence of events for the audience?

✓ Are all words spelled correctly?

Publishing You may wish to complete the writing process by sharing your writing with a friend or family member.

Writing to Inform and Explain

QuickGuide

Informative Writing page 261	**Informative writing** supplies readers with facts, directions, examples, background information, and explanations.
Prewriting pages 262–271	To develop an informative essay, first choose and limit a topic, then gather and organize details, and finally develop an outline.
Drafting pages 271–273	Get your ideas down on paper.
Revising pages 274–275	Remember that you can move back and forth among the stages of the writing process.
Editing and Publishing page 275	Prepare your writing for your intended audience.

Informative Writing

Informative writing **explains something or informs the reader of something.**

Instructions that show you how to put together a piece of furniture, an article that explains weather systems, an encyclopedia entry that describes the culture of an African nation, or a book that relates the history of the Spice Trade are all examples of informative writing. This type of writing is also known as **expository writing.**

The Structure of Informative Writing

No matter the length or the purpose, most informational writing has a common structure. In the introduction, the main idea is presented; in the body supporting sentences or paragraphs provide details, examples, or steps in a process; and in the conclusion the main idea is summarized.

The purpose of the following paragraph is to inform the reader about how a computer can "smell." (Note that the topic and concluding sentences are in blue type.)

An Electronic Nose

Topic Sentence

Computers can be programmed to do many things, even tell the difference between roses and lilacs. Computers, of course, need a special kind of "nose" to do this.

Supporting Sentences

This electronic nose samples the air and sends signals to a memory chip in the computer. The signals are compared to information stored in the memory chip. If the signals match the information for "rose," the computer identifies

Concluding Sentence

the smell. Through clever programming, the computer nose knows!

—Seymour Simon, *Computer Sense, Computer Nonsense*

Prewriting

Before you write, you need to decide on a subject.

Discover and Choose a Subject

Ideas for informative essays may come from your own interests and knowledge or from your reading or research. First identify subjects that you already know about from your own experiences. For example, you may have learned enough about a favorite sport, a software game, or baby-sitting to write about one of those subjects.

Strategies for Finding a Subject for Informational Writing

- Look through your journal, particularly your Learning Log and interest inventory, for ideas.
- Think about books, magazines, or newspaper articles you have read lately on subjects of special interest to you.
- Think about an interesting television documentary or educational program you have watched recently.
- Think about a recent conversation that made you stop and think.
- Think about what interests you in your other classes.
- Start freewriting and see where it takes you.
- Use the clustering technique starting with the phrase *things I can explain*.

Consider Your Audience

Sometimes your choice of a subject will depend on who will be reading your essay. A classmate, a teacher, and a school newspaper editor, for example, may prefer to read about very different subjects. Whether you choose a subject to suit your audience or choose an audience for the subject you want to write about, you will need to consider the interests, knowledge, opinions, and needs of your audience.

Audience Profile

- Who will read my work?
- What subjects might interest my audience?
- Who is the logical audience for my subject?

Limit and Focus Your Subject

Many informative topics may be too broad to be developed adequately in a short essay. Therefore, after you choose a subject, you usually need to narrow, or limit, it. To limit a subject, think of specific aspects or examples of it. If your new subject is still too broad, continue the process of limiting. The example below shows how a writer might limit the subject of space exploration.

Subject: Space Exploration	
Limited Subjects	**More Limited Subjects**
early space flights	moon probes
firsts in space	first moon landing
Soviet achievements	*Sputnik*
space flight projects	*Skylab*
space encounters	*Vega*'s encounter with Halley's Comet

One good way to limit a subject is to ask yourself questions about it. Here are some possibilities:

Strategies for Limiting a Subject

- Who are some of the people associated with my subject?
- What are some specific examples of my subject?
- Where is my subject usually done or found?
- Why should people learn more about my subject?
- When was my subject first discovered? When did it become popular?

Focusing Your Subject After you have limited a subject, your next step is to find a focus for your thoughts. One way to find a focus is to make a preliminary survey of your subject by reading about it in a reference book or searching the Internet. Another way is to brainstorm general questions you could ask about the subject, based on what you already know about it. For example, if you chose moon probes as your limited subject, you might decide to focus on the adventures of *Surveyor I* as an example of an early moon probe, or you might focus on information scientists learned from moon probes before astronauts first landed on the moon.

Strategies for Focusing a Subject

- Focus on a specific event or incident.
- Focus on a specific time and place.
- Focus on one example that best represents your subject.
- Focus on one person or group that represents your subject.

The example below shows how a limited subject may have more than one possible focus.

Limited Subject: *Sputnik*	
Possible Subject Focuses	• how *Sputnik* started a space race between the United States and the Soviet Union
	• the story of Laika, the first dog in space, on *Sputnik II*
	• the effect of *Sputnik* on education in the United States
	• how *Sputnik II* differed from *Lunik I*—the first missile to reach the moon
	• why putting an object into orbit for the first time was so difficult

Gather Information and List Details

Once you have a focused subject, start gathering information. Use brainstorming, freewriting, clustering, inquiring, or researching to explore your subject and find details that will help you to inform others about it. Collect as much information as possible so that you will be able to choose the details that will best explain your subject. The kinds of details will depend on your main idea and your purpose for writing. If your purpose is to inform, you will probably use facts and examples. If your purpose is to explain or to give directions, your details will be the steps in a process.

To help you think of details, first make a list of questions that readers might have about your subject. Then jot down any details that will help you answer those questions. Your list could include any of the types of details shown in the box on the next page.

Types of Details Used in Informative Essays		
facts and examples	analogies	similarities
reasons	incidents	differences
steps in a process	definitions	causes and effects

Here are some facts one writer listed for an essay about the La Brea Tar Pits in Los Angeles, California.

Limited Subject	Tar Pits at Rancho La Brea
Focus	how prehistoric animals were trapped in pits
Fact	rainwater gathered on surface of tar pools and gave appearance of lake
Fact	animals came to drink and got caught in tar
Fact	their dead bodies attracted scavenging animals that also became trapped
Fact	tar helped preserve bones of animals
Examples	animals trapped include mammoths, saber-toothed tigers, and mastodons

A simulation of how a mastodon became trapped in the La Brea Tar Pits

Organize Your Information

The final step in the prewriting stage is arranging your list of support-ing details in a logical order. A **logical order** is an arrangement that makes sense—an arrangement your readers will be able to follow clearly. In planning an informative essay, you will usually be handling a great deal of informa-tion, so you will have to organize the information by developing an outline. Before you start an outline, however, you should group your information into categories and then arrange those categories in a logical order.

Grouping Information into Categories A **category** is a group, or class, of related pieces of information. To group information, write your categories at the top of a sheet of paper, then list information under the ap-propriate column. The following example shows two categories that represent what an astronaut might see from outer space.

Geographical Features	Man-made Features
• Antarctic ice flows	• Great Wall of China
• Ganges River	• irrigated land
• Caribbean Sea	• airports
• mountain ranges	• city lights at night
• "boot" of Italy	• oil slicks
• Sahara desert	• piers in large harbors

Arranging Categories in Logical Order Once you have cat-egorized your information, you should arrange those categories in the order in which you want to include them in your essay. The order you choose will depend largely on your purpose. For example, if your purpose is to give information, arrange your details in the order of importance, interest, size, or degree. If your purpose is to give directions or to explain a process, arrange your details in the order in which they occur. The chart on the next page lists some commonly used orders.

Types of Order	
Chronologi-cal Order	Information is presented in the order in which it occurred. First Rome was a Republic, then Rome had an emperor, finally the Roman Empire fell apart.
Sequential Order	Information is presented in the order in which it occurs. First you open the Web browser, next you select a search engine, then you type in your search term.
Spatial Order	Information is given according to location. 41 miles above earth; near the coast of Florida
Order of Importance	Information is given in order of importance, interest, size, or degree. bicycle, car, airplane (increase in size and speed)
Developmen-tal Order	Information of equal importance is arranged to lead up to a conclusion. Hurricane Katrina caused hardship; people from all over the United States went to help; people come together when they see others in trouble.
Comparison/ Contrast	Information is arranged to point out similarities and differences. Astronauts reached moon by spacecraft in three days—the same amount of time required for Thomas Jefferson to make a 90-mile trip in a horse-drawn carriage.

Organizing Comparison and Contrast Essays If you have chosen to compare and contrast two subjects in your essay, there are two ways to organize your information. One way is to write first about one subject and then about the other subject. For example, if you were comparing *Mercury* flights (subject A) to *Gemini* flights (subject B), you would first write all your information about subject A (*Mercury* flights). Then you would write all your information about subject B (*Gemini* flights). This is called the **AABB pattern** of comparison and contrast. The partial essay on the next page shows how the AABB pattern works.

Conflict Between the North and the South
(AABB Pattern of Organization)

As Americans pushed westward during the early 1800s, conflict grew between **the North (subject A)** and **the South (subject B)**. Since the nation's early days, the northern and southern parts of the United States had followed different ways of life. Each section wanted to extend its own influence into the western lands.

(A) The North had a diversified economy with both farms and industry. **(A) Northern farmers** raised a variety of crops that fed the thriving northern cities. **(A) Mills and factories in the North** competed with Great Britain in making cloth, shoes, iron, and machinery. For both its farms and factories, **(A) the North** depended on free workers. Such workers could move from place to place to meet the needs of industry. They could also be laid off when business slumped.

(B) The South depended on just a few cash crops, mainly cotton. To raise cotton, **(B) planters in the South** needed a large labor force year-round. They relied on slave labor. **(B) Southerners** traded their cotton for manufactured goods from Europe, especially from Great Britain. **(B) The South** had little industry of its own.

The second way to organize comparison and contrast compositions is called the **ABAB pattern.** As you might expect, in the ABAB pattern, first you compare both subject A and subject B in terms of one similarity or difference. Then, you compare both of them in terms of another similarity or difference. The following continuation of the essay on the conflict that led to the Civil War switches to the ABAB pattern. In the passage below, the writer first discusses the differences between the North and the South regarding attitudes toward slavery. Then the writer discusses differences in political power.

> The economic differences between the two sections of the country soon led to political conflicts. The worst of them arose over slavery. **(A) Many people in the North** considered slavery morally wrong. They wanted laws that would outlaw the practice in the new western territories. Some wanted to abolish slavery altogether. **(B) Most white Southerners,** on the other hand, believed slavery was necessary for their economy. They wanted laws to protect slavery in the West so that they could raise cotton on the fertile soil there.
>
> **(A) Northerners** had great political power in the national government. **(B) Southerners** feared the North's rising industrial power and growing population. Soon, they reasoned, the North would completely dominate the federal government. The election of 1860 seemed to confirm their worst fears. Abraham Lincoln, a Northern candidate who opposed the spread of slavery, was elected president.

Targeting the Six Traits: Ideas and Organization

Gathering information and details can help you determine the organization of your essay—but you may also find that the form of organization you choose will determine what types of information you will gather. For example, a comparison and contrast essay requires that you collect information and details about the two things being compared. As you research or brainstorm for information, you may find that your subject is not easily compared to something else. In such a case, you may decide to let the information dictate the type of organization you use.

Making an Outline With an outline you can plan the whole body of your essay. The first two supporting paragraphs of the essay titled "Conflict Between the North and the South" were written from the following outline.

Subject	**Conflict grew as Northerners and Southerners followed different ways of life.**
Main Topic	I. The way of life in the North
Subtopic	A. Had farms
Supporting Points	1. Raised a variety of crops 2. Fed thriving cities
Subtopic	B. Had industry
Supporting Points	1. Both mills and factories 2. Competed with Great Britain in making goods such as cloth, shoes, iron, and machinery
Subtopic	C. Work force
Supporting Points	1. Depended on free workers 2. Could move from place to place to meet the needs of industry 3. Could be laid off when business slumped
Main Topic	II. The way of life in the South
Subtopic	A. Grew mainly cotton
Subtopic	B. Had little industry of its own
Supporting Points	1. Traded cotton for manufactured goods 2. Traded mainly with Great Britain
Subtopic	C. Work force
Supporting Points	1. Needed a large labor force year-round 2. Depended on slave labor

Follow these guidelines when writing a formal outline.

Guidelines for Making an Outline

- Use Roman numerals for topics.
- Use capital letters for subtopics and indent them under the topic. If you use subtopics, always include at least two of them.
- Use Arabic numerals for supporting points and indent them under the subtopic. If you use supporting points, include at least two of them.
- Use lowercase letters for any other details and indent them under the supporting point to which they refer.

Drafting

Through prewriting you have explored your topic and examined what you know about it. You have also selected ideas and arranged them in a logical order. At this stage you are ready to write a first draft. The first draft need not be polished. It should, however, contain the basic parts of your essay—an introduction, body with supporting information, and conclusion.

Drafting the Introduction In an informative essay, the introduction has several functions other than stating the main idea. For example, in the introduction, you also set the tone of your essay and capture the reader's interest. Because the purpose of writing an informative essay is to inform or explain, a candid, matter-of-fact tone is usually appropriate. The following are common ways to attract the reader's attention in an informative essay.

Ways to Introduce Informative Essays

- Tell about an incident that shows how you became interested in your subject.
- Give some background information.
- Cite an example that illustrates your main idea.
- Cite a startling statistic about the subject.
- Define or describe the subject.
- Quote an expert on the subject.

(Note that some writers find it easier to begin with the body of the essay and to write the introduction later.)

The model below presents an introduction for the essay you read earlier about conflicts between the North and the South that led to the Civil War. Notice how the introduction captures interest, and sets the tone while expressing the main idea.

Main Idea

> As Americans pushed westward during the early 1800s, conflict grew between the North and the South. The main cause for this conflict was the different ways of life that had developed in these regions. As each section of the country tried to extend its own way of life to the new western lands, those differences began to threaten the nation's unity. By the 1860s, the contrast between the ways of life in the North and the South had brought the nation to the brink of war.

Drafting the Body When you draft the body of your essay, you should follow your outline. Each main topic, with some or all of the subtopics and supporting points, will become at least one paragraph. If you have a number of supporting details, you may need two or more paragraphs to cover each topic adequately. Pause occasionally to read over what you have written and to check the flow of your writing. Connect your words, sentences, and paragraphs with transitions to give the essay unity and coherence.

Strategies for Achieving Unity and Coherence

- Use transitional words and phrases.
- Repeat a key word from an earlier sentence.
- Use synonyms for key words from earlier sentences.
- Use a pronoun in place of a word used earlier.

Drafting the Conclusion An informative essay is not complete without a conclusion. The concluding paragraph sums up your information and reinforces your thesis.

Strategies for Writing a Conclusion

- Summarize the body of the essay.
- Restate the thesis in new words.
- Draw a conclusion based on the body of the essay.
- Add an insight about the thesis.
- Write a memorable clincher sentence.

The following paragraph concludes the essay about conflicts that led to the Civil War in the United States. Notice that the conclusion adds interesting details about the start of the Civil War and also restates the main idea in a memorable clincher sentence.

Clincher Sentence

After Lincoln's election, 11 southern states made the fateful decision to withdraw from the United States. They established a separate nation called the Confederate States of America. On April 12, 1861, Confederate guns opened fire on Fort Sumter, a fort in South Carolina held by soldiers of the federal government. This event marked the beginning of the Civil War—a tragic clash between Americans following different ways of life.

Sunset at Fort Sumter, Conrad Wise Chapman

Revising

If you are like most writers, your first draft will not be the best you can do. In the revising stage of the writing process, you have a chance to improve your writing in a second or third draft. When **revising,** look at your draft as if you were the reader instead of the writer.

Checking for Unity and Coherence One way to improve your draft is to check it carefully for **unity.** An essay has unity when all of the supporting information in the body relate directly to the main idea stated in the introduction. Paragraphs within the essay should each have unity as well, with sentences in the paragraph supporting the topic of the paragraph. Sentences that stray from the main idea cause readers to become confused and distracted.

Another way to improve a first draft is to make sure that it is **coherent.** In an essay with coherence, the ideas are presented in a logical order with clear transitions. As you revise, check your writing to see if any idea is out of place, or if transitions could improve the flow.

Using the Six Traits of Good Writing Use the Six Traits of Good Writing checklist during the revising and editing stages. (The first five traits follow. You will work on the sixth trait, *conventions,* when you edit your paper.)

Six Traits of Good Writing Checklist

Ideas
✓ Is your main idea clear?
✓ Do your ideas take your audience into consideration?
✓ Do you include enough details for your reader to understand your subject?
✓ Did you present your ideas in logical order?

Organization
✓ Does your introduction establish your main idea and set the tone?
✓ Does your essay have unity?
✓ Is your essay coherent?
✓ Does each paragraph have adequate development?
✓ Do you have a strong conclusion?

Voice

✓ Does your interest in your subject come through in your writing?

✓ Does your writing draw the audience into your subject?

Word Choice

✓ Does each word express clearly and precisely what you want to say?

✓ Do the words you've used help the reader understand the subject?

✓ Did you use precise details and examples?

✓ Did you use vivid words?

Sentence Fluency

✓ Did you vary your sentences and sentence beginnings?

✓ Are transitions clear and smooth?

✓ Do the sentences flow naturally?

Editing and Publishing

Editing When you are satisfied with the content of your essay, move on to editing—correcting mistakes in grammar, usage, mechanics, and spelling. Use proofreading symbols as a shorthand way of showing corrections.

Targeting the Six Traits: Conventions

The conventions of spelling, grammar, and usage are particularly important in informational writing. If a reader sees that you have taken care to get the conventions correct, that reader is more likely to trust your facts, examples, and other details. Pay particular attention to the spelling of technical terms, names, historical places, and other details in your informational writing.

Publishing Complete the writing process by sharing your informative essay with someone whom you think might have an interest in it.

Writing to Persuade

CHAPTER
27

QuickGuide

Persuasive Writing pages 277–279	**Persuasive writing** offers an opinion on a subject and uses facts, reasons, and examples to convince readers that the opinion is valid.
Prewriting pages 280–284	Choose and develop a topic that you would like to convince others is important.
Drafting pages 285–288	Get your facts, reasons, and examples down on paper.
Revising and Editing pages 288–289	Revise your essay to make certain your arguments support your opinion. Then prepare it for those you hope to persuade.

Persuasive Writing

Persuasive writing offers an opinion on a subject and uses facts, reasons, and examples to convince readers that the opinion is valid.

What do TV ads, political speeches, charity fund-raisers, and recycling campaigns all have in common? They all involve forms of persuasion. They try to convince readers to buy, vote, give, or recycle. The ability to persuade others is important in many areas of life. It also plays a part in sharpening thinking skills.

A big part of writing persuasively is taking a stand. To persuade others, you need to know what you think about a topic. Believing strongly in your position is vital to persuasive writing. No matter what the issue—great or small—you need to be sure of your own opinion. And if you are going to convince others, you need to be sure that your opinion is supported by experience, facts, or logic. Then, by applying various persuasive strategies, you can attempt to convince others.

The Structure of a Persuasive Essay

Like all essays, a persuasive essay has three main parts: an introduction, a body, and a conclusion. The following list shows how each part helps develop an argument.

Structure of a Persuasive Essay

- The introduction captures the reader's attention, presents the issue, and expresses the writer's opinion in a thesis statement.
- The body presents reasons, facts, examples, and expert opinions to back up the writer's ideas.
- The conclusion presents a summary or strong conclusive evidence that drives home the writer's opinions.

In the example on the next page, the writer presents the issue in the first sentence and follows with several reasons.

Fire Drills at Home

Introductory Sentence

Fire drills should be conducted in homes as well as in schools and other public buildings. First of all, having regular fire drills at home would allow all family members to practice what to do in an emergency. This

Body

practice would reduce panic during a fire and perhaps make the difference between escaping safely and being trapped. Second, having home fire drills would set a good example in the neighborhood. Nearby families may be encouraged to have their own drills. Most important, having fire drills at home would probably lead people to be more safety-conscious so that fires would not get started in

Concluding Sentence

the first place. A few minutes a few times a year can help save lives.

Facts and Opinions

If you intend to change someone's mind, you must provide a convincing argument. Sticking to the facts, rather than just giving opinions, is essential to building a strong case.

Facts are statements that can be proved. **Opinions** are beliefs or judgments that cannot be proved. Opinions definitely have their place, but they cannot be used as proof. Learn to recognize opinions by watching for words such as *should, must, ought, better, best,* and *worst.* Phrases such as "I think," "some people feel," or "many believe" also indicate that opinions are being expressed.

Facts and opinions are presented together in persuasive essays. The main idea is an opinion. The body of the essay backs up this idea with facts and examples.

There are several ways to test whether a statement is a fact or an opinion. First, ask yourself, "Can I prove this statement through my own experience?"

Fact   Some physical education programs stress competitive sports.

Another test of a fact is to ask, "Can I prove this statement by referring to accepted authorities and experts?"

Fact   Muscle tension increases the risk of injury during sports. (To prove this statement you could ask a sports doctor.)

Opinions, unlike facts, can never be proved. They are judgment calls, personal likes or dislikes, and interpretations that vary from person to person.

Opinion   Movies are **more satisfying** on a big screen than on TV.

Opinion   Competition **should be** downplayed in school sports.

The following words often signal opinions.

Opinion Words		
should	good, better, best	probably
ought	bad, worse, worst	might
can	beautiful	perhaps
may	terrible	maybe

Opinions gain strength when they are supported by factual evidence, logical arguments, or both.

Unsupported Opinion   Volleyball is more fun than soccer. (There are no supporting facts available.)

Supported Opinion   Noncompetitive volleyball may teach positive social skills. (Experts in sports and society can offer supporting facts and observations based on experience.)

Prewriting

Thinking your subject through carefully and gathering the best possible evidence are the surest ways to develop a good argument. If you take your time during prewriting, you will be able to anticipate any arguments that might be offered against your opinion and be ready for them.

Choose a Subject

The two most important aspects of a good persuasive subject are (1) that the subject is something that really matters to you and (2) that you are able to find enough facts and examples to make a convincing argument. Brainstorm a list of possible subjects about which you can say, "I believe," and about which another person might say, "I don't believe."

Guidelines for Choosing a Persuasive Essay Subject

- Choose a subject involving a local or national issue that is important to you.
- Choose a subject involving an issue on which people hold very different opinions.
- Choose a subject you can support with examples, reasons, and facts from your own experience or from other reliable sources.
- Choose a subject for which there is an audience whose beliefs or behavior you would like to influence.

Identify Your Audience

You need to identify your target audience when writing a persuasive essay. Readers who initially disagree with your viewpoint will mentally try to block your ideas. The following questions will help you understand your audience.

Questions for Analyzing an Audience

- What does my audience already know about my subject?
- What is my audience's point of view about my subject? Do they already agree or disagree with my position?
- What are the chances of changing the opinions and behavior of my audience?
- Are there any sensitive issues I should be aware of?

Targeting the Six Traits: Voice

Voice is an important element of persuasive writing. You want your voice to sound authentic—like a real person sharing something important. In addition, you want to sound authoritative and confident, so the reader will know that you actually believe the arguments you are using and that your facts and examples are reliable. It is important to remember, however, that *authoritative* and *confident* do not mean *cocky* and *rude*. You always want to be polite and respectful of your reader.

To help you develop the right voice for your persuasive writing, think about someone whom you would really like to talk to about your ideas, someone who would be sympathetic and interested even if he or she didn't agree with you. Keep this person in mind as you write.

Develop a Thesis Statement

Once you have chosen your subject and identified your audience, you can begin to develop your thesis statement. The **thesis statement** is a sentence that sums up the main idea of your essay—the opinion you will be presenting. A strong thesis statement expresses a supportable opinion, not just a simple preference. Often a thesis statement will take the form of a recommendation for action.

Simple Preference	Horseback riding is a better pastime than watching television. (unacceptable as a thesis statement)
Supportable Opinion	Although horseback riding is a pleasurable pastime, it should not be enjoyed at the expense of the horses' well-being. (unacceptable)
Call for Action	Until the care of retired race horses improves, people should not support horse racing. (acceptable)

The following guidelines will help you develop your thesis statement.

Guidelines for Developing a Thesis Statement

- Choose a debatable opinion—one that has two sides.
- State the main idea simply in one sentence. This is your thesis statement.
- Avoid hasty generalizations by limiting your statement.
- Give a supportable opinion or a recommendation for action.
- As you gather information, keep revising your thesis statement, so that it covers all your evidence.

If you find that you cannot develop a thesis statement according to these guidelines, do not hesitate to try again on a different topic or to rethink your viewpoint.

Develop an Argument

In some ways, writing a persuasive essay is like gathering facts and evidence for a courtroom trial. After you have defined your thesis, you need to build a sound case to convince your jury of readers. In addition to listing all the **pros**—facts, reasons, examples, and expert opinions that support your view— you should also be prepared to answer your opponents by anticipating the **cons**—the evidence used to oppose your position. The following guidelines will help you develop your argument.

Guidelines for Developing an Argument

- List pros and cons in separate columns in your prewriting notes. Be prepared to address any opposing views
- Use facts and examples to support your opinions.
- If those with an opposing view have a good point, admit it. Then show why the point is not enough to sway your opinion. Such an admission is called *conceding a point,* and it will strengthen your credibility.
- Use polite and reasonable language rather than words that show bias or overcharged emotions.
- Refer to well-respected experts and authorities in the field who agree with your position.

Organize an Argument

Presenting your evidence in a well-organized way will strengthen your position. Perhaps the most common pattern for persuasive compositions is **order of importance**—starting with the least important point and building up to the most important. Saving your best point for last will help your readers remember your most convincing evidence.

Listing your facts, reasons, examples, and other details will help you decide which organizational pattern will work best for the opinion or call to action you wish to address in your essay.

Targeting the Six Traits: Organization

A persuasive essay is strongest when it is well organized. Arguments can lose strength if connected points are too far apart, or if points do not build logically. Here are some organizational models that work well in persuasive essays.

Order of importance is a dramatic way to organize a persuasive argument. In this organization, the writer starts with the weaker points and builds up to the fact or example that clinches the argument.

Cause and effect arguments work well with facts that can be presented as "because A happened, B happened, and because B happened, then C happened" and so on.

Compare and contrast arguments are based on comparing or contrasting facts and examples. As a part of an argument about American eating habits, you might compare a person with poor eating habits to one with healthy habits.

Write an Outline

Use your facts and examples, together with the organizational pattern, to build an outline such as the one on the next page.

New Games

Thesis: Alternatives to competitive sports should be the rule rather than the exception in physical education.

I. (Introduction) Choosing sides for games can make students feel inadequate.

II. Some say athletes need competition to perform at their best.

    A. Competition can have a negative effect on athletes' performance.

    B. Removing competition from games can help to strengthen rather than weaken skills.

III. Competition can diminish the positive effects of playing games.

    A. Competition can create frustration rather than pleasure.

    B. Competition can increase the possibility of injury.

    C. Competition can limit the development of social skills.

IV. Physical education programs in school should incorporate "New Games" into their programs.

V. Infinity volleyball is an example of a "New Game."

    A. The object is to keep volleying for as long as possible.

    B. All players on both teams share the score.

VI. (Conclusion) Noncompetitive games will bring pleasure back to physical education classes.

Drafting

Your outline will guide you as you draft your persuasive essay. Pay special attention to the introduction. You may want to begin with an incident or example to show the importance of the issue. Many writers save their thesis statement for the end of the introduction.

When drafting the body, follow your outline ideas unless you see a better way to organize. Write one full paragraph for each of your main supporting points. At appropriate spots, address your opponents' possible differing viewpoints. To achieve a smooth flow, use transitional words and phrases.

In your conclusion, combine your ideas in a compelling and memorable summary. Restate your recommendations for action, if you are including any.

Use Persuasive Language

Overly emotional language weakens your arguments. Language should be polite and reasonable—but also strong and direct.

Emotional Language	The **slave-driving** owners of the **sickeningly run-down** stables **deserve the same treatment as their animals.**
Forceful Language	**The unsympathetic** owners of the **poorly kept** stables should begin to consider the animals' welfare.

Use Transitions

If you have organized your argument by order of importance, you might use some of the following transitions.

Transitions for Order of Importance			
also	another	for example	more important
first	besides	furthermore	most important
second	moreover	similarly	to begin with
third	finally	in addition	in conclusion

If you have chosen to compare and contrast opinions or viewpoints, you may find the following transitions useful.

Transitions for Comparing and Contrasting		
although	instead	nonetheless
admittedly	nevertheless	still
however	on the other hand	while it is true that

In the following draft, the writer develops her outline on the topic of new games. As you read the essay, notice the transitions the writer uses between ideas.

New Games

Introduction
Captures attention and provides background

Can you recognize yourself in the following scene? On a cold winter day, students prepare to play a game of volleyball in the gym. For some, eagerness turns to anxiety when it comes time to choose sides. The team captains call on the best players first, and within a few minutes, the remaining players are feeling left out and inadequate. As the choosing continues, the last few players are feeling very small indeed. Nobody seems to want them, and maybe even worse, everyone <u>knows</u> nobody wants them. When the game gets underway, the last-chosen play timidly, afraid to confirm their reputation. Too often, the competitive nature of sports and games interferes with the learning and pleasure

Thesis Statement

that they could be providing. Enjoyable, relaxing alternatives to competitive sports should be the rule rather than the exception in physical education.

First Body Paragraph
Addresses opposing views; offers expert evidence

Some people argue that without competition, athletes would not perform at their very best. In fact, competition sometimes has the opposite effect. Tennis pro Tim Gallwey believes that a key part of success in any sport is conquering "such obstacles as lapses in concentration, nervousness, self-doubt, and self-condemnation." For the dedicated athlete, competition may help enhance the ability to overcome these inner obstacles. However, for the vast majority of students in physical education, the team-choosing, score-keeping scene described would only make the obstacles all the more insurmountable. Remove the competition, however, and students are free to experiment, make mistakes, and—by so doing—improve their skills in a sport.

Second Body Paragraph
Provides additional reasons

Besides sometimes getting in the way of improving in a sport, competition can also reduce other positive side effects of play. When winning becomes more important than playing, pleasure may give way to frustration. The joy that comes from a relaxed body at play is out of reach if players are only trying for another notch on the scoreboard. Also, as players face off against an imagined enemy, their muscles could become tense, increasing the risk of injury. Finally, sports help young people learn social skills. If competition and winning are stressed, the skills learned might help shape an isolated, aggressive, self-centered outlook. Less competition might foster cooperation and trust.

Third Body Paragraph
Offers alternative

Instead of competitive sports, physical education programs should incorporate "New Games." These made-up games have three basic rules, which are reflected in the motto of the "New Games" Association. The rules are "Play hard, play fair, nobody gets hurt."

Fourth Body Paragraph
Elaborates on alternative with clear example

One of the games suggested in the "New Games" Association's guidebook is "infinity volleyball." According to the guide, "The object of this game is to keep the ball on the volley indefinitely. In general, the normal rules of volleyball apply, except that no specified number of players is required. As in regular volleyball, one team may hit the ball no more than three times before sending it over the net. Players of both teams chant aloud the number of times the ball has been volleyed. Both teams share the final score. For average players, any score over 50 is very good; 100 or more is phenomenal."

Conclusion	"New Games," or other innovative approaches to
Drives home the main point	sports that steer clear of competition, can help restore the kind of joy young people should have when they get together to play. And, along the way, the players are more likely to develop confidence in their physical abilities. When the outer obstacle of competition is removed, students can begin to master their inner obstacles and at the same time enjoy their time in the gym or on the playing field. Everyone is always chosen first; everyone is a winner.

Revising and Editing

You can revise your work on your own by studying it carefully for flaws in unity, coherence, and clarity.

Consider Unity Ask yourself, "Have I stuck faithfully to my intended subject? Do all of my supporting points relate directly to my thesis statement? Do I include any unnecessary information that might distract my readers?"

Check for Coherence Review your organizational pattern. Does it follow a logical order? Does one idea flow smoothly and logically to the next? Do you include clear and ample transitions?

Check for Clarity Make sure there is no possibility that your points could be misunderstood. Replace vague language with forceful, specific words. Make sure all terms are clearly defined within the context of your subject. Fully explain any reasons or examples that fail to support your thesis clearly.

One way to check for clarity is to erase from your mind all that you already know about your subject. Then imagine that you are a reader who is completely unfamiliar with the issues of your essay. Will the pros and cons be clear to such a reader?

Use the Six Traits of Good Writing

Use the following checklist as you revise and edit.

Ideas

✓ Did you pick a subject about which you have a strong opinion?

✓ Have you gathered enough facts, examples, and reasons to support your opinion?

✓ Have you considered opposing views honestly and effectively?

✓ Do any of your sentences stray from the main idea?

Organization

✓ Does your introduction clearly state your opinion?

✓ Have you developed your arguments well and organized them in the most logical way?

✓ Are transitions clear and smooth?

✓ Have you supported your main points with facts, real-life examples, and expert opinions?

✓ Does your writing exhibit unity, coherence, and clarity?

✓ Does your conclusion draw your ideas together in a forceful summary?

✓ Did you include a recommendation for action, if appropriate to your essay?

Voice

✓ Is your voice in the essay authoritative and confident?

✓ Will your interest in the topic be clear to the reader?

Word Choice

✓ Is your language polite and respectful of the reader?

✓ Have you used forceful words, rather than emotional ones?

Sentence Fluency

✓ Are your sentences complete and well constructed?

✓ Do the sentences flow naturally?

Conventions (Editing)

✓ Are your sentences free of errors in grammar and usage?

✓ Did you spell each word correctly?

✓ Did you use capital letters where needed?

✓ Did you punctuate sentences correctly?

QuickGuide

The Creative Work page 291	**Creative writing** allows writers to share their ideas, dreams, emotions, and observations with others.
Writing a Short Story pages 291–296	A short story is a brief but well-developed piece of fiction about characters facing a conflict or problem.
Prewriting pages 297–301	Find a topic that engages your imagination and creativity.
Drafting pages 302–303	Find or create the structure that will help your ideas come to life.
Revising pages 303–304	Revise your story until it communicates your ideas clearly and effectively.
Editing and Publishing page 304	Prepare your essay for readers by editing it for conventions.
Writing a Scene for a Play pages 305–308	Develop characters and set them in a dramatic conflict.
Writing a Poem pages 309–311	Find a topic that inspires you, and play with the music of language.

The Creative Work

Creative writing allows writers to share their ideas, dreams, emotions, and observations with others.

The world of plays, stories, and poems has been built by creative writers. The creative writer creates a work that communicates the writer's thoughts, beliefs, or perceptions. The author can manipulate characters and situations in order to examine human foibles and strengths. This may cause the reader to ask questions: What made the author think of this? What does this work reveal about the author? What message does this work have for me?

Creative writing takes many forms. It can be humorous, tragic, suspenseful, or whimsical. Creative writing may or may not include fictional elements. A historical novel may have fictional characters participating in real events, such as the American Revolution. Science fiction may include fictional characters, places, and events, but include elements of real science. A play may include real characters in real events, but with additional dialogue or commentary from an outside narrator. A poem can be entirely factual—real events, real people, or real emotions—but be transformed by the creative process into something that transmits that reality to the reader in a special way.

Writing a Short Story

A **short story** is a well-developed fictional story about characters facing a conflict or problem. Once you know how to write a good short story, you can carry that skill in any direction you wish, expanding it to book length, switching from realistic fiction to science fiction to fantasy, or spinning it into the funny tales told by a comedian. The basic skills can take you wherever you want to go with your creativity.

Though the characters you create are only one aspect of a short story, an interesting character thrust into a threatening, confusing, or desperate situation always makes a good basis for a short story.

Read the following short story by Langston Hughes and think about how the author has created a vivid scene and lively characters.

Thank You, M'am

She was a large woman with a large purse that had everything in it but hammer and nails. It had a long strap and she carried it slung across her shoulder. It was about eleven o'clock at night, and she was walking alone, when a boy ran up behind her and tried to snatch her purse. The strap broke with the single tug the boy gave it from behind. But the boy's weight, and the weight of the purse combined, caused him to lose his balance so, instead of taking off full blast as he had hoped, the boy fell on his back on the sidewalk, and his legs flew up. The large woman simply turned around and kicked him right square in his blue-jeaned sitter. Then she reached down, picked the boy up by his shirt front, and shook him until his teeth rattled.

After that the woman said, "Pick up my pocketbook, boy, and give it here." She still held him. But she bent down enough to permit him to stoop and pick up her purse. Then she said, "Now ain't you ashamed of yourself?"

Firmly gripped by his shirt front, the boy said, "Yes'm."

The woman said, "What did you want to do it for?"

The boy said, "I didn't aim to."

She said, "You a lie!"

By that time two or three people passed, stopped, turned to look, and some stood watching.

"If I turn you loose, will you run?" asked the woman.

"Yes'm," said the boy.

"Then I won't turn you loose," said the woman. She did not release him.

"I'm very sorry, lady, I'm sorry," whispered the boy.

"Um-hum! And your face is dirty. I got a great mind to wash your face for you. Ain't you got nobody home to tell you to wash your face?"

"No'm," said the boy.

"Then it will get washed this evening," said the large woman starting up the street, dragging the frightened boy behind her.

He looked as if he were fourteen or fifteen, frail and willow-wild, in tennis shoes and blue jeans.

The woman said, "You ought to be my son. I would teach you right from wrong. Least I can do right now is to wash your face. Are you hungry?"

"No'm," said the being-dragged boy. "I just want you to turn me loose."

"Was I bothering you when I turned that corner?" asked the woman.

"No'm."

"But you put yourself in contact with *me*," said the woman. "If you think that that contact is not going to last awhile, you got another thought coming. When I get through with you, sir, you are going to remember Mrs. Luella Bates Washington Jones."

Sweat popped out on the boy's face and he began to struggle. Mrs. Jones stopped, jerked him around in front of her, put a half-nelson about his neck, and continued to drag him up the street. When she got to her door, she dragged the boy inside, down a hall, and into a large kitchenette-furnished room at the rear of the house. She switched on the light and left the door open. The boy could hear other roomers laughing and talking in the large house. Some of their doors were opened, too, so he knew he and the woman were not alone. The woman still had him by the neck in the middle of her room.

She said, "What is your name?"

"Roger," answered the boy.

"Then, Roger, you go to that sink and wash your face," said the woman, whereupon she turned him loose—at last. Roger looked at the door—looked at the woman—looked at the door—*and went to the sink.*

Jim, William H. Johnson, 1930

"Let the water run until it gets warm," she said. "Here's a clean towel."

"You gonna take me to jail?" asked the boy, bending over the sink.

"Not with that face, I would not take you nowhere," said the woman. "Here I am trying to get home to cook me a bite to eat and you snatch my pocketbook! Maybe you ain't been to your supper either, late as it be. Have you?"

"There's nobody home at my house," said the boy.

"Then we'll eat," said the woman. "I believe you're hungry—or been hungry—to try to snatch my pocketbook."

"I wanted a pair of blue suede shoes," said the boy.

"Well, you didn't have to snatch *my* pocketbook to get some suede shoes," said Mrs. Luella Bates Washington Jones. "You could of asked me."

"M'am?"

The water dripping from his face, the boy looked at her. There was a long pause. A very long pause. After he had dried his face and not knowing what else to do dried it again, the boy turned around, wondering what next. The door was open. He could make a dash for it down the hall. He could run, run, run, run, *run!*

The woman was sitting on the day-bed. After a while she said, "I were young once and I wanted things I could not get."

There was another long pause. The boy's mouth opened. Then he frowned, but not knowing he frowned.

The woman said, "Um-hum! You thought I was going to say *but*, didn't you? You thought I was going to say, *but I didn't snatch people's pocketbooks*. Well, I wasn't going to say that." Pause. Silence. "I have done things, too, which I would not tell you, son—neither tell God, if he didn't already know. So you set down while I fix us something to eat. You might run that comb through your hair so you will look presentable."

In another corner of the room behind a screen was a gas plate and an icebox. Mrs. Jones got up and went behind the screen. The woman did not watch the boy to see if he was going to run now, nor did she watch her purse which she left behind her on the daybed. But the boy took care to sit on the far side of the room where he thought she could easily see him out of the corner of her eye, if she wanted to. He did not trust the woman not to trust him. And he did not want to be mistrusted now.

"Do you need somebody to go to the store," asked the boy, "maybe to get some milk or something?"

"Don't believe I do," said the woman, "unless you just want sweet milk yourself. I was going to make cocoa out of this canned milk I got here."

"That will be fine," said the boy.

She heated some lima beans and ham she had in the icebox, made the cocoa, and set the table. The woman did not ask the boy anything about where he lived, or his folks, or anything else that would embarrass him. Instead as they ate, she told him about her job in a hotel beauty-shop that stayed open late, what the work was like, and how all kinds of women came in and out, blondes, redheads, and brunettes. Then she cut him a half of her ten-cent cake.

"Eat some more, son," she said.

When they were finished eating she got up and said, "Now, here, take this ten dollars and buy yourself some blue suede shoes. And next time, do not make the mistake of latching on to *my* pocketbook *nor nobody else's*—because shoes come by devilish like that will burn your feet. I got to get my rest now. But I wish you would behave yourself, son, from here on in."

She led him down the hall to the front door and opened it. "Good-night! Behave yourself, boy!" she said, looking out into the street.

The boy wanted to say something else other than, "Thank you, m'am," to Mrs. Luella Bates Washington Jones, but he couldn't do so as he turned at the barren stoop and looked back at the large woman in the door. He barely managed to say, "Thank you," before she shut the door. And he never saw her again.

Short Story Structure

All short stories have three main parts. The **beginning** introduces the characters and the problem or conflict. The **middle** tells the main events of the narrative. The **ending** shows how the problem was finally resolved.

The following chart shows some of the other elements most short stories have.

Elements of a Short Story	
Narrator	the person telling the story; may be first person (if he or she is in the story) or third person (if he or she is outside the story telling what happened to others)
Setting	the time and place in which the story takes place
Characters	the people involved in the story
Conflict	the problem at the heart of the story
Triggering Event	the event that starts the story rolling
Climax	the point in the story where the conflict or problem is most serious
Resolution	how the problem or conflict is solved
Outcome	the way the story ends
Dialogue	words spoken by the characters
Description	writing that helps the reader see, hear, feel, taste, or smell what is happening

Most short stories also have a **theme,** or main idea. The theme might be the healing power of love, the rewards of showing courage, or the wastefulness of despair. The outcome of the story may then imply some lesson or moral about the theme, or it may affirm some meaningful observation or conclusion about life. Some short stories aim chiefly to surprise or entertain readers rather than to give a message.

Prewriting

Short stories, like other kinds of writing, usually do not spring out of a writer's imagination fully completed and ready to write down. Most writers follow a process of prewriting, drafting, revising, and editing to shape their ideas into meaningful stories.

Many good stories tell about events that are out of the ordinary. Unusual happenings, such as a celebrity moving in next door, keep readers interested. The main characters may be ordinary individuals with whom readers can identify, but the situations in which you place the characters should be something that keeps the reader reading. This can be because the situation is dangerous, exciting, or even very familiar to the reader, but one where the reader wants to know how the character handles a problem or conflict. When choosing a subject, search your memory and imagination for experiences that stand out as unusual, important, or interesting.

Think of a Plot

Many of your best ideas for a plot will come from your own experiences and observations, while others will come from your imagination. The following strategies may stimulate your thinking about plot ideas.

Strategies for Thinking of a Plot

- Brainstorm a list of story ideas based on conflicts you have experienced or observed firsthand.
- Scan newspaper headlines and news items for an unusual event.
- Think of conflicts or events in history—including your family history and local history.
- Observe people and events in your life. Sometimes even small events or snatches of conversation will suggest a conflict on which to build a plot.

Once you have a story idea and a conflict, you can build the plot around them. A plot usually unfolds from the event that triggers the conflict to the event that resolves it. Therefore, you will need to arrange the details of your plot so that they naturally unfold as the story progresses. The list on the next page shows some steps for developing a plot.

Strategies for Developing a Plot

1. Introduce the event or circumstance that triggers the action. Include descriptive details to make the source of the conflict clear.
2. Develop details describing the nature of the conflict.
3. Develop details about the obstacles the characters will struggle against or overcome to resolve the central conflict.
4. Develop details about how the main character overcomes the obstacles.
5. Decide how the conflict will be resolved and how the story will end.

Determine Point of View

Every story has a narrator, the person whose "voice" is telling the story. Readers see the story unfolding through the eyes, or **point of view,** of the narrator. If the narrator takes part in the story, the narrative is said to have a **first-person** point of view. If the narrator tells what happens to others and is not a character in the story, the narrative has a **third-person** point of view.

Compare the two story openers below. Both introduce the same narrative from different points of view.

First-Person Point of View

Last year, on an early spring evening, **I** was looking forward to having the house to **myself. My** parents were going out to dinner, and **my** younger sister was staying overnight at a friend's house. For about four hours, **I** would be alone in the house. **I** could play **my** CDs as loudly as **I** wanted.

Third-Person Point of View

Last year, on an early spring evening, **Mark** was looking forward to having the house to **himself. His** parents were going out to dinner, and **his** younger sister was staying overnight at a friend's house. For about four hours, **he** would be alone in the house. **He** could play **his** CDs as loudly as **he** wanted.

Using first-person point of view can give the story a sense of realism, as if you are talking directly to the reader. It has its limitations, however. If the character is in the story, the character cannot know the thoughts or motives of other characters. The first-person narrator may wonder what others are thinking and try to figure out what is happening.

With the third-person point of view, the writer has a choice: have a limited narrator who learns things as they develop, or have the narrator know everything, including what characters think and feel, and what they did in the past or will do in the future.

Once you pick a point of view for a story, stick with it.

Targeting the Six Traits: Voice

The point of view has an effect on the voice of a story. In a first-person narrative about an imaginary day at the beach, you may want the voice to be filled with enthusiasm, showing some flashes of your own thoughts and insights, as if you are sharing an experience with a friend. If you are writing a third-person mystery in which the narrator is relating the efforts of a detective to solve a murder, you want the voice to be confident as it leads the reader through the story.

Whichever point of view you select, you should strive for a genuine voice—a real person "talking" to the reader. There should always be enough of your personality in the narrator that you can keep the "realness" going without too much trouble. Even if people think, "Wow, what an imagination," you still want them to think they are connecting with another person.

Sketch Your Characters

Draw upon your own personality and habits when sketching, or describing, characters. You might create a story character by mixing together details of yourself and other people, such as the determined way you approach challenges, the way your third-grade teacher walked, the color of your best friend's hair, and the laugh of your great-aunt Matilda.

Be as specific as you can when creating your character sketches. If you use aspects of your own personality, you can easily create new details without much effort. If you created a fresh character, you may not know how that person would behave in a given situation. The more detailed your sketch, the easier it will be to figure out how the character will act.

Below are sketches of the characters created by Langston Hughes in "Thank you, M'am." Notice how the description includes both physical characteristics as well as personality traits.

Luella Bates Washington Jones	Urban, large, physically strong, stern, intimidating, kind, no-nonsense, uses *ain't* in speech, hardworking, works in a hotel beauty shop, middle-aged, may have a "past"
Roger	Urban, skinny, fourteen or fifteen, speech reflects urban street culture, probably poor and feeling defeated, desperately wants blue-suede shoes, a potentially good kid inside

Create a Setting

Once you have chosen a subject, defined your character, and chosen a point of view, you can plan the details of your story's **setting.** First determine the location and time of your story. Then add details that will bring the setting to life. You might make a list of details, as in this brief list of the setting of "Thank you, M'am."

Setting of "Thank You, M'am"	
Where	**When**
city	evening
a quiet street	recent past
a rooming house	11:00 P.M.
large kitchenette-furnished room	probably summer

Try to be as detailed as possible. For example, the setting of the kitchenette in "Thank You, Ma'm" is accomplished with just a few telling details. There is a gas plate rather than a stove, and an icebox in the place of a refrigerator. These few details suggest that the kitchenette is rather old and modest, and it adds a sense of Luella Jones's poverty. This in turn adds to the sense of dignity—that she acts kindly in spite of the fact that she is not well off. Details like these help define the setting, but also contribute to our understanding of the character and the circumstances.

List Events in Chronological Order

The last step before writing your short story is to list all the events that make up the story. When listing events, answer the following questions. Your list will then be in chronological order, the order in which the events occurred. This order will help your readers follow the story as it unfolds.

Listing Events in Chronological Order

- What happens to start the story rolling?
- What happens next? Next? Next?
- What is the climax, or highest point of the action in the story?
- What finally happens to resolve the conflict?
- How does the story end?

Drafting

Create a structure that will help your ideas come to life.

Good stories draw readers into the action and make them feel involved. Before you begin writing your short story, think about what you enjoy most as you read stories. Do you like characters with whom you can identify? Do you like a lot of action, humor, or suspense?

Keep your audience in mind. Add details that will make your narrative more interesting to readers, and leave out unnecessary details that slow the story down or lead your readers to false predictions.

Draft the Beginning

The beginning of a short story introduces the main characters, the setting, and the main conflict. You can begin your story any way you like, but remember the beginning is the place where you "hook" your readers and draw them into the world you have created.

Guidelines for Beginning a Story

- Set the time and place of the story, adding details that capture the reader's attention.
- Introduce the characters in the story.
- Provide any background information needed.
- Include the event that starts the story in motion.

Remember that for each of these points, you need to include enough details to make things real to readers. "A boy in a room" tells us a little, but we don't really connect with the character or the setting. "A small, sad, 12-year-old boy with dark hair sat slumped on the edge of an unmade bed in a tiny, dark room with peeling wallpaper" hooks readers into wanting to know what's going on, why the boy is sad, why the room is dark.

You don't have to include every detail—the description above doesn't mention the boy's eye color, weight, or what he's wearing, and we don't know if the room has other furniture besides the bed, but we know the key details that establish for us who the character is and where, and suggests something of what he is feeling. You can add more details as necessary, but remember to focus on details that are important to the reader's understanding.

Draft the Middle

The middle of your narrative tells the story, event by event.

Guidelines for Drafting the Middle

- Use chronological order and transitions to show the passing of time.
- Build on the conflict until the action reaches a climax, or high point.
- Use dialogue to show what the characters are thinking.
- Use description to bring the events to life.

Draft the Ending

The ending of your story should make readers feel satisfied that the conflict or problem has reached an appropriate conclusion.

Revising

Review your story and rework it until it communicates your ideas clearly.

Use the Six Traits of Good Writing checklist during the revising and editing stages, to help ensure that your work is as good as you can make it.

Six Traits of Good Writing Checklist

Ideas
✓ Do you have well-defined characters?

✓ Will the setting be clear to the reader?

✓ Is your plot well thought out?

✓ Do your details help establish your characters and setting?

✓ Did you pick an appropriate point of view?

Organization
✓ Does your introduction grab your reader's attention and introduce the main characters, the setting, and the main conflict?

✓ Does the middle of your story tell the events in chronological order?

✓ Does your story build on the conflict until the action reaches a climax?

✓ Did you use dialogue and description to bring your story to life?

✓ Does the ending show how the conflict was resolved?

Voice

✓ Does your interest in your subject come through in your writing?

✓ Is your personality reflected in your writing?

✓ Did you stick to one point of view throughout the story?

Word Choice

✓ Do the words you've chosen help readers "see" the characters and events?

✓ Did you use strong verbs that move the action forward appropriately?

✓ Did you use the active voice most of the time?

Sentence Fluency

✓ Are your sentences varied in length and structure?

✓ Do the sentences flow naturally?

Editing and Publishing

Polish your work before presenting it to the intended audience.

Editing When you are satisfied with your short story, read through one more time for errors in grammar, spelling, usage, and mechanics. This is the sixth of the traits of good writing. Use the proofreading symbols in Chapter 19 when you edit.

Editing Conventions Checklist

✓ Are your sentences free of errors in grammar and usage?

✓ Did you spell each word correctly?

✓ Did you use capital letters where needed?

✓ Did you punctuate sentences correctly?

✓ Did you indent each paragraph?

Publishing After you have read your edited version over several times, prepare a neat final copy that is either typed or in cursive writing to share with a classmate.

Writing a Scene for a Play

A **play** is a piece of writing intended to be performed on stage by actors. A play has many things in common with the short story—both use character, setting, and plot. However, a playwright uses dialogue and action alone to tell the story, without using narrative to explain the plot.

Along with the dialogue in a script, modern playwrights (people who write plays) provide information about how the characters should perform. This information is called **stage directions.** Playwrights have always supplied some information, such as when an actor leaves the stage or if there is a sound off stage. In the past, playwrights provided less information than writers typically provide today. William Shakespeare, a 16th-century English playwright, did not use many stage directions; he expected his actors to understand the characters well enough to interpret his words effectively.

The following scene is from one of Shakespeare's most famous plays, *Romeo and Juliet.* In this scene, Juliet, a girl from a wealthy family, anxiously asks her nurse for news of her fiancé, Romeo. (In Shakespeare's time, a nurse was like a nanny.) As you read the scene, imagine how you would say the dialogue. Does the language give you clues about the characters? What can you tell about the relationship between Juliet and her nurse from the way they speak to one another?

---

from *Romeo and Juliet*

JULIET   The clock struck nine when I did send the nurse;
In half an hour she promised to return.
Perchance she cannot meet him. That's not so.
O, she is lame! Love's heralds should be thoughts
which ten times faster glide than the sun's beams
Driving back shadows over low'ring hills.
Therefor do nimble-pinioned doves draw love,
And therefor hath the wind-swift Cupid wings.
Now is the sun upon the highmost hill
Of the day's journey, and from nine till twelve
Is three long hours; yet she is not come.
Had she affections and warm youthful blood,

She would be as swift in motion as a ball;
My words will bandy her to my sweet love,
And his to me.
But old folks, many feign as they were dead—
Unwieldy, slow, heavy and pale as lead.

[Enter Nurse and Peter.]

O God, she comes! O honey nurse, what news?
Hast thou met with him? Send thy man away.

NURSE   Peter stay at the gate. *[Exit Peter.]*

JULIET   Now, good sweet nurse—O Lord, why lookest thou sad?
Though news be sad, yet tell them merrily;
If good, thou shamest the music of sweet news
By plating it to me with such a sour face.

NURSE   I am aweary, give me
leave awhile. Fie, how my
bones ache. What a jaunce
have I had!

JULIET   I would thou hadst
my bones, and I thy news.
Nay, come, I pray thee speak.
Good, good nurse, speak.

NURSE   Jesu, what haste!
Can you not stay awhile?
Do you not see that I am out
of breath?

Juliet, John William Waterhouse

Choose a Conflict or Problem

Like stories, plays are based on conflict. A conflict may be between two or more people, as when Juliet tries to get her nurse to hurry and tell her about Romeo. A conflict may also exist within a single person, as when Juliet talks to herself before the nurse returns.

Sketch Your Characters

As in a story, the characters are usually the most important element of a play. In drama the characters are brought to life by actors—people who use gestures, facial expressions, and tones of voice to capture the essence of a particular character in a unique way.

Decide on a Setting

In a book or movie, the writer can create scenes that move from setting to setting. One scene might take place inside an apartment, and the next might be in the middle of a forest. In contrast, most plays have only a few scenes with different settings. Because of the difficulty of changing sets quickly and easily between scenes, an entire play might take place inside one room.

If the play you have in mind requires more than one location, you need to think about how this might be shown on stage. For example, you might use a wall with a door—one side of the door might represent the inside of a house, the other might represent the garden. Even the reactions of the characters can be used to establish a setting. For example, on a bare stage, an actor could say, "The fall colors of those trees remind me that winter is coming."

Use Dialogue

Dialogue is the medium through which the playwright shows the plot development, expresses the characters' emotions, and creates conflict. As in a story, the dialogue in a play should seem real. Each character should have his or her own way of speaking. In addition, the dialogue in plays needs to deliver information to the audience.

For example, we learn about Juliet's impatience when she says, "from nine till twelve is three long hours; yet she is not come." And we learn of the nurse's exasperation with Juliet when she replies, "what haste! Can you not stay awhile? Do you not see that I am out of breath?" The need to express information and characterization at the same time makes the dialogue in plays particularly rich in content.

Targeting the Six Traits: Sentence Fluency

Sentence fluency is particularly important in a play. There may be times when a character stumbles over his or her words to show confusion or surprise. On the whole, however, the dialogue in a play needs to flow easily and comfortably. Remember, an actor needs to be able to recite your speeches. Read your dialogue out loud and listen to the rhythm. Are your lines easy to deliver?

Dialogue should sound natural—but also better and smoother than natural speech. Watch a movie or TV show in which the characters talk a lot. Notice how the sentences flow. Look back at the scene from *Romeo and Juliet*. There is a great variety of sentence lengths, which helps create emotion and energy.

Use Stage Directions

Playwrights usually supply stage directions to suggest how the characters should speak and move. Stage directions are usually found in italic print. Some playwrights create lengthy, detailed directions that establish the appearance of characters and sets, tone of voice, movements, and lighting. Because the dialogue itself often conveys what the audience learns about the characters, some playwrights like to keep their stage directions brief.

Some stage directions are necessary, however. They express meaningful actions, such as one character pushing another. At the beginning of the play, there is usually a brief description of the set. When a new character appears, there is usually a brief physical description of the character, perhaps including how the character is dressed. **Props**—short for properties—are the physical objects important to a scene (for example, a table and chairs, a golf club, or a flower vase full of roses). Props are also mentioned in stage directions.

Writing a Poem

Poetry is a writing form that can express powerful feelings through sound, images, and other imaginative uses of language. Read this poem written by the American poet Walt Whitman.

When I Heard the Learn'd Astronomer

When I heard the learn'd astronomer,
When the proofs, the figures, were ranged in columns before me,
When I was shown the charts and diagrams, to add, divide, and
    measure them,
When I sitting heard the astronomer where he lectured with much
    applause in the lecture-room,
How soon unaccountable I became tired and sick,
Till rising and gliding out I wander'd off by myself,
In the mystical moist night-air, and from time to time,
Look'd up in perfect silence at the stars.

Find an Idea for a Poem

Poetry is the form of writing that depends most upon the emotions and thoughts of the writer. In choosing a subject for a poem, find something that moves you. One good way to discover the emotionally powerful ideas that are already within you is to make an Idea Chart like the one below. List general subject areas on the left side of the chart. Write down some specific examples on the right-hand side.

Idea Chart	
Event	getting an *A*; buying shoes; playing trumpet
Scene	an empty schoolyard at night; a crowded beach; a sail-boat skimming the waves
Sensation	the sound of a subway train; the taste of hot peppers; the sight of sunset

Use Sound Devices

The sound of language is extremely important in poetry. In fact, the full effect of a poem comes through only when it is read aloud. Not only can the sounds of the words be beautiful, interesting, or strange, but they can make interesting connections among ideas in the poem.

Poets use particular sound devices to achieve special effect. Try to use some of these devices when you write your poetry.

Sound Devices	
Alliteration	Repetition of a consonant sound or sounds at the beginning of a series of words **B**aa, **B**aa, **b**lack sheep
Consonance	Repetition of a consonant sound or sounds, used with different vowel sounds, usually in the middle or at the end of words the pa**tt**er of li**tt**le fee**t**
Assonance	Repetition of a vowel sound within words the b**ow**ling b**a**ll r**o**lled **o**ver and **o**ver
Onomatopoeia	Use of words whose sounds suggest their meaning hum, splash, whistle, hoot, murmur, fizz, zap
Repetition	Repetition of an entire word or phrase O **Captain!** my **captain! rise up** and hear the bells; **Rise up—for you** the flag is flung—**for you** the bugle trills —Walt Whitman, "Oh Captain! My Captain!"
Rhyme	Repetition of accented syllables with the same vowel and consonant sounds The woods are lovely, dark, and **deep**, But I have promises to **keep**, And miles to go before I **sleep** —Robert Frost, "Stopping by Woods on a Snowy Evening"

Use Rhyme

Many poems have a pattern, or **rhyme scheme,** that can be shown by letters.

Sally, will you come out to **play**?	a
Yes, my dearest **friend**.	b
I'll play with you till the sky turns **gray**	a
And the day has reached its **end**.	b

Notice that the rhyme pattern for the poem above is **abab.** The first line rhymes with the third, and the second line rhymes with the last.

Rhythm and Meter

Almost all poems have **rhythm**—a sense of flow produced by the rise and fall of accented and unaccented syllables. In many poems, the rhythm is a specific beat called a **meter.** The accented and unaccented syllables of metered poetry follow a regular, countable pattern like the beats in a piece of music. In the lines below, the accented syllables are marked with ´ and unaccented syllables are marked with ˘. Read the lines from William Blake's poem "The Tyger." Notice the strong, regular rhythm.

Tyger, tyger, burning bright,

In the forests of the night:

Targeting the Six Traits: Word Choice

Word choice is always important, but nowhere is it more vital than in poetry. Because fewer words are used, every word must do more work. In addition, the words must function in the meter you have selected. You may need to change a word that breaks up your meter. For example, "green" will have an entirely different impact on the meter than the phrase "emerald-hued."

Your words may also need to be selected with rhyme as part of the consideration. For example, you might need to use "golden" instead of "yellow," if you need to rhyme with "olden."

CHAPTER 29

Writing About Literature

QuickGuide

The Literary Essay **pages 313–320**	A **literary essay** is a formal written response to a piece of literature.
Prewriting **pages 320–326**	Part of prewriting is reading. Read the literary work carefully, and respond to it from both personal experience and literary knowledge.
Drafting **pages 327–328**	While drafting you may discover how you feel about a piece of writing.
Revising **pages 328–329**	Revise your essay for unity, coherence, and clarity.
Editing and Publishing **page 329**	Prepare your essay for readers by editing it for conventions.

The Literary Essay

A *literary essay* is a formal written response to a piece of literature.

Almost everybody has a response after seeing a movie, reading a book, or attending a concert. Works of literature are meant to have an effect. Sometimes the effect is a fizzle, and sometimes it's volcanic—powerful enough to change someone's life.

Writing about literature can help you connect with the literature. You can write freely about a poem, story, play, or novel to explore your responses to it. You can also use a more formal piece of writing, such as a literary essay, to share your understanding of a literary work with readers.

When you respond to a work of literature by writing about it, you can develop a greater appreciation for the craft of the writer. You can also enhance your own critical and imaginative abilities as a reader and writer. In this chapter you will learn and practice the skills you need to write about literature.

Develop Your Skills of Literary Analysis

A **literary analysis** presents an interpretation of a work of literature and supports that interpretation with appropriate details and quotations from the work. Writing about a literary work helps you digest and appreciate it. The elements—characters, setting, word choice, ideas, plot, problems, resolutions, rhyme scheme, rhythm, organization, theme, or whatever else makes up the piece of writing being analyzed—are examined, individually and together, to reach a conclusion about what the literature is saying. This process enables a reader to respond to a work of literature—to write a literary essay.

The form in which you write about a work of literature can range from the informal to the formal. An informal piece might take the form of quick notes jotted in your **journal**. Creating a carefully developed composition, on the other hand, requires not only more thought but also clear and concise writing.

Literary Genres

A **genre** is a form of literary expression, such as the short story, the novel, and the poem. While there is a great deal of variety within a genre, there are also some common characteristics of a literary form. These characteristic are among the elements you will analyze when you write a literary essay.

Characteristics of Literary Genres	
Short Story	A **short story** is a short work of narrative fiction that focuses on a single central conflict. The short story often occurs within a short period of time and involves few characters and settings.
Novel	A **novel** is a long work of narrative fiction with a plot that is unfolded by the actions, speech, and thoughts of the characters. A novel presents a central conflict and its resolution, but may also include one or more subplots and many minor characters.
Poem	A **poem** presents images through condensed, vivid language and word choices that emphasize sounds as well as meaning. Characteristics commonly include the use of meter, rhyme, and figurative language.
Play	A **play** is a work written for dramatic performance on the stage. Like a short story, a play usually revolves around a central conflict. The playwright relies on dialogue, stage sets, and action to present the story to the audience.

Responding to Literature

As a reader, you help create the meaning of a literary work. No work has a single, correct meaning. Instead, the meaning grows out of the relationship between the writer's words and each reader's response. That response comes from several sources.

Sources of a Reader's Response to Literature

- Reader's characteristics—such as age, sex, and personality
- Cultural or ethnic origins, attitudes, and customs
- Personal opinions, beliefs, and values
- Life experiences and general knowledge

- Knowledge of literature and literary genres
- Knowledge of the historical and cultural context of a work
- Reading and language skills

All of these sources combine to affect your response to anything you read. Who you are, where you live, and what your life has been like so far, for example, may enable you to identify with a character, situation, or feeling in a work. When you identify with characters, you put yourself in their shoes; you see what they see and feel what they feel. The more closely you can identify with characters, the more enjoyment and meaning you will usually find in reading and writing about a literary work.

Responding from Personal Experience One of the reasons you may enjoy reading and writing about a particular work is the pleasure you get from recalling your own past. A story, play, or poem will often trigger memories of your feelings and experiences. You use these memories to identify with characters.

In the process of identifying, you may recall times in your life when you were in similar situations. For example, you may remember a time when you were in conflict with others over behaviors that you felt were wrong. This type of memory may give the story a deeper meaning for you. Or you might be reading a story about a circus, and if you once had a fun experience at a circus, chances are those pleasant memories will be rekindled and color your reaction to the work.

The following strategies will help you explore your personal responses to a literary work.

Personal Response Strategies

1. In your journal, freewrite answers to the following questions:
   - Do you see yourself in the poem, story, novel, or play?
   - What experiences from your own life come to mind as you read this work?
   - Which character(s) do you identify with?
   - Are there characters that remind you of people you know?
   - How does the work make you feel? Why?
   - If you were a character in the work, would you have behaved differently?
2. Write a personal response statement. In this statement, explain what the work means to you.

3. In small discussion groups, share your reactions to the questions above. Feel free to adjust your reactions if your classmates suggest ideas that make sense to you. After the discussion write freely about how, if at all, your ideas about the work changed after talking with your classmates.

Responding from Literary Knowledge As a reader, you not only respond to each work on the basis of your past experience and background, but you also apply your knowledge of other stories, poems, or plays that you have read. Through reading, you develop a deeper understanding of the characteristics that distinguish each genre. This knowledge helps you interpret a work and appreciate a writer's skill. When you respond to literature on the basis of your literary knowledge, you analyze its **elements**.

The following chart describes some of the main elements of fiction, poetry, and drama. (Because drama has most of the same elements as other works of fiction, the elements listed under the Drama head on the next page show only how reading a dramatic work differs from reading other kinds of fiction.)

Elements of Literature	
Fiction	
Plot	the events in a story that lead to a climax (high point) and to a resolution of the central conflict
Conflict	the main problem in a story. A conflict can be **internal** (in a character's mind) or **external** (between a character and something outside, such as another character, events, nature, and so on)
Setting	the place and time in which a story occurs
Characters	the people in the story who advance the plot through their thoughts and actions
Dialogue	conversations among characters that reveal their personalities, actions, and motives
Tone	the writer's attitude toward his or her characters
Point of View	the "voice" telling the story—first person (*I*) or third person (*he, she,* or *they*)
Theme	the main idea or message of the story

Poetry	
Speaker	the "voice" of the poem that reveals the character the poet is assuming
Meter	the rhythm of stressed and unstressed syllables in a line of poetry
Rhyme Scheme	the pattern of rhymed sounds, usually at the ends of lines
Sound Devices	techniques for playing with sounds to create certain effects, such as **alliteration** and **onomatopoeia**
Figures of Speech	imaginative comparisons such as **similes** and **metaphors**
Shape	the way a poem looks on the printed page; may contribute to the underlying meaning of the poem
Theme	the overall feeling or underlying meaning of the poem
Drama	
Setting	the time and place of the action; lighting and stage sets, as described in the stage directions
Characters	people who participate in the action of the play
Plot	the story of the play divided into acts and scenes and developed through the characters' words and actions
Theme	the meaning of a play, revealed through the setting and the characters' words and actions

How Literary Elements Contribute to Meaning The
elements of each genre contribute to the meaning of a work. The following
list of questions can help you explore the meaning of a poem, a play, a short
story, or a novel.

Questions for Finding Meaning in Fiction

Plot

- What are the key events in the story?
- What is the impact of each key event in the development of the plot?
- How does each event affect the main characters?
- What details in the plot reveal the narrator's attitude toward the central conflict?
- What do the climax and the ending reveal about the theme?

Setting

- What are the most important details in the setting?
- What overall feeling does the setting convey?
- How do details of the setting help define the characters?
- What details of the setting are most important in the development of the plot?
- How do details relate to the theme?

Characters

- How do the characters relate to their setting?
- How does each character contribute to the development of the plot?
- How do the details of characterization reveal personalities?
- What does the dialogue reveal about each character's personality and motivation?

Theme

- What is the theme or message of the story?
- Which passages and details in the story best express the main theme?
- Does the title help you identify the theme?
- What else have you read that has a similar theme?

Questions for Finding Meaning in Poetry

- Who is the speaker (persona) in the poem?
- Can you describe the rhythm of the poem?
- How does that rhythm add to the feeling of the poem?
- How does the rhyme scheme affect the expression of ideas and feelings?
- What sounds do you hear in the poem?
- What images do the sound devices create in your mind?
- What images do the figures of speech create?
- What feelings do the images in the poem suggest?
- Does the shape of the poem relate to the subject, mood, or theme?
- What specific word choices are memorable and effective?
- What effect does the poem have on you?
- What meaning does the poem have for you?
- What feeling, theme, or message does the poem express?

Questions for Finding Meaning in Drama

- What details of setting and character do the stage directions emphasize?
- How do the stage directions contribute to the impact of the play?
- What are the key relationships among the characters?
- How do the relationships reveal the central conflict?
- What changes in the relationships help resolve the conflict?
- How does the dialogue advance the plot?
- What plot developments occur with each change of act and scene?
- What is the subject and theme of the play?
- What in the play has meaning for you?

Evaluating a Literary Work Analyzing the elements in a story or a poem helps you make judgments about the work. Because there are many different standards of evaluation, your personal judgment will not always agree with the judgments of literary critics, historians, biographers, teachers, and classmates. You may find it helpful to know the criteria by which any great work of literature, or classic, is usually judged. **Classics** are literary works that withstand the test of time and appeal to readers from generation to generation and from century to century. When you evaluate a literary work, consider the characteristics listed on the next page.

Some Characteristics of Great Literature

- Explores great themes in human nature and the human experience that many people can identify with—such as growing up, family life, personal struggles, love, or war
- Expresses universal values—such as truth or hope—to which people from many different backgrounds and cultures can relate
- Conveys a timeless message that remains true for many generations of readers
- Presents vivid impressions of characters, settings, and situations that many generations of readers can treasure

Not all works of literature, of course, are classics. You may discover a contemporary story about which you wish to write. Some of the characteristics listed above may apply to a new work you have read. Whether or not a literary work you are reading is regarded as a classic, you can apply other standards of evaluation. When you are making judgments about a work, ask yourself the following questions.

Questions for Evaluating Literature

- How inventive and original is the work?
- How vivid and believable are the characters, settings, dialogue, actions, and feelings portrayed?
- In fiction, how well structured is the plot?
- Is there a satisfying resolution of the central conflict?
- How strongly did you react to the work?
- Did you identify with a character, situation, or feeling?
- Did the work touch your memories and emotions?
- Did the work have meaning for you?
- What do you think you will remember about it in the future?

Prewriting

The prewriting stage is probably the most important stage in preparing a literary analysis. Of course, you start with careful reading of the literature about which you will write. Then the planning and choosing of a subject help prepare you for drafting.

Choose a Subject

You can now draw on your previous work to develop a subject for writing about literature. In some cases you will be assigned a subject. In other cases, however, you may be expected to choose a subject. The questions below may help.

Questions for Choosing a Subject

- What parts of the work puzzle me? What would I like to understand better?
- What parts of the work especially move me? Why do they have that effect?
- How do the characters in the work differ?
- What makes each character "tick"?
- What images or details made a strong impression on me? What do they contribute to the overall work?
- With which character do I identify, and why?
- What message does the work convey to me?

You will probably find the answers to some of these questions in the responses you have already made in your journal. Carefully review your written responses looking for aspects of the literary work that hold the most interest for you. It is also a good idea to reread the literary work to see if you have any fresh, new responses now that you have had a chance to become better acquainted with the work.

Synthesizing Personal and Literary Responses Another strategy for choosing a subject is to **synthesize,** or combine, your personal responses with responses based on your literary knowledge. If the central conflict of a story centers on honesty, you might be able to tell about a time when you were the beneficiary of a stranger's honesty. By synthesizing your personal and literary response, you can focus your thoughts for a literary analysis.

Limit Your Subject

A clearly focused, limited subject will keep your analysis from wandering aimlessly through a general discussion of the literary work. To test whether your subject is suitably limited, ask yourself whether you can express your subject in a phrase rather than a single word. If you can express your subject only in a single word, then ask yourself a series of questions. On the next page is an example of how you might limit a subject based on the fairy tale "Cinderella."

Too General	Who is the fairy godmother?
Probe Deeper	What do I want to say about the fairy godmother?
Better Question	Why does the fairy godmother help Cinderella?
Focused Question	What are the qualities of Cinderella that make the fairy godmother help her?

Develop Your Thesis

Like other kinds of compositions, writing about literature develops one main idea, or **thesis.** Your specific purpose in writing a literary analysis is to prove that your thesis is true. Your essay provides the evidence that will convince the reader that your interpretation is valid.

Your clearly focused subject is just a step away from your thesis. Pin down the exact statement you want to make about your subject. In the following example, notice how the thesis goes one step further and makes a complete statement about the subject.

Focused Question	What are the qualities of Cinderella that make the fairy godmother help her?
Thesis	In "Cinderella," the title character has qualities and virtues that make the fairy godmother want to help her—and make the reader glad she does.

To develop your thesis, cast your focused question into the form of a complete declarative sentence. Pin your subject down by saying something definite and concrete about it. Once again, you can ask yourself, "What about my subject?" until you have a statement that is expressed in a complete sentence.

Remember you can adjust and improve your thesis statement during drafting and revising. Even in its rough form, however, your thesis statement will help you develop the rest of your composition.

Targeting the Six Traits: **Ideas**

The idea you choose is where the potential success or failure of your composition lies. Of course, your fact gathering and writing still need to be good, but everything that follows is built on the foundation of a good idea. The idea you select needs to explore an idea, make a point, teach a lesson, share an insight, offer an interpretation, or answer a question about the literature.

In the "Cinderella" example, the thesis sets up an essay that can demonstrate the idea that, in traditional tales, virtue is rewarded, and we all like to see the "good guy" win. Another type of essay might explore why a character came to believe what he or she believes or how a rhyme scheme contributes to the meaning of a poem. The possible topics are almost limitless.

Just remember that there needs to be a point, message, or idea behind your essay, and it needs to be something that you find interesting and that you think will interest your audience.

Gather Evidence

After clearly expressing your composition's thesis, you can gather evidence to support it. In most cases the evidence you use will come out of the literary work itself.

When developing a list of supporting details for your analysis, skim the literary work from start to finish looking for details that support your thesis statement.

On sticky notes or note cards, jot down each detail as you come across it, and put a page reference beside it so you can return easily to that spot if you need to read it again. You may also want to make a brief note to yourself about why you think the detail is important.

The notes that follow show how a writer gathered evidence to support his thesis statement about Langston Hughes' short story "Thank You, M'am." (If you are not familiar with the story you can find it on pages 292–295.) Notice that the writer has identified details that support the thesis statement.

Thesis: In "Thank You, M'am," Langston Hughes uses mother-son imagery to stress the importance of Roger's encounter with Mrs. Jones.

After that the woman said, "Pick up my pocketbook, boy, and give it here." She still held him. But she bent down enough to permit him to stop and pick up her purse. Then she said, "Now ain't you ashamed of yourself?"

Firmly gripped by his shirt front, the boy said, "Yes'm."

1. Mrs Jones's statements show that she is not afraid of Roger; she treats him as a disappointed mother would treat a son; Roger reacts as a son might by agreeing that he is ashamed.

The woman said, "You ought to be my son. I would teach you right from wrong. Least I can do right now is to wash your face. Are you hungry?"

"No'm," said the being-dragged boy. "I just want you to turn me loose."

"Was I bothering you when I turned that corner?" asked the woman.

2. Mrs. Jones tells Roger plainly "You ought to be my son," says she would teach him right from wrong, and wants him to wash his face. Her actions and words show that she treats him as she would a misbehaving child, with firmness but with compassion and concern for his well being.

When they were finished eating she got up and said, "Now, here, take this ten dollars and buy yourself some blue suede shoes. And next time, do not make the mistake of latching onto my pocketbook nor nobody else's—because shoes come by devilish like that will burn your feet. I got to get my rest now. But I wish you would behave yourself, son, from here on in.

She led him down the hall to the front door and opened it. "Good night! Behave yourself, boy!" she said, looking out into the street.

The boy wanted to say something else other than, "Thank you, m'am," to Mrs. Luella Bates Washington Jones, but he couldn't do so as he turned at the barren stoop and looked back at the large woman in the door. He barely managed to say, "Thank you," before she shut the door. And he never saw her again.

> 3. Mrs. Jones feeds Roger and gives him money and calls him "son" and "boy." Roger reacts by wanting to "say something else." The language and actions work to reinforce the mother-son relationship.

Minnie, William H. Johnson, 1930

Create an Informal Outline

After you have collected supporting details, think carefully about the best order in which to present them. It might help to group your details into categories, or you might arrange them in the order in which they appear in the story.

The nature of your thesis will help determine the best order for your supporting details.

Ordering Evidence	
Kind of Thesis	**Type of Order**
Trace character or plot development	Chronological order
Show similarities and differences between characters or two different works	Comparison/contrast, using the AABB or the ABAB pattern of development
Analyze a character's motivation	Cause and effect
Explain the significance of the setting	Order of importance
Draw conclusions about the theme	Developmental order

After deciding on a logical order for your details, make a simple list, chart, or informal outline showing the order. The following is an informal outline for a composition about "Thank You, M'am."

Thesis statement: In "Thank You, M'am" mother-son imagery is used to describe the encounter between the characters.

1. Introduction

2. Body

> 1st detail: Mrs. Jones disciplines Roger, yet at same time tells him she will make sure he washes his face. Roger reacts by saying "Yes m'am" and saying he is ashamed of his behavior.

> 2nd detail: Mrs. Jones's own words ("you ought to be my son")

> 3rd detail: Mrs. Jones feeds Roger, calls him "son" and "boy," gives him money, tells him to "behave."

> 4th detail: Mrs. Jones's own words "you are going to remember Luella Bates Washington Jones."

> 5th detail: Roger wants to say something other than thank you; the encounter with Mrs. Jones has taken larger meaning for him.

3. Conclusion

Drafting

With your informal outline as a guide, drafting your literary essay is a matter of putting your ideas into flowing sentences. As you read the following essay, notice how each part of the composition works to clarify or support the main idea. Your first draft will no doubt be less polished than this finished analysis.

Title Suggests focus of essay	Thank You, Mom: Mother-Son Imagery in "Thank You, M'am"
Introduction Identifies title, author, and thesis	In the short story "Thank You, M'am," Langston Hughes uses mother-son imagery to stress the lasting importance of the encounter between the two main characters. When a young man named Roger attempts to steal a purse from Luella Bates Washington Jones, not only does the "frail and willow-wild" Roger not get Mrs. Jones's purse, but she publicly disciplines him. Mrs. Jones quickly turns the dynamics of their relationship from victim and criminal to angry mother and regretful son—teaching Roger a lesson he will never forget.
First Body Paragraph	From the moment Mrs. Jones and Roger encounter one another, Mrs. Jones is portrayed as a strong disciplinarian set on teaching a misbehaving child an important lesson. After Roger falls to the ground while trying to steal her purse, Mrs. Jones holds on to him, demanding, "Now ain't you ashamed of yourself?" She reacts to Roger as a disappointed mother would react to her own son: not only with firmness but also with compassion and concern for his well-being. And Roger reacts in kind, acknowledging that he is, in fact, ashamed of his behavior.
Second Body Paragraph	As the story develops, other words and actions work to reinforce the mother-son imagery established in the story's opening scene. Even as Mrs. Jones lectures Roger, she tells him she has a "great mind to wash [his] face for [him]." Later, Mrs. Jones says to Roger directly, "You ought to be my son. I would teach you right from wrong." She takes Roger to her home, fixes him dinner, and asks that he comb his hair so he will look "presentable."

	After they eat Mrs. Jones gives Roger money so that he can buy a pair of shoes, and, calling him "son," tells him to "behave . . . from here on in."
Third Body Paragraph	The relationship between Mrs. Jones and Roger is, of course, surprising. Although these two people have just met under negative circumstances, an immediate, positive relationship has formed. The importance of this relationship is shown by the mother-son imagery. No relationship is more important than the relationship between a parent and a child. Mrs. Jones tells Roger that his contact with her will "last awhile....When I get through with you, sir, you are going to remember Luella Bates Washington Jones." Roger's contact with Mrs. Jones is, in fact, relatively brief.
Conclusion Reinforces thesis statement	But when he sees Mrs. Jones's large body filling the door in the last scene of the story, and feels that he wants to say something—something other than just "thank you"—it is clear that the impact will be permanent.

Revising

After completing your first draft, set it aside for a day or two, so that you can return to it with a critical eye.

Using the Six Traits of Good Writing

Use the Six Traits of Good Writing checklist as you revise.

Ideas
✓ Does your thesis statement clearly state your point or idea?
✓ Does the body of your composition provide ample details and evidence from the work to support your thesis?
✓ Did you use quotations from the work to strengthen your points?

Organization

✓ Is the author and work you will discuss mentioned in your introduction?

✓ Does your introduction contain a clearly worded thesis statement?

✓ Does your conclusion reinforce your thesis statement?

Voice

✓ Does your interest in your subject come through in your writing?

✓ Do you sound as if you believe what you are saying about the literature?

Word Choice

✓ Did you use lively, specific words?

✓ Did you include transition words to guide readers to the conclusion?

Sentence Fluency

✓ Are your sentences varied in length and structure?

✓ Do the sentences flow naturally?

Editing and Publishing

Editing When you are satisfied that your composition clearly conveys your interpretation of the work you have chosen to write about, you can move on to polishing it and presenting it to readers. Read carefully for errors in grammar, spelling, punctuation, and capitalization.

Publishing Some ways of publishing your composition are listed below.

- Write to the National Council of Teachers of English (1111 Kenyon Road, Urbana, IL 61801), or visit the *Students* section of their Web site (http://www.ncte.org/) for information on places to publish student writing.

- If your school has a literary magazine, submit your paper to the editor.

- Hold a Reader's Roundtable. At this meeting each participant reads his or her literary analysis aloud. The rest of the group responds with questions and/or shares other interpretations of the same work.

CHAPTER

30

Writing Research Reports

QuickGuide

Report Writing page 331	**Report writing** is a skill that is useful throughout life.
Prewriting pages 332–340	After you pick your subject, the research begins.
Drafting pages 340–349	Organize the information you have gathered to create your first draft.
Revising and Editing pages 350–351	Consider the development and accuracy of your report.

Report Writing

Much of the information you read in newspapers, magazines, nonfiction books, and on the Internet, as well as much of what you watch on the news or in documentaries, is research reporting. Knowing how to gather interesting and accurate information and present it in a pleasing and meaningful way is an important skill that can help you in school, in business, and in life.

Research reports can fall into several of the categories described in previous chapters. Some reports are designed to persuade, while others will simply present information to the reader. A report can also focus on a literary work.

The Structure of a Report

A **research report** is a factual composition of three or more paragraphs that uses information from books, magazines, the Internet, and other sources. The three main parts of a report are the introduction, the body, and the conclusion. In addition, a report ends with a page that lists your sources of information.

Structure of a Report	
Introduction	• captures the reader's attention
	• provides any background information that the reader may need to know
	• contains your thesis statement
Body	• supports the main idea stated in the introduction
	• follows the order of your outline
	• includes specific information from your sources
Conclusion	• brings the report to a close
	• summarizes the main idea
	• includes a comment that shows the importance of your subject
Works Cited Page	• lists your sources of information
	• appears at the end of the report

Prewriting

Planning a research report requires some detective work to find the resources you need. You may want to visit the library at school or the public library. You may have books in your classroom, or you may search on the Internet. The right supplies will help you keep track of your information as you collect it. These supplies include a folder with pockets, index cards, paper clips, and rubber bands.

Choose and Limit a Subject

The following suggestions may be helpful when you begin searching for a good subject for your report.

Finding Ideas for Research Reports

- Using an online or traditional card catalog, find a section in the library or media center that interests you. Then walk up and down the stacks, looking for book titles that catch your eye.
- Skim through magazines and other periodicals, in print or online.
- Skim through any volume of an encyclopedia, in print or on CD-ROM.
- Ask your potential readers what they would like to know more about.
- Check the assignments in your other courses to see if any of them require a research paper.
- Do a keyword search and browse Web sites that interest you.
- Watch documentary television programs or videos that might contain report topics.

After you have listed five to ten possible subjects for a research paper, choose one for which the following statements hold true.

Choosing a Suitable Research Subject

- I would like to know more about this subject.
- My audience would like to know more about this subject.
- This subject is appropriate for my purpose; that is, I can explain it well in a short research report.
- I can find enough information on this subject by using resources in the library or media center and through other sources, such as interviewing or searching on the Internet.

One way to limit a subject is to break it down into its different aspects. Suppose, for example, that you decided to write a report on the film *The Wizard of Oz*. Since this subject is too broad for a short report, you could list the following elements as possible limited subjects.

Subject	*The Wizard of Oz*

Limited Subjects	the story	the cast
	the music	the special effects
	the sets	the costumes

Gather Information

A good way to plan your research is to jot down some questions that you want your report to answer. Suppose you had chosen the subject of special effects in *The Wizard of Oz*. Your research questions might appear as follows.

- How were the tornado, flying monkeys, melting witch, and other effects created?
- Which effects were easiest to make? Hardest? Most expensive?
- Who created the effects?
- How do effects in this film compare to special effects in today's movies?

The strategies below will help you find the answers to your questions.

Strategies for Gathering Information

- Begin by checking an encyclopedia. This will give you an overview of your subject.
- Use the card catalog to find more books on your subject.
- Check *The Readers' Guide to Periodical Literature* and a news index such as Facts on File for magazine and newspaper articles.
- Use an Internet search engine to search Web sites about your subject.
- Make a source card for each of your sources. Use a 3-by-5-inch index card to record the necessary information. For each source, record the proper information in the proper format. (See page 334.)
- Remember to always evaluate the quality of your sources. Watch for information that is outdated, biased, inaccurate, or unreliable.

The following examples show how you can prepare source cards so they contain all necessary information. Note that if you cannot find complete information for a source, include whatever information you have.

Encyclopedia

Hoffman, Frederick J. "L. Frank
Baum," World Book
Encyclopedia, 1998 ed.

Book

Scarfone, Jay and William Stillman.
The Wizardry of Oz: The
Artistry and Magic of The 1939
MGM Classic, New York: Applause
Books: 2004 (revised edition).

Magazine

Hall, Jane. "The Wizard of Oz,"
Good Housekeeping.
Aug. 1939: 40-1.

Web site

Dirks, Tim. Rev. of The Wizard
of Oz in "The 100 Best Movies
Ever Made." Movieline
Magazine. Dec. 1995. 9 Nov.
2001 <http://www.filmsite.org>.

Take Notes

After you have developed a list of print and online sources, gather the books and periodicals together along with printouts of any online source materials. Skim each source, looking for the information you need for your research report. With books, you will find the tables of contents and the indexes especially helpful in your search.

Once you have located the relevant portion of a reliable source, take a note card and, in the upper right-hand corner of the card, identify the source (see "source" labeled on sample card on the next page). On the note cards, summarize what you learn from your sources. When you **summarize,** you write information in a condensed, concise form, touching only on the main ideas. To record direct quotations, you copy the words exactly and enclose them in quotation marks. Always write the name of the person who made the statement you are quoting and the page number where you found the statement in the source.

The following excerpt is from a book on *The Wizard of Oz*. Read it, and then study the sample note card and guidelines on the following page.

Basically, what Gillespie [the special-effects director] knew about tornados in 1938 was that "we couldn't go to Kansas and wait for a tornado to come down and pick up a house." Everything beyond that was an experiment…. "I was a pilot for many years and had an airplane of my own. The wind sock they used in airports in the old days to show the direction of the wind has a shape a little bit like a tornado and the wind blows through it. I started from that. We cast a cone out of thin rubber. We were going to whirl the rubber cone and rotate it. But tornadoes are called twisters and the rubber cone didn't twist. So that was rather an expensive thing down the drain. We finally wound up by building a sort of giant wind sock out of muslin." The giant thirty-five foot muslin tornado was—technically—a miniature.

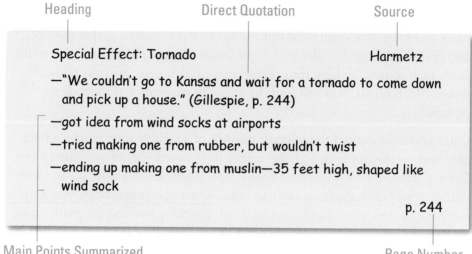

Special Effect: Tornado   Harmetz

—"We couldn't go to Kansas and wait for a tornado to come down and pick up a house." (Gillespie, p. 244)

—got idea from wind socks at airports

—tried making one from rubber, but wouldn't twist

—ending up making one from muslin—35 feet high, shaped like wind sock

p. 244

Taking Notes

- Write the title of your source in the upper right-hand corner of your index card.
- Identify the part of the subject being discussed with a heading in the upper left-hand corner.
- Begin a new card for each new part of your subject.
- Summarize main points in your own words.
- Record the page number(s) containing the information.
- Clip together all cards from the same source.

Develop a Thesis

After you have gathered information and have taken notes from many sources, your next step is to pull together your ideas and information to form a working thesis. A **working thesis** is a statement that expresses a possible main idea for your research paper. Keep in mind that you may change your working thesis as you continue to develop your research report.

To create your working thesis, think about what you have discovered about your subject. For example, while researching *The Wizard of Oz,* the researcher learned that the filmmakers used a 35-foot wind sock to create the impression of a tornado. From this and similar examples, the researcher decided that the creation of special effects in the movie would make a good working thesis.

| **Limited Subject** | special effects in *The Wizard of Oz* |
| **Working Thesis Statement** | Much wizardry went into creating the special effects in *The Wizard of Oz.* |

Organize Your Notes

Building a system of categories is the first step in organizing your notes into an outline. To create meaningful categories, review the information in your note cards, looking for ideas that are closely related. Then think of a category that would cover each group of related ideas. If some of your notes do not fit into any of the categories, clip them together separately for possible use in your introduction or conclusion. Once you have determined your categories, you can easily sort through your notes and clip together all the cards that belong in each category.

The writer of the research report on the special effects in *The Wizard of Oz* initially sorted the notes into the following categories.

Category 1   general information: cost, year of release, quotations from reviews, name of special-effects director

Category 2   the tornado

Category 3   the melting witch

Category 4   Glinda's arrival in the glass bubble

Category 5   the flying monkeys

Category 6   the horse-of-a-different-color

Category 7   the crystal ball

Category 8   the lifting and dropping of the house

After reviewing all of the information in the eight categories, the writer decided to combine some categories. For example, the special effects in categories 3, 4, 7, and 8 had something in common; they were all simple tricks that were easy to achieve.

The following revised organization consists of only four categories, which are broad enough to cover all the information.

Category 1   general information

Category 2   hardest effect to achieve—tornado

Category 3   simple tricks—house being picked up and dropped, crystal ball, glass bubble, melting witch

Category 4   tricks that should have been simple but proved difficult— flying monkeys, horse-of-a-different-color

Based on these categories, the writer chose to arrange the information in order of importance. For a memorable effect, the writer decided to place the more interesting information at both the beginning and the end of the report.

Make an Outline

The final step in the prewriting stage is to develop an outline as a guide to drafting. Your outline will be based on the order of categories that you have already created for your notes.

The following brief outline organizes the main ideas for the report on special effects in *The Wizard of Oz*.

Special Effects in *The Wizard of Oz*

I. Hardest special effect: tornado

II. Simple tricks

III. Simple tricks made difficult by unexpected problems

When you are satisfied with the organization of your main topics, study the information in your note cards again and add **subtopics** with capital letters under the Roman numerals. Then add **supporting points** with numbers under the subtopics and if necessary to cover all the facts you gathered, add **supporting details** with lowercase letters under each point. Use the outline on the next page as a model when you outline your research report.

Title The Wizardry of Oz

Subject Special effects in the film *The Wizard of Oz*

Main Topic	I. Hardest special effect: tornado
Subtopic	A. First attempt
Supporting Points	1. Cost and materials
	2. Why it failed
Subtopic	B. Attempt that succeeded
Supporting Points	1. Cost and materials
	2. How it moved
	3. Related effects
Supporting Details	a. Storm clouds
	b. Dark sky
Main Topic	II. Simple tricks
	A. House's lifting and dropping
	B. Crystal ball
	C. Glinda's glass bubble
Main Topic	III. Simple tricks made difficult by unexpected problems
	A. Flying monkeys
	1. Technique
	2. Problems
	B. Horse-of-a-different-color
	1. Technique
	2. Problems
	a. Objection of ASPCA
	b. Horses' licking off colored gelatin

Outline Form

- Include a title and a statement of the main idea.
- Use Roman numerals for main topics, capital letters for subtopics, numbers for supporting points, and lowercase letters for supporting details.
- Always include at least two subtopics under each main topic.
- Indent as shown in the model on the previous page.
- Capitalize the first word of each entry.

Drafting

After outlining your report, you are ready to write the first draft.

Copying Is Not Reporting

With the amount of information on the Internet, it is tempting—and very easy—to simply copy and paste your report, lifting paragraphs from resources and other reports and dropping them into your document. This is called *plagiarism*, and it is a crime. You are stealing someone else's words and saying they are your own. As a student, you will receive a lower or failing grade if you are caught. As an adult, you can receive heavy fines and other penalties.

Draft the Introduction

Think about your readers as you write the introduction. Remember that they have not done the research you have just completed. They will not even know what your report is about until they begin reading.

A strong introduction—

- captures the reader's attention.
- provides any necessary background information.
- contains your thesis statement.

Notice that a major objective of your introduction is to make your thesis clear to readers. As you draft your introduction, therefore, you should refine your working thesis into an appropriate thesis statement.

Guidelines for Refining a Thesis Statement

- Make the thesis statement specific enough so the main point of your research paper is clear to the readers.
- Make the thesis statement general enough to include all the main topics in your outline.

Draft the Body

As you draft the body of your research paper, think of ways to work your source materials smoothly into your own writing.

Tips for Using Sources

- Use a quotation to finish a sentence you have started.
- Quote a whole sentence. If you omit words from a quoted sentence, indicate the omission with an ellipsis (. . .).
- Quote only a few words as part of a sentence.
- Paraphrase information from a source. When you paraphrase, reword the text, in your own words. When you summarize on note cards, you are often paraphrasing.

Original Source	"To match the appearance of the swirling pools of water in the real Yellowstone, Alex used evaporated milk and white poster paint, mixed with water and poured into the set's pools. The pressure of the steam caused just the proper amount of movement in the pale white whirlpools and eddies duplicated in this enormous outdoor set."
Paraphrase	With condensed milk, paint, and steam, Alex made a model of a Yellowstone hot spring.

Draft the Conclusion

Use the strategies below to write a strong conclusion.

Writing a Conclusion
- Restate your main idea in new words.
- Add a comment that shows the importance of your subject or an insight about it.

Compose a Title

Once you have finished your first draft, give your report an interesting title. Your title should catch your reader's interest and indicate what your report is about.

Cite Your Sources

To **cite** means "to make reference to, to give recognition to, to quote." So when you cite your sources, you are making sure readers know the books and writers who supplied the information you used. This is where your source cards will come in handy.

In a research report, you cite the sources used for research for two reasons. First, it lends authority to your work. Your word on a new medical procedure would not hold much weight, but the word of the doctor who invented it would. Your paper gains authority from the authority of those whose work you studied.

The other reason is to give credit to those whose words and ideas you may be quoting. It is another protection against plagiarism. Whenever you use source materials, you must give credit to the authors—even if you only paraphrase. You have already taken steps to avoid plagiarism by taking notes in your own words and by recording the author, the page number, and the exact words of any quotation you plan to use. The chief methods of citing sources are parenthetical citations and footnotes or endnotes.

Parenthetical Citations Brief parenthetical citations are used within the text of a report to provide the reader with information about the source of the material you have borrowed. For complete information about each source, readers can refer to the Works Cited page at the end of your paper.

Formats of Parenthetical Citations	
Book by One Author	Give author's last name and a page reference: (Harmetz 244).
Book by Two or More Authors	Give both authors' names and a page reference: (Morella and Epstein 27).
Article	Give author's last name and a page reference: (Hall 40).
Article, Author Unnamed	Give shortened form of title of article and page reference: ("Fabulous Land of Oz" 24).
Article in a Reference Work, Author Unnamed	Give title (full or shortened) and page number, unless title is entered alphabetically in an encyclopedia: ("Special Effects").
Article from an Online Database with a Print Version	Give title (full or shortened) and page number if author is unnamed. ("Munchkins Aplenty" 16). If author is named, give name and date site was updated. (Worth 6/4/98).
Online Material That Has No Print Version	Give name of the author, if available, and page numbers. If no author is given, give title of material and page numbers. No page number is needed if reference is to a single page from an encyclopedia ("Baum, L. Frank").

Parenthetical citations should be placed as close to the words or ideas being credited as possible. To avoid interrupting the flow of the sentence, place them at the end of a phrase, a clause, or a sentence. If a parenthetical citation falls at the end of a sentence, place it before the period. If you are using quotation marks, the citation goes after the closing quotation mark but before the period.

Footnotes and Endnotes If your teacher directs you to use footnotes or endnotes instead of parenthetical citations, you will use a different form. For either footnotes or endnotes, you put a small numeral halfway above the line immediately after the borrowed material. This numeral is called a **superscript**. It sends readers to a note at the bottom, or foot, of the page.

The number is repeated in the footnote or endnote, so readers know which citation goes with which item in your report. Your teacher will tell you whether to number your notes consecutively throughout your report or to begin the first note on each page with the numeral 1. Endnotes are the same as footnotes, except that they are listed at the end of the paper.

Format of Footnotes and Endnotes	
General Reference Works	[1] Frederick J. Hoffman, "L. Frank Baum," World Book Encyclopedia, 1998 ed.
Books by One Author	[2] Aljean Harmetz, The Making of the Wizard of Oz (New York: Alfred A. Knopf, 1977) 244.
Books by Two or More Authors	[3] Joe Morella and Edward Epstein, Judy: The Films and Career of Judy Garland (New York: Citadel Press, 1969) 34.
Articles in Magazines	[4] Jane Hall, "The Wizard of Oz," Good Housekeeping, Aug. 1939: 137.
Articles in Newspapers	[5] Frank S. Nugent, "A Critic's Adventure in Wonderland," New York Times 5 Feb. 1939, sec. 9: 5.
Article from an Online Database with a Print Version	[6] Tim Dirks, review, "The Wizard of Oz" in "The 100 Best Movies Ever Made," Movieline Magazine Dec. 1995. 9 November 2001 <http://www.filmsite.org>.
Online Material with No Print Version	[7] "Frank L. Baum" Compton's Encyclopedia 13 Sept. 1999 <http://www.optonline.net/plweb-cgi>.

Whenever you cite a work that you previously cited in full, you can use a shortened form of footnote for all repeated references to that work.

First Reference	[2] Aljean Harmetz, The Making of the Wizard of Oz (New York: Alfred A. Knopf, 1977) 244.
Later Reference	[6] Harmetz 247.

Works Cited Page A **works cited page** is a listing of sources cited in a research report. List sources alphabetically by the author's last name or by the title if no author is given. The following examples show the correct form for works-cited entries. In each example note the order of information, the indentation, and the punctuation. When citing online sources, always give the date you accessed the site before the Web address.

Formats of Works Cited Page Entries	
General Reference Works	Hoffman, Frederick J. "L. Frank Baum." World Book Encyclopedia. 1998 ed.
Books by One Author	Harmetz, Aljean. The Making of the Wizard of Oz. New York: Alfred A. Knopf, 1977.
Books by Two or More Authors	Morella, Joe, and Edward Epstein. Judy: The Films and Career of Judy Garland. New York: Citadel Press, 1969.
Articles, Author Named	Hall, Jane. "The Wizard of Oz." Good Housekeeping Aug. 1939: 40–1+.
Articles, Author Unnamed	"The Fabulous Land of Oz: Dream World via Cyclonic Ride Recreated in Technicolor." Newsweek 21 Aug.1939: 23–4.
Articles in Newspapers	Nugent, Frank S. "A Critic's Adventure in Wonder-land." New York Times 5 Feb. 1939, sec. 9: 5.
Reviews	Rev. of The Wizard of Oz, dir. Victor Fleming. Senior Scholastic 18 Sept. 1939: 32–33.
Article from an Online Database with Print Version	Dirks, Tim. review, "The Wizard of Oz" in "The 100 Best Movies Ever Made." Movieline Magazine December, 1995. 15 Sept. 1999 <http://www.filmsite.org>.
Article from an Online Database That Has No Print Equivalent	"Baum, L. Frank" Compton's Encyclopedia Online. 1997. 13 Sept. 1999 <http://www.optonline.net/plweb-cgi>.

Sometimes your teacher may ask you to include a **works-consulted page**—often called a **bibliography**—on which you include all the works you consulted but did not necessarily cite in your research report. A works-consulted page or bibliography uses the same form as the works cited page.

The following passage is the final draft of the research report on special effects in *The Wizard of Oz*. As you read, notice how the writer incorporated source material, with quotations and paraphrases worked into the sentences and paragraphs. You will see that the writer chose parenthetical citations instead of using footnotes for citing sources. Notice also how the writer added transitions—such as *although, instead, first,* and *meanwhile*—to connect the parts of the outline into coherent paragraphs.

Title	The Wizardry of Oz
Introduction	<u>The Wizard of Oz</u> was released in 1939 after two years in production at a cost of three million dollars. One motion picture reviewer remarked that "the wizards of Hollywood have turned on their magic full force in the making of this film" (Rev. of <u>The Wizard of Oz</u> 32). The "magic" referred to the movie's special effects, such as the "realistically contrived cyclone" praised by <u>Newsweek</u> ("The Fabulous Land of Oz" 23). Other reviewers raved about the Good Witch's arriving in a golden bubble, the Wicked Witch's skywriting and her later melting away to nothing, the monkeys' flying, the trees' talking, and the horse's changing colors. The movie won an Oscar in 1939 for these creative effects by special-effects director A. Arnold (Buddy) Gillespie.
Thesis Statement	Although these effects looked effortlessly magical, much real wizardry went into creating the special effects in <u>The Wizard of Oz</u>.
First Body Paragraph (Roman numeral II in outline)	The most challenging effect was the twister. Gillespie knew he "couldn't go to Kansas and wait for a tornado to come down and pick up a house" (Harmetz 244). Instead he got an idea from watching cone-shaped wind socks used at airports to indicate wind direction. First he made a similar cone out of rubber at a cost of $8,000; but when the rubber did not twist properly,

he had to start over. After several experiments he built a 35-foot miniature cyclone out of muslin. He attached it to a machine that moved along a track and blew a dusty substance through the model twister to create a dust cloud. The $12,000 machine moved and twisted the muslin cone in a convincing way. Meanwhile a worker perched above the machine made huge clouds of yellowish-black smoke from carbon and sulfur. In front of the cameras, glass panels covered with gray cotton gave the tornado scene a dark, menacing quality on film and at the same time hid all the machinery (Harmetz 247–48).

Second Body Paragraph (Roman numeral III in outline)

A much simpler effect was the illusion that the cyclone lifted Dorothy's house off the ground. Gillespie's crew filmed a three-foot-high model of the house falling onto a floor painted like the sky. Then the film was simply run in reverse. The crystal ball in the witch's castle was also a simple trick. It was a big glass bowl placed over a small screen. Film shot earlier was projected onto the screen, giving the illusion of real images appearing in the crystal ball. Another simple effect was the glass bubble that transports Glinda into Munchkinland. Gillespie's crew first filmed a silver ball, "just like a Christmas tree ornament, only bigger," by moving the camera closer and closer, making the ball seem to grow larger (Harmetz 254–55). Then, by layering the films, they added the scene of Munchkinland and Billie Burke, the actress playing Glinda.

Third Body Paragraph (Roman numeral IV in outline)

Some effects that should have been simple became complicated because of unexpected problems. The flying monkeys, for example, were models suspended from a trolley, attached by 2,200 piano wires that moved them and their wings (McClelland 92). The wires kept breaking, however, which forced the crew to reshoot the scene repeatedly. Another problem was the horse-of-a-different-color, the creature that keeps changing hues. Six matching white horses were used for the trick photography—each colored a different shade.

When the crew proposed to paint the horses to achieve the desired effect, however, the American Society for the Prevention of Cruelty to Animals protested. As a creative solution, the horses were "painted" with colored gelatin, but the crew had to work fast because the horses kept licking it off (McClelland 92–3)!

Conclusion

While the cyclone was the most difficult effect, the melting disappearance of the Wicked Witch was the simplest of all. "As for how I melted," said Margaret Hamilton, the actress playing the witch, "I went down through the floor on an elevator . . . leaving some fizzling dry ice and my floor length costume" (McClelland 96–7). While the demise of the Wicked Witch was truly effortless, the other tricks and illusions in The Wizard of Oz required both effort and skill. Every bit of "magic," from the cyclone to the electric tail wagger in the Cowardly Lion's costume (Hall 137), was created by Gillespie's wizards of special effects. The enduring story and all of these technological achievements have made the film a frequent item on many lists of "best films" ever made (Dirks 1995).

Works Cited

"The Fabulous Land of Oz: Dream World via Cyclonic Ride Recreated in Technicolor." Newsweek 21 Aug. 1939: 23-4.

Dirks, Tim. review, "The Wizard of Oz" in "The 100 Best Movies Ever Made." Movieline Magazine, December, 1995. 8 November 2001 <http://www.filmsite.org>.

Hall, Jane. "The Wizard of Oz." Good Housekeeping Aug. 1939: 40-1+.

Harmetz, Aljean. The Making of the Wizard of Oz. New York: Alfred A. Knopf, 1977.

McClelland, Doug. Down the Yellow Brick Road: The Making of the Wizard of Oz. New York: Pyramid Books, 1976.

Rev. of The Wizard of Oz. dir. Victor Fleming. Senior Scholastic 18 Sept. 1939: 32-33.

Targeting the Six Traits: Sentence Fluency

You may feel that it is impossible to maintain sentence fluency when you have to include footnotes or parenthetical citations. It may take a little more effort, but it's definitely not impossible. If you review the model composition, you'll note that parenthetical citations are inserted where natural breaks occur, at the end of sentences or before commas.

To make it easier to focus on sentence fluency during your first draft, put a check mark or star where you think a citation is needed. Then write the actual citation in the margin. When you feel the sentences are flowing well, you can insert the citations at the place where they seem to work best—close to the information to which they refer, but at a natural pause, such as a comma or period.

Revising

Two qualities of a research paper are especially important—adequate development and accuracy.

Check for Adequate Development As you read over your draft, check the development of your main ideas. Did you use sufficient supporting details to back up your thesis? Have you adequately covered all the main points on your outline? Have you consulted enough sources to write authoritatively about your subject? If your answer to any of these questions is "no," consider doing additional research to improve the content of your report.

Check for Accuracy Check for accuracy in your use of sources by examining all the quotations in your report. Have you accurately represented each source? Have you quoted any source out of context, thus distorting the author's real meaning? Have you used enough sources so that you are not relying too heavily on one viewpoint? The more accurate and balanced your report is, the greater will be its power to explain or inform.

Get a Second Opinion A second opinion is valuable when you are preparing the final draft of your research report. If possible, ask a reader to review and critique your work. Ask your reviewer to summarize in his or her own words the main idea of your report and to point out any words, sentences, or paragraphs that seem unclear. Then, as you revise, take into account the reader's specific comments and suggestions. If your reviewer cannot summarize your main idea, you may need to make your focus or thesis clearer.

Use the Six Traits of Good Writing

Use the Six Traits of Good Writing checklist during the revision and editing stages, to help ensure that your work is as good as you can make it.

Ideas
✓ Is your thesis clearly stated, and does it appear in your introduction?

✓ Does the body support your main points with specific information and examples?

✓ Is your information accurate and balanced?

Organization

✓ Does your introduction grab your reader's attention and make him or her want to keep reading?

✓ Are transitions clear and smooth?

✓ Does your paper have a beginning, a middle, and a conclusion?

✓ Did you include a works-cited page?

Voice

✓ Does your own style come through?

✓ Do you sound as though you are speaking with an authoritative voice?

Word Choice

✓ Have you chosen words that help convey the topic in your own words?

✓ Did you use strong verbs and vivid adjectives?

Sentence Fluency

✓ Did you vary the length and beginnings of your sentences?

✓ Did you avoid rambling sentences?

✓ Are your sentences free of repetition and empty expressions?

Editing and Publishing

Editing You are now ready to find and correct any errors in your work. The Editing Conventions Checklist can remind you what to look for.

Editing Conventions Checklist

✓ Are your sentences free of errors in grammar and usage?

✓ Did you spell and capitalize each word correctly?

✓ Did you punctuate sentences correctly?

✓ Did you indent each paragraph?

Publishing During the process of writing a research report, the writer learns about his or her subject in order to pass the information on to an interested reader. When deciding how to publish a research report, keep in mind the subject and who might benefit from reading about it.

Written Communication

QuickGuide

The Purpose of Written Communication page 353	Writing is still one of the most common ways to connect with others.
Writing Informal Letters pages 353–356	Use your writing skills to craft informal letters and notes.
Writing Business Letters pages 357–364	Knowing how to write business letters can help you place an order, communicate with a company, get into a program, get a job, or do your job.
Writing E-mail pages 365–369	E-mail messages: They're easy, they're fast, and they can benefit from a little thought and care.

The Purpose of Written Communication

Written communication takes many forms, from a handwritten note your parents might send with you to school to a formal letter sent to a major corporation asking them to sponsor a project. In spite of the many forms of instant communication such as cell phones and text messaging, letter writing is still one of the most common ways to communicate.

With written correspondence, whether in the form of a letter or an E-mail message, you can take time to compose your thoughts and get the language just right before you send it. Time for reflection is not always possible during phone calls and other forms of instant communication.

Written communication is also more permanent than other forms. You can save letters and E-mail messages for reference. Unless you tape your phone conversations, the only records of a phone call are your recollections and an entry on your phone bill.

There are also situations when written correspondence is the only acceptable form of communication. You may be applying for a job or filing a complaint, both situations in which written communication is the correct form to use.

As with all other forms of writing, the point of written communication is to get your ideas and information across. The formats for written communication are different from those for essays, but the skills covered in this text still apply. You need to develop a voice appropriate for your audience, topic, and purpose, and you need to pay attention to spelling and grammar conventions. Of course, the degree to which you need to craft your letters varies with the purpose, but remember, even an informal E-mail needs to be understood.

Writing Informal Letters

An **informal letter** is one that you write to a friend or relative. Informal letters can be handwritten, typed, or produced on your computer. If you use a typewriter or word processor, you still need to sign the letter yourself.

A Girl Writing, Henriette Browne, 19th century

Parts of an Informal Letter	
Heading	This includes your full address with ZIP code. Use the full name of your state or the abbreviation. Always include the date after your address. Follow the rules of capitalization and comma use.
Salutation	This is your personal greeting. Always capitalize the first word and all proper nouns. Use a comma after the salutation. Dear Aunt Sally, Dear Dad,
Body	This is your message. Remember to indent each paragraph.
Closing	The closing is followed by a comma. Capitalize the first word only. Your nephew, Love always,
Signature	Sign your name below the closing.

With close friends to whom you write often, you may be able to leave off the address, but always date your letters. Knowing when a letter was sent is one of the things people want to know when they reread it later.

Informal Letter Form The following model shows the correct form for an informal letter.

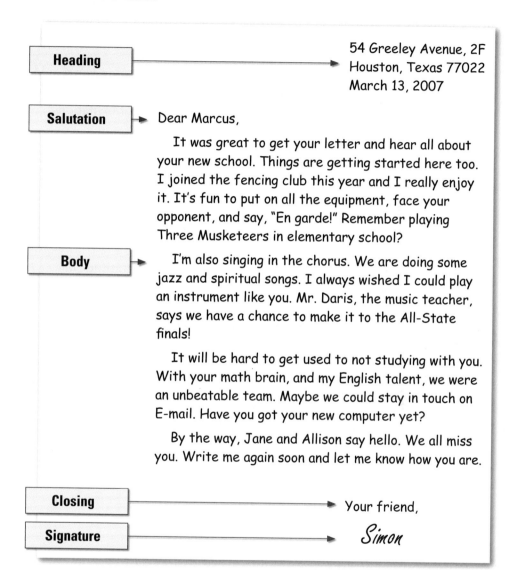

Heading → 54 Greeley Avenue, 2F
Houston, Texas 77022
March 13, 2007

Salutation → Dear Marcus,

It was great to get your letter and hear all about your new school. Things are getting started here too. I joined the fencing club this year and I really enjoy it. It's fun to put on all the equipment, face your opponent, and say, "En garde!" Remember playing Three Musketeers in elementary school?

Body → I'm also singing in the chorus. We are doing some jazz and spiritual songs. I always wished I could play an instrument like you. Mr. Daris, the music teacher, says we have a chance to make it to the All-State finals!

It will be hard to get used to not studying with you. With your math brain, and my English talent, we were an unbeatable team. Maybe we could stay in touch on E-mail. Have you got your new computer yet?

By the way, Jane and Allison say hello. We all miss you. Write me again soon and let me know how you are.

Closing → Your friend,

Signature → Simon

Social Letters

A **social letter** usually has a specific purpose, such as to thank someone, to invite someone to an event, or to inform someone that you cannot accept an invitation. Social letters use the same form as informal letters.

Invitations An invitation informs someone about an occasion you would like that person to attend. It includes the time and place and any other details your guests might need to know. You can use smaller paper for invitations.

Invitations often include R.S.V.P. at the end. This is an abbreviation for the French phrase *respondez, s'il vous plait,* which means "respond, if you please." It says that the person who is inviting you would like to know if you will be attending or not. Respond as soon as you know one way or the other. That way the person planning the event can get an idea of the number of people attending.

Thank-you Letters A thank-you letter expresses your gratitude or appreciation. You can be saying thank you for a gift, a kindness, or anything else you appreciate. You don't need to write a note for every thoughtful gesture or act of service, but in most cases, if a gift is given, you should write a thank-you letter or note.

A thank-you note, written inside a special card that says "thank you," can exclude the address but should still include the date and all the other elements of a letter. Thank-you cards are most common when many notes need to be sent out at once, such as after a graduation party where many gifts were received.

Letters of Regret A letter of regret informs someone that you will be unable to attend an event to which you have been invited. In it you explain why you will be unable to attend, and you express your regret. Invitations that include an R.S.V.P. should be responded to in a timely fashion. This will help the person planning the event know how many people to expect.

Writing Business Letters

A **business letter** is a formal letter that requires action on the part of the receiver. Business letters you receive will ask you to do something, business letters you write will ask the receiver to do something.

You may write a letter requesting information about some research that you are doing. You may order merchandise from a catalog, asking the receiver to send the desired items. You may write a letter requesting a form that you need to fill out in order to register for a service. You might write to a company asking them to sponsor your team. To ensure you get the results you want, keep your letter brief and state your business clearly.

Things to Remember When Writing a Business Letter

- Use white stationery when you write a business letter, preferably 8½ by 11 inches.
- Whenever possible, type or word process your business letter.
- Leave margins at least 1 inch wide on all sides.
- Be sure to keep a copy of every business letter you send. You can keep an electronic copy on your computer, but you should also keep a hard copy.

Because business letters are formal and often important, you will want to go through more of the steps of the writing process, including producing a draft, to make certain you are including all the necessary information, using an appropriate voice and concise words, and organizing your information in a way that will be clear to the person who receives the letter.

There are many styles for writing business letters. The **block style** puts each part of the letter at the left margin of the page. A blank line is left between each paragraph in the body of the letter. The paragraphs are not indented.

In the **modified block style,** the heading, closing, and signature are on the right. The inside address, salutation, and body all start at the left margin. Paragraphs are indented.

Business Letter Form

Business letters have six main parts, one part more than friendly letters. This extra part is called the inside address. The inside address includes all the information about the receiver that you will put on the envelope.

Parts of a Business Letter	
Heading	The heading is the same as the heading of a friendly letter. Include your full address and the date. Follow the rules for capitalizing proper nouns and using commas.
Inside Address	Start two to four lines below the heading. Write the name of the person who will receive the letter, if you know it. Use Mr., Ms., Mrs., Dr., and so on, before the name. If the person has a title, like General Manager, write it on the next line. Then write the receiver's address.
Salutation	Start the salutation, or greeting, two lines below the inside address. In a business letter, use a colon after the salutation. Dear Mrs. Walters: Dear Sir or Madam:
Body	Two lines below the salutation, begin the body or message of the letter. Skip a line between paragraphs and indent each new paragraph.
Closing	In a business letter, use a formal closing. Start two or three lines below the body. Line up the closing with the left-hand edge of the heading. Capitalize the first word only and use a comma. Sincerely, Sincerely yours,
Signature	In the signature of a business letter, your name appears twice. First type or print your name four or five lines below the closing. Then sign your name in the space between the closing and your typed name. Do not use Mr. or Ms. to refer to yourself.

When you are writing a business letter, always make sure it is clearly written, has a neat appearance, and follows the correct form. The sample on the next page uses the modified block form.

Heading

1411 Vista Drive
Oakland, CA 94611
July 16, 2007

Inside Address

Customer Service Department
Sports Barganza, Inc.
352 Rosemont Avenue
Olympia, WA 98502

Salutation

Dear Sir or Madam:

Body

I received four baseballs that I ordered from your company. Three of them are fine. The fourth one, however, is defective. Some of the stitching has come undone.

I am returning the defective ball, which I would like you to replace. I would appreciate it if you would send a new one as soon as possible. Also, I think you should reimburse me for the shipping charge to send the ball back. It cost me $2.47.

Closing

Yours truly,

Signature

Robert Tessler

Robert Tessler

Types of Business Letters

Letters of Request When writing a letter of request, be as specific as possible about the information you want and state your request politely. "Please" and "thank you" are essential. Notice how the form of a business letter is used to request information.

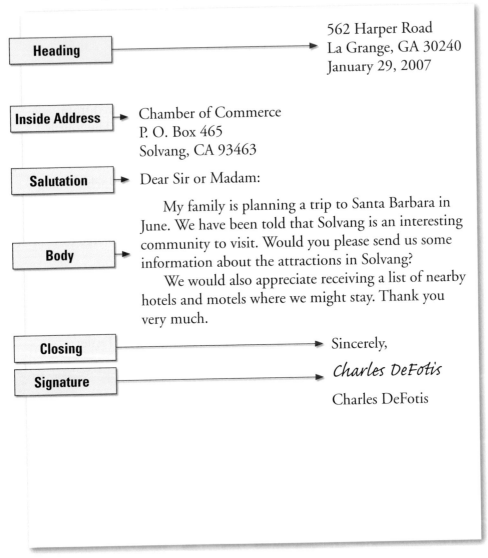

Heading

562 Harper Road
La Grange, GA 30240
January 29, 2007

Inside Address

Chamber of Commerce
P. O. Box 465
Solvang, CA 93463

Salutation

Dear Sir or Madam:

Body

My family is planning a trip to Santa Barbara in June. We have been told that Solvang is an interesting community to visit. Would you please send us some information about the attractions in Solvang?

We would also appreciate receiving a list of nearby hotels and motels where we might stay. Thank you very much.

Closing

Sincerely,

Signature

Charles DeFotis

Charles DeFotis

Letters of Complaint If you have a complaint about a product, express yourself courteously in a letter to the company. The following letter uses a polite but firm tone, which is appropriate for a letter of complaint. The sample letter below is in the block form.

313 Lavender Way
Millville, PA 17846
September 30, 2007

Subscription Department
Stars and Sky Magazine
36 Parkway Drive
Evanston, IL 60201

Dear Sir or Madam:

On July 17, I mailed you an order form and a check for $19.95 for a one-year subscription to your magazine. Two weeks later I received a card indicating that my first issue would arrive by September 1. My check was cashed on July 21. So far I have not received a magazine.

Please look into this and let me know what is being done to resolve this problem.

Thank you for your cooperation.

Very truly yours,

Michael Chin

Michael Chin

Letters of Application When you want to apply for something—a special art program, summer music camp, or a job—you need to write a letter of application.

459 West Avenue
Glenview, IL 60025
March 30, 2007

Dr. Allan Clegger
Biology Department
University of Chicago
14 Academic Way
Chicago, IL 60226

Dear Dr. Clegger:

My biology teacher, Mr. James Hoyt, whom I believe you know, has recommended that I apply for the summer program you offer to students who have shown promise in the sciences. I feel that I am qualified for this program, and I would like to apply for the session that will begin this coming June.

I have maintained a 4.0 grade point average during my first two years at Washburne Middle School. I have created presentations for science fairs for the last four years, and I placed second in the state last year.

As you can see, I am very interested in science. I think my science fair success and my grade point average both show that I am qualified for your program. Mr. Hoyt has said that he will notify you with his own comments on why I should be in this program.

I would be happy to come in for an interview. You can contact me at 222-555-1212. Thank you for considering my application.

Very truly yours,

Claire Johnson

Claire Johnson

Envelopes

The model below shows the correct form for an envelope. Print or type your own name and address in the upper left-hand corner. The receiver's address is the same as the inside address in the letter. It is centered on the envelope. Use the abbreviation for the state and remember to include the zip code.

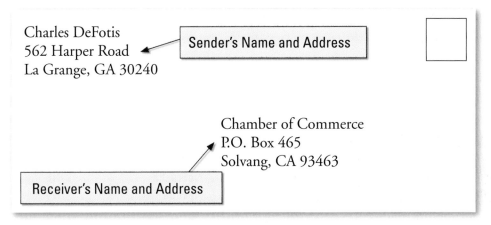

The way you fold your letter depends on the size of your envelope. If you use envelopes that are as wide as your stationery, fold the letter in thirds as shown in the diagram below.

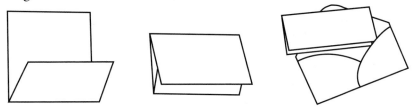

Commas and Capitalization in Letters

Commas When you write the date in the heading of a letter, use a comma to separate the month and day from the year.

March 11, 2007

Always use commas to separate parts of an address on the same line (the city from the state, for example). Do not use a comma to separate the state from the ZIP code.

455 Wilmington Drive, Apartment 2-C
Bozeman, MT 59715

Capitalization Capitalize the names of all streets, cities, states, and months.

> 2119 Spring Street
> Skokie, IL 60025
> October 24, 2007

Capitalize the first word of your salutation, as well as all names and titles.

> Dear Terry,   Dear Mr. Saddlebrook:

Capitalize the first word only of the closing, and capitalize your name.

> Sincerely yours,   Shelley Garfield

State Postal Abbreviations

Alabama	AL	Montana	MT
Alaska	AK	Nebraska	NE
Arizona	AZ	Nevada	NV
Arkansas	AR	New Hampshire	NH
California	CA	New Jersey	NJ
Colorado	CO	New Mexico	NM
Connecticut	CT	New York	NY
Delaware	DE	North Carolina	NC
District of Columbia	DC	North Dakota	ND
Florida	FL	Ohio	OH
Georgia	GA	Oklahoma	OK
Hawaii	HI	Oregon	OR
Idaho	ID	Pennsylvania	PA
Illinois	IL	Puerto Rico	PR
Indiana	IN	Rhode Island	RI
Iowa	IA	South Carolina	SC
Kansas	KS	South Dakota	SD
Kentucky	KY	Tennessee	TN
Louisiana	LA	Texas	TX
Maine	ME	Utah	UT
Maryland	MD	Vermont	VT
Massachusetts	MA	Virginia	VA
Michigan	MI	Washington	WA
Minnesota	MN	West Virginia	WV
Mississippi	MS	Wisconsin	WI
Missouri	MO	Wyoming	WY

Writing E-mail

E-mail—short for Electronic Mail—is the most commonly used feature of the Internet. E-mail can be a great way to send a note, ask a question, check plans, or send files. It is also a useful way of gathering information.

Each E-mail program has a slightly different format. But the main features of all E-mail programs are the same.

Once you open your E-mail program, click on the button that says Compose, Compose Mail, New, or New Message. This will open a new, blank E-mail form similar to the one pictured below. Next, fill in the blanks.

To: Type the recipient's E-mail address here.

Cc: Cc stands for carbon copy (also known as courtesy copy). Type additional E-mail addresses in this area to send a copy of the message to other people.

Bcc stands for blind courtesy copy. By typing one or more E-mail addresses here, you can send a copy of the message to others without the original recipient knowing that other people have received the same message.

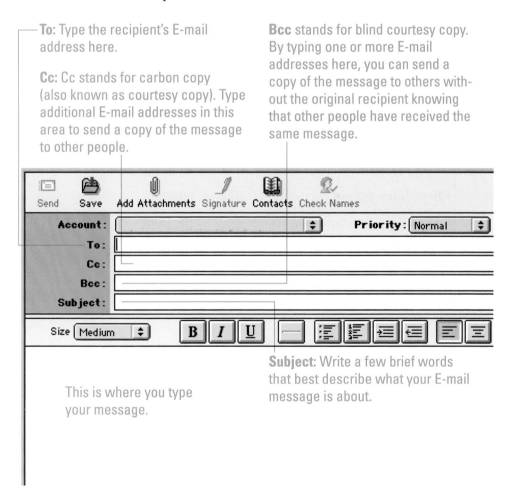

This is where you type your message.

Subject: Write a few brief words that best describe what your E-mail message is about.

Say It with Style

Like regular letters, E-mail can assume different tones and styles. Informal E-mails to close friends can be light and brief. In the case of more formal messages keep the following guidelines in mind.

- Make sure your message is clear and concise.
- Use proper grammar and punctuation.
- Check your spelling. (Some E-mail programs have their own spell-check function.)
- Double-check the person's E-mail address to be sure you've typed it correctly.

Internet Shorthand E-mail and other communication formats such as Instant Messaging are designed for quick communication. To keep pace, users have developed a shorthand that helps them write their messages even faster. Here are a few commonly used abbreviations.

Common Messaging Abbreviations			
BRB	be right back	J/K	just kidding
BTW	by the way	LOL	laughing out loud
F2F	face-to-face	L8R	later
FYI	for your information	OIC	Oh, I see
HAND	Have a nice day	ROFL	rolling on the floor laughing
IMHO	in my humble opinion	TTYL	talk to you later
IOW	in other words	WU	What's up?

Emoticons When conversing in person, you can usually tell when a friend is joking around with you. You can hear in his or her voice. This is not the case with written communication. You might type something in a message that is meant as a joke. The receiver, on the other hand, may misinterpret your "voice" and get upset. Using **emoticons**—faces turned sideways made out of keyboard symbols—can help solve this problem. When you are joking, or sad, or kidding, you can add the appropriate symbol to communicate your tone.

Emoticons	
:-) happy	:-(sad
:-D laughing	:`-(crying
;-) winking	:-} smirking
:-O shocked	:-/ skeptical
:-# my lips are sealed	:<> bored

You can also add static or animated **smiley face emoticons** to your E-mail and instant messages. There are many Web sites that let you download these for free.

Attachments An **attachment** is a file that you attach to an E-mail message. You can attach text documents, photos, illustrations—even sound and video files.

Follow Up Just because you have sent a message, don't automatically assume that the other person has received it. The person you sent your E-mail to might be away from his or her computer or may not check messages regularly. Also, the Internet is not perfect. From time to time, servers go down or other "hiccups" in electronic transmissions can occur, leaving your message stranded somewhere in cyberspace. If you don't get a reply in a reasonable amount of time, either resend your original E-mail message or call the person and let him or her know that your message is waiting.

Responding to E-mail When someone sends you an E-mail message, you have several options, which are listed in the chart on the next page.

Responding to E-mail	
Reply	Click Reply, and you can automatically send a new message without having to retype the person's E-mail address. (Be sure you keep a copy of the sender's E-mail address in your Address Book for future use.)
Reply to All	Most E-mail programs have a "Reply All" or "Reply to Everyone" option, which sends the reply to every person copied on the original E-mail. Only use this if you really want your response to go to everyone.
Forward	Suppose you receive a message that you would like to share with someone else. Click Forward, and you can send a copy of the message, along with a few of your own comments, to another person.
Print	In some instances, you may need to have a paper copy of the E-mail message. For example, if someone E-mails you directions to a party, click Print to make a hard copy of the instructions.
Store	Do you want to keep a message to refer to later? Some E-mail programs allow you to create folders to organize stored messages.
Delete	You can discard a message you no longer need just by clicking Delete. It's a good idea to throw messages away regularly to keep them from accumulating in your mailbox.

If there are buttons you don't recognize, or if the buttons do not all carry the labels given above, look on the menu bar for the "Help" option for your E-mail program. This will help you learn more about the specifics of the program you are using.

Manners on the Internet

As in any social setting, there are a few guidelines to follow when you are talking to people online—whether it's through E-mail, in a chat room, or in a newsgroup. This conduct is called **netiquette,** short for Internet etiquette. The following suggestions will help you avoid conflicts in cyberspace.

E-mail and Chat

- Never use harsh or insulting language. This is called *flaming* and is considered rude. A continuing argument in which insulting or unkind words are swapped back and forth is called a *flamewar.* Avoid this situation. (On many blogs or chat groups, you can be blocked or kicked off if you are unpleasant. So it's not just about being nice, it's also about staying connected.)
- Type your messages using both uppercase and lowercase letters. WRITING IN ALL CAPITAL LETTERS IS DIFFICULT TO READ AND IS REFERRED TO AS "SHOUTING."
- Respect other people's ideas and work. Don't forward a message or attach documents written by someone else without first asking the author's permission.
- Don't send spam. *Spamming* refers to sending messages to entire lists of people in your address book, on mailing lists, or in newsgroups for the purpose of selling something.
- Respect other people's privacy. The Internet is an enormous public forum, so be careful what you write and post. Hundreds or even thousands of people might see it. Don't use the Internet to spread rumors or gossip.

A Word of Warning Remember that E-mail is not secure. Do not put credit card numbers or your Social Security number in an E-mail. This data can be intercepted, and it is an easy way for thieves to gather this information from you.

Be careful when opening E-mail attachments. Attachments can contain programs called viruses or worms that may damage your computer or intercept and forward vital information such as credit card numbers. Be sure you know the origin of an E-mail attachment before you open it.

Critical Thinking

QuickGuide

Thinking Skills pages 371–377	Use the following **basic thinking skills** when reading, writing, and speaking: recalling, classifying, comparing, fact/opinion, inferring, generalizing, problem-solving, analyzing, summarizing, and evaluating
Propaganda pages 378–379	Watch for **propaganda techniques** designed to mislead: bandwagon, testimonial, loaded words, snob appeal, and appeal to fear.

Thinking Skills

Critical thinking refers to the mental discipline of analyzing and evaluating what is read, seen, and heard. The pages that follow illustrate the range of thinking skills beginning with the most basic and moving to the more complex and abstract.

Recalling

Recalling simply means remembering things. The challenge is to tap into this information. For instance, concentrate on an experience you have had. Perhaps you recall a family reunion. Use a chart like the one below to help you recall the details. Next to each heading, list all the details you can remember.

Experience: Visit to Mammoth Cave	
Sights	Aunt Susan and Mom hugging, five families in canoes
Sounds	Uncle Terry playing the guitar, singing around the campfire
Touch	feel of mud in lake between my toes
Smells	microwave popcorn while playing card games
Reactions	loved playing games until late at night; sad to say good-bye

Classifying

Classifying is a process of grouping items into classes, or categories. The following chart, for example, classifies various games and party activities.

Board Games	Card Games	Party Activities
Apples to Apples	hearts	Twister
chess	rummy	capture the flag
checkers	euchre	croquet
Monopoly	Uno	

While classifying, you may add categories as needed. In the above chart, for example, you could add the category "Word Games" to classify charades, crossword puzzles, and Pictionary.

Comparing

When you **compare,** you think of similarities between people, places, things, or even ideas. One effective way to compare is to create a simile or metaphor. For example, if you compared the human brain to a computer, you would find several similarities. Both a brain and a computer process information. They both have extensive memories, and they both can classify related pieces of information into groups.

Effective similes and metaphors use creative comparisons that allow people to see things in new and different ways.

> His eyes are **like** lasers. (simile)

> The moon **is** a flower blooming in the garden of the stars. (metaphor)

For more about similes and metaphors see Chapter 25.

Distinguishing Facts from Opinions

A **fact** is a statement that can be proved. An **opinion** is a judgment that cannot be proved. One way to test whether a statement is factual is to look for confirmation of it within your own experience. You can, for example, test the following statement against your own experience. You know that balloons full of helium float up.

> **Fact**   Helium is lighter than the air around us.

Some statements cannot be verified by your own observation and experience. Consider the following sentence.

> **Fact**   Helium was discovered by Sir William Ramsay in 1895.

Since you were not part of the discovery of helium, you cannot use your own experience to verify this statement. You can, however, consult a reference source to check the validity of the statement. Consulting reliable authorities is the second way to verify facts.

Unlike fact, **opinions** can never be proved. They are judgments, interpretations, predictions, or preferences that vary from person to person. Some opinions, however, are more sound than others. In any discussion or persuasive essay about important issues, the soundest opinions are those that can be supported by convincing factual evidence.

Supported Opinion	Students should get plenty of rest the night before a big test. (Supporting Fact: Many test-taking experts suggest that test takers get plenty of rest before an important test.)
Unsupported Opinion	Tacos taste better than pizza. (No facts are available to back up this statement.)

Learn to recognize opinions in what you read and write, and check every opinion for facts that back it up. The following words are often used in statements of opinion.

Opinion Words		
should	good, better, best	probably
ought	bad, worse, worst	might
can	beautiful	perhaps
may	terrible	maybe

Inferring

Making inferences or **inferring,** means filling the gaps in your knowledge based on what you already know. For example, the following chart shows how you might make inferences about a literary character by using details from the story.

Question: In "Thank You, Ma'm," does Mrs. Jones fear the boy?	
Type of Clue	**Detail**
Description of Character	She was a large woman with a large purse that had everything in it but hammer and nails.
Statements About Character's Actions	. . . she reached down, picked the boy up by his shirt front, and shook him until his teeth rattled.
Character's Own Words	"When I get through with you, sir, you are going to remember Mrs. Luella Bates Washington Jones."
Logical Inference About Mrs. Jones'	Mrs. Jones does not appear to fear the boy.

Generalizing

Generalizing is the process of drawing conclusions based on facts and experiences. To write a topic sentence, you often use the thinking skill of generalizing. In other words, you look at specific details, facts, and examples to form a general observation or principle.

Not all generalizations are true. To persuade your parents to get you a cell phone, you might pose this unsound generalization: *Everybody else's parents buy cell phones for their kids.*

Making a chart like the one on the next page can help you examine the soundness of your generalizations. Start by listing a preliminary generalization. Then add exceptions. Finally, rewrite your limited generalization to reflect the new information by using words such as *some, many,* or *most.*

Revising a Generalization	
Preliminary Generalization	Hobbies are just a way to pass time.
Exceptions	My uncle's hobby of building model airplanes led to a career as an aeronautical engineer. My sister's love of computer games got her interested in programming.
Revised Generalization	*Some* hobbies are just ways to pass time.

Problem/Solution

When you have a problem to solve, a logical approach is more likely to result in a positive solution. To solve a problem, follow the steps in the chart below, which shows how the process can be applied to improving an art program.

Steps	Example
Problem	How can my school improve the art program?
List Possible Solutions	**Solution 1** Have families pay extra for art classes **Solution 2** Have volunteer artists teach some art classes
Evaluate Each Solution	**Solution 1** **Pro:** there would be money for art classes **Con:** some families could not afford the extra expense **Solution 2** **Pro 1:** students would be exposed to practicing artists **Pro 2:** artists will expand their audience **Con:** there might not be enough qualified volunteers
Make Decision	**Decision** Have volunteer artists help teach some art classes.

Analyzing

Analyzing means breaking down a whole into its parts to see how the parts fit together to form the whole.

Suppose, for example, you are writing about how to release a bowling ball. You go bowling so often that releasing the ball is second nature to you. When you try to explain it clearly to someone else, you may need to analyze the action, or break it down into its parts, so the other person can understand it.

As you analyze the way you release the ball, you see that you are actually following several different steps. What seemed like one continuous motion was actually a series of smaller, intermediate movements that can be explained. You take a series of steps. As you move, your arm straightens and swings the bowling ball back behind you. The opposing hand and arm follow through in a smooth motion as you release the ball. Analyzing helps you recognize the smaller parts, or steps, within a whole so that you can explain them clearly.

Analysis: Releasing a Bowling Ball
1. pick a target
2. without removing your eye from the target—
3. take a series of steps forward
4. as you move, straighten your bowling arm
5. swing the ball straight back behind you
6. take a final step
7. swing the ball forward toward the target
8. use the other arm to follow through in a smooth motion
9. release the ball

Summarizing

A **summary** is a concise condensation of a longer work or event. While conversations, discussions, film plots, and so forth can all be summarized, you may find that you use this skill most frequently with nonfiction texts.

Your main task when you write a summary is to restate the original ideas accurately and in your own words. A summary does not include personal comments, interpretations, or insights. Its purpose is to state clearly the most important ideas of a work by omitting the unnecessary details. The ideas are presented in the same order as in the original and with the same meaning. Writing a good summary takes some skill. You must remain true to the original as you restate the main ideas and condense the details.

Features of a Summary

- Usually, it is no more than one-third the length of the original.
- It extracts the main ideas of the original, omitting all but the most important details.
- It presents the main ideas in the same order as the original.
- It restates the main ideas of the original in the summary writer's own words.

Evaluating

Evaluating means making reasoned judgments about whether something is right or wrong, good or bad, valuable or worthless.

While opinions often reflect feelings and emotions—*I loved this book, I hated that movie*—evaluations are formed by measuring information against established criteria or standards. For example, a teacher develops criteria in order to evaluate student writing. A film critic judges a movie based on the criteria he or she has decided represent motion picture quality.

You might use evaluation, for example, to determine the validity of information found on the Web or in print. Here are some of the criteria that could be used.

Criteria for Validity of Information

- Is the information up-to-date?
- Is the information thorough?
- How does this information compare to other sources on the topic?
- Is the source objective and unbiased?
- What evidence do I have that this source is knowledgeable?

Propaganda

When you listen or read critically, you evaluate the content or message and make judgments about it. As a critical listener or reader, you must be able to recognize propaganda devices, which people sometimes use to mislead.

The purpose of propaganda is to get you to accept a particular point of view or take some action. Rather than facts, evidence, proved generalizations, and logical reasoning, however, speakers who use propaganda techniques misrepresent or distort information, or they present opinions as if they were facts. Propaganda also appeals to people's emotions through the use of emotional language, stereotypes, and exaggeration. Following are some examples of propaganda techniques.

Bandwagon Appeal

The **bandwagon appeal** tries to get you to do or think something because "everyone else is doing it." Often bandwagon appeals are used in advertising to make customers feel inadequate if they do not buy a certain product. A bandwagon statement can be misleading because it suggests that if you do not jump on the bandwagon, you will be different from everyone else.

> Don't be left out. Join the healthy generation and take
> Peak-of-Health vitamins.

Testimonial

A famous person's endorsement of a product is called a **testimonial**. A testimonial, however, can be misleading because it often suggests that because the famous person uses the product or endorses it, the product is so good that everyone else should also use it. A testimonial may suggest that using the product will give you the same success as the famous person endorsing it.

> Hi! I'm baseball star Bob Mose. Bran Buds gives me the energy
> I need to hit the ball out of the park!

Loaded Words

Another type of misleading statement is one that contains loaded words. **Loaded words** are ones that are carefully chosen to appeal to your hopes or fears rather than to reason or logic. In the following advertisement, the word *embarrassment* was chosen to stir up the listener's emotions.

> When standing close to that special person, avoid embarrassment by using Why Worry Antiperspirant.

Snob Appeal

Snob appeal is a technique often used in advertising. In this case, a reader or viewer is urged to do, think, or buy something in order to become part of an elite, aristocratic group. Look at how the following phrases employ this device.

> For those who insist on the best . . .
>
> Only a select few can own these incredible athletic shoes.

Appeal to Fear

An **appeal to fear** tries to frighten people into supporting a particular idea. It is commonly used in marketing and politics. Look at these examples.

> Unless you elect Candidate X, your taxes will go up and so will the crime rate.
>
> If neglected, those little aches and pains could turn into something much more serious. Brand Y can help.

CHAPTER 33

Critical Reading

QuickGuide

Creating Meaning pages 381–382	Readers have an important role in creating meaning.
Before You Read pages 382–385	Like writing, reading is a process. Getting your mind set for what you are about to read can help focus your thoughts and increase your understanding.
Skills to Use While You Read pages 386–393	When you dig into a text and read it carefully, your mind is busy. Successful readers continually look for connections.
Strategies to Use While You Read pages 394–397	Reading strategies include questioning, connecting, summarizing, synthesizing, and monitoring.
After You Read pages 398–399	The reading process continues even after you have finished the text. To get the most out of what you read, evaluate it, go back and re-read parts, and reflect on its meaning.

Creating Meaning

The writer and editor Norman Cousins wrote, "The way a book is read—which is to say, the qualities a reader brings to a book—can have as much to do with its worth as anything the author puts into it."

You can probably relate to this from your own experience. You know that while you read you don't just sit still while a writer pours his or her words into your head. Instead, you read interactively. You let your mind create images from the words you take in. You ask questions, and you put yourself into the text.

Read the following excerpt from the novel *Hatchet* by Gary Paulsen. In the story, a thirteen-year-old boy struggles to survive in the Canadian wilderness after an airplane crash.

At first he thought it was a growl. In the still darkness of the shelter in the middle of the night his eyes came open and he was awake and he thought there was a growl. But it was the wind, a medium wind in the pines had made some sound that brought him up, brought him awake. He sat up and was hit with the smell.

It terrified him. The smell was one of rot, some musty rot that made him think only of graves with cobwebs and dust and old death. His nostrils widened and he opened his eyes wider but he could see nothing. It was too dark, too hard dark with clouds covering even the small light from the stars, and he could not see. But the smell was alive, alive and full and in the shelter. He thought of the bear, thought of Bigfoot and every monster he had ever seen in every fight movie he had ever watched, and his heart hammered in his throat.

Then he heard the slithering. A brushing sound, a slithering brushing sound near his feet—and he kicked out as hard as he could, kicked out and threw the hatchet at the sound, a noise coming from his throat. But the hatchet missed, sailed into the wall where it hit the rocks with shower of sparks, and his leg was instantly torn with pain, as if a hundred needles had been driven into it. "Unnnnghh!"

Now he screamed, with the pain and fear, and skittered on his backside up into the corner of the shelter, breathing through his mouth, straining to see, to hear.

If you are like most readers, your reading experience probably goes something like this:

1) You temporarily leave the world around you and focus your attention on the text. You don't know enough yet to figure out exactly what you are "getting into," so you ask mental questions or look for clues about the kind of world you have stepped into. In the case of *Hatchet*, you probably plunged into the excerpt with only a little information about the book and didn't yet know what was going on. But you began to get the scene in your head as you pictured what Paulsen wrote.

2) Once you have figured out the world of the text, you move through it as you read. In the process, you ask yourself, "How does this fit with what I know or have experienced?" In the case of *Hatchet*, you might have found yourself remembering camping trips you have taken, or times when you have needed courage. You compared what you know of those topics with what the text was offering.

3) As you move through the text, you step back from time to time to figure out if what you are reading is changing any understandings or outlooks you had before. In just a short excerpt, you may not step back very much, but in a longer text you will often rethink your understandings.

4) When you finish reading, you step back into the world around you. You reflect on what you read and evaluate it. With the *Hatchet* excerpt, you probably considered whether or not you should read the whole book.

In all of these ways, you have been making meaning—lighting up your imagination by fusing the text with your own experiences and knowledge. In school or in a book or study group you can go even farther than this in creating meaning. You can share your ideas with other readers and listen to the understandings of others. Your own understandings may very well change as you share your responses to what you have read.

Before You Read

You wouldn't step outside without knowing what the weather was like and dressing for conditions. In the same way, readers who want to get as much as possible from their reading do not open the door to a new text without knowing at least something about it. Instead, they use the strategies listed on the next page to preview the text.

Strategies for Before Reading

- **Skim the Text.** Skim the text to get a general idea of the kind of text you are reading. Look at the illustrations, too.

- **Note the Title and Section Headings.** The title and section heads (if any) will help you know what to expect when you read.

- **Connect to Other Texts.** Ask yourself if you have read other texts like the one you are about to read. If so, what might they lead you to expect in this text?

- **Predict.** If you are starting a new text, you can use the impressions you get from the title and from skimming to predict what it will be about. If you are continuing in a reading, you can predict what might happen in the section you are about to read.

- **Set a Purpose for Reading.** When you have a rough idea of the kind of text you will be reading, you can set your mind for the purpose at hand. Maybe you will be reading for pleasure. Maybe you will be reading to find information you need for a report.

- **Use Your Prior Knowledge.** Thinking about what you already know about a subject, or what experiences you have had that relate to it, will help you get the most out of your reading. That becomes your starting point for creating meaning.

- **Learn New Vocabulary.** Especially in school, many of the books you read will have new vocabulary words identified at the beginnings of chapters and sections. Becoming familiar with key terms is one helpful pre-reading strategy.

Use these strategies before reading the selection on the next page. Ask yourself and answer the following questions.

1) What do I notice when I skim the text?

2) What is the title? Are there any headings?

3) What other texts like this have I read?

4) What do I think this selection will be about?

5) What will be my purpose in reading this selection? Do I think I will share in a personal experience of the writer, or will I gain information?

6) What do I already know about the subject?

7) When I skimmed the text, did I see any unfamiliar words I might want to learn before reading?

Thomas Jefferson's Library

Thomas Jefferson (1743-1826), who had one of the finest libraries in America, intended that his collection should benefit the nation. All through his years of public service—as minister to France, as vice president, and as president—he used every opportunity to add to his collection of documents about America and its past, as well as volumes in many languages about philosophy and history, science and technology, agriculture and horticulture, architecture and painting, poetry and rhetoric. He shared the vision of the nation's Founders that liberty and learning are inseparable and that a free democratic people must have free access to information in order to carry out their civic responsibilities.

After the War of 1812, during which the British burned the Capitol and with it all the volumes of the Library of Congress, Jefferson offered his own collection to Congress, which they purchased in 1815. The former president, then living in retirement in Monticello, was paid $23,950 for nearly 6,500 books, almost twice the number lost in the fire. Thus, the Library of Congress has grown from the seed of Jefferson's own library, universal in subject matter and format, into a library that serves as Congress's working research collection, as the nation's library, and as a symbol of the central role that free access to information plays in our knowledge-based democracy.

—from the American Treasures of the Library of Congress Web site
www.loc.gov/exhibits/treasures/tr66003.html

Library of Congress entry hall

Using Writing in Prereading

You can use writing to help set your mind for your reading. For example, you might want to keep a **two-column journal.** In the left-hand column, you could write your predictions. In the right-hand column, while you are reading, you can note whether your predictions were right. You can also use the two-column journal to write prereading questions in the left column and the answers you find when you read, in the right.

Two-Column Journal	
Questions About *Hatchet* Excerpt	**Answers Found While Reading**
What danger is the boy going to face in the wilderness?	It doesn't say what it was, but it was probably an animal.
Will he get hurt?	He gets hurt with a feeling that 100 needles stabbed him.
Will he be okay?	Still reading to find out.

A three-column **K-W-L chart** is another good graphic organizer. In the first column you record what you already **k**now about the subject. In the second column you write down what you **w**ant to know. After reading, you can fill in the third column with what you **l**earned.

Three-Column K-W-L Chart		
What I Know About Thomas Jefferson	**What I Want to Know**	**What I Learned**
• wrote the Declaration of Independence	• What was so special about his library?	He had books on almost every subject.
• lived at Monticello • was a president • was tall	• Why is it called a treasure?	The books of Congress were burned in the War of 1812 and these were a great replacement.
	• Did a lot of people have their own libraries?	Don't know—wasn't mentioned.

Skills to Use While You Read

After you have set your mind to read, you begin the active part of the reading process. During this stage, successful readers draw on all of the following skills to help them understand.

Sequencing

Sequencing is the skill of putting events in time order. Successful readers use sequencing to keep track of events in both fictional narratives and non-fictional narratives. The signal words that show the sequence of events in the following paragraph are highlighted.

> Photographing pets can sometimes be a dangerous hobby. One day last week I went next door to take some pictures of Raggs and her newborn puppies. As I walked close to her and her pups, she charged at me, barking in a wild, high-pitched voice. Before I knew it, I was racing to the door, dropping my camera on the way. Only later did I learn that all animals are very protective of their young.

Graphic Organizers for Sequencing To help you with sequencing, you can make a timeline, such as the simple one below based on the article about Thomas Jefferson's library.

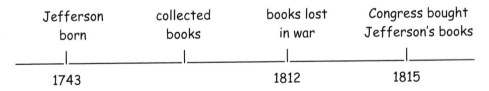

Jefferson born	collected books	books lost in war	Congress bought Jefferson's books
1743		1812	1815

You could also represent the events in a storyboard, like the following based on the story of Raggs.

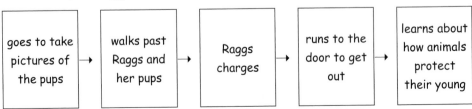

goes to take pictures of the pups → walks past Raggs and her pups → Raggs charges → runs to the door to get out → learns about how animals protect their young

Identifying Main Idea and Details

Being able to identify the main idea helps readers focus on the most important point. There are several ways to look for the main idea. One is to look for sentences that contain a general idea rather than a specific fact. Often, but not always, these sentences are the first or last in a paragraph.

Another is to use some of the features of the text, such as titles, headings, and introductory comments. These may point clearly to the main idea. Can you identify the main idea in the paragraph about ancient Egypt below?

> . . . The rituals of mummy-making and burial reflected the Egyptians' belief in life after death. Egyptians believed a person had not only a body but a spirit. After death a person's spirit could go on living if it had a body in which to dwell. The body, however, had to preserve the dead person's appearance. A mummified body did just that. Preparing mummies was a religious rite. A priest wearing a jackal-shaped mask—symbol of Anubis, god of embalming—directed the ritual. Other priests treated the body to protect it from decay. The process was called embalming. Priests drained the fluids and wrapped the corpse in cloth.
>
> —from nationalgeographic.com

If you thought the first sentence contained the main idea, you were right. It is the most general statement in the paragraph. The other statements all contain more specific information that helps explain the main idea—the religious reason for the practice, the role of the priests, the clothing of the chief priest.

19th-Dynasty painting of Anubis preparing a mummy

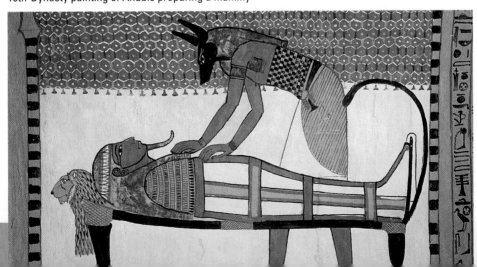

Graphic Organizer for Main Idea and Details You can use your two-column journal to help you keep track of main ideas and supporting details. Write the main ideas in the left column and the details that support them in the right. Or you could use an organizer like the one below.

Main Idea Egyptian burial practices reflect beliefs about life after death.		
Detail 1 A person's spirit could go on living if it had a body in which to dwell.	**Detail 2** Preparing a mummy was a religious rite.	**Detail 3** Priests directed the ritual and prepared the body for burial.

Comparing and Contrasting

When you **compare** two or more subjects, you look for likenesses. When you **contrast** two or more subjects, you look for differences. Readers often can recognize a comparison or contrast because of the signal words that accompany it. For comparisons these include such words and phrases as *like, both, in the same way,* and *similarly.* For contrasts the words and phrases highlight differences. Examples of these signal words include *in contrast, on the other hand, unlike, however,* and *another difference.* Look for the comparisons and contrasts in the following paragraph. The signal words are highlighted.

Insects and spiders are both small creatures that at first glance look very much alike. Both have many legs, and both crawl. Insects and spiders both reproduce by laying eggs, and they both use camouflage as a natural defense. However, insects and spiders are different from each other in many ways. Insects usually have six legs (in three pairs) and a body that is divided into three parts. In contrast, spiders always have eight legs, attached to the front section of their two-sectioned bodies. Adult insects usually have wings, often two pairs. Spiders, however, do not have wings. While people often think of insects as pests, spiders are seen as pest controllers because they prey on insects.

Graphic Organizers for Comparing and Contrasting

Following are two of many possible organizers you can use as you read a passage that compares and contrasts two or more subjects. Both are based on the passage about insects and spiders.

Similarities	Differences
• small • many legs • crawl • lay eggs • use camouflage	• number of legs (6 for insects, 8 for spiders) • body parts (3 for insects, 2 for spiders) • wings (insects yes, spiders no) • insects are pests; spiders control pests

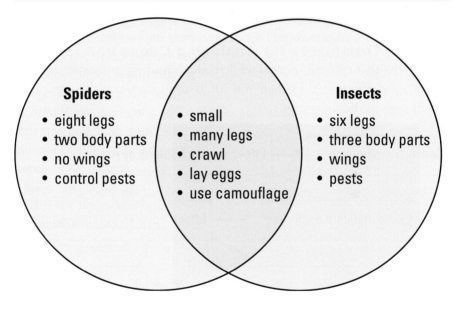

Analyzing Cause and Effect

A **cause** is an action or situation that results in some outcome. The outcome or result of a cause is called an **effect**. Seeing the relationships between causes and effects will help you understand what you are reading. Such signal phrases as *because, for this reason*, and *as a result* can help you see these relationships.

Sometimes you will see a chain of causes and effects, as in the following paragraph. In a chain, an effect becomes a new cause that then has its own effects. Signal words are highlighted.

> As human populations grow and more houses are built, city limits extend further and further into the countryside. The immediate impact on wild animals is that they lose their natural habitat and find themselves with a choice of either sharing their space with human neighbors or moving to open, undeveloped space. Some animals, like coyotes, often remain near new housing developments. Fed by well-meaning people, these coyotes become more used to and less afraid of humans. As a result, they become more aggressive. In the end, coyotes are often perceived as a menace and met with hostility.

Graphic Organizers for Analyzing Cause and Effect You can use the two-column journal while you are reading to record causes in one column and effects in the other. You could also map out a chain of causes and effects such as the following.

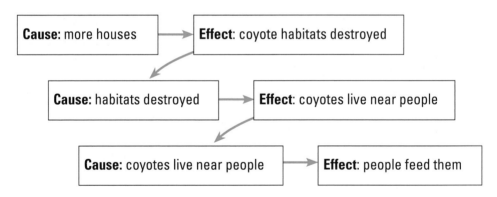

Cause: more houses → **Effect**: coyote habitats destroyed

Cause: habitats destroyed → **Effect**: coyotes live near people

Cause: coyotes live near people → **Effect**: people feed them

Identifying Fact, Opinion, and Bias

While you read, you take in a lot of information and statements. Knowing which statements are facts and which are opinions can help you understand and evaluate what you are reading, especially if you are reading persuasive writing. As you know, a **fact** is a statement that can be proved true. As a critical reader, ask yourself if the opinions you read are backed up by facts.

The **opinions** in the following paragraph are highlighted.

Skateboarding is a healthy, exciting way to spend time. Some people complain that kids watch too much television, or play too many video games. Many kids are developing strong muscles, quick reflexes, and healthy lungs and hearts by skateboarding. The Surgeon General recommends that people exercise every week. Skateboarding is one of the best exercises, and it can be done almost anywhere. Any sidewalk or parking lot can serve as a place to ride. Finally, skateboarding provides kids with an alternative to the kinds of troubles that idleness can bring about. All in all, a skateboard is a good investment in any kid's health and future.

A critical reader may feel that more facts would be helpful in backing up the opinions in this paragraph. What about the injuries sometimes associated with skateboarding? Some facts comparing skateboarding injuries to other sports injuries would help make the point about the safety of skateboarding.

As a critical reader, you also need to be on the lookout for bias. **Bias** is the slant that certain writing may have that makes it less likely to be completely objective. One way to detect bias is to check the source. For example, if the paragraph above had been written by someone working for a skateboarding company, you might wonder how accurate the statements are. On the other hand, if it had been written by a doctor who has nothing to gain from the information, you would have little reason to suspect bias.

Inferring

The expression "reading between the lines" means that you take away a meaning that is not stated directly. That is also what **inferring** means. When you infer, your mind supplies an understanding that is not actually in the text. You blend what you have read with your own experiences and knowledge to come up with this meaning. For example, suppose you read the following sentence:

> Joanna left her lunch on the kitchen counter when she ran out the door for school.

Your mind is probably busy remembering times when you forgot your lunch. Putting what you have read together with what you remember from your own experience, you can *infer* that Joanna was hungry by the time she got home from school, even though the text does not say that.

Following are several important ways readers infer meaning.

Drawing Conclusions Conclusions are understandings you come to when you add up specific ideas and facts. Read the following reflection by author E. B. White and see what conclusion the specific ideas lead to.

> Many years ago I went to bed one night in a railway sleeping car, and during the night I dreamed about a tiny boy who acted rather like a mouse. That's how the story of Stuart Little got started. It took about twelve years to do *Stuart,* but most of the time I did not think I was writing a book. I was busy with other matters.
>
> I like animals and my barn is a very pleasant place to be, at all hours. One day when I was on my way to feed the pig, I began feeling sorry for the pig because, like most pigs, he was doomed to die. This made me sad. So I started thinking of ways to save a pig's life. I had been watching a big gray spider at her work and was impressed by how clever she was at weaving. Gradually I worked the spider into *Charlotte's Web,* a story of friendship and salvation on a farm.
>
> —from *Pauses,* by Lee Bennett Hopkins

The specifics in this excerpt are about how E.B. White got his ideas for two of his famous books. But nowhere in the excerpt does he state directly how he usually gets his ideas. Using the examples he discusses, what conclusion can you draw about how he gets his ideas? For a conclusion to be reasonable, all of the specifics must fit with it. So if you concluded that E .B. White gets his ideas from his farm, your conclusion would not fit with the first example, which shows that he got one idea by dreaming it. However, you could draw this conclusion, which works with both examples: E.B. White got his ideas for some of his books by just going about his regular life and waiting for them to appear.

Predicting Outcomes Closely related to drawing conclusions is the skill of predicting outcomes. That skill calls for taking the conclusions you have drawn and applying them to something unknown. For example, if you are reading a novel and the character has lied about something important twice already, you might have concluded that he lies about everything important. You might predict that the next time he will also lie.

However, suppose you also noticed as you were reading that each time the boy lies, he feels worse and worse. His lies seem to be bothering him so much that he is in a great conflict about them. While you are reading, you make connections to your own life. You think about everything you have read, you think about any personal experience you have had in lying, and then you make a prediction about how the boy will handle the truth at his next chance. Successful readers briefly stop and make predictions as they read.

Understanding Figurative Language While reading, you are likely to come upon figurative language, or language that uses such figures of speech as similes and metaphors. You may recall that similes are comparisons that use the words *like* or *as* to show similarities. Metaphors imply a comparison but do not use the words *like* or *as.*

Simile	The storm, *like* a bird of prey, swooped down on the town.
Metaphor	The talons of the fierce storm caught the town by surprise.

The use of the word *talons,* which means the claws of a bird of prey, creates the comparison. Critical readers use both the skill of comparing and the skill of inferring to draw meaning from figurative language. The meaning is not stated directly. Instead, the reader needs to call to mind all the association he or she has to birds of prey and then apply them to the storm.

Strategies to Use While You Read

In addition to using skills for understanding, readers use a toolbox of strategies to help them get the most out of their reading. Some of these are continuations of the strategies used before reading.

Asking Questions

Question everything! In your mind, question the author about what he or she means or what evidence there is to support it. Question the text, too. Ask why there is a chapter devoted to one subject but not another one that seems logical to you. Ask yourself questions: why do I think that? Why do I disagree with this? Why does that make me laugh?

Techniques for Questioning Some readers like to make notes of their questions in the margins of books as they are reading. If you are reading a book you do not own or do not wish to mark up, you can use sticky notes to write your questions. You can also write your questions in the left column of a two-column journal, putting the answers you find or come up with in the right column.

Questioning the author is another technique you can use. In this approach, you realize that authors can be imperfect, just like readers. They may not always be as clear as they could be. They may be presenting outdated information. They may have left out an important step. Discussing questions like the following with your classmates can help you deepen your own understanding of the subject.

- What does the author mean here?
- What is the author's message?
- Does this fit with other things the author wrote?
- Is this explained clearly?
- Why did the writer include this information?
- Why did the writer organize the information this way?

Making Connections

Before you started reading a text, you began to make connections in three ways. You thought about connections between the text and your own experience. You reflected on the connections between the text and other texts you have read—how they might be similar or different. And you thought about connections there may be between the text and your own knowledge of the world. As you dig into the reading, continue to make those connections to help you understand what you are reading in a deep way.

Techniques for Making Connections One way to highlight connections you make is to use sticky notes every time a connection occurs to you. You can place the sticky note at the point of the text that made you think of the connection. If it is a connection to your experiences, you can write an "S" on the note, showing it is a connection to "Self." If you see something that reminds you of another text you read, you can place a sticky note and write "T" on it, for "Text." If you make a connection between something in the text and your world knowledge, you can place a sticky note and write "W" on it.

Making Mental Pictures

Reread the excerpt from *Hatchet* on page 381. If you are like most readers, your mind was busy picturing the boy in his dark and frightening environment. In fact, you probably not only pictured the scene but also heard the growl, the wind, the slithering sound. You probably called to mind a rotting smell. And you probably imagined very vividly what it must feel like to get 100 needles in your leg. Creating mental pictures and using all of your senses as you read aids understanding. It also accounts for a good deal of the pleasure of reading.

Summarizing

While you are reading, you are taking in a lot of information and detail. Successful readers often pause and summarize what they have read so far so they can keep the most important points clear in their minds. When you summarize, you express in just a few words or sentences the main ideas of what you have read. You leave out a lot of detail.

Techniques for Summarizing One very good way to focus your mind on the main ideas is to *retell* what you have read to someone else. In textbooks, you can sometimes also look back over the key words, which might be in bold type, and use them to summarize what you have read. You can also use writing to help you summarize. You can write a sentence or two in your journal after you finish each section or chapter in a book, or each paragraph in an article, to capture the most important ideas.

Synthesizing

Before you started reading a text, you considered what you already knew about the subject. During your reading, you began to try to fit what you were reading into the framework of what you already knew. That is one part of **synthesizing,** or bringing together old information and new information. However, synthesizing does not stop there. As you read and learn more, you no longer just try to fit the new information into the old framework. You rebuild your framework to account for the new information.

Techniques for Synthesizing A good way to keep track of the synthesizing you do as you read is to go back to your pre-reading notes and see how your ideas are changing. Regular discussions with classmates or others who are reading the same text will also help you synthesize what you read.

Monitoring Understanding

During active reading, successful readers are always making mental checks about how well they are understanding. This process is called **monitoring,** or watching over, understanding. If you find when you check your understanding that you are confused, there are a number of strategies you can use to get back on track. These are often called "fix-up strategies." They help you clarify what you have read.

Fix-up Strategies Successful readers use some of these strategies and others to keep moving even if they hit a snag in their understanding.

- Skip a hard word or small problem and keep reading.
- Go back and reread a confusing part.

- Skip ahead to see if the confusion is cleared up later in the text.
- Slow down your reading.
- Use strategies to figure out unfamiliar words, such as identifying context clues and word parts. Take a good guess at the meaning of a word if those strategies don't work.
- Talk about your confusion with another reader.

Read the following passage from the book *Pilgrim at Tinker Creek*, by Annie Dillard. This section is about the memory of feeling a cocoon in a classroom.

We passed the cocoon around; it was heavy. As we held it in our hands, the creature within warmed and squirmed. We were delighted, and wrapped it tighter in our fists. The pupa began to jerk violently, in heart-stopping knocks. Who's there? I can still feel those thumps, urgent through a muffling of spun silk and leaf, urgent through the swaddling of many years, against the curve of my palm. We kept passing it around. When it came to me again it was hot as a bun; it jumped half out of my hand. The teacher intervened. He put it, still heaving and banging, in the ubiquitous Mason jar.

A reader monitoring understanding and using fix-up strategies might think something like this while reading.

I can picture the scene. The cocoon is getting passed around. I don't know the word pupa *but I have a feeling it's the thing inside the cocoon, because it starts to move. I don't understand the sentence that has the word* urgent *in it a couple of times. What does "a muffling of spun silk and leaf" or the "swaddling of many years" mean? I'll try rereading it slower. Okay, maybe the muffling of spun silk refers to the outer part of the cocoon...I know on a car the muffler is what keeps the engine quiet, so maybe this means a layer of something that keeps it quiet inside. I still don't really understand the "swaddling of many years" but I think I can still keep reading and get the main idea. I don't know the word* intervened. *The teacher did something...maybe it just means he got it back from the students. Though actually if* inter- *is a prefix, I know that means* between, *like in inter-galactic warfare. So maybe it means something like the teacher got in between the students who were passing the cocoon around? I don't know the meaning of* ubiquitous, *but I think I can still get the main point.*

After You Read

When you have finished reading, the reading process wraps up with additional skills and strategies to process what you have just read and "make it your own." Some of them are similar to the ones you have used all through the reading process.

Strategies for After Reading

- **Rereading.** Looking back over the text and rereading passages that you especially liked or that you found especially challenging is a useful strategy after you have finished active reading. Rereading the whole work, or key parts, can also help you see things you might have missed on the first pass.

- **Evaluating the Success of the Reading Purpose.** When you have finished reading, you can judge whether your reading purpose was met or not. If it was not met, you can think through why and make adjustments in setting reading purposes the next time you read. Or you can look for another text that will meet your reading purpose.

- **Checking Your Predictions.** Did the story come out the way you thought? If you are reading nonfiction, did the explanation unfold in the way you predicted?

- **Discussing Favorite Parts.** Talking about your favorite parts of a text can help you understand why you liked it or why you got out of it what you did. Talking with your classmates also gives you ideas that might not have occurred to you otherwise. These ideas can help you evaluate the text.

- **Reflecting.** When you reflect on something you have read, you ask yourself what meaning it had and what of value it conveyed to you. How did it influence the way you see things? What did it teach you?

- **Applying.** When you apply what you have read to your own knowledge and life experience, you can really make it your own. For example, if you had been reading fiction, what if you tried to write a different story with the same characters? Through that process, you would be applying what you knew about the characters to a new situation. Or if you had been reading nonfiction, try applying what you learned to a new subject area. For example, if you read a book about how to train horses, ask yourself how much of what you read might apply to training dogs or even to how people learn behavior.

Using Writing After Reading

Think of the reading process, and the writing you do after it, as a recipe or a formula. For example, when you mix red paint with blue paint you get an entirely new color: purple. When you read, you are mixing your own background and experiences with the text. What results is a brand-new understanding. Writing about what you have read will help you develop that understanding.

When you have finished reading, you can complete any two-column journals you have been using or any KWL charts or other graphic organizers. You can also do any of the following kinds of writing to help lead you to new understandings.

Personal Writing   You can use a journal or any other kind of paper to write a personal response to what you read. For this kind of writing, just write freely. Explore in your writing what you learned from the reading or how it made you feel. Explore how you will use what you learned. Reflect on the connections you made while reading. Raise questions. In this kind of writing, you don't need to worry about spelling and punctuation.

Informational Writing   You can also use what you have learned or gotten out of a reading to develop a more formal piece of writing that you will share with a reader. Answering these questions will help you focus your writing: What topics did your reading bring to mind? What did you learn from your reading about these topics? Which of those would interest you the most to write about? For whom will you be writing this piece? Since this piece of writing will be shared with a reader, it should follow the usual conventions, with correct spelling, punctuation, and usage.

Critical Writing   Another kind of formal writing you can do is a book review. For this kind of writing, you focus on the text itself and how well it accomplished its purpose. In the course of exploring that topic, you will probably want to compare it to other texts you have read or experiences you have had. The difference between this kind of writing and informational writing is that now you are *evaluating* the work, making a judgment about it.

All of these ways of using writing will aid your understanding of what you read. So will other expressions, such as dramatizing, illustrating, or discussing. Sharing your expressions with other readers will help create a community of understanding where learning is both fun and meaningful.

Study and Test-Taking Skills

QuickGuide

Learning Study Skills **pages 401–405**	You can learn and retain more if you study effectively.
Taking Standardized Tests **pages 405–411**	There are strategies that can help improve your scores on standardized tests.
Taking Essay Tests **pages 411–415**	The steps used in the writing process can help you with essay tests.

Learning Study Skills

Practicing good study habits will help you when taking tests as well as when completing daily classroom assignments. In addition, the better your study habits, the more easily you can learn new things outside of school, from new hobbies to career changes.

Improve your study habits by using the following strategies.

Strategies for Effective Studying

- Choose an area that is well lighted and quiet.
- Equip your study area with everything you need for reading and writing, including a dictionary and a thesaurus.
- Keep an assignment book for recording assignments and due dates.
- Allow plenty of time for studying. Begin your reading and writing assignments early.
- Adjust your reading rate to suit your purpose.

Adjusting Reading Rate to Purpose

Your **reading rate** is the speed at which you read. Depending on your purpose, you may appropriately choose to read certain materials quickly or slowly, using the techniques of scanning, skimming, or close reading. For example, if your purpose is to get a quick impression of the contents of a newspaper, you should scan the headlines. If you want to learn the main ideas in a certain article, you should skim it. If your purpose is to learn new facts or understand details, you may choose to read the article closely.

Scanning is reading to get a general impression. To scan, you should read the title, headings, subheadings, picture captions, words and phrases in boldface or italics, and any focus questions. Using this method you can quickly determine what the reading is about and what questions to keep in mind. Scan the table of contents, appendix, glossary, and index of a book before reading.

Skimming is reading to identify quickly the purpose, thesis, main ideas, and supporting ideas of a selection. After scanning a chapter, section, or article, you should quickly read, or skim, the introduction, the topic sentence of each paragraph, and the conclusion.

Close reading is for locating specific information, following the logic of an argument, or comprehending the meaning or significance of information. After scanning the selection or chapter, read it more slowly, word for word.

With literature close reading also offers you a chance to appreciate style, word choice, figurative language, and other elements that differentiate literature from informational texts.

Reading a Textbook

In studying a textbook, the techniques of scanning, skimming, and close reading are combined in the **SQ3R** study strategy. This method helps you to understand and remember what you read. The *S* in *SQ3R* stands for *Survey,* the *Q* for *Question,* and the *3R* for *Read, Recite, and Review.*

The SQ3R Study Method	
Survey	First get a general idea of what the selection is about by scanning titles, subtitles, and words that are set off in a different type or color. Also look at maps, tables, charts, and other illustrations. Then read the introduction and conclusion or summary.
Question	Decide what questions you should be able to answer after reading the selection. You can do this by turning the headings and subheadings into questions or by looking at any study questions in the book.
Read	Now read the selection. As you read, try to answer your questions. In addition, find the main idea in each section and look for important information that is not included in your questions. After reading, review the important points in the selection and take notes.
Recite	Answer each question in your own words by reciting or writing the answers.
Review	Answer the questions again without looking at your notes or at the selection. Continue reviewing until you answer each question correctly.

Taking Notes

Here are three methods of taking notes.

In an **informal outline**, you use words and phrases to record main ideas and significant details. Notes in this form are helpful in studying for an objective test because they emphasize specific facts.

In a **graphic organizer**, words and phrases are arranged in a visual pattern to indicate the relationships between main ideas and supporting details. This is an excellent tool for studying information for an objective test, for an open-ended assessment, or for writing an essay.

In a **summary**, you use sentences to express important ideas in your own words. A good summary should express relationships between ideas and draw conclusions. Summaries are useful in preparing for an essay test.

In the passage below, the essential information is underlined. On the next page this information is expressed in an informal outline, a graphic organizer, and a summary.

Leonardo da Vinci, an Italian man of the Renaissance, is believed to be one of the greatest artists of all time. He was also, however, a genius in many other areas of study. Because his notebooks survived, we know that he laid out plans for hundreds of inventions and machines. Among them are designs for a flying machine, a helicopter, a parachute, a movable bridge, artillery, an alarm clock, and revolving stages. He was fascinated by anatomy and produced the first accurate drawings of the human body. However, he is probably most famous for his paintings, such as *The Last Supper*. His work inspired many other artists—among them another giant of the Renaissance, Michaelangelo.

Da Vinci drawing of a helicopter

Leonardo da Vinci

Informal Outline

- Great Renaissance artist and inventor
- Sketched plans for hundreds of inventions and machines
- Created first accurate drawings of human anatomy
- Most famous for his paintings
- Inspired Michaelangelo

Graphic Organizer

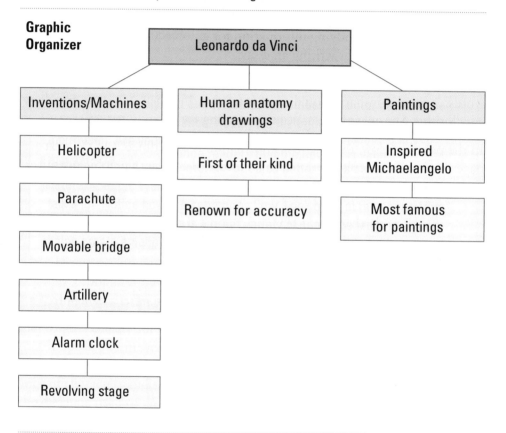

Summary

Leonardo da Vinci was a great Renaissance artist and a great scientist, laying out plans for many inventions and machines. His scientific work was also concerned with accurate drawings of the anatomy of the human body. He influenced other greats like Michaelangelo.

Whichever note-taking method you use, the following strategies will help you make those notes clear and well organized.

Strategies for Taking Notes

- Label your notes with the title and page numbers of the chapter or the topic and date of the lecture.
- Record only the main ideas and important details.
- Use the titles, subtitles, and words in special type to help you select the most important information.
- Use your own words; do not copy word for word.
- Use as few words as possible.

Taking Standardized Tests

A **standardized test** measures your academic progress, skills, and achievement in such a way that results can be compared with those of other students who have taken the same test. Standardized tests that assess your ability to use language skills include vocabulary tests, analogy tests, sentence-completion tests, reading tests, and tests of standard written English.

The best way to do well on standardized tests is to work consistently on your school subjects throughout the year, to read as much as possible from a variety of sources, and to learn the strategies of test taking.

Strategies for Taking Standardized Tests

- Read the test directions carefully, always taking time to answer the sample questions to be sure you understand what the test requires.
- Relax. Although you can expect to be a little nervous, concentrate on doing the best you can.
- Preview the whole test quickly by skimming to get an overview of the kinds of questions on the test.
- Plan your time, allotting a certain amount of time to each part of the test.
- First answer the questions you find easiest. Skip hard questions, coming back to them later if you have time.
- Read and reread all choices before you select an answer. If you are not sure of the answer, try to eliminate choices that are obviously wrong.
- If you have time, check your answers.

Vocabulary Tests

One kind of vocabulary test asks you to find **antonyms**—words most nearly opposite in meaning. For instance, in the following test item, you must find the antonym for *slumber* among the five choices.

SLUMBER: (A) dream   (B) hibernate   (C) snore

                  (D) awaken   (E) sleep

(The answer is *(D)* because *awaken* is an antonym for *slumber.* The other choices are wrong for various reasons. The word *sleep* is a synonym for *slumber,* not an antonym. None of the other three choices means the opposite of *slumber.)*

COMPLEX: (A) mysterious (B) complicated   (C) simple

                 (D) fancy   (E) harmless

(The answer is *(C)* because *simple* is the opposite of *complex.* The word *complicated* is a synonym for *complex,* and the other words do not have the opposite meaning of *complex.)*

Synonym items have the same format as antonym items, but in this case, the answer means the same thing as the word in capital letters.

WANDER: (A) tempt   (B) ask   (C) hide

               (D) stray   (E) walk

(The answer is *(D)* because *stray* has close to the same meaning as *wander.* The word *walk* is related to *wander* in that when one wanders, one is usually walking, but it is not the same meaning. The words *hide, tempt,* and *ask* do not have the same meaning as *wander.)*

Analogies

Analogy questions test your skill at figuring out relationships between words. The first step is to decide how the given words—the first capitalized pair of words—are related to each other. The next step is to decide which other pair has the same kind of relationship as the first pair.

STALE : FRESH : : old : new

The above example reads, "Stale is to fresh as old is to new." That is, *stale* has the same relationship to *fresh* as *old* has to *new*. *Stale* is the opposite of *fresh*, just as *old* is the opposite of *new*. Explaining an analogy to yourself in one sentence can help you to figure out the answer. In the following item, for example, you might say to yourself, "One kind of tree is an oak."

TREE : OAK : :

(A) deer : buffalo   (B) fever : virus   (C) music : jazz

(D) plumber : wrench   (E) rose : flower

(The answer, *(C) music : jazz,* expresses the same category-to-item relationship.)

Keep in mind that the word order in an analogy is very important. If the given pair of words in the analogy expresses a part-to-whole order, the words in the correct answer will also be in part-to-whole order, not whole-to-part.

Some analogies are written in sentence form.

Rapid is to *slow* as *raw* is to _____.

(A) bitter   (B) cooked   (C) hard

(D) quick   (E) cold

(The first two italicized words are antonyms. Therefore, the correct answer is *(B) cooked,* which is the opposite of *raw.*)

Knowing some of the common types of analogies, like those in the following chart, will help you figure out word relationships.

Common Types of Analogies	
Analogy	**Example**
word : synonym	slim : slender
word : antonym	exciting : dull
part : whole	wing : airplane
whole : part	hand : finger
cause : effect	drought : famine
worker : tool	carpenter : hammer
worker : product	baker : bread
item : purpose	ruler : measure

Sentence-Completion Tests

Sentence-completion tests measure your ability to comprehend what you read and to use context clues. Each item consists of a sentence with one or more words missing. First read the entire sentence. Then select the choice that completes the sentence in a way that makes the most sense.

Dr. Sawyer's mechanical servant Robbie is the ideal use of ___.

(A) friendship   (B) automation   (C) gasoline

(D) nurses   (E) hospitals

The answer is *(B) automation.* The clue *mechanical servant* tells you that the use of *automation* is a robot Dr. Sawyer uses for assistance.

Some sentence-completion questions have two blanks in the same sentence, with each answer choice including two words. Find the correct answer in this example.

> While all the other members of the jury thought the man was ___, a single ___ held on to her "not guilty" vote.
>
> (A) friendly . . . witness (B) guilty . . . juror
>
> (C) mean . . . officer (D) innocent . . . defense lawyer
>
> (E) nice . . . judge
>
> The answer is (B) *guilty . . . juror.* The other choices do not fit the context. A *juror* sits on a jury, and since the the single juror found the man not guilty, the other jurors must have found him guilty.

Reading Tests

Reading tests assess your ability to understand and analyze written passages. The information you need to answer the test questions may be either directly stated or implied in the passage. You must study, analyze, and interpret a passage in order to answer the questions that follow it. The following strategies will help you answer questions on reading tests.

Strategies for Reading Test Questions

- Begin by skimming the questions that follow the passage.
- Read the passage carefully and closely. Notice the main ideas, organization, style, and key words.
- Study all possible answers. Avoid choosing one answer the moment you think it is a reasonable choice.
- Use only the information in the passage when you answer the questions. Do not rely on your own knowledge or ideas on this kind of test.

Most reading questions will focus on one or more of the following characteristics of a written passage.

- **Main idea** At least one question will usually focus on the central idea of the passage. Remember that the main idea of a passage covers all sections of the passage—not just one section or paragraph.
- **Supporting details** Questions about supporting details test your ability to identify the statements in the passage that back up the main idea.

- **Implied meanings** In some passages not all information is directly stated. Some questions ask you to interpret information that is merely implied.
- **Purpose and Tone** Questions on purpose and tone require that you interpret or analyze the author's purpose in writing and the author's attitude toward his or her subject.

The Double Passage You may also be asked to read two paired passages, called the **double passage,** and answer questions about each passage individually and about how the two passages relate to each other. The two passages may present similar or opposing views or may complement each other in various ways. A brief introduction preceding the passages may help you anticipate the relationship between them.

Tests of Standard Written English

Objective tests of standard written English assess your knowledge of language skills used for writing. They contain sentences with underlined words, phrases, and punctuation. The underlined parts will contain errors. You are asked to find the error in each sentence, or, on some tests, to identify the best way to revise a sentence or passage. Read the following sentence and identify the error.

The <u>people</u> of <u>Haiti</u> won their <u>Independence</u> from <u>France</u> in 1804.
     A   B   C   D

(The answer is *C.* The word *independence* should not be capitalized.)

The following list identifies some of the errors you should look for on a test of standard written English.

- lack of agreement between subject and verb
- lack of agreement between pronoun and antecedent
- incorrect spelling or use of a word
- missing, misplaced, or unnecessary punctuation
- missing or unnecessary capitalization
- misused or misplaced italics or quotation marks

Remember that the parts of a sentence that are not underlined are presumed to be correct. You can use clues in the correct parts of the sentence to help you search for errors in the underlined parts.

Sentence-Correction Questions In a sentence-correction question, you must select the most appropriate and effective way to write the sentence. A sentence or passage is presented with a section underlined followed by choices showing different ways of writing the underlined part. Errors, if they exist, may involve grammar, usage, capitalization, punctuation, or word choice. Be sure that the answer you choose does not change the meaning of the original sentence.

The statue *Venus de milo* is displayed in a french museum.

(A) *Venus de milo* is displayed in a french museum.

(B) *Venus de Milo,* is displayed in a french museum.

(C) *Venus de Milo* is displayed in a French museum.

(D) *Venus de Milo* is displayed, in a french museum.

(E) *Venus de Milo* is displayed in a French Museum.

(The answer is *(C)*. *Venus de Milo* is a proper noun and should be capitalized. *French* should also be capitalized, but *museum* should not.)

Revision-in-Context Another type of multiple-choice question that appears on some standardized tests is called revision-in-context. These questions are based on a short passage that is meant to represent an early draft of student writing. The questions following the reading ask you to choose the best revision of a sentence, a group of sentences, or the essay as a whole. This type of test assesses your reading comprehension, your composing skills, and your understanding of the conventions of standard written English.

Taking Essay Tests

Essay tests are designed to assess both your understanding of important ideas and your ability to see connections, or relationships, between those ideas. To do well, you must be able to organize your thoughts quickly and to express them logically and clearly.

Kinds of Essay Questions

Always begin an essay test by carefully reading the instructions for all the questions on the test. Look for key words, such as those listed in the following chart. Such key words will tell you precisely what kind of question you are being asked.

Essay Questions May Ask You to—	
Analyze	Separate into parts and examine each part.
Compare	Point out similarities.
Contrast	Point out differences.
Define	Clarify meaning.
Discuss	Examine in detail.
Evaluate	Give your opinion.
Explain	Tell *how*, *what*, or *why*.
Illustrate	Give examples.
Summarize	Briefly review main points.
Trace	Show development or progress.

As you read the instructions, jot down or underline key words and phrases in the instructions, as in the following example.

The women's suffrage movement in the late 1800s had several key women leaders. Write four paragraphs that describe the life of one of these women, giving specific examples of how she was an influence on women's right to vote.

Writing an Effective Essay Answer

The steps in writing a well-constructed essay are the same for an essay test as for a written assignment. The only difference is that in a test situation you have a strict time limit for writing. As a result, you need to plan how much time you will spend writing each answer and how much time you will devote to each step in the writing process. As a rule of thumb, for every five minutes of writing, allow two for planning and one for revising and editing.

Prewriting Begin planning your answer by brainstorming for main ideas and supporting details. Then organize your main ideas into a simple informal outline. Your outline will help you present your ideas in a logical order, cover all your main points, and avoid omitting important details.

Informal Outline

Indian Writing Systems

1. Mayan glyphs used as a calendar

2. Aztec pictographs kept records

3. Inca quipu knots kept count of crops

You can also plan your answer by using a graphic organizer to indicate the relationships between your main ideas and supporting details.

Graphic Organizer

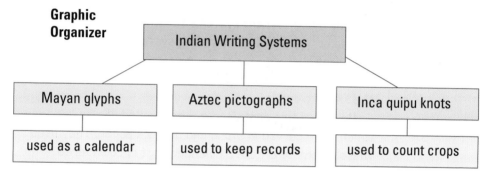

Your next step is to write a statement that presents your main idea and covers all your supporting ideas. Often you can write a suitable main idea statement by rewording the test question.

Essay Question

Compare and contrast the types of Indian writing systems and their purposes.

Main Idea Statement

There are many types of Indian writing systems and many purposes for these systems.

Drafting As you write your essay, keep the following strategies in mind.

Strategies for Writing an Essay Answer
- Write an introduction that includes the main idea statement.
- Follow the order of your outline. Write one paragraph for each main point.
- Be specific. Support each main point by using supporting details such as facts and examples.
- Use transitions to connect your ideas and examples.
- End with a strong concluding statement that summarizes your main idea.

Main Idea Statement   In the United States today, we use a Roman alphabet to write our ideas and keep records. Of course, we have computers today, but we have had paper for writing for a very long time. Before the arrival of the Europeans, Indians had different systems for writing. There are many types of Indian writing systems and many different purposes for these systems. The most highly developed systems came from the Maya, the Aztec, and the Inca.

Mayan writing contained symbols called glyphs, which were carved in stone and on bark paper. They used these glyphs to create a calendar that is considered by some to be more accurate than those of the ancient Egyptians, Greeks, or Romans.

Aztec writing was made up of pictures called pictographs. These pictographs were used mainly to keep records. Even the Spanish explorers learned to read Aztec writing.

The Inca had a system of tying knots on a string called a *quipu*. The *quipu* used the decimal system, much as we do. The knots at the end stood for 1, those farther up each counted for 10, and those still higher up stood for 100. Crop records and population information were recorded by this method.

Concluding Statement   Records of all types have always been important to society. How we keep records will change as technology and our needs change.

Revising Leave time to revise and edit your essay answer. To keep your paper as neat as possible, use proofreading symbols to mark any corrections or revisions. As you revise, think of the following questions.

- Did you follow the instructions completely?
- Did you interpret the question accurately?
- Did you begin with a main idea statement?
- Did you include facts, examples, or other supporting details?
- Did you sequence your ideas and examples logically in paragraphs according to your informal outline?
- Did you use transitions to connect ideas and examples?
- Did you end with a strong concluding statement that summarizes your main idea?

Editing After you have made any necessary revisions, quickly read your essay to check for mistakes in spelling, usage, or punctuation.

Timed Writing

Throughout your school years, you will be tested on your ability to organize your thoughts quickly and to express them in a limited time. (This is, in fact, a skill that will most likely be useful throughout your life.) Your teacher may ask you to write a twenty-minute, two-hundred-word essay that will then be judged on how thoroughly you covered the topic and organized your essay. The more you practice writing under time constraints, the better you will be able to apply these effective writing strategies during timed tests.

Strategies for a Timed Writing Test

- Listen carefully to instructions.
- Find out if you may write notes or an outline on your paper or in the examination book.
- Find out if you should erase mistakes or cross them out by neatly drawing a line through them.
- Plan your time carefully.

Vocabulary Development

QuickGuide

Varieties of English pages 417–418	There are often differences between spoken and written English.
Words That Communicate pages 418–419	When you write or speak, use words that truly communicate your ideas to the reader.
Determining Word Meaning pages 420–424	Numerous strategies can help you determine word meanings as you read.
Dictionary Skills pages 424–435	There is no better way to develop your vocabulary skills—or to polish your writing—than knowing how to use the dictionary well.

Varieties of English

The English language is spoken in many different countries around the world. Although English is one language, there are variations in the accents and even meanings of the same words. For example, the device that Americans call an *elevator* is called a *lift* in England, and in Australia, to be *bushed* is to be lost, while in the United States, it is to be tired.

American Dialects Even across the United States, because of the rich mix of people, there are differences in the way English is spoken. These different ways of speaking are called **dialects.** There are basically two types of American dialects: regional dialects and ethnic dialects.

Regional Dialects People from the same region tend to use the same pronunciation or accent. In the United States, scholars often divide the country into three dialect regions: Northern, Midland, and Southern. Some scholars, however, also identify New England, the West, and the Great Lakes area as different dialect regions as well. New Englanders are said to speak with a twang and Southerners with a drawl. Besides the variety in accents, there are also local usages. For example, in Philadelphia, Pennsylvania, a large sandwich may be called a *hoagie;* in Boston, Massachusetts, that same sandwich may be called a *submarine.* A similar sandwich in the South is called a *po'boy.*

Ethnic Dialects A person's cultural background can also be a factor in how he or she speaks. A variety of English spoken by a large number of members of a particular ethnic group is called an **ethnic dialect**. Some of the most widely spoken ethnic dialects in the United States are black, Hispanic, and Asian-influenced English.

Standard American English is the most widely used and accepted form of English. It is the variety of English used in newspapers, scholarly writings, and in most nonfiction books. It is the formal English that is expected in your schoolwork and in most business situations. This is not to say that other forms of English are wrong, just that different forms are appropriate to different situations. Using Standard English helps people of different regions and cultures communicate clearly with one another.

Nonstandard American English is English that does not follow the rules and guidelines of Standard American English. It is not incorrect or wrong, but simply language that is inappropriate in certain situations. Nonstandard English is the variety of English you probably use when speaking to friends and family members or when you write journal entries, personal letters, or E-mails. It has a conversational and informal tone.

Colloquialisms are informal phrases or colorful expressions that have nonliteral meanings. They can be used when nonstandard English is appropriate. Colloquialisms are appropriate for conversation and informal writing but not for formal writing.

Colloquialisms	As soon as Dan and Luis met, they **hit it off**. (got along well together)
	That horror movie sure **gave me the creeps**. (scared me)

Slang consists of nonstandard English expressions that are developed and used by particular groups. For example, teenagers often come up with their own slang expressions. Such expressions are highly colorful, exaggerated, and often humorous. Although most slang goes out of fashion quickly, a few slang expressions—such as those that follow—have become a permanent part of the language.

Slang Expressions	Simone earned ten **bucks** by mowing the Henshaws' lawn. (dollars)
	I'm going to **hang out** with Sheila and Marcus. (spend time)

Words That Communicate

Scholars estimate that English has between 700,000 and 900,000 words. With this many words, there are lots of choices, both for speaking and, more especially, for writing. Pick the words that communicate precisely what you want to say.

Tired Words and Clichés

A **tired word** is a word that has been so overused that it has been drained of meaning. Take, for example, the word *wonderful.* This word literally means "full of wonder." Now, through overuse, the word means "good."

A **cliché** is a tired expression. These are also bland and powerless due to overuse. Some examples of clichés follow.

Clichés	
good as gold	light as a feather
heavy as a rock	cold as ice
crafty as a fox	bright and early

Denotations and Connotations

The **denotation** of a word means its specific definition—the definition you will find in the dictionary. Through usage many words take on additional meanings, or **connotations**. For example, *lazy* and *idle* have similar denotative meanings. They have very different connotative meanings, however. *Lazy* has come to mean "not willing to work," while *idle* means "not working." The difference in connotation is important to consider when choosing a word.

Jargon

Jargon is specialized vocabulary used by a particular group of people. It is usually shared among group members who engage in the same activity or profession. For example, photographers use the word *zoom,* meaning "to move the camera's lens in toward the subject." The word *zoom* might not be understood to have that meaning outside a group of photographers.

Jargon can be useful when you are speaking to a group of people who are sure to understand it. It should not be used, however, when you are speaking to or writing for a general audience who may not be familiar with a specialized meaning.

Determining Word Meaning

If you come across a word that is new to you, what do you do? Suppose you came across this sentence.

Mario was indecisive when it came to choosing which hat to wear.

Perhaps you already know that *indecisive* means "prone to indecision" or "hesitant." If you didn't know the meaning, you could look up the word in a dictionary. In this section, you will learn several additional ways to unlock the meaning of an unfamiliar word.

Context Clues

The **context** of a word is the sentence and surrounding words and paragraphs in which the word is used. You can use the context to give you clues to the meaning of a new word. The following examples show the three most common kinds of context clues.

Types of Context Clues	
Definition	Objects in space that emit strong radio signals are **quasars**. (The word *quasars* is defined within the sentence.)
Examples	**Fossil fuels**, such as coal, oil, and natural gas, are nonrenewable resources. (The words *fossil fuels* are followed by examples that are known to readers and listeners.)
Synonym	Much of our knowledge about Norse explorers comes from **sagas**. These long stories were recited and passed from one generation to the next. (A synonym for the word *saga* is used in the sentence that follows it.)

Suncraft (sculpture representing Norse explorer ships), Jon Gunner Arnason, 1986

Root Words, Prefixes, and Suffixes

In addition to using context clues, you can also unlock the meanings of unfamiliar words by looking for familiar root words. In these examples, the root words are boldfaced. You probably know these words, even if you don't know what the prefixes or suffixes mean.

Root Words   mis**read**, un**touch**able, re**appear**ance, **wish**ful

Prefixes

A **prefix** is one or more syllables added to the beginning of a root word to change its meaning. For example, in the word *rename,* the prefix is *re-.* If you know that *re-* means "again," you can figure out that *rename* means "name again." Following are some common prefixes and their meanings.

Prefix	Meaning	Example
anti-	against	**anti**freeze
co-	together	**co**author
dis-	do the opposite, not	**dis**appear
il-	not	**il**legal
in-	not	**in**secure
inter-	between, among	**inter**national
mis-	incorrect	**mis**place
non-	not	**non**sense
pre-	before	**pre**historic
re-	again, back	**re**gain
super-	more than	**super**human
trans-	across	**trans**continental
un-	opposite of	**un**happy

Suffixes

A **suffix** is a syllable or group of syllables added to the end of a word to change its meaning. Unlike prefixes, many suffixes can change a word from one part of a speech to another. Just as with prefixes, however, knowing a few suffixes can help you determine the meaning of some words. Below, the part of speech identified for each suffix is the part of speech created by adding the suffixes shown.

Common Suffixes		
Noun Suffixes	**Meaning**	**Examples**
-ance, -ence	state of	correspond**ence**
-ment	state of	amaze**ment**
-ist	one who or that	art**ist**
-ness	state of	well**ness**
Verb Suffixes	**Meaning**	**Examples**
-en	make, become	bright**en**
-ize	make, cause to be	material**ize**
Adjective Suffixes	**Meaning**	**Examples**
-able, -ible	capable of	flex**ible**
-ful	full of	hope**ful**
-less	without	pain**less**
-ous	full of	danger**ous**
Adverb Suffix	**Meaning**	**Example**
-ly	in a certain way	careful**ly**

Be careful when reading for prefixes and suffixes. The word *unify* is not *ify* with the prefix *un*. It is the word *unit* with the suffix *–fy*.

Using context clues will help you determine whether or not your guess about a word is correct. If a definition does not make sense in context, then look the word up and find out what it means.

Compound Nouns

Compound nouns are nouns that are formed by combining two or more words. For example, *railroad, football,* and *raincoat* are compound nouns. So are *dog house* and *warm-up*. You can often determine the meaning of a compound noun by breaking it into parts. For example, if you didn't know the meaning of the word *raincoat*, you could get a pretty good idea by breaking it into the two words *rain* and *coat*—a coat for wearing in the rain.

Synonyms

When you write or speak, you want to express your meaning exactly. English is so rich in words that you can often choose among several with similar meanings to find just the right one. A word that has nearly the same meaning as another word is called a **synonym**.

Although synonyms mean about the same thing, they often convey slightly different shades of meaning. In the following sentences, for example, the verb *padded* paints a more precise picture.

> The wolf **walked** through the deep forest
>
> The wolf **padded** through the deep forest.

Dictionaries often include synonyms for words. A special dictionary called a **thesaurus** lists only synonyms.

When trying to determine the meaning of a word, synonyms can be helpful if they are used nearby. Consider this sentence.

> She returned swiftly to her domicile, knowing that the small cottage would cheer her up.

Even if you don't know the word *domicile,* the synonym *cottage* would help you figure out that she is returning home.

In the Garden, Yeend Kind

Antonyms

An **antonym** is a word that means the opposite of another word. Dictionaries as well as thesauruses list antonyms for many words.

Some Antonyms	
abundant : scarce	ban : allow
negative : positive	drab : colorful
precise : inexact	exterior : interior
descendent : ancestor	effect : cause
temporary : permanent	meek : bold

As with synonyms, antonyms can aid you in determining word meaning in context. For example, if you read, "You're not the hero in this story, you're the antagonist," you can tell that *antagonist* is the opposite of *hero,* because of the "not" before hero. So *antagonist* is the opposite of *hero.*

Dictionary Skills

A **dictionary** is a reference source that gives the pronunciations, definitions, parts of speech, and other information about the words of a particular language. Whenever you need to confirm the spelling, definition, pronunciation, or part of speech of a word, you will use a dictionary. In addition, you can use the dictionary to research the origin or history of a word. Some dictionaries also provide synonyms and antonyms.

Dictionary Structure

There are some variations among dictionaries, but all of them are organized in the same general manner. Dictionaries are structured so that you will be able to quickly and easily find the information you are looking for. As you look over the following dictionary entries, notice how the information is organized. Especially notice that the entries are listed in alphabetical order.

abbreviation — **Ne** The symbol for the element **neon**.
NE *abbr.* An abbreviation of: **1.** Northeast. **2.** Nebraska. **3.** New England.
Ne·an·der·thal (nē ăn′ l′) *n.* Neanderthal

capitalization — far away, close by. A brook ran nearby.
Near East (nîr). A region of southwest Asia generally thought to include Turkey, Lebanon, Israel, Iraq, Jordan, Saudi Arabia, the other countries of the Arabian Peninsula, and sometimes Egypt and

spelling — **near·ly** (nîr′lē) *adv.* **1.** Almost but not quite: *That*
definitions — *coat nearly fits.* **2.** Closely or intimately: *The two girls are nearly related.*
near·sight·ed (nîr′sī′tĭd) *adj.* Unable to see distant
pronunciation — objects clearly; myopic. —**near′sight′ed·ly** *adv.*
related forms — —**near′sight′ed·ness** *n.*
part of speech — **neat** (nēt) *adj.* **neat·er, neat·est. 1.** Orderly and clean; tidy: *a neat room; neat handwriting.* **2.** Orderly, as in appearance; not careless or messy: *a neat person.* **3.** Performed with precision and skill: *a neat, graceful takeoff.* **4.** *Slang.* Wonderful; fine: *a*
word origin — *neat party.* [First written down in 1542 in Modern English, from Latin *nitidus*, elegant, gleaming.] —**neat′ly** *adv.* —**neat′ness** *n.*

synonyms — **Synonyms: neat, tidy, trim, shipshape.** These adjectives mean marked by good order and cleanliness. **Neat** means pleasingly clean and orderly: *Marcia pulled back her hair into a neat ponytail.* **Tidy** suggests precise arrangement and order: *Even their closets and drawers were kept tidy.* **Trim** stresses a smart appearance because of neatness, tidiness, and pleasing proportions: *The trim little boat was all ready to set sail.* **Shipshape** means both neat and tidy: *We'll have the kitchen shipshape in no time.* **antonyms** — **Antonyms: messy, sloppy.**

Guide words are the words printed in **boldface** type at the top of each dictionary page. They show you the first and last words defined on that page. The guide words *pinch/pioneer,* for example, let you know that *pine* and *pinto bean* are listed on that page. The words *pistachio* and *pit,* however, would appear on a later page.

Alphabetical Order A dictionary includes many different kinds of entries. Notice the strict letter-by-letter alphabetical order in the examples below. A compound word is alphabetized as if there were no space or hyphen between each part of the word. An abbreviation is alphabetized letter by letter, not by the word it stands for.

Entry Type	Example
Single Word	valentine
Two-Word Compound	vampire bat
Hyphenated Compound	Venus's-flytrap
Prefix	vice-
Phrase	vice versa
Abbreviation	V.I.P.

Information in an Entry The dictionary presents a wealth of information about each word. All of the information for each word is called the **entry**. The four most important parts of the entry are the entry word, pronunciation, definitions, and word origin. The following entry for the word *disk* shows these four main parts.

pronunciation

entry word — **disk** also **disc** (dĭsk) *n.* **1.** A thin, flat, circular object, such as a plate or coin. **2.** Something that resembles such an object: *the moon's disk reflected in the pond.* **3.** Often **disc. a.** A phonograph record. **b.** A round flat plate coated with a magnetic substance on which computer data is stored. **c.** An optical disk, especially a compact disk. [First written down in 1664 in Modern English, from Greek *diskos,* quoit, from *dikein,* to throw.]

definitions

word origins

The Entry Word

A quick glance at the entry word will give you three pieces of useful information. It shows you (1) how to spell a word, (2) whether a word should be capitalized, and (3) where a word should be divided into syllables.

Spelling The entry word shows how to spell a word correctly. Some words have more than one correct spelling. The most common spelling is called the **preferred spelling**. It will be listed first. The second spelling is called the **variant spelling**. Always use the preferred spelling in your writing.

preferred spelling   variant spelling

the·a·ter   or   **the·a·tre**

A dictionary also shows you how to spell the plurals of nouns, the principal parts of verbs, and the comparative and superlative degrees of adjectives and adverbs. These are given only if the form or spelling is irregular.

pronunciation ———
principal parts ———
com·mute (kə myoot´) *v.* com·mut·ed, com·mut·ing, com·mutes.

adjective forms ———
mouse (mous) *n., pl.* mice.
rust·y (rŭs´ tē) *adj.* rust·i·er, rust·i·est.

Words formed by adding a suffix to the entry word are often shown at the end of the entry. This most commonly occurs when the spelling of the root word is altered by the addition of the suffix. These related forms are called **derived words**.

nois·y (noi´zē) *adj.* **nois·i·er, nois·i·est. 1.** Making a lot of noise: *a noisy engine.* **2.** Full of, characterized by, or accompanied by noise: *noisy streets.*
derived words —**nois´i·ly** *adv.* —**nois´i·ness** *n.*

Capitalization When a word should be capitalized, the entry word will be printed with a capital letter. If a word is not always capitalized, the word will be shown with a capital letter near the appropriate definition.

> **web** (wĕb) *n.* **1.** A woven fabric, especially one on or just removed from a loom. **2.** A latticed or woven structure: *A web of palm branches formed the roof of the hut.* **3.** A structure of fine silky strands woven by spiders or by certain insect larvae. **4.** Something that traps or snares by or as if by entangling: *a web of deceit.* **5.** A fold of skin or thin tissue connecting the toes of certain water birds or other animals. **6.**
>
> capital letter ——— **Web.** World Wide Web. —*tr.v.* **webbed, web·bing, webs.** To provide with a web or webs. [First written down about 725 in Old English and spelled *webb.*]

Syllables Sometimes when you are writing a composition, you need to divide a word at the end of a line. The dictionary shows you where each syllable ends.

as·tro·naut   **I·tal·ian**   **pri·va·cy**

Homographs are words that are spelled alike but have different meanings and different origins. They are also sometimes called **homonyms**. Homographs will have separate listings preceded by superscripted numbers, as in ¹**mail,** ²**mail.** For example, one listing for *compound* reveals a Latin root— *com-* + *ponere*—and means "to put together, make a whole," while another listing for *compound* reveals a Malaysian root—*kompong*— and means "enclosure or fenced-in area." Homographs are not the same as multiple-meaning words. Multiple-meaning words have the same origins and are not listed separately.

Pronunciation A phonetic spelling is shown in parentheses after each entry word. The phonetic spelling shows how to pronounce the word correctly.

knee (nē)   **ra·di·o** (rā′dē·ō)

A complete pronunciation key at the beginning of the dictionary explains all the symbols used in the phonetic spellings. In addition, most dictionaries provide a shortened form of the key on every other page for easy reference.

Partial Pronunciation Key			
Symbol	**Example**	**Symbol**	**Example**
ă	pat	ō	toe
ā	pay	ô	caught, paw, for
âr	care	o͝o	took
ä	father	o͞o	boot
ĕ	pet	th	this
ē	bee	ŭ	cut
hw	whoop	ûr	urge, term, firm, word, heard
ĭ	pit	ü	rule, youth
ī	pie, by	zh	vision, pleasure, garage
îr	dear, deer, pier	ə	about, item, edible, gallop, circus
ŏ	pot	ər	butter

Diacritical Marks In the pronunciation key, there are marks over some of the vowels. They are called diacritical marks. Diacritical marks are used to show the different sounds a vowel can make. For example, the different sounds of the vowel *a* are shown in the following ways.

Diacritical Marks   ă as in hat   ā as in age   â as in far

The Schwa Sometimes vowels are pronounced like the sound *uh*. Dictionaries use the symbol **ə** to represent this sound. This symbol is called a schwa.

a·bove (ə bŭv′)   **lem·on** (lem′ ən)   **to·ken** (tō′ kən)

Accent Marks An accent mark (′) in a phonetic spelling tells you which syllable should be pronounced with the most stress.

fa·mous (fā′ məs)   in·jus·tice (ĭn jŭs′ tĭs)

Some words have two accent marks. The darker one, called the **primary accent,** receives the most stress. The lighter one, called the **secondary accent,** receives slightly less stress.

Primary Accent

Secondary Accent

in·ex·pen·sive (ĭn ĭk spĕn′ sĭv)

Definitions Many words have more than one definition. Look at the entry for the word *program.* Notice that eight definitions are given. When looking for the meaning of a word, be sure to read all of the definitions and examples carefully. Then decide which meaning makes sense in your sentence.

pro·gram (prō′grăm′ *or* prō′grəm) *n.* **1.** A list of the order of events and other information for a public presentation or entertainment: *a printed program of the concert.* **2.** A public performance, presentation, or entertainment: *We presented a program of folk music.* **3.** A radio or television show. **4.** An ordered list of activities, courses, or procedures; a schedule: *arranged her program so that she could have Mondays off.* **5.** A course of academic study or extracurricular activities: *an excellent African studies program.* **6.** A system of services or projects designed to achieve a goal: *the space program.* **7.a.** The set of steps necessary for a computer to solve a problem, including the collection and processing of data and the presentation of results. **b.** The set of instructions that a computer must execute in carrying out these steps. —*tr.v.* **pro·grammed, pro·gram·ming, pro·grams** *or* **pro·**

Parts of Speech Labels To indicate a word's **part of speech** most dictionaries use the following abbreviations.

n.	noun	*pron.*	pronoun
v.	verb	*prep.*	preposition
adj.	adjective	*conj.*	conjunction
adv.	adverb	*interj.*	interjection

tug (tŭg) *v.* **tugged, tug·ging, tugs.** —*tr.* **1.** To pull at vigorously; strain at: *The puppy was tugging the leash.* **2.** To move by pulling with great effort or exertion; drag: *I tugged a chair across the room.* See Synonyms at **pull. 3.** To tow by a tugboat. —*intr.* To pull hard: *kept tugging until the boot came off.* —*n.* **1.** A strong pull or pulling force. **2.** A tugboat. [First written down before 1200 in Middle English and spelled *toggen,* from Old English *tēon.*]

Many words may be used as more than one part of speech. Notice that the word *tug* can be used as either a verb or a noun. Be sure to find the right part of speech when searching for the definition of a word.

Synonyms At the end of some entries, the dictionary will list synonyms. Synonyms are words that have similar definitions.

> **glad** (glăd) *adj.* **glad·der, glad·dest. 1.** Experiencing or showing joy and pleasure: *We were so glad to get your letter.* **2.** Providing joy and pleasure: *The wedding was a glad occasion.* **3.** Pleased; willing: *I would be glad to help.* —**glad'ly** *adv.* —**glad'ness** *n.*

synonyms ——— > **Synonyms: glad, happy, cheerful, lighthearted, joyful.** These adjectives mean being in or showing good spirits. **Glad** often means satisfied with immediate circumstances: *I am so glad we finally met.* **Happy** can mean feeling pleasurable contentment, as from a sense of fulfillment: *Jane is happy with her new job.* **Cheerful** means having good spirits, as distinct from being pleased: *Leroy tried to remain cheerful while he was in the hospital.* **Lighthearted** means free of cares and worries: *Summertime always puts you in a lighthearted mood.* **Joyful** means having great happiness and liveliness: *Their wedding was a joyful occasion.*

Word Origins As you read at the beginning, the English language has gone through many changes. The following examples show how the words we use today have changed over time.

Old English	Middle English	Modern English
modor	*moder*	mother
faeder	*fader*	father
wudu	*wode*	wood
geolu	*yelwe, yelow*	yellow
brecan	*breken*	break
fealdan	*folden*	fold

The dictionary provides information about the history of words in the English language. This information, called the **word origin**, is generally found in brackets at the end of an entry. The following entry shows that the word *compute* comes from two Latin words meaning "to reckon together."

word origin ——

> **com·pute** (kəm pyoot′) *v.* **com·put·ed, com·put·ing, com·putes.** —*tr.* **1.** To work out (a result, an answer, or a solution) by mathematics; calculate: *The bank computes the interest on savings accounts.* **2.** To determine by use of a computer: *compute the most efficient design of a sailboat.* —*intr.* **1.** To determine an amount or a number. **2.** To use a computer. [First written down in 1631 in Modern English, from Latin *computāre* : *com-*, together + *putāre*, to reckon.]

Not all dictionaries spell out the names of the languages of the words of origin. Often, you will see *L* for Latin, *ME* for Middle English, *Gk* for Greek, *F* for French, and so on. Look for a listing near the front of the dictionary that identifies the abbreviations and their meanings.

Words from Foreign Languages

The English language is constantly growing as well as changing. Although there are many different sources for new words, more than half of the words in the English language have been adopted from other languages. As you read at the beginning of this chapter, English has adopted useful words wherever they were found. Often, the words are clearly related to the countries from which they were adopted, such as *kimono* from Japan. But some adopted words may surprise you. Look at the charts on the following page.

Words from Foreign Languages			
Spanish	canyon	rodeo	bonanza
Dutch	cookie	landscape	skipper
Italian	cartoon	spaghetti	violin
Arabic	algebra	coffee	harem
Hindi	pajama	khaki	shampoo
Afrikaans	trek	commando	aardvark
Egyptian	paper	ivory	barge
Japanese	kimono	kamikaze	sushi
Chinese	tea	typhoon	wok
Malay	bamboo	sarong	gecko

Words with Native American Origins

Native American groups have added numerous words to English.

Words of Native American Origin			
avocado	chocolate	muskrat	squash
barbecue	hickory	opossum	tobacco
canoe	hurricane	pecan	toboggan
caribou	igloo	potato	tomahawk
caucus	jaguar	powwow	tomato
chili	maize	raccoon	totem
chipmunk	moose	skunk	wigwam

Words with Unusual Origins

Borrowing words from other languages is only one way our language grows. New words come into our language in a variety of other ways. Some words, called compounds, are formed by combining two words.

Compounds   fingerprint, raincoat, houseboat

Some words need to be created to name things that did not exist before. One example is *astronaut,* which combines the Greek words meaning *star (astro)* and *sailor (naut).* So an astronaut is someone who travels among the stars.

Some words are a blend of two words.

Blends   television + broadcast = telecast

squirm + wiggle = squiggle

situation + comedy = sitcom

Some words are shortened forms of longer words.

Shortened Forms   ad = advertisement

lunch = luncheon

radio = radiotelegraphy

fax = facsimile machine

Some words imitate sounds. (If you have studied poetry, you may remember that the use of a word that imitates a sound is called *onomatopoeia.*)

Sounds   crunch, plunk, strum, yap, whiff

Some words are derived from the names of people.

People's Names   Adolf Sax: Belgian inventor of the **saxophone**

Rudolf Diesel: German inventor of the **diesel** engine

Some words are acronyms. **Acronyms** are words that are formed by the first letters or syllables of other words.

Acronyms   SONAR: **so**und **na**vigation **r**anging

RADAR: **ra**dio **d**etecting **a**nd **r**anging

SCUBA: **s**elf-**c**ontained **u**nderwater **b**reathing **a**pparatus

CHAPTER 36

Spelling Strategies

QuickGuide

Learning Spelling Strategies pages 437–438	Master key strategies for correct spelling.
Spelling Patterns pages 438–440	Use spelling patterns to become a better speller.
Plurals pages 440–444	Follow a few simple rules for spelling plurals.
Prefixes and Suffixes pages 445–448	Prefixes and suffixes follow specific spelling rules.
Words to Master page 449	Make it your goal to learn to spell these fifty words.

Learning Spelling Strategies

Misspelled words, whether in a composition for school or in a letter to a friend, call attention to themselves. Unfortunately, that means they are likely to distract readers from the thoughts being expressed and may even leave readers wondering what you meant. This chapter will introduce you to strategies and generalizations to help improve your spelling.

Strategy **Use a dictionary.** If you're not sure how to spell a word, or if a word doesn't "look right," check its spelling in a dictionary. Don't rely on guessing to help you spell accurately.

Strategy **Proofread your writing carefully.** If you use a computer, do not rely on your word processing program to catch spelling errors. When you type the word *strait,* the computer can't know if you really meant to type *straight, strait, trait,* or even *strain.*

Strategy **Be sure you are pronouncing words correctly.** "Swallowing" syllables or adding extra syllables can cause you to misspell a word.

Strategy **Use mnemonic devices.** Look for memorable small words or word patterns in difficult words: "I want a **pie**ce of **pie**," "pull a**part** to se**pa**rate," or "The first two syllables of Antarctica begin with *a*'s followed by two consonants." Inventing a sentence like "**Re**placing **cur**tains **ren**ovates **cel**lars" can help you remember the letter groups in *recurrence.*

Strategy **Keep a spelling journal.** Use it to record the words you have had trouble spelling. Here are some suggestions for organizing your journal.

- Write the word correctly.
- Write the word again, underlining or circling the part of the word that gave you trouble.
- Write a tip that will help you remember how to spell the word in the future.

stationery station<u>e</u>ry	A w<u>ri</u>ter writes on station<u>e</u>ry. (An <u>art</u>ist needs a station<u>a</u>ry model.)
accidentally <u>a</u>ccidental<u>ly</u>	The first and last consonants are doubled; the consonants in the middle are single.

Strategies That Use Your Senses

The senses of hearing, sight, and touch are useful tools for learning to spell correctly. Try this five-step strategy.

1. Auditory Say the word aloud. Answer these questions.
- Where have I heard or read the word before?
- What was the context in which I heard or read the word?

2. Visual Look at the word. Answer these questions.
- Does this word divide into parts? Is it a compound word? Does it have a prefix or a suffix?
- Does this word look like any other word I know? Could it be part of a word family I would recognize?

3. Auditory Spell the word to yourself. Answer these questions.
- How is each sound spelled?
- Are there any surprises? Does the word follow spelling rules I know, or does it break the rules?

4. Visual/Kinesthetic Write the word as you look at it. Answer these questions.
- Have I written the word clearly?
- Are my letters formed correctly?

5. Visual/Kinesthetic Cover up the word. Visualize it. Write it. Answer this question.
- Did I write the word correctly?
- If the answer is "no," return to step 1.

Spelling Patterns

Some people are naturally good spellers. They can "see" the correct spelling of a word in their minds, or they can "hear" the word, remembering how the syllables sound. If you are not a naturally good speller, learning some patterns should make spelling easier for you. And if you are a good speller, these strategies can make you better.

Words with *ie* and *ei*

Words with *ie* and *ei* often cause confusion. Use the following familiar rhyme to help you spell such words.

> Put *i* before *e*
> Except after *c*
> Or when it sounds like long *a*
> As in *neighbor* and *weigh*.

As the poem reminds you, when you spell words with *ie* or *ei*, *i* frequently comes before *e*, except when these letters follow *c* or when they stand for the long *a* sound.

Words with *ie* and *ei*		
i* before *e		
belief	achieve	niece
piece	field	brief
except after *c*		
ceiling	conceit	deceive
perceive	receipt	receive
sounds like *a*		
eight	reins	sleigh
veil	weight	feign

Exceptions: These words do not follow the pattern			
either	foreign	height	ancient
sufficient	species	forfeit	conscience
glacier	weird	their	leisure

When you look at exceptions to spelling generalizations, ask yourself if you can see patterns in them. For example, you might notice that *c* is followed by *ie* in words like *ancient, conscience,* and *sufficient*. Pronouncing these words may help you. None of them are pronounced with the long *e* sound that you find in *piece, belief,* and so on.

Words Ending in *–cede, –ceed,* or *–sede*

Some other words that cause problems are those that end with a "seed" sound. This sound can be spelled *–cede, –ceed,* or *–sede.* Most words that end with this sound are spelled *–cede.*

-cede			
precede	recede	concede	intercede
secede	accede	supercede	

There are only four words with the "seed" sound that are not spelled with *–cede.* You'll have no trouble spelling these words if you memorize the four exceptions.

-ceed and -sede			
exceed	proceed	succeed	supersede

Plurals

The following generalizations will help you spell the plurals of nouns correctly. When in doubt, check a dictionary.

Regular Nouns

To form the plural of most nouns, simply add *s*.

Most Nouns				
Singular	moon	moth	nova	age
Plural	moons	moths	novas	ages

If a noun ends in *s, ch, sh, x,* or *z,* add *es* to form the plural.

Nouns Ending in *s, ch, sh, x,* or *z*				
Singular	lens	peach	blush	box	chintz
Plural	lenses	peaches	blushes	boxes	chintzes

Follow the same generalizations to make proper nouns plural.

the Garcia family = the Garcias

the James family = the Jameses

the Walsh family = the Walshes

An apostrophe is never used to make the plural form of proper nouns. It is used to show possession.

Nouns Ending in *y*

Add *s* to form plurals of nouns ending in a vowel and a *y.*

Nouns Ending in Vowel and *y*				
Singular	decoy	alley	delay	chimney
Plural	decoys	alleys	delays	chimneys

Change the *y* to *i* and add *es* to a noun ending in a consonant and a *y.*

Nouns Ending in Consonant and *y*				
Singular	galaxy	recovery	paddy	balcony
Plural	galaxies	recoveries	paddies	balconies

Nouns Ending in *o*

Add *s* to form the plural of a noun ending with a vowel and an *o*.

Nouns Ending in Vowel and an *o*			
Singular	ratio	cameo	embryo	taboo
Plural	ratios	cameos	embryos	taboos

Add *s* to form the plural of musical terms ending in *o*.

Musical Terms That End with *o*			
Singular	trio	soprano	piccolo	tango
Plural	trios	sopranos	piccolos	tangos

Add *s* to form the plural of words borrowed from the Spanish language.

Spanish Words That End in *o*			
Singular	lasso	rodeo	pinto	presidio
Plural	lassos	rodeos	pintos	presidios

The plurals of nouns ending in a consonant and an *o* do not follow a regular pattern.

Nouns Ending with Consonant and an *o*			
Singular	yo-yo	silo	veto	echo
Plural	yo-yos	silos	vetoes	echoes

When you are not sure how to form the plural of a word that ends in *o*, consult a dictionary. Sometimes you will find that either spelling is acceptable. In this case, use the first form given. If the dictionary does not give a plural form, the plural is usually formed by adding *s*.

Nouns Ending in *f* or *fe*

To form the plural of some nouns ending in *f* or *fe*, just add *s*.

Nouns Ending in *f* or *fe*				
Singular	belief	staff	giraffe	carafe
Plural	beliefs	staffs	giraffes	carafes

For some nouns ending in *f* or *fe*, change the *f* to *v* and add *es* or *s*.

Nouns Ending in *f* or *fe* That Change to *v*				
Singular	calf	scarf	thief	life
Plural	cal**ves**	scar**ves**	thie**ves**	li**ves**

Other common words where *f* turns to *v* are *knife, wife, loaf, wolf,* and *half.* Because there is no sure way to tell which generalization applies, consult a dictionary to check the plural form of a word that ends with *f* or *fe*.

Compound Words

Most compound nouns are made plural by adding an *s* or *es* at the end.

Compound Nouns				
Singular	teammate	dragonfly	tryout	bathing suit
Plural	teammates	dragonflies	tryouts	bathing suits

Sometimes it makes more sense to add the ending to the first word. When the main word in a compound noun appears first, that word is made plural.

Exceptions				
Singular	father-in-law	part of speech	attorney general	passerby
Plural	fathers-in-law	parts of speech	attorneys general	passersby

Numerals, Letters, Symbols, and Words as Words

To form the plurals of most numerals, letters, symbols, and words used as words, add an *s*.

> Those *8*s look too much like *B*s.

> The 1870s and 1880s were called the Gilded Age.

> Proofreaders' *#*s tell printers to add space.

To prevent confusion, it's best to use an apostrophe and *s* with lowercase letters, some capital letters, and some words used as words.

> How do you pronounce the *i*'s in *giving*? (Without the apostrophe, *i*'s might be confused with the verb *is*.)

> There are a lot of *I*'s in his conversation.

> These two *theirs*'s should be *they're*'s.

Other Plural Forms

Irregular plurals are not formed by adding *s* or *es*. These are words you must memorize.

Irregular Plurals		
foot, feet	tooth, teeth	goose, geese
child, children	man, men	woman, women
die, dice	mouse, mice	louse, lice

Some nouns have the same form for both singular and plural.

Same Form for Singular and Plural		
Swiss	French	British
deer	sheep	moose
pliers	species	politics

When in doubt, check the dictionary. If the plural is irregular, the dictionary will show how it is spelled.

Prefixes and Suffixes

Prefixes

A **prefix** is one or more syllables placed in front of a base word to form a new word.

When you add a prefix, the spelling of the base word does not change.

Prefixes	
in + sincere = **insincere**	**im** + patient = **impatient**
pre + caution = **precaution**	**over** + rated = **overrated**
dis + honest = **dishonest**	**mis** + heard = **misheard**
re + arrange = **rearrange**	**un** + noticed = **unnoticed**
ir + resistible = **irresistible**	**il** + legible = **illegible**

Occasionally, it is necessary to add a hyphen after a prefix to avoid confusion. Check a dictionary if you are in doubt.

Hyphenated Prefixes	
re-cover (Add hyphen to distinguish from the verb *recover*.)	**semi**-independent (Add hyphen to avoid double *i*'s.)

It's easy to leave out one of the *r*'s in *irresistible* or *overrated*. Remember that these words are created by adding prefixes to base words. If you're not sure whether a word has double letters in the beginning, ask yourself whether it could be one of these prefix-base word combinations.

Suffixes

A **suffix** is one or more syllables placed after a base word to change its part of speech and possibly its meaning.

In many cases, especially when the base word ends in a consonant, you simply add the suffix.

Suffixes	
eager + **ness** = eager**ness**	right + **ful** = right**ful**
treat + **ment** = treat**ment**	vague + **ly** = vague**ly**

Words Ending in *e*

Drop the final *e* before a suffix that begins with a vowel.

Words Ending in *e*; Suffix Starts with a Vowel	
pause + **ing** = paus**ing**	size + **able** = siz**able**
narrate + **ion** = narrat**ion**	universe + **al** = univers**al**

Keep the final *e* in words that end in *ce* or *ge* if the suffix begins with an *a* or *o*. The *e* keeps the sound of the *c* or *g* soft before these vowels.

Words Ending in *ce* and *ge*	
manage + **able** = manage**able**	replace + **able** = replace**able**
advantage + **ous** = advantage**ous**	notice + **able** = notice**able**
knowledge + **able** = knowledge**able**	

Keep the final *e* when adding a suffix that begins with a consonant.

Words Ending in *e*; Suffix Begins with a Consonant	
peace + **ful** = peace**ful**	amuse + **ment** = amuse**ment**
hope + **less** = hope**less**	wise + **ly** = wise**ly**
same + **ness** = same**ness**	

Exceptions	
true + **ly** = truly	judge + **ment** = judgment
awe + **ful** = awful	argue + **ment** = argument

Words Ending in *y*

To add a suffix to most words ending in a vowel and a *y*, keep the *y*.

Words Ending in Vowels and a *y*	
play + **able** = play**able**	mislay + **ing** = mislay**ing**
enjoy + **ment** = enjoy**ment**	replay + **ed** = replay**ed**

Exceptions	
day + **ly** = dai**ly**	gay + **ly** = gai**ly**

To add a suffix to most words ending in a consonant and a *y*, change the *y* to *i* before adding the suffix except when adding the verb ending *–ing*.

Words Ending in Consonants and a *y*	
envy + **able** = env**iable**	bounty + **ful** = bount**iful**
thrifty + **ly** = thrift**ily**	dreary + **ness** = drear**iness**
mercy + **ful** = merc**iful**	identify + **able** = identif**iable**

Exceptions	
identify + **ing** = identify**ing**	solidify + **ing** = solidify**ing**

One-syllable words that end in *y* pronounced long *i* do not change their spellings when the suffix *–ness* or verb ending *–ing* are added. They *do* change their spellings when the verb ending *–ed* is added.

Words Ending in *y* pronounced long *i*	
shy + **ness** = shy**ness**	dry + **ed** = dr**ied**
dry + **ness** = dry**ness**	pry + **ed** = pr**ied**
sly + **ness** = sly**ness**	spy + **ed** = sp**ied**

Doubling the Final Consonant

Sometimes the final consonant in a word is doubled before a suffix or verb ending is added.

Double the final consonant in a word before adding a suffix or verb ending only when all three of the following conditions are met:

    (1) The suffix begins with a vowel.

    (2) The base word has only one syllable or is stressed on the last syllable.

    (3) The base word ends in one consonant preceded by a vowel.

One-Syllable Words	
plot + **ing** = plotting	char + **ed** =charred
trap + **er** =trapper	mad + **est** = maddest
Final Syllable Stressed	
befit + **ing** = befitting	transfer + **ed** = transferred
rebut + **al** = rebuttal	recur + **ence** = recurrence

Don't double the final *r* in words that end in *fer* when you add the suffix *–ence* or *–able.* Notice how the pronunciation of the base word changes when the suffix is added. This is your clue that only one *r* is needed.

Final *r*	
refer + **ence** = reference	infer + **ence** = inference
defer + **ence** = deference	transfer + **able** = transferable

Be sure not to double the final letter if it is preceded by two vowels.

Two Vowels	
creep + **ing** = creeping	seat + **ed** = seated
train + **er** = trainer	proud + **est** = proudest

Words to Master

Make it your goal to learn to spell these fifty words this year. Use them in your writing and practice writing them until spelling them comes automatically.

accelerate	hygiene
accessory	ingredient
accommodate	intercede
accumulate	irregular
acquaintance	liable
admittance	maneuver
advisable	miscellaneous
alliance	noticeable
appreciation	occurrence
ascend	pageant
carburetor	paralysis
circuit	physics
coincidence	pneumonia
committee	possibility
conceit	precipitation
consequence	preference
convenience	recruit
counterfeit	regrettable
defendant	siege
defiance	stationary
dissatisfied	stationery
efficient	succession
existence	tariff
exquisite	temporary
furlough	vacuum

CHAPTER 37

Speaking and Listening

QuickGuide

Developing Your Speaking Skills pages 451–452	Both informal and formal speaking skills will help you throughout your life.
Preparing Your Speech pages 453–455	Identify and develop a subject that suits the purpose and audience for your speech.
Practicing Your Speech page 455	Practice your speech until you feel comfortable with it.
Delivering Your Speech page 456	Remember that you are presenting your speech orally, not in writing.
Developing Your Listening Skills pages 456–459	Listening well increases enjoyment and appreciation.

Developing Your Speaking Skills

You have probably seen and heard countless conversations—in real life, on television, or in the movies. No doubt you focused on *what* was being said, but what about *how* it was said—and received? Did the speaker look relaxed, excited, or nervous? Did the listener look interested, distracted, or bored? Were the two people really listening to each other?

Informal Speaking Skills

Informal speaking is a form of speech that is suitable for everyday use or for casual occasions. This section of the chapter will help you sharpen your informal speaking skills so that even in everyday speech, you will be better understood by your listeners.

Everyday Speech Clear communication is something you can practice all the time. Whenever possible, think before you speak. If the person to whom you're talking doesn't understand what you're saying, try to think of a different way to say it.

Giving Directions Giving directions is an important type of informal speech. Clear directions show organized thinking. Clear directions are also easier to listen to and to follow. Read the two sets of directions below. Then compare them to determine why the second set of directions would be clearer to a listener who is unfamiliar with the area.

Unclear	The football stadium. Yup. Follow this road for a while until you come to a light. Then go west. The stadium should be near there.
Clear	To get to the football stadium, continue on Maple Street until you come to the second traffic light. That's Spring Street. You'll see a gas station on one corner and a medical building on another corner. Turn left on Spring and go half a mile. The stadium will be on your right.

The second set of directions would be clearer to a listener because it includes a specific distance, street names, and landmarks. The first set of directions is vague. You won't always know as many details as the second speaker, but make an effort to be clear and include as many details as you can.

Following are some important steps to keep in mind when you give directions.

Guidelines for Giving Directions
- Use *right, left,* or *straight* rather than *north, south, east,* or *west.*
- Use names of streets if you know them.
- Mention landmarks whenever possible.
- Include the approximate number of miles if you know this information.
- If possible, draw a map.
- Do not give directions for a difficult shortcut.
- If you are unsure of the correct directions, direct the person to someone who might know.
- Repeat the directions or have the other person repeat the directions to you.
- Speak clearly.
- Look directly at the person as you give them directions.
- Pay attention to nonverbal clues that might indicate that the listener does not understand.

Formal Speaking Skills

A formal speech is different from an informal speech in two basic ways. A **formal speech** is prepared in advance and is usually longer than an informal speech. Formal speaking does not mean that you have to sound stuffy or stiff. Depending on the purpose and intended audience, the speech writer can vary the tone and mood of the speech, making it more or less personal, as the occasion demands.

Occasions for Formal Speaking
- A student has to give an oral report for history class.
- A museum guide wants everyone to know why a new exhibit is important.
- You have been asked to introduce and explain the music being performed at the next band concert.
- A science fair winner must accept an award.
- The mayor dedicates a memorial for firefighters from your town.

Preparing Your Speech

The preparation of a formal speech is similar to the preparation of a written report. The main difference is that you will practice your speech and deliver it orally rather than write it.

Choosing and Limiting a Subject

For formal speeches, the subject and audience often need to be considered at the same time. Of course, if you have an assigned topic and the audience is your class, your decisions are made for you. However, you will often need to pick the topic, pick the audience, or pick both.

Sometimes the audience will determine the subject, and sometimes the subject will help determine the audience. For example, if your audience is the astronomy club, your subject will probably be something related to space. If your subject is why you should be elected student body president, your audience will be the students who might vote for you.

When you need to choose a subject, first make a list of topics you know something about. Then choose one that will interest both you and your audience. For example, if you were speaking to parents about your school's need for new athletic equipment, you might inform them about your school's athletic programs and explain the need for new equipment. If, however, you were speaking to your classmates, you could attempt to persuade them to help raise money for the new equipment.

After deciding on a subject, you need to consider the amount of time you have to deliver your speech. If you have only ten minutes, you may not be able to cover all the athletic programs your school offers. Instead, you could limit your subject to the athletic programs that attract the largest number of participants.

Understanding Your Purpose

Once you have chosen and limited your subject, you should think about the purpose of your speech. Most speeches have one of the following three purposes: to inform, to persuade, or to entertain.

Purpose	Examples
To Inform	• to explain about the effect of the moon on ocean tides • to explain the structure of icebergs
To Persuade	• to encourage students to join after-school volleyball games • to convince the school administration to sponsor a school newspaper
To Entertain	• to tell about the first time you made Thanksgiving dinner for your family • to tell about the first and only time you tried to ice-skate

Gathering and Organizing Information

After choosing and limiting your subject and deciding on your purpose, you should begin to gather and organize information.

Gathering Information

- List what you already know about your subject.
- Gather more information in the library or through an interview.
- Find interesting examples and quotations to include.
- Write your information on note cards.

Organizing Information

- Make an outline of your speech.
- The introduction should capture the attention of your audience. It should also include the main idea of your speech.
- The body of your speech should include the supporting points. Arrange your points in a logical order. Use transitions to connect your ideas.
- The conclusion of your speech should summarize your main idea.

Practicing Your Speech

Practicing aloud is a necessary step in delivering a successful speech. You may want to use a tape recorder, so you can listen to yourself and make certain you are speaking at a good rate of speed and speaking clearly. If possible, practice in front of a friend or a family member and ask for suggestions.

Practicing Your Speech

- Read your complete outline several times until you are familiar with all the information.
- Make only a few notes to use as you begin to practice aloud. You want to *talk* about your subject, not read about it from a script.
- Practice in front of a long mirror so that you will be aware of your facial expressions and gestures, such as biting your lips or clenching your hands.
- Practice looking around the room as you talk. Good eye contact is important.
- Time the length of your speech. If it is too long, decide what information you can omit. If it is too short, find more information.
- Practice over a period of several days.

Delivering Your Speech

It is important to be well prepared before a speech. Write and practice carefully, and the actual delivery will be much easier. Depending on the audience, the occasion, and the location of your speech, you may need to take additional measures. Make certain your appearance is appropriate for your audience and the occasion. Try to arrive early, because being in a rush can make you feel more nervous. Try to relax. Most people in your audience will realize that it takes work to give a formal speech, and they will be sympathetic.

Following are some guidelines for delivering your speech.

Guidelines for Delivering a Speech
- Be well prepared and have all the necessary materials.
- Wait until your audience is quiet and settled.
- Take a deep breath and begin.
- Stand with your weight evenly divided between both feet. Avoid swaying back and forth.
- Speak slowly, clearly, and loudly enough to be heard.
- Use rehearsed gestures and facial expressions to emphasize your main points.
- Look directly at the people in your audience, not over their heads. Try to make eye contact.
- Use pictures and other audiovisual aids to increase the attention of your audience.

Developing Your Listening Skills

Listening is more than just hearing words. It involves understanding what another person has said. It also requires critical thinking skills. You must evaluate what a speaker is saying by separating fact from opinion. Listening, like speaking, is a skill that can be practiced and improved.

Listening to Enjoy and Appreciate

One of the most important aspects of listening is enjoying and appreciating the subject. You will remember more about a presentation you enjoyed than one you did not enjoy. Some speakers use humor or descriptions to solidify their points and keep their speech interesting. Paying attention and listening carefully will help you enjoy the speech.

Listening for Information and Taking Notes

Taking notes is one way to focus your attention while listening to a speech. Taking notes requires you to listen carefully for important points and to organize the information. Taking notes also makes what you hear more memorable, even if you don't look at your notes again.

The following guidelines will help you take clear notes while listening.

Taking Notes on Speeches

- Write the main idea presented in the introduction of the speech.
- Write the main topics, using Roman numerals (I, II, III) in an outline form.
- Under each main topic, write the subtopics, or supporting points, using capital letters (A, B, C). Listen for clues to the supporting points, such as "There are three main reasons why . . ." or "I will explain the four main causes of . . ."
- In the conclusion of the speech, write the restatement of the main idea.

Do not try to note everything. Write only the most important points. Following is an outline of a speech about the development of gymnastics.

Main Idea	Gymnastics—sport in which physical feats are performed in artistic manner—has long history.
Main Topic	I. Began in ancient Greece
Subtopics	A. Greeks had gymnasiums with fields for throwing discuses and javelins
	B. Romans adopted Greek ideas; added them to their military training
	II. Died out between 392 A.D. and the 1700s
	A. Revived in Germany by Frederick Jahn
	B. He added side bar with pommels, horizontal bars, parallel bars, balance beams, jumping standards
	III. Brought to the U.S. in the 1800s by immigrants
	A. Americans participated in first international competition in 1881
	B. Four Americans won first gold medals in gymnastics in 1904 Olympics
Summary Statement	Gymnastics started in ancient Greece but died out for many centuries until it was revived in the 1700s. Americans did not become involved in gymnastics until the 1880s. They have participated in international competition since then.

Listening Critically

When listening, it is important to evaluate what is being said.

Fact and Opinion A **fact** is a statement that can be proved; an **opinion** is a personal feeling or judgment. Because opinions are often stated as facts, you must listen carefully to tell them apart.

Fact	Dogs belong to the canine family.
Opinion	A dog is a person's best friend.

Bandwagon Commercials and advertisements sometimes include a bandwagon statement. A **bandwagon** statement is one that leads you to believe that everyone is using a certain product so you should too. A bandwagon statement can be misleading because it suggests that if you do not jump on the bandwagon you will be different from everyone else.

Bandwagon Statement	Don't be left out. Join your friends and neighbors and pick up Ultra-Shine Car Polish. You will be glad you did.

Testimonial In a **testimonial** a famous person encourages you to buy a certain product. A testimonial can be misleading because it implies that if a famous person uses the product it must be worth buying.

Testimonial Statement	Hi! I'm quarterback Hank Hawkins. I need to have lots of pep and zip to run and throw the ball. I get all the energy I need from Grizzlies. Eat Grizzlies for breakfast every day, and you'll be just like me—ready to go.

Loaded Words Another type of misleading statement is one that contains loaded words. **Loaded words** are ones that are carefully chosen to appeal to your hopes or fears rather than to reason or logic. In the following advertisement, the word *embarrassed* was chosen to stir up the listener's emotions.

Loaded Word	Don't be embarrassed by unsightly blemishes. Use ZitZap Cleanser.

A Guide to Literature

QuickGuide

All About Authors pages 461-480	Find out more about your favorite authors from these short biographies of 101 authors
Good Reading for Young Adults pages 481-491	At a loss for a good book to read? Look over this list of favorite titles, from *Across Five Aprils* to *Z for Zachariah.*
Famous Characters from Literature pages 492-501	Characters from literature are an important part of any culture. Find many of the most memorable in this list.
Characters, Places, and Creatures from Mythology pages 502-512	Mythology is a vast source of stories, characters, and even words. Here is a list of some of the most important mythological places and characters.
Characters and Creatures from Folklore pages 513-515	From King Arthur to the Yeti, here is a list of characters and creatures from tall tales, fables, fairy tales, folktales, and legends.
A Guide to Literary Genres pages 517-521	There are many types of fiction—the fable and the tall tale, to name two. Refer to this guide for definitions of the many types of fiction, nonfiction, poetry, and drama.
A Glossary of Literary Terms pages 522-526	In this list you will find important literary terms from *allegory* to *voice.*

All About Authors

Douglas Adams (1952–2001) Author of the beloved cult science fiction novel *The Hitchhiker's Guide to the Galaxy*, Douglas Adams expanded that novel into a series of five books and a multimedia empire that included radio shows, a television series, a movie, and computer games. *The Hitchhiker's Guide* records the adventures of an alien and his human companions as they explore the universe after earth is destroyed. Adams grew up in England, and he was said to have no interest in writing until he a received a top grade on a writing assignment from one of his most exacting teachers. Adams was fascinated with technology—he was an early advocate of the Internet—and had an abiding passion for environmental issues.

Joan Aiken (1924–2004) Born and raised in England, Aiken spent her birthday money when she was five on a writing tablet and began to fill it with poems and stories. She finished her first full-length novel when she was seventeen. In her series of novels entitled the *Wolves Chronicles*, including *The Wolves of Willoughby Chase*, she re-imagines the course of history in the hopes of taking steps towards a better future. Other titles by Joan Aiken include *Black Hearts in Battersea, Nightbirds on Nantucket,* and *The Whispering Mountain.*

Lloyd Alexander (1924–2007) Lloyd Alexander began reading at an early age. He was determined to be an author, although he was vague about how to do it. To gain experience, Alexander dropped out of college and sought adventure by joining the U.S. Army during World War II. After returning to the United States, his manuscripts were rejected for seven years before his first novel was accepted. Alexander's acclaimed works include *Taran Wanderer,* named the School Library Journal's Best Book of the Year, and *The High King*, winner of a Newbery Medal in 1969.

Julia Alvarez (1950–present) Julia Alvarez was born in New York during her parents' first stay in the United States. She and her family went back to the Dominican Republic when she was three. While there her father became involved with an underground political organization. His life became endangered and resulted in the family's return to New York in 1960. Alvarez spoke some English, but she had to pay close attention to each word while conversing with her peers. This was great training for her ear as a writer. In 1991, Alvarez published her first novel, *How the Garcia Girls Lost Their Accents.* Following the success of that book, she wrote *In the Time of the Butterflies, Before We Were Free, How Tía Lola Came to Stay,* and *In the Name of Salome.* Alvarez's writing reflects the multiple identities she has assumed as a woman, a Latina, and an American.

Laurie Halse Anderson (1961–present) Laurie Halse Anderson was born in Potsdam, which she describes as "a cold place in Northern New York State." She became interested in writing in the second grade when she was taught how a haiku is structured. Her first novel, *Ndito Runs,* was inspired by a National Public Radio report about Kenyan Olympic runners. Her novel *Speak* was a National Book Award Finalist and a Printz Honor book. Other works include *Catalyst; Thank You, Sarah: The Woman Who Saved Thanksgiving;* and *Prom.*

Judie Angell (1937–present) Judie Angell sees a close correlation between music and writing. "The music was always there as background for the stories in my head, a rhythm to fit the mood," she says. As a little girl she composed stories in crayon while records played in the background. In her adolescent years she listened to the radio as she wrote in her journal. Her books include *Dear Lola: Or How to Build Your Own Family; Leave the Cooking to Me;* and *First the Good News.*

Isaac Asimov (1920–1992) It's hard to think of a writer more prolific than Isaac Asimov. In his seventy-two years, he wrote or edited more than five hundred books. Although he is best known for his science fiction novels, he wrote about other subjects as well. Born in Russia, Asimov immigrated to the United States with his family when he was three years old. He began writing at eleven, and by the time he was eighteen, he had sold his first story. *I, Robot* and *The Foundation Trilogy* are two of his best-known science fiction titles.

Avi (1937–present) Avi's pen name was bestowed on him at an early age by his twin sister. He grew up in a household that prized reading and writing. Every night he was read to, so the writer's seed was planted. But it was tough going. Avi had a learning disability called dysgraphia that made writing difficult. However, after the birth of his first child, he was inspired to write children's books, and there he found success. He received the Newbery Medal for *Crispin: The Cross of Lead* in 2003 and a Newbery Honor for *Nothing But the Truth: A Documentary Novel* in 1992. He is also the author of *The Fighting Ground* and *The True Confessions of Charlotte Doyle.*

Joan Bauer (1950–present) Joan Bauer grew up in Illinois feeling "like a water buffalo at a tea party," she reports. She is now a graceful adult and the author of several comedic novels for young people. "I believe that humorous books teach young people to use laughter against the storms of life." Bauer saw little of her father after her parents divorced, and his absence remained a source of pain into adulthood. Consequently, many of her stories contain characters that have complex yet humorous relationships with their fathers. One of her most popular titles is *Hope Was Here.*

Judy Blume (1938–present) Judy Blume says she never considered becoming a writer as a child. It didn't occur to her that the stories she made up in her head could be enjoyed by a wider audience. Blume's books have broken the mold by exploring important and sometimes uncomfortable topics such as racism, divorce, sexuality, and menstruation, at times making her books a target of censorship. Yet they have also brought praise and numerous awards. Blume's most recognizable titles include *Are You There, God? It's Me Margaret; Tales of a Fourth Grade Nothing; Freckle Juice;* and *Superfudge.*

Ray Bradbury (1920–present) Ray Bradbury has described the act of writing as "a fever—something I must do. And it seems I always have some new fever developing, some new love to follow and bring to life." As if to back up that claim, he wrote his first story at age eleven on butcher paper. Since then, Bradbury has published more than five hundred short stories, novels, plays, screenplays, television scripts, and poems, including best sellers *The Martian Chronicles, The Illustrated Man, Fahrenheit 451,* and *Something Wicked This Way Comes.* Bradbury blends contemporary issues with science fiction elements to explore the impact of technology on our lives.

Ann Brashares (1967–present) Ann Brashares found instant success with her first novel, *The Sisterhood of the Traveling Pants.* She says that the most important ingredients of female friendships are loyalty, unconditional love, and the commitment to communicate and stay involved in each other's lives.

Sue Ellen Bridgers (1942–present) Sue Ellen Bridgers grew up in North Carolina and spent much of her childhood bedridden with rheumatic fever, being entertained and read to by friends and family. She began writing poetry for the school newspaper in first grade, and in college she continued to submit work. Bridgers took a hiatus from writing to marry and raise her children before publishing her acclaimed novel *Home Before Dark.*

Bruce Brooks (1950–present) Brooks started his literary journey by writing comic books. When the plots and dialogues began to squeeze out the pictures in the frames, he knew it was time to rethink his interests. Brooks says he's happy to be a writer for young adults—a group he considers far more observant and perceptive than adults give them credit for. His two Newbery Honor books are *The Moves Make the Man* in 1985 and *What Hearts* in 1993.

Martha Brooks (1944–present) Martha Brooks' childhood was unconventional; she was raised in a medical family that lived on the grounds of the Manitoba Sanatorium. And as an adult she continues to forge her own unique path, enjoying a career as a children's author and a well-regarded jazz singer and lyricist. Brooks says that her two parallel lives balance each other nicely—the jazz is a great escape from the intensive character examination that comes with writing a book. Her critically acclaimed titles include *Being with Henry* and *True Confessions of a Heartless Girl.*

Joseph Bruchac (1942–present) A well-known storyteller from upstate New York, Joseph Bruchac draws heavily from his Abenaki Indian ancestry. He works with family members on projects to preserve Abenaki culture, language, and traditional skills. Bruchac tells traditional Native American stories that advise people to respect the earth and to behave well towards others. He has also edited several highly praised anthologies of contemporary poetry and fiction. His best-known books include *Arrow over the Door, The Dark Pond,* and the collection *Native American Stories.*

Betsy Byars (1928–present) Unlike many of her author peers, Betsy Byars was never encouraged or mentored by a teacher to become a writer. Indeed, the thought of being a writer seemed like an unappealing, solitary job. Since then she's written a number of highly regarded novels including 1971 Newbery Medal winner *The Summer of the Swans* and *The Night Swimmers,* for which she received the American Book Award. She is also the author of *The Pinballs.*

Orson Scott Card (1951–present) Orson Scott Card is known primarily for his science fiction/fantasy novels, including the *Ender* series (*Ender's Game* and *Ender's Shadow* among them). Card is a voracious reader, keeping up with the latest in science, politics, civic affairs, and so on. He also maintains a blog featuring social commentary, reviews, and advice on writing. Although he writes in a variety of literary styles, Card always emphasizes moral issues. His novels *Ender's Game* and *Speaker for the Dead* won both the Hugo and Nebula awards.

Sandra Cisneros (1954–present) Sandra Cisneros was born into a family of six brothers in Chicago, Illinois. She recalls moving often from one dilapidated neighborhood to another. To deal with the pain of the frequent moves, she retreated inside herself and found solace in writing. It was while at the University of Iowa's Writer's Workshop that she found the voice of Esperanza Cordero—a Mexican-American girl living in the plain, harsh reality of a poor Chicago barrio. The result was *The House on Mango Street*, in which Esperanza tells of her experiences through poignant short vignettes.

Beverly Cleary (1916–present) Beverly Cleary knows a little about childhood angst, as she was relegated to the lowest reading level in elementary school. Cleary has tried to make sure that children view reading as a pleasurable activity through her smart, delightful characters and plots filled with the rich, normal experiences of kids and families. She has accomplished her goal of writing about real kids, the ones who make messes and mistakes and use their imaginations in poignant, funny ways. She is best known for *Dear Mr. Henshaw, Henry Huggins*, and the *Ramona Quimby* series.

Andrew Clements (1949–present) As a college student Andrew Clements found writing an arduous process, and it was something he rarely did unless it was assigned. After teaching in public school for seven enjoyable years, Clements and his family moved to New York City so he could pursue a career in singing and songwriting. Instead he found work in publishing, which led him to explore his own strengths as a writer. On his first try he wrote *Frindle*, the wildly popular children's novel.

Judith Ortiz Cofer (1952–present) Brought up as a Puerto Rican Latina in the United States, Cofer writes her poems, essays, and stories as a woman from two cultures, incorporating both backgrounds and languages into her work. Her *An Island Like You: Stories of the Barrio* won the first Pura Belpre Award. She has said that "being both [Puerto Rican and American] makes me feel rich in cultures and languages."

James Lincoln Collier (1928–present) Making history accessible and relevant for kids is not always easy, but James Lincoln Collier, who collaborates with his brother Christopher on many historical novels, seems to have a knack for it. His brother comes up with the central idea and research, and Collier fills in the outline with an engaging, vivid story. Collier was born into an extensive family of writers and he eagerly joined the family business. His critically acclaimed books include *My Brother Sam Is Dead* and *Jump Ship to Freedom*.

Ellen Conford (1942–present) Ellen Conford loves games. She has been dubbed an authority on cryptic crossword puzzles and is a Scrabble champion. She lives with her husband, whom she claims to have been married to for 107 years despite the fact that he won't let her adopt any more dogs. She has written more than 50 children's books. Her characters embody the trials and tribulations of childhood and adolescence, and Conford treats them with humor, sensitivity, and creativity. Her popular titles include *I Love You, I Hate You, Get Lost!* and *Dear Mom, Get Me Out of Here!*

Robert Cormier (1925–2000) After thirty years as a newspaper journalist, Robert Cormier made a seamless transition to writing fun, provocative books for young adults. One of his favorite topics is intimidation and the manipulation of power. Cormier attended parochial school, and although he had some run-ins with the nuns, it was also a nun that pronounced him a writer. His best known titles are *The Chocolate War*, *I Am the Cheese*, and *After the First Death*. Cormier is the recipient of the American Library Association's Margaret A. Edwards Award, citing this trio of books as "brilliantly crafted and troubling novels that have achieved the status of classics in young adult literature."

Bruce Coville (1950–present) Before Bruce Coville could embark on his journey as a writer, he endured a list of offbeat jobs (toymaker, gravedigger, cookware salesman, and assembly line worker) until finding his rightful place as a writer. Coville's books tend to fall into the sci-fi and fantasy categories, but he doesn't take himself too seriously. His stories are full of funny, realistic characters. His popular titles include *Sarah's Unicorn*, *My Teacher Is an Alien*, and *Aliens Ate My Homework*.

Sharon Creech (1945–present) Sharon Creech grew up in a boisterous family in a suburb of Cleveland. During the summers everyone would pile into the car and take road trips to nearby states, leaving Creech with a lasting appreciation for the vast and potential adventures the landscape held—which would figure into her Newbery Medal-winning novel *Walk Two Moons*. Growing up, Creech wanted to be many things including a reporter, but she gave that up when she realized that she had a habit of changing the facts to fit her writing needs. Like many other young-adult authors, Creech started out writing for adults. She says she has to write in order to allow the characters and plot to reveal themselves to her, and that she goes into the process without knowing what direction the story will take. Creech's well-known works include *The Wanderer*, *Absolutely Normal Chaos*, and *Ruby Holler*.

Chris Crutcher (1946–present) Chris Crutcher's books, with their gritty, realistic young adult situations, are deeply appealing to his audience but not always to their parents. He's been a defining voice of the young adult genre since he started writing his sports-themed novels in the 1980s. Although he was not athletic, the small size of his school allowed him to play on several teams, where he learned the importance of sports in the lives of adolescents. Crutcher feels justified in championing his pet cause—fighting censorship of children's literature. "Banning books is senseless . . . . It doesn't do what they want it to do, and it lets kids . . . know we think they can't handle tough subjects." Crutcher's books include *Running Loose* and *Staying Fat for Sarah Byrnes*.

Christopher Paul Curtis (1953–present) Christopher Paul Curtis spent thirteen years working on an auto-body assembly line. Although that job didn't provide much creative fodder, his need to find an escape and his impressive family lineage, filled with Negro League baseball players and musicians, certainly did. It was during that time that Curtis attended college at night and began to write *The Watsons Go to Birmingham—1963*, which received a Newbery Honor Award and the Coretta Scott King Award. As a youth, Curtis had difficulty finding books he could relate to—they never seemed to be about him. His books seek to remedy the absence of young adult novels about children of color, and he delves into issues that are relevant to him and his readers. His second novel, *Bud, Not Buddy* won the Newbery Medal in 2000 and a Coretta Scott King medal.

Roald Dahl (1916–1990) Roald Dahl was born in 1916 to Norwegian parents who had immigrated to Wales. His father and older sister died when he was four, but his mother managed to send him to boarding school. Dahl hated the school, however. The cruelty of his teachers and classmates left a keen impression on him that sometimes shows up in his stories. His first children's book, *The Gremlins,* became a Disney movie in 1943, and many others (including *Charlie and the Chocolate Factory*) followed. Dahl won three Edgar Allan Poe Awards and a World Fantasy Convention Lifetime Achievement Award. Another popular title from Dahl is *James and the Giant Peach.*

Roald Dahl

Paula Danziger (1944–2004) Paula Danziger did a great deal of traveling and visiting schools to keep her in touch with how to build her characters. Although she knew she wanted to be a writer from an early age, it took a painful car accident for her to rethink her career as an educator and to begin writing for young adults. Her first book, *The Cat Ate My Gymsuit,* came out in 1974. Her books are refreshing, realistic snapshots of the young adult experience, and the fact that they are all still in print is a testament to their enduring popularity. Included in an encouraging checklist for aspiring writers, Danziger, true to her quirky fashion, reminded kids not to "eat tuna fish salad with mayo if it's been out in the sun too long."

Kate DiCamillo (1964–present) Kate DiCamillo was motivated to write when she got a job working in the children's book section of a warehouse where she was employed for more than four years. DiCamillo says she realized later in life that talent takes you only so far—hard work is equally important, if not more so. She says that even though she never wants to write, she's always glad when she does. Her goal is to write two pages a day, five days a week. After the popular success of her book *Because of Winn-Dixie*, DiCamillo won a Newbery Medal for *The Tale of Despereaux*.

Lois Duncan (1934–present) Lois Duncan is a suspense novelist who keeps her readers eagerly turning pages to get to the bottom of a mystery. Although she writes for different audiences, Duncan says, " I still choose to write primarily for teenagers because I love the sensitivity, vulnerability, and responsiveness of that age reader." Duncan meticulously constructs her plots and knows long in advance what the outcome will be. However, she is still in search of answers to the shooting death of her daughter, which she chronicled in the book *Who Killed My Daughter?* Other books include *Killing Mr. Griffin* and *I Know What You Did Last Summer.*

Nancy Farmer (1941–present) Nancy Farmer grew up in a strange hotel on the Arizona-Mexico border where she met and befriended rodeo riders and circus performer guests. She kept her adventures going by joining the Peace Corps after college and living in India for two years. When she returned, she taught science in the Bay Area of Northern California. She was again drawn to the exotic and moved to Africa for three years. She now stays in one place, at least to write, which took over her life after she read a children's book to her son. Her unusual life experiences provide all the material she needs to write fascinating books for kids. Her award-winning novels include *The Ear, the Eye, and the Arm*; *The Sea of Trolls*; and *The House of the Scorpion.*

Jack Finney (1911–1995) Jack Finney experimented with many genres of writing, but he was most famous for his thrillers. His novel *Invasion of the Body Snatchers* was twice made into a major motion picture. Finney died in 1995, after writing the sequel to his popular novel *Time and Again.*

Paul Fleischman (1952–present) Paul Fleischman's work spans many genres and has won many awards: *Graven Images,* the Newbery Honor Book, and *Bull Run,* the Scott O'Dell Award for Historical Fiction, for example. Fleischman does not write for recognition but because he is, he says, "a maker at heart." He constructs his stories slowly and carefully, taking pleasure in every page. He is also the author of *Whirligig.*

Paula Fox (1923–present) To say that Paula Fox had a difficult childhood would be an understatement. Born to parents that didn't want her, she was in an orphanage during infancy, then lived with a minister (who taught her to read and introduced her to the magical powers of storytelling), and finally with grandparents who moved around the country and to Cuba. Fox's straightforward, beautiful writing and unflinching examination of difficult topics matches her belief that "We must never,

ever try to pull the wool over children's eyes by 'watering down' powerful stories." Her young adult novels include *The Slave Dancer*, a Newbery Medal winner, and *One-Eyed Cat*, a Newbery Honor Book.

Russell Freedman (1929–present) Russell Freedman is a nonfiction writer who prefers to call himself a "factual writer" because writing about factual topics sounds more interesting than *not* writing about fiction. Freedman has written almost forty books on various topics including animal behavior and admirable people such as Eleanor Roosevelt, Crazy Horse, and Abraham Lincoln. His books often include carefully chosen photographs about his topics. They include *The Wright Brothers: How They Invented the Airplane, Immigrant Kids,* and *Kids at Work: Lewis Hine and the Crusade Against Child Labor.*

Jack Gantos (1951–present) In first grade Jack Gantos was placed in the group for slow readers. But he was too busy playing games to care. He moved to Barbados at seven and claims that ninety percent of what he knows today he learned by fifth grade from his teachers there. In sixth grade, his writing career received a boost when he surreptitiously read his sister's diary. Believing he could write better than that, he started his own diary to record stories, over heard conversations, and anything else of interest. He uses that notebook to this day for ideas for his books. His novels include *The Love Curse of the Rumbaughs, Hole in My Life,* and the *Joey Pigza* books.

Jean Craighead George (1919–present) Jean Craighead George learned a deep appreciation for nature from her naturalist parents. They spent weekends camping, studying animals, and learning about flora and fauna. A prodigious writer, George has penned more than one hundred novels, including two award-winning books about the relationships between humans and animals, *Julie of the Wolves* and *My Side of the Mountain*. One of George's writing goals is to emphasize the importance of protecting nature—nature that she hopes her audience becomes familiar with through her books.

David Gifaldi (1950–present) Like many authors who write for young adults, David Gifaldi first became interested in books while a child himself. He credits his third grade teacher for introducing him to the book that remains his favorite to this day, *The Adventures of Tom Sawyer*. It wasn't until he was a substitute teacher that he found inspiration to write his first novel. "My father's in jail," a fifth grade student said during sharing time, and Gifaldi used the shock and embarrassment of this revelation to write about a boy in similar circumstances in *One Thing for Sure*. Gifaldi says, "Growing up is hard. But it's also a time of wonder and discovery. Writing keeps me on my toes, wondering and discovering."

Jamie Gilson (1933–present) Just like the kids she writes for, Jamie Gilson uses school as a resource for ideas and learning. She credits school visits and field trips with giving her a steady supply of information and experiences she incorporates into her books. Gilson was born on the Fourth of July, and as a child she celebrated her birthdays in a number of small towns as her family moved from place to place because of her father's job. These locales are the inspiration for a number of Gilson's books (*Harvey, the Beer Can King* and *Hello, My Name Is Scrambled Eggs* set in Pittsfield, Illinois, and *Wagon Train 911* set in Independence, Missouri).

Nikki Giovanni (1943–present) Yolande Cornelia Giovanni, Jr., was born in Knoxville, Tennessee. Called Nikki from an early age, she is a leader in the black poetry movement. Her work is renowned for its urgent call for black people to embrace their own identity and to fully understand white-controlled culture. Her poetry collections *Black Feeling, Black Talk* and *Black Judgment,* both published in 1968, capture the militant attitude of the civil rights and black arts movements of that time.

Virginia Hamilton (1936–2002) Virginia Hamilton grew up listening to her parents and grandparents as they spun stories out of their personal, historical, and familial experiences. This immersion in the storytelling tradition at a young age paved the way for Hamilton to celebrate her African American and Native American heritage by using the techniques of oral storytelling in her writing. Hamilton knew how to engage children, and her stories covered everything from science fiction to history to folklore. Her extensive work has won numerous awards, and the novel *M. C. Higgins, the Great* won both a Newbery Medal and a National Book Award. Other titles include *The House of Dies Drear.*

Karen Hesse (1952–present) At the age of ten, Karen Hesse knew that she was "good with words." Because of a supportive fifth grade teacher, Mrs. Datnoff, Hesse believed that she might one day become a professional writer. It took more than thirty years, but that childhood dream finally came true. During those years she earned her living as a nanny, a waitress, a laborer, a secretary, a proofreader, and a substitute teacher—all the time writing poetry and stories whenever she could. Her book *Out of the Dust* was awarded the Newbery Medal in 1998.

S.E. Hinton (1950–present) S.E. Hinton was dissatisfied with the literature she read as a teenager, so she took matters into her own hands. When she was only seventeen, she wrote the break-out novel *The Outsiders* about class and the coming of age of a group of boys. Suddenly Hinton was the voice of youth, and she felt the pressure of representing so many people. But Hinton says she's always been better at writing than talking about writing, so she wrote—three more books, *That Was Then, This Is Now; Rumble Fish;* and *Tex,* before having her own child. Because she frequently writes from a male perspective, she uses her initials instead of her name (Susan Eloise) so she'll have more credibility with her audience. Hinton says that she writes for many reasons, one of which is that kids let her know they might not read much, but they read her books, and they want more.

S.E. Hinton

Irene Hunt (1907–2001) After a long career of college teaching, Irene Hunt changed course and pounded out stories on the typewriter at her kitchen table, learning from every one that was completed—and rejected. Her first novel was published when she was 57—and it was worth the wait. *Across Five Aprils*, Hunt's interpretation of her grandfather's Civil War story, won a Lewis Carroll Shelf Award, the Dorothy Canfield Fisher Award, the Clara Ingram Judson Memorial Award, the Charles W. Follett Award, and was the sole runner-up for the Newbery Medal. She went on to win the Newbery for her book *Up a Road Slowly*.

Angela Johnson (1961–present) Angela Johnson has produced a number of beautifully written novels that carry a strong message about love and mutual admiration as ingredients of a successful life. Although she lives alone, Johnson is constantly surrounded by her characters who make themselves at home in her world, taking up space and time like any demanding house guest. Johnson doesn't practice the rigid schedule of some authors—she prefers to let her characters' need to escape her thoughts dictate when she writes. Her books include *Toning the Sweep,* which won the Coretta Scott King Award, and *Humming Whispers*, among others.

M.E. Kerr (1927–present) Her real name is Marijane Meaker, and while M.E. Kerr has always loved books, she has not always loved her name. Thus, she has written stories under several different pseudonyms, including Ann Aldrich, Mary James, M.J. Meaker, and Vin Packer. She began her career as an office assistant working for E. P. Dutton. After one of her stories was published, she quit her job to begin writing full time. She is still writing today. Her titles include *Dinky Hocker Shoots Smack!; Is That You, Miss Blue?; If I Love You, Am I Trapped Forever?*; and *The Son of Someone Famous.*

Ron Koertge (1940–present) Ron Koertge isn't shy about his gifts as a writer, and he says he writes for the sheer exploration of it. Koertge keeps his life simple: He writes a great deal, swims, hangs out with his wife, and goes to the horse races. His writing companion is his cat Jo-Jo, who offers a supportive, noncritical presence. Koertge says, "I write dialogue well, and I'm funny," and indeed these are attributes of his highly praised novel *Stoner & Spaz*. Koertge took a very different approach with his first young adult book, *The Brimstone Journals*, an edgy novel of poems written by adolescent characters, rife with tension and violence.

E.L. Konigsburg (1930–present) E.L. Konigsburg excelled in chemistry. She studied and taught science, but after her children were in school, she picked up a pen and turned her life in a completely different direction. Through teaching and raising children, Konigsburg realized that she might have light to shed on the questions young adults have about identity and place, and this has become an underlying theme for many of her books. Konigsburg won the Newbery Medal for the beloved children's novel *From the Mixed-Up Files of Mrs. Basil E. Frankweiler.* She also wrote *The View from Saturday.*

Ursula K. LeGuin (1929–present) When it comes to writing, Ursula K. LeGuin can do almost anything. She has published six books of poetry, several books of children's fiction, twenty novels, and more than a hundred short stories. She has also published translations and books of essays. Her work has repeatedly won awards such as the National Book Award, the Pushcart Prize, Hugo and Nebula Awards, and others. LeGuin's series *Earthsea Trilogy* has been translated into sixteen languages.

Madeleine L'Engle (1918–present) Born in New York City, Madeleine L'Engle moved with her family to the French Alps when she was twelve. She returned to the states and studied theater in college, writing her first novel backstage during rehearsals. Her best-known works, Newbery Medal winner *A Wrinkle in Time* (which was rejected twenty-six times before finding a publisher) and its sequels, reveal her deep interest in the science aspect of science fiction. Her idea for *A Wrinkle in Time*, the story of a group of kids who are transported to another galaxy through a tesseract—or a wrinkle in space or time—came to her as she drove cross-country with her husband.

C.S. Lewis (1898–1963) Born in Northern Ireland as Clive Staples Lewis, Lewis was content to lose himself in his parents' extensive library rather than play outside. He was a close friend of J.R.R. Tolkien, who had a strong influence on his life choices and career path. The *Chronicles of Narnia*, a series of seven books with strong Christian and mythological themes, are Lewis's most enduring works for children. His creative, fantastic stories about three children who discover another world have captured the imaginations of readers for generations.

Robert Lipsyte (1938–present) Robert Lipsyte's first job was as a copyboy for the *New York Times*, where he worked his way up to sports columnist. In 1964 he began covering professional boxing, especially the career of Muhammad Ali. He drew on this experience in his writing of *The Contender*, which became an award-winning book and has been required reading in many American schools for the past four decades.

Lois Lowry (1937–present) Lois Lowry claims she is happy to have been born a middle child because it allowed her the time and energy to be alone and explore what she loved to do, like using her imagination and reading. The untimely deaths of her sister and her oldest son solidified Lowry's resolve "to convey my passionate awareness that we live intertwined on this planet and that our future depends upon our caring more, and doing more, for one another." Among Lowry's best known works are Newbery Medal winners *Number the Stars* and *The Giver.*

Norma Fox Mazer (1931–present) Mazer spent much of her twenties procrastinating—leaving stories half finished and making excuses. But when she turned twenty-eight she and her husband got serious and struck a deal in which both would write for at least one hour per day. Her commitment paid off. Her books have been nominated for the National Book Award, and have won the Newbery Honor title and the Lewis Carroll Shelf Award. Her titles include *Girlhearts; Silver; Good Night, Maman;* and *When She Was Good.*

Anne McCaffrey (1926–present) As a teenager, Anne McCaffrey wrote a novel in Latin class (in English), but after being reprimanded by her parents and teacher, she turned to acting and singing as a career. When she returned to writing, she made her first book a protest novel against the characterization of females in science fiction and fantasy literature. She has been breaking down barriers in the male-dominated genre ever since. She lives in a house she calls Dragonhold-Underhill, which she dug out of a hill in Ireland. She is best known for the books in her *Dragonriders of Pern* series.

Patrick F. McManus (1933–present) Patrick McManus worked in construction and saved enough money to attend college, where he decided to become a writer. When a magazine picked up a humor piece he wrote on a whim, he realized he was good at writing humor. This pleased him, as he found that it took much less effort than researching and writing factual essays. His humorous works, often based on life in the outdoors, include *Deer on a Bicycle; Into the Twilight, Endlessly Grousing;* and *Never Cry "Arp!"*

Nicholasa Mohr (1938–present) Immigrants from Puerto Rico, Nicholasa Mohr's parents settled in New York City, where she was born and raised with five siblings. Many of her books center around children growing up in Latino neighborhoods and being saddled with others' expectations, roles, and stereotypes based on their heritage. Mohr has said, "In American literature, I, as a Puerto Rican child, did not exist . . . and I, as a Puerto Rican woman, do not exist now." She is determined to fill this void, and has won awards and praise for her books including *El Bronx Remembered* and *Nilda*.

Pat Mora (1942–present) An author of Mexican-American descent, Pat Mora has written more than twenty five books of poetry, fiction, and nonfiction for children, teens, and adults. Her grandparents immigrated to the United States during the Mexican Revolution. They spoke only Spanish. Their daughter Estela, who was Pat's mother, grew up translating English into Spanish for them. Estela raised her daughter to be bilingual. Thus, many of Mora's books contain both English and Spanish text. They include *My Own True Name* and *Nepantla: Essays from the Land in the Middle*.

Jim Murphy (1947–present) Reading was the last thing on Jim Murphy's mind until his teacher forbade students to read a particular book. Naturally, Murphy tracked it down, read it, and hasn't stopped reading since. His historical fiction and nonfiction books for young adults reflect both his intensive research and deep fascination for his subjects. He has earned numerous awards for his efforts, including two Newbery Honors, an ALA Robert J. Sibert Informational Book Award and Honor Book Award, and a National Book Award Finalist Medal. His titles include *An American Plague, Great Fire*, and *The Boys' War*.

Walter Dean Myers (1937–present) As a youngster with a serious speech impediment, Myers discovered writing as an outlet for self-expression. He grew up in a poor but lively Harlem, very different from the violent Harlem he saw depicted in books and TV. That sense of positive potential and values is at the core of Myers' work, as are his own experiences. In an autobiographical essay, he commented, "Books took me, not so much to foreign lands and fanciful adventures, but to a place within myself that I have been exploring ever since. The public library was my most treasured place. I couldn't believe my luck in discovering that what I enjoyed most—reading—was free." His young adult novel *Scorpions* was a Newbery Honor Book. Other Myers titles include *Hoops, Monster*, and *Harlem*, which was illustrated by his son and became a Caldecott Honor Book.

Lensey Namioka (1929–present) Born in Beijing, China, Lensey Namioka wrote her first book at the age of eight and published it herself. Namioka immigrated with her parents to the United States when she was nine years old. She still remembers her early childhood in China, and some of her stories include memories of her experience there. In her more than thirty years as a writer, Namioka has written twenty-three books ranging from picture books for toddlers to Samurai tales for young adults. Her titles include *Half and Half, Ailins Weg*, and *Mismatch*.

Phyllis Reynolds Naylor (1933–present) A three-ringed binder holds Phyllis Reynolds Naylor's evolving ideas for the books she wants to write. Each time she brainstorms a new character or plot twist for one of the books, she jots it down. Naylor knew from the time she was a little girl that she wanted to write her own stories. She creates them from a combination of things she reads or hears and her own imaginative thoughts. Naylor says she's constantly observing and taking note of kids and their interactions, so she's able to form realistic characters. Her books include *Alice in the Know, Who Won the War?, Shiloh,* and *Witch Water*.

Naomi Shihab Nye (1952–present) Naomi Shihab Nye is a celebrated poet and author, and her children's books include *A Maze Me: Poems for Girls* and *Come with Me: Poems for a Journey*. She's also the editor of seven poetry anthologies for young adults. As a child, Nye started keeping a journal so that she could remember everything she observed. She uses her five senses to document the events in her life: "The neat whop of a baseball rammed perfectly with a bat. My father's funny Palestinian stories. The feeling of a breeze as my brother and I rode our bicycles down the hill." As a berry-picker during her first job on a farm, Nye would wander down the rows of berries, composing poems as she walked.

Scott O'Dell (1898–1989) Odell Gabriel Scott was "renamed" Scott O'Dell by a misinformed typesetter. He liked the mistake so much that he changed his name. When O'Dell was born in Los Angeles, there were more horses in the streets than cars and more jackrabbits than people. O'Dell's family moved around Southern California, and his memories of the frontier and the sea directly affected the settings and plots of his stories. Although his Newbery Medal-winning novel *Island of the Blue Dolphins* was based on a true event, his telling of it was entwined with his experiences as a boy who smelled the ocean and looked for adventures.

Katherine Paterson (1932–present) When Katherine Paterson was ten, she wanted to be either a movie star or a missionary. When she was twenty, she wanted to get married and have lots of children. But after her church hired her to write some educational materials, she became a writer. Paterson confesses that she sometimes thinks she will never have another good idea. Then a character crosses her imagination, and she writes a new novel. She feels lucky to be living a writer's life. Her well-known books include *Bridge to Terabithia, The Great Gilly Hopkins,* and *The Invisible Child.*

Gary Paulsen (1939–present) At the age of fourteen, Gary Paulsen ran away from an unhappy home to travel with a circus. This experience spurred an enduring sense of adventure, and it was the first of his many varied endeavors—engineer, farmer, construction worker, ranch hand, truck driver, and sailor. He has even competed in the Iditarod Trail Sled Dog Race, a grueling 1,150-mile race held yearly in Alaska. Many of Paulsen's life experiences are reflected in the more than 175 books he has written. His success as a writer stems from his ability to tap into the human spirit in a way that encourages the reader to observe and care about the world. His novels *Hatchet, Dogsong,* and *The Winter Room* were each given the Newbery Award. He is also the author of *How Angel Peterson Got His Name, Nightjohn,* and *Soldier's Heart.*

Richard Peck (1934–present) Richard Peck did not write any fiction at all until the age of thirty-seven, and even now, he does not begin a story until he gets a concrete idea from talking to a young person. Peck dislikes technology and types his stories on a typewriter. He investigates issues that are important to young people, such as peer pressure, censorship, and the journey toward independence. He has written more than a dozen novels and has won a Newbery Award and other honors for his work. His titles include *Here Lies the Librarian, The Teacher's Funeral: A Comedy in Three Parts, A Long Way from Chicago,* and *A Year Down Yonder.*

Robert Newton Peck (1928–present) Robert Newton Peck grew up on a farm in New England and was heavily influenced by one of his teachers. Coming of age and the tough realities of life are themes Peck uses to expose his young characters' imperfect resourcefulness. His best-known books are *A Day No Pigs Would Die* and the *Soup* books. Peck believes that children are the same through time, whether living through the American Revolution or growing up in the present day. They are all susceptible to the draw of engaging storytelling that smacks of truth.

Susan Beth Pfeffer (1948–present) Her first story was written at age six—a romance between an Oreo cookie and a pair of scissors—but Susan Beth Pfeffer's career really began in 1970 with the publication of *Just Morgan.* Since then, she has written more than 60 books for children and young adults. Her work includes *The Pizza Puzzle, Nobody's Daughter,* and *Family of Strangers.* Pfeffer's young adult novels *About David* and *The Year Without Michael* were both recipients of the South Carolina Young Adult Book Award. She is also the author of the popular *Portraits of Little Women* series, which features each of the March sisters from Louisa May Alcott's *Little Women.*

Rodman Philbrick (1951–present) Rodman Philbrick wrote eight novels after college, none of which was accepted by publishers. He found success writing commercial adult suspense books and although he enjoyed the work, he says that it was a very different experience from what he felt when he composed his first young adult novel. "The writing was almost effortless. It wasn't work—it was playing; it was fun." Philbrick has been writing from the kid's voice in his head ever since, including his books *Freak the Mighty*, *The Fire Pony*, and *The Young Man and the Sea*.

Tamora Pierce (1954–present) Born to a poor family in rural Pennsylvania, Tamora Pierce grew up telling herself stories about girl warriors. She credits her father with suggesting she write the stories down. Pierce wrote her first novel after graduating from college. It was never published—until a friend and literary agent where she worked suggested she carve her long novel into four young-adult fantasies. These books—the *Circle of Magic* series—launched Pierce's writing career. She has published many fantasy books for young readers and edited, with Josepha Sherman, the anthology *Young Warriors: Stories of Strength*. She continues to specialize in heroines she describes as "girls who kick butt."

Terry Pratchett (1948–present) By selling his first story at age thirteen, Terry Pratchett was able to purchase an old typewriter, that enabled him to further his craft and career. He went on to become a best-selling British author of fantasy, science fiction, and young adult novels. Even his adult fans are rabid readers of his kids' books. His *Discworld* series includes thirty-three novels at present. Writing is Pratchett's life, and he has described himself as living behind a keyboard, and not having "a life" despite the fact that he's so busy he feels that he's trying to live three simultaneously. Recent titles include *Wintersmith, Thud!*, and *A Hat Full of Sky*.

Wilson Rawls (1913–1984) Wilson Rawls wrote the American childhood classic *Where the Red Fern Grows*, a book as much about friendship, hunting, and adventures in the Ozark Mountains as it is about Rawls' own childhood and struggles. Rawls lived in an area so remote there were no schools, so his mother taught him at home. Initially Rawls didn't like books—he just couldn't relate to the stories. Then his mom gave him Jack London's *Call of the Wild*, opening his eyes to literature's potential. Because of his informal education, his first stories were unpolished and unacceptable to publishers. His wife helped him edit his first draft of *Red Fern,* and by the 1960s it was an important part of the young adult literary canon, where it remains, popular as ever, today.

Barbara Robinson (1927–present) After graduating from Allegheny College, where she fed her passion for writing and acting, Robinson found success as a short story writer and has published more than fifty stories. Her books for children include *The Best Christmas Pageant Ever*, *The Best School Year Ever*, and *My Brother Louis Measures Worms*.

J.K. Rowling (1965–present) J.K. Rowling says she was riding on a train when the idea for Harry Potter "fell into my head." Rowling had been writing from age six, but it wasn't until that moment that she discovered something she wanted to write a book about. The *Harry Potter* series featuring an orphaned half-human, half-wizard sparked what can only be described as a reading frenzy among children and adults alike around the world. The books have set records as the fastest selling titles in history. Twelve publishing houses rejected her first manuscript before one finally decided to take a chance on it. Besides being inundated with awards and credited with reigniting imaginations and literary interest in children, Rowling has had an asteroid and a newly discovered dinosaur named in her honor.

J.K. Rowling

Pam Muñoz Ryan (1951–present) Pam Muñoz Ryan considers herself truly American because of her ethnically diverse makeup; she claims Mexican, Italian, Spanish, and Oklahoman in her lineage. Growing up in a big family in California's hot San Joaquin Valley, Ryan stayed cool by spending her summers in the air-conditioned local library reading the days away. Before she became an author, she was a teacher, and she learned from first-hand experience what her audience wanted and needed in a book. Ryan writes between twenty and thirty drafts to get a book just right. She's the author of the award-winning novels *Esperanza Rising* and *Riding Freedom* as well as *Becoming Naomi Leon.*

Cynthia Rylant (1954–present) Cynthia Rylant writes from her experience growing up in a poor region of West Virginia's Appalachia. She admits that as a child she preferred playing cops and robbers on bikes to sitting and writing—but she maintains that playing is the best training for a writer because it helps a person love life and come up with exciting story ideas. Her first book *When I Was Young in the Mountains,* won the American Book Award. She focuses on bittersweet themes of life—family, growing old, and living in Appalachia.

Louis Sachar (1954–present) When he was nine years old, Louis Sachar moved from New York City to a neighborhood surrounded by orange groves. One of his fondest childhood memories was of having fights with neighborhood kids using oranges, mostly rotten ones, as ammunition. After earning college credits as a teacher's aide, Sachar decided he wanted to write children's books. He worked on his first novel at night and labored in a sweater factory by day—a job from which he was eventually fired. Sachar writes for about two hours a day and refuses to tell anyone, including his family, about his book until it's complete. Sachar is the author of *Sideway Stories from Wayside School, There's a Boy in the Girl's Bathroom,* and *Holes.*

Neal Shusterman (1962–present) As a youngster, Neal Shusterman felt more comfortable holding a pencil than a baseball bat, and he's been writing and telling stories ever since. He carves out time from his busy writing schedule to do tours of schools—enthralling students with his stories and leading workshops where students can use their own creativity to become aspiring writers. His acclaimed children's science fiction and fantasy books, including *Kid Heroes* and *Darkness Creeping*, have won many awards and allowed him to expand into the field of television writing.

Zilpha Keatley Snyder (1927–present) Since she didn't have television or watch movies Zilpha Keatley Snyder filled her childhood with animals and books. She recognized her path early, deciding at age eight that she would be a writer. Snyder felt out of place in junior high and found solace and escape in the library. "Libraries were treasure houses. I always entered them with a slight thrill of disbelief that all their endless riches were mine for the borrowing," she says. She found her stride in college and after graduating spent the next nine years teaching. Her Newbery award-winning novels are *The Egypt Game*, *The Headless Cupid*, and *The Witches of Worm*.

Gary Soto (1952–present) Gary Soto grew up in Fresno, California, in a Mexican-American community. As a child he thought about becoming a priest or a paleontologist. In an interview, Soto said, "I don't think I had any literary aspirations when I was a kid. We didn't have books, and no one encouraged us to read. So my wanting to write poetry was a sort of fluke." Soto writes novels, short stories, and poetry for both youth and adults. His work often explores the lives of Mexican-Americans. His young adult titles include *Taking Sides, Buried Onions, Local News*, and *The Skirt*.

Armstrong Sperry (1897–1976) Armstrong Sperry said that he had been a doodler and scribbler for as long as he could remember. His true inspiration for storytelling and fondness for the setting of remote islands came from his grandfather, a mariner who captivated Sperry with his daredevil tales. Sperry's life was multifaceted—part artist, one-time sailor, farmer, and writer. He used his collective experiences and imagination to create graphic illustrations and write award-winning books including Newbery Award winner *Call It Courage*.

Jerry Spinelli (1941–present) Initially Jerry Spinelli fancied himself as an author for adults, but luckily the rejection letters from publishing houses steered him toward writing children's books instead. As it turns out, he had all the material he needed to write engaging, true-to-life stories that kids could relate to simply from absorbing all the experiences of growing up. For example, he lists "John Ribble's blazing fastball," "Dovey Wilmouth, so beautiful a fleet of boys pedaled past her house ten times a day," and "Mrs. Seeton's whistle calling her kids in to dinner" as inspirations. He sums himself up with the appropriate title of "berry-picking, pony-touching, star-marveler." He's the author of the Newbery Medal winning book *Maniac Magee*, as well as *Wringer, Stargirl*, and many others.

Nancy Springer (1948–present) A versatile writer of fiction, nonfiction, stories, and poetry for children and young adults, Nancy Springer has won more than a dozen awards for her work. Her books include *The Silver Sun, Colt,* and *Blood Trail.*

Todd Strasser (1950–present) Todd Strasser was a member of a commune, a street performer, an adman, a newspaperman, and a fortune cookie manufacturer before deciding to devote himself to writing full time. He spent the early part of his career writing novels based on existing movies, then found a unique perspective through his *I'm Trapped . . .* books, beginning with *Help! I'm Trapped in My Teacher's Body.* Strasser has written more than 100 books including *The Wave.*

May Swenson (1919–1989) English was May Swenson's second language. She spoke Swedish in her childhood home in Utah. Despite not being a native speaker, Swenson is considered one of America's most inventive poets. The author of more than ten poetry collections including *Another Animal: Poems* and *In Other Words: Poems,* Swenson's writing often delights in the natural world, sometimes featuring scientific inquiries, particularly space research.

Mildred Taylor (1943–present) Mildred Taylor draws from her family and community history for the inspired writing about race, class, and family bonds that have made her works required reading. She wanted to write the version of history that African American children lived before the civil rights movement but that could not be found in history books. Taylor was born in Mississippi, but her family moved to the North in search of opportunities that would not be available to Taylor in the segregated South. After graduating from college, she lived in Ethiopia for two years as a Peace Corps volunteer. Taylor eventually moved to California, where she wrote *Song of the Trees* and the Newbery Medal-winning novel *Roll of Thunder, Hear My Cry.*

Theodore Taylor (1921–2006) Because Taylor claims that he doesn't have a very active imagination, he relies on his own experiences and adventures to fuel his novels. His primary training has been in newspaper reporting, but he was also a press agent in Hollywood, rubbing shoulders with the big stars of the day. He recently wrote a sequel for his best-known novel, *The Cay,* and at age 81 traveled around the country on a book signing tour for *Timothy of the Cay,* meeting legions of fans.

J.R.R. Tolkien (1892–1973) John Ronald Reuel Tolkien didn't just create *The Hobbit* and *The Lord of the Rings* trilogy, he created an entirely new world—one that seems as familiar to his fans as planet Earth. Tolkien called it Middle-Earth, complete with its own species, language, conflicts, and folklore. Tolkien had an affinity for ancient languages, and his first job was working for the Oxford English Dictionary researching words. He then became a professor of Anglo-Saxon. Tolkien loved to tell fantastic stories for the enjoyment of his children—originally *The Hobbit* was written just for them. His devotion to language inspired him to create more than one of his own invented languages. Throughout his career he maintained a close friendship and received the support and advice of another prolific children's fantasy writer, C.S. Lewis.

Mark Twain (1835–1910) Samuel Clemens, better known as Mark Twain, is an integral part of the American literary landscape. Twain grew up in Missouri, where the Mississippi River took on a significant presence in his imagination as he watched the commerce and travel of river boats. He spent a short stint as a boat pilot before heading West to seek his fortune at the height of the gold rush. Instead he found work as a reporter, writing humorous pieces about the prospectors' experiences. He turned his "sketches" into a lecture series, touring the country giving humorous talks. Through his lectures, Twain became a beloved celebrity before he ever wrote the classics *The Adventures of Tom Sawyer, The Adventures of Huckleberry Finn, The Prince and the Pauper,* and *A Connecticut Yankee in King Arthur's Court.*

Mark Twain

Vivian Vande Velde (1951–present) Vivian Vande Velde loves stories, but she didn't start writing them herself until she became a mother and spent time at home with her daughter. She found her first book hard to write and even more difficult to get published. She sent it to thirty-three publishers over two years before one finally accepted her manuscript. But she has hit her stride, with the support of two active writers' groups and her editor, Jane Yolen. Her books include *Dragon's Bait, All Hallows' Eve,* and *Being Dead.*

Cynthia Voight (1942–present) Cynthia Voight says that her writing process begins with a question. She writes down her thoughts and lets them swim around her head for a year before having her characters take shape. She was awarded the Newbery Medal for *Dicey's Song* and, in 1990, the California Young Reader's Award for *Izzy, Willy-Nilly.* Recently Voight has tackled serious issues such as child abuse, racism, and emotional abandonment. She says that when she discovered writing "it was as if somebody had opened a window for me, to show me a whole new landscape."

Nancy Werlin (1961–present) A writer of thrillers and suspense novels for young adults, Nancy Werlin finds it particularly ironic that her career focuses on a stage of life that she disliked so much at the time. "I find it hilarious that I was desperate not to be a teenager, and yet, as a writer, I am forever fascinated by the teenage years." As a teenager, she read more than a dozen books a week, and she admits that young adult literature is still what she enjoys reading most today. "I think suspense is the perfect form for young adult novels," Werlin says. As evidence for that belief, she points to the natural feeling of being "in between" during the teen years, and consequently, the suspicious feeling of waiting to encounter "what comes next." Werlin has won numerous awards for her work, most notably the Edgar Award for her novel *The Killer's Cousin.*

Budge Wilson (1928–present) Budge Wilson describes herself as a "very late bloomer," because she did not begin writing fiction until her fifties and was not published until she was fifty-six years old. Since publishing her first book, Wilson has written and published nearly thirty books for children and adults including *Fractures: Family Stories, The Dandelion Garden,* and *Harold and Harold.*

Tim Wynne-Jones (1948–present) Tim Wynne-Jones is eager to point out that the word *imagine* has the word *image* embedded within it, which dovetails with his philosophy that writing and storytelling are closely linked to pictures, whether they're on paper or in our imaginations. The Canadian writer published his first book in 1974. His titles include *A Thief in the House of Memory, The Boy in the Burning House,* and *Zoom at Sea.*

Laurence Yep (1948–present) Laurence Yep had an unusual childhood, growing up as a Chinese American in a predominantly African American neighborhood in San Francisco. He was drawn to sci-fi and fantasy because he could relate it to his own experience of having to adapt and adjust in his community. After a high school English teacher vowed to give *A*'s only to students who had a story published in a national magazine (a pronouncement later retracted), Yep became hooked on writing and began to publish stories in a science fiction magazine. His works include Newbery Honor books *Dragonwings, Dragon's Gate*, and *Child of the Owl. The Lost Garden* is another of his popular titles.

Jane Yolen (1939–present) Jane Yolen has been called "America's Hans Christian Anderson" for her immensely popular children's fantasy books. After graduating from Smith College, where she wrote poetry and worked on the school paper, Yolen moved to New York City to become an editor. She wrote stories and poems on her lunch breaks and over the weekends. Her first book, *Pirates in Petticoats,* was published when she was twenty-three, and she has since published more than 200 titles for children and adults, including *The Pit Dragon Chronicles* and *The Devil's Arithmetic.* Her book *Owl Moon* won the Caldecott Medal. Yolen has become one of the acknowledged masters of fantasy writing.

Paul Zindel (1936–2003) Paul Zindel's first love was writing plays, and he won the prestigious Pulitzer Prize for Drama for his play *The Effect of Gamma Rays on Man-in-the-Moon Marigolds.* Then a friend suggested he write a novel for kids. His goal was to let teenagers know that they aren't alone and that he recognizes how difficult adolescence can be. His autobiography *The Pigman and Me* exemplifies his style of writing from the perspective of a young adult: "Eight hundred and fifty-three horrifying things had happened to me by the time I was a teenager . . . . If you haven't croaked before finishing this book, you will know how I survived . . . ."

Good Reading for Young Adults

Across Five Aprils, **Irene Hunt (1964)** The heartache and agony of the Civil War as reflected in the life of a young Illinois boy.

The Adventures of Huckleberry Finn, **Mark Twain (1884)** As Huck and runaway slave Jim make their way down the mighty Mississippi, Huck is forced to ponder the nature of friendship and to find a sense of his own moral vision.

The Adventures of Tom Sawyer, **Mark Twain (1876)** This is the lighthearted excursion into boyhood—a nostalgic return to the simple, rural Missouri world of Tom Sawyer and his friends Huck and Becky, and his Aunt Polly.

Airborn, **Kenneth Oppel (2004)** Matt, a cabin boy aboard an airship, and Kate, a wealthy girl traveling with her chaperone, team up to search for the existence of mysterious creatures reportedly living hundreds of feet above the earth's surface.

Al Capone Does My Shirts, **Gennifer Choldenko (2004)** A 12-year-old boy named Moose moves to Alcatraz Island in 1935 when guards' families were housed there, and has to contend with his extraordinary new environment in addition to life with his autistic sister.

And Then There Were None [Ten Little Indians], **Agatha Christie (1939)** Ten strangers are gathered together on an isolated island by a mysterious host. One by one, the guests share the darkest secrets of their wicked past . . . and one by one they die.

Anne Frank: The Diary of a Young Girl, **Anne Frank (1952)** The true story of a young Jewish girl who lived with seven other people in secret rooms in Amsterdam during World War II.

Ashes of Roses, **Mary Jane Auch (2002)** Sixteen-year-old Margaret Rose Nolan, newly arrived from Ireland, finds work at New York City's Triangle Shirtwaist Factory shortly before the 1911 fire in which 146 employees died.

Because of Winn-Dixie, **Kate DiCamillo (2000)** Winn-Dixie, a big, ugly, happy dog, helps 10-year-old Opal make new friends, begin to find her place in the world, and let go of some of the sadness left by her mother's abandonment seven years earlier.

Becoming Joe DiMaggio, **Maria Testa (2002)** Twenty-four poems describe the relationship between a boy and his grandfather.

Becoming Naomi Leon, **Pam Muñoz Ryan (2004)** When Naomi's mother, absent for seven years, resurfaces to claim her, Naomi runs away to Mexico with her great-grandmother and younger brother in search of her father. 2006 Pura Belpre Honor Award.

Belle Prater's Boy, **Ruth White (1997)** Everyone in Coal Station, Virginia, has a theory about what happened to Belle Prater, but 12-year-old Gypsy wants the facts.

The Best Christmas Pageant Ever, **Barbara Robinson (1972)** The worst kids in town take over the Christmas pageant with hilarious and tender consequences.

The Boy Who Saved Baseball, **John H. Ritter (2003)** The fate of a small California town rests on the outcome of one baseball game, and Tom Gallagher hopes to lead his team to victory with the secrets of the now-disgraced player, Dante Del Gato.

Bridge to Terabithia, **Katherine Paterson (1977)** The story of a very special friendship between a boy and girl.

Bud, Not Buddy, **Christopher Paul Curtis (1999)** Ten-year-old Bud hits the road in search of his father and his home.

The Call of the Wild, **Jack London (1903)** The icy tale of a sled dog's adventures.

The Cay, **Theodore Taylor (1969)** An exciting adventure of two survivors of a shipwreck washed ashore on a desolate island.

Charlie and the Chocolate Factory, **Roald Dahl (1964)** The adventures of Charlie and his friends in Mr. Willy Wonka's chocolate factory.

Charlotte's Web, **E.B. White (1952)** "Some Pig"—these are the words in Charlotte's web, high in the barn. Her spiderweb tells of her feelings for a little pig named Wilbur, as well as the feelings of a little girl named Fern . . . who loves Wilbur, too.

Cheaper by the Dozen, **Frank B. Gilbreth Jr. & Ernestine Gilbreth Carey (1948)** The story of the 12 lively Gilbreth children and their remarkable parents.

The Chocolate Touch, **Patrick Skene Catling (1979)** Instead of gold, everything John Midas touched turns to precious chocolate.

Crispin: The Cross of Lead, **Avi (2002)** Falsely accused of theft and murder, an orphaned peasant boy in 14th-century England flees his village and meets a larger-than-life juggler who holds a dangerous secret.

Criss Cross, **Lynne Rae Perkins (2005)** Teenagers in a small town in the 1970s experience new thoughts and feelings, question their identities, connect, and disconnect as they search for the meaning of life and love.

Cuba 15, **Nancy Osa (2003)** Violet Paz, a Chicago high school student, reluctantly prepares for her upcoming "quince," a Spanish nickname for the celebration of an Hispanic girl's 15th birthday. Pura Belpre Honor Book.

***A Day No Pigs Would Die,* Robert Newton Peck (1972)** The story of growing up on a Shaker farm touches the whole cycle of life and death with simplicity.

***Dear Mr. Henshaw,* Beverly Cleary (1983)** Leigh Botts, the new kid in town, pours his heart out to his favorite author.

***The Devil's Arithmetic,* Jane Yolen (1988)** Time travel about a young Jewish girl, Hanna, who goes back to Communist Poland, where she is taken to a death camp.

***Dogsong,* Gary Paulsen (1985)** Inspired by an Eskimo shaman, Russel takes a dog team and sled to escape the modern ways of his village and to find the "song" of himself.

***Dragonwings,* Laurence Yep (1975)** In the opening years of the 20th century, eight-year-old Moon Shadow travels from China to San Francisco to join his father, Windrider, whom he has never met.

***The Egypt Game,* Zilpha Keatley Snyder (1967)** Eleven-year-old April and her friend Melanie become intrigued with ancient Egypt and invent a game that soon culminates in the capture of very real criminals.

***Esperanza Rising,* Pam Muñoz Ryan (2000)** Esperanza and her mother are forced to leave their life of wealth and privilege in Mexico to go work in the labor camps of Southern California on the eve of the Great Depression.

***The Fighting Ground,* Avi (1984)** Thirteen-year-old Jonathan is captured in the war against the British. This novel describes the experiences of war personally rather than through history or events.

***Flowers for Algernon,* Daniel Keyes (1967)** The heart-rending tale of a retarded man who becomes a genius through a bold experiment.

***Flush,* Carl Hiaasen (2005)** With their father jailed for sinking a river boat, Noah and his younger sister, Abbey, must gather evidence that the owner of this floating casino is emptying his bilge tanks into the protected waters around their Florida Keys home.

***Freak the Mighty,* Rodman Philbrick (1993)** An emotionally charged novel about two boys, a slow learner too large for his age and a tiny, crippled genius, who forge a unique friendship when they pair up to create one formidable human force.

***Freckle Juice,* Judy Blume (1971)** Andrew wants freckles more than anything else, so Sharon offers to sell him her secret freckle recipe.

***Frindle,* Andrew Clements (1996)** Of all of Nick Allen's great ideas, the frindle is his most successful. What's a frindle? It's a pen, or what used to be called a pen before Nick began his brilliant campaign.

From the Mixed-up Files of Mrs. Basil E. Frankweiler, **E.L. Konigsburg 1967)**
Having run away with her younger brother to live in the Metropolitan Museum of Art, 12-year-old Claudia strives to keep things in order in their new home.

The Giver, **Lois Lowry (1994)** The Elders of the Committee choose Jonas to be the person responsible for receiving and keeping all the memories of the past—a huge task for this exceptional boy.

The Grape Thief, **Kristine L. Franklin (2003)** In 1925, in a small Washington State community made up of families from different ethnic backgrounds, 12-year-old Cuss tries to stay in school as he watches those around him struggle with various financial difficulties.

The Great Gilly Hopkins, **Katherine Paterson (1978)** A rebellious and unmanageable foster child learns the true meaning of love and family.

Guys Write for Guys Read: Boy's Favorite Authors Write About Being Boys, **compiled by Jon Scieszka (2005)** A fast-paced, high energy collection of short works: stories, essays, columns, cartoons, anecdotes, and artwork by today's most popular male writers and illustrators.

Harriet Tubman: Conductor on the Underground Railroad, **Ann Petry (1971)**
The story of the courageous black woman who escaped to freedom on the Underground Railroad and then returned again and again to lead others.

Hatchet, **Gary Paulsen (1987)** After a plane crash, 13-year-old Brian spends 54 days in the wilderness, learning to survive with only the aid of a hatchet given to him by his mother.

Holes, **Louis Sachar (1998)** In a compelling novel that is both serious and funny, with a rich vein of tenderness running through it, Louis Sachar has created a narrative puzzle in which the characters cannot escape their destinies.

Homeless Bird, **Gloria Whelan (2000)** When 13-year-old Koly enters into an ill-fated arranged marriage, she must either suffer a destiny dictated by India's tradition or find the courage to oppose it.

Hoot, **Carl Hiaasen (2002)** Roy, who is new to his small Florida community, becomes involved in another boy's attempt to save a colony of burrowing owls from a proposed construction site.

Hope Was Here, **Joan Bauer (2000)** Sixteen-year-old Hope moves to Wisconsin with her aunt to run the Welcome Stairways Diner and finds herself involved in the leukemia victim owner's run for mayor.

The House of Dies Drear, **Virginia Hamilton (1968)** An African American family tries to unravel the secrets of their new home, which was once a stop on the Underground Railroad.

***The House of the Scorpion,* Nancy Farmer (2002)** In a future where humans despise clones, Matt enjoys special status as the young clone of El Patron, the 142-year-old leader of a corrupt drug empire nestled between Mexico and the United States.

***The House on Mango Street,* Sandra Cisneros (1991)** Told in a series of short vignettes, this is the story of Esperanza Cordero, a young girl growing up in a Mexican American barrio in Chicago. Winner of the American Book Award.

***How Angel Peterson Got His Name and Other Outrageous Tales About Extreme Sports,* Gary Paulsen (2003)** Author Gary Paulsen relates tales from his youth in a small town in northwestern Minnesota in the late 1940s and early 1950s, such as skiing behind a souped-up car and imitating daredevil Evel Knievel.

***How to Eat Fried Worms,* Thomas Rockwell (1973)** A hilarious story that will revolt and delight young readers.

***I Am the Cheese,* Robert Cormier (1977)** Adam bicycles through New England to meet his father and journeys into the far reaches of his mind to unlock a devastating past he cannot accept.

***The Indian in the Cupboard,* Lynne Reid Banks (1980)** It all starts with a birthday present Omri doesn't even want—a small plastic Indian of no use to him at all. But when an old wooden cupboard and a special key bring the unusual toy to life, Omri's Indian becomes his most important secret: precious, dangerous, wonderful, and above all, magical.

***Island of the Blue Dolphins,* Scott O'Dell (1960)** A young Indian girl lives alone for years on a Pacific island.

***James and the Giant Peach,* Roald Dahl (1961)** An orphaned boy becomes a worldwide celebrity thanks to an oversized peach and its resident collection of outsized insects.

***Joey Pigza Loses Control,* Jack Gantos (2000)** Joey, ADD but under control with meds, goes to spend time with his estranged, non-medicated ADD dad and must decide between control and his newfound friendship with his father. Parents' Choice Award. Sequel to *Joey Pigza Swallowed the Key.*

***Johnny Tremain,* Esther Forbes (1943)** After injuring his hand, a silversmith's apprentice in Boston becomes a messenger for the Sons of Liberty in the days before the American Revolution.

***Julie of the Wolves,* Jean Craighead George (1972)** The story of a girl caught between two cultures—Eskimo and white. She learns to communicate with a small pack of wolves and thus gets food when she is starving.

***Killing Mr. Griffin,* Lois Duncan (1978)** A group of high school students plan to scare their tough, demanding English teacher into being more lenient. Their attempt brings on Mr. Griffin's fatal heart attack.

***Kira-Kira*, Cynthia Kadohata (2004)** Chronicles the close friendship between two Japanese American sisters growing up in rural Georgia during the late 1950s and early 1960s, and the despair when one sister becomes terminally ill.

***The Light in the Forest*, Conrad Richter (1953)** The unforgettable story of a white boy raised by Indians and returned to white society.

***The Lion, the Witch and the Wardrobe*, C.S. Lewis (1950)** Four adventurers step through a wardrobe door and into the world of Narnia—a land enslaved by the power of the White Witch. But when almost all hope is lost, the return of the Great Lion, Aslan, signals a great change . . . and a great sacrifice.

***Lizzie Bright and the Buckminster Boy*, Gary D. Schmidt (2004)** It's 1911, and Turner Buckminster hates his new home of Phippsburg, Maine. But things improve when he meets Lizzie Bright, a girl from a poor island community.

***Locomotion*, Jacqueline Woodson (2003)** In a series of poems, 11-year-old Lonnie writes about his life after the death of his parents, separated from his younger sister, living in a foster home, and finding his poetic voice at school.

***A Long Way from Chicago*, Richard Peck (1998)** A boy recounts his annual summer trips to rural Illinois with his sister during the Great Depression to visit their larger-than-life grandmother.

***The Lost Garden*, Laurence Yep (1973)** Laurence Yep's autobiography. Discusses growing up Chinese American and how writing helped him solve the puzzle of where he fit in.

***A Mango-Shaped Space*, Wendy Mass (2003)** Afraid that she is crazy, 13-year-old Mia, who sees a special color with every letter, number, and sound, keeps this a secret until she becomes overwhelmed by school, changing relationships, and the loss of something important to her.

***Maniac Magee*, Jerry Spinelli (1990)** Not every boy becomes a legend in his own time. That's what happened to Maniac Magee, who earned his nickname by doing brave and foolish things, like running away from an unloving home, living in the zoo, and bringing people closer.

***The Miracle Worker*, William Gibson (1959)** A drama depicting Annie Sullivan's titanic struggle to release a young blind and deaf girl from her terrifying prison of darkness and silence.

***Mrs. Frisby and the Rats of NIMH*, Robert C. O'Brien (1971)** A widowed mouse, Mrs. Frisby, attempts to save her family by acquiring some help from the well-taught rats of NIMH.

My Brother Sam Is Dead, **James Lincoln Collier & Christopher Collier (1974)** Tim is torn between his brother's patriotism and his father's Tory sympathies.

My Brother's Keeper, **Patricia McCormick (2005)** Thirteen-year-old Toby, a prematurely gray-haired Pittsburgh Pirates fan and baseball card collector, tries to cope with his brother's drug use, his father's absence, and his mother dating Stanley the Food King.

My Side of the Mountain, **Jean Craighead George (1959)** The story of a young boy's adventures in the Catskill Mountains.

Nightjohn, **Gary Paulsen (1993)** Twelve-year-old slave Sarny risks terrible punishment as, letter by letter, an adult slave, Nightjohn, teaches her how to read.

No More Dead Dogs, **Gordon Korman (2000)** Eighth-grade football hero Wallace Wallace is sentenced to detention, which means attending rehearsals of the school play. He becomes wrapped up in the production and begins to suggest changes that improve not only the play but his life as well.

Nothing but the Truth, **Avi (1992)** A ninth-grader's suspension for singing the National Anthem during homeroom becomes a national news story.

Number the Stars, **Lois Lowry (1989)** An inspiring story of a little Danish girl's bravery when Nazis threatened her best friend's safety.

October Sky, **Homer H. Hickam Jr. (1999)** Originally titled *Rocket Boys,* this is the coming-of-age memoir of a distinguished NASA scientist that looks back on his childhood in a coal mining town and the roots of his obsession with space.

Old Yeller, **Fred Gipson (1956)** Travis gets help from a big, ugly, yellow dog.

Out of the Dust, **Karen Hesse (1997)** In a series of poems, 15-year-old Billie Jo relates the hardships of living on her family's wheat farm in Oklahoma during the dust bowl years of the Depression.

The Outsiders, **S.E. Hinton (1967)** The story of a rough gang of long-haired teenagers from the wrong side of the tracks.

The Pearl, **John Steinbeck (1947)** A poor Mexican fisherman finds a pearl beyond price, and tragedy follows.

Pictures of Hollis Woods, **Patricia Reilly Giff (2002)** A troublesome 12-year-old orphan, staying with an elderly artist who needs her, remembers the only other time she was happy in a foster home, with a family that truly seemed to care about her.

The Pinballs, **Betsy Byars (1987)** Three lonely foster children learn to care about themselves and each other.

***Princess Academy,* Shannon Hale (2005)** While attending an academy for potential princesses, 14-year-old Miri discovers unexpected talents and connections to her homeland. Bandits come to kidnap the future princess and Miri uses a unique power to save herself and her classmates.

***Red Kayak,* Priscilla Cummings (2004)** First hailed as a hero for his dramatic water rescue of a little boy, 13-year-old Brady soon makes a discovery that puts him at the heart of a tragedy. Alone with his dark secret, Brady is forced to choose between his friends and the right thing.

***Roll of Thunder, Hear My Cry,* Mildred D. Taylor (1976)** A Southern black family is determined to maintain their pride and independence against hard times and racial inequities.

***Ruby Holler,* Sharon Creech (2002)** Thirteen-year-old fraternal twins Dallas and Florida have grown up in a terrible orphanage, but their lives change forever when an eccentric but sweet older couple invites them each on an adventure, beginning in an almost magical place called Ruby Holler.

***Rumble Fish,* S.E. Hinton (1975)** James is the number one tough guy in junior high until a series of explosive events shatters his world.

***Sarah, Plain and Tall,* Patricia MacLachlan (1986)** When their father invites a mail-order bride to come to live with them in their prairie home, Caleb and Ann are captivated by her and hope that she will stay.

***The Sea of Trolls,* Nancy Farmer (2004)** After Jack becomes apprentice to a Druid bard, he and his sister are captured by Viking Berserkers and taken to the home of King Ivar the Boneless and his half-troll queen, leading Jack to undertake a vital quest to Jotunheim, home of the trolls.

***Shackleton's Stowaway,* Victoria McKernan (2005)** A fictionalized account of the adventures of Perce Blackborow, who stowed away for the 1914 Shackleton Antarctic expedition and, after their ship was crushed by ice, endured many hardships, including the loss of the toes of his left foot.

***Shiloh,* Phyllis Reynolds Naylor (1992)** Marty's deception in secretly keeping a beagle pup that he knows belongs to a cruel owner causes him heartache and trouble as one lie leads to another. A near tragedy reveals his secret and brings Marty face-to-face with the owner.

***The Sign of the Beaver,* Elizabeth George Speare (1983)** Left alone to guard the family's wilderness home in 18th-century Maine, a boy is hard-pressed to survive until local Indians teach him their skills.

***A Single Shard,* Linda Sue Park (2001)** Tree-ear, a 13-year-old orphan in medieval Korea, lives under a bridge in a potters' village, and longs to learn how to throw the delicate celadon ceramics himself.

***Soldier's Heart,* Gary Paulsen (1998)** Eager to enlist, 15-year-old Charley has a change of heart after experiencing both the physical and mental anguish of Civil War combat.

***Stargirl,* Jerry Spinelli (2000)** In this story about the perils of popularity, the courage of nonconformity, and the thrill of first love, an eccentric student named Stargirl changes Mica High School forever.

***Summer of My German Soldier,* Bette Greene (1973)** The moving story of a dangerous friendship between a 12-year-old Jewish girl and a German POW during World War II.

***Surviving the Applewhites,* Stephanie S. Tolan (2002)** Jake, a budding juvenile delinquent, is sent for home schooling to the arty and eccentric Applewhite family's Creative Academy, where he discovers talents and interests he never knew he had.

***Tangerine,* Edward Bloor (1997)** Paul Fisher's older brother, Erik, is a high school football star, but to Paul he's no hero.

***Tears of a Tiger,* Sharon M. Draper (1996)** The death of high school basketball star Rob Washington in an automobile accident affects the lives of his close friend Andy, who was driving the car.

***Tex,* S.E. Hinton (1979)** Against his will, Tex gets acquainted with hate. It forces him to grow up fast and pushes him right to the point of murder.

***That Was Then, This Is Now,* S.E. Hinton (1971)** Sixteen-year-old Mark and Bryon have been like brothers since childhood, but now, as their involvement with girls, gangs, and drugs increases, their relationship seems to gradually disintegrate.

***There's a Boy in the Girls' Bathroom,* Louis Sachar (1987)** A hilarious tale of an 11-year-old misunderstood misfit, Bradley Chalkers, who becomes a reformed character once he starts believing in himself.

***Touching Spirit Bear,* Ben Mikaelsen (2001)** After his anger erupts into violence and to avoid prison, Cole agrees to participate in a sentencing alternative based on Native American Circle Justice at a remote Alaskan Island and encounters a huge Spirit Bear that changes his life.

***The True Confessions of Charlotte Doyle,* Avi (1991)** The only passenger on the long Atlantic Ocean crossing, Charlotte Doyle finds herself caught between the madness of a ruthless captain and the rage of a mutinous crew. This is her terrifying account of that fateful voyage.

***Tuck Everlasting,* Natalie Babbitt (1975)** Ten-year-old Winnie discovers the secret of a spring whose waters impart immortality—a questionable gift.

***Under the Persimmon Tree,* Suzanne Fisher Staples (2005)** During the Taliban's reign in Afghanistan, the lives of Najmah, a young refugee from Kunduz, and Nusrat, an American-Muslim teacher who is awaiting her husband's return from Mazar-i-Sharif, intersect at a school in Peshawar, Pakistan.

***The View from Saturday,* E.L. Konigsburg (1996)** For the first time in the history of Epiphany Middle School, there is a chance that a sixth-grade team will beat the seventh-grade in the Academic Bowl, putting them on the path to the state finals.

***Walk Two Moons,* Sharon Creech (1994)** After her mother leaves home, 13-year-old Sal and her grandparents take a car trip retracing her mother's route. Along the way, Sal recounts the story of her friend Phoebe, whose mother also left.

***The War with Grandpa,* Robert Kimmel Smith (1984)** When Grandpa comes to live in the family's house, in Peter's room, Peter plans for war.

***The Watsons Go to Birmingham—1963,* Christopher Paul Curtis (1995)** Story narrated by Kenny, 10, about his family, the Weird Watsons of Flint, Michigan, and their trip to Birmingham, Alabama, during one of the civil rights movement's most tragic events.

***The Wave,* Todd Strasser, writing as Morton Rhue (1981)** The classroom experiment that went too far. The powerful forces of group pressure that pervaded such movements as Nazism are re-created in a classroom.

***The Westing Game,* Ellen Raskin (1979)** A puzzling mystery of 16 players who are all suspects in the curious murder of millionaire Sam Westing—and heirs to his fabulous fortune.

***When Zachary Beaver Came to Town,* Kimberly Willis Holt (1999)** Set during the Vietnam War, Cal and Todd befriend Zachary, "the fattest boy in the world," after he is abandoned in their small Texas town. 1999 National Book Award Winner for Young People's Literature.

***Where the Red Fern Grows,* Wilson Rawls (1961)** A young boy's dogs win the gold cup in a contest, but tragedy strikes.

***Whirligig,* Paul Fleischman (1998)** Sixteen-year-old Brent Bishop is sent on an unusual journey of repentance—building wind toys across the land—after he inadvertently causes the death of a young woman.

***The Witch of Blackbird Pond,* Elizabeth George Speare (1959)** When Kit's friendship with the old woman is discovered, she is accused of witchcraft.

***Woodsong,* Gary Paulsen (1990)** A memoir about Paulsen's intimate relationship with Minnesota's north woods, the dog team he trained for Alaska's Iditarod race, and the mesmerizing day-by-day account of his first try at this 1,180-mile race.

***A Wrinkle in Time,* Madeleine L'Engle (1962)** It was a wild, stormy night when the unearthly visitor arrived to change the lives of Meg; her small brother, Charles; and their scientist mother.

***The Young Man and the Sea,* Rodman Philbrick (2004)** After his mother's death, 12-year-old Skiff Beaman decides that it is up to him to earn money to take care of himself and his father.

***Z for Zachariah,* Robert C. O'Brien (1975)** Seemingly the only person left alive after a nuclear war, a 16-year-old girl is relieved to see a man arrive in her valley until she realizes that he is a tyrant, and she must somehow escape.

Famous Characters from Literature

If a literary work is memorable, it is usually due to a cast of memorable characters. We might be drawn into a work because we identify with the main character at some level. More often we are captivated by the extraordinary challenges the protagonist faces. A character might be completely fictional in a fantastic world, such as Aladdin or Harry Potter, or based on a historical figure such as Captain Bligh of *Mutiny on the Bounty*. Whether historical or fictional, the characters in the list below are memorable.

Aladdin One of the best-known characters from the *Arabian Nights,* Aladdin came to possess a magical lamp. When he rubbed the lamp, a powerful genie would appear and grant Aladdin's wishes.

Ali Baba In "Ali Baba and the Forty Thieves," one of the most popular tales in the *Arabian Nights,* a poor woodcutter named Ali Baba sees a band of thieves enter a cave using the words "Open, Sesame." When the thieves depart, Ali Baba uses the magic words and discovers a fortune in gold.

Alice A young girl who visits a strange, illogical land filled with peculiar characters in the Lewis Carroll fantasy classic *Alice's Adventures in Wonderland* and *Through the Looking-Glass.*

Artful Dodger Nickname of Jack Dawkins, a young, skilled thief in Charles Dickens's novel *Oliver Twist.*

Aslan The great lion who is creator and ruler of the land of Narnia in C.S. Lewis's classic fantasy series, the *Chronicles of Narnia.*

Babar In a series of French children's books, Babar is a young elephant who makes his way to Paris after his mother is killed by hunters. He later returns home, where he is crowned king, marries, and introduces French culture to the elephants.

Alice in Wonderland, John Tenniel

Mr. Badger Character in Kenneth Grahame's classic tale *The Wind in the Willows.* Mr. Badger is a wise, kind, solitary creature.

Bilbo Baggins Central character of J.R.R. Tolkien's fantasy classic *The Hobbit*. It is Bilbo who recovers the One Ring from Gollum and carries it back to the Shire.

Frodo Baggins Central character of J.R.R. Tolkien's trilogy *The Lord of the Rings*. Frodo is the ring-bearer who must carry the One Ring to Mount Doom and destroy it, before the evil Sauron finds it.

Black Beauty A magnificent black horse in Anna Sewell's famous novel *Black Beauty*. The book was written to encourage better treatment of animals.

Harrison Bergeron Title character of a short story by Kurt Vonnegut about a world where everyone is forced to be equal, with masks for people who are attractive, drugs to slow down those who are intelligent, and weights to hobble those who are athletic. Fourteen-year-old Harrison tries to escape the weights and limitations imposed by the Handicapper General.

William Bligh Real-life captain of the British ship *H.M.S. Bounty*. Captain Bligh sailed to Tahiti to get breadfruit for Britain's colonies in the Caribbean, but his crew mutinied during the return trip. Bligh succeeded in navigating across 4,000 miles in a small boat and lived to carry out his mission. His adventures were recounted in a poem by Lord Byron and in the novel *Mutiny on the Bounty*.

Brom Bones In Washington Irving's "The Legend of Sleepy Hollow," Abraham "Brom Bones" Van Brunt pretends to be the legendary Headless Horseman in order to scare away the gawky schoolmaster Ichabod Crane, his rival for the love of a young woman.

Buck Dog hero of Jack London's famous novel *The Call of the Wild*. Buck is stolen from his family and made to work as a sled dog in the frozen Klondike gold fields. Buck survives the abuse he receives by learning to fight. He is in time rescued by a better owner, John Thornton, but when Thornton is murdered, Buck breaks away and joins a wolf pack.

Natty Bumppo The central character of James Fennimore Cooper's *Leatherstocking Tales*, a series of novels that movingly recounts frontier life of the 1700s from the point of view of both Native Americans and European settlers. Natty (Nathaniel) is the son of a farmer, but he becomes a scout and eventually chooses the wilderness and his Indian friend Chingachgook over being a farmer. He is adopted into an Indian tribe, where he is known as Deerslayer and Hawkeye. The five books in the series are *Last of the Mohicans, The Pathfinder, The Deerslayer, The Prairie,* and *The Pioneers*.

Rhett Butler Rugged, worldly hero of Margaret Mitchell's historical novel *Gone with the Wind*.

Casey In the humorous 1888 poem "Casey at the Bat," by Ernest L. Thayer, "mighty Casey" is the star batter for the team from Mudville, who comes to the plate with the team behind and bases loaded—and strikes out.

Charlotte A talking spider who befriends the pig Wilber in the classic *Charlotte's Web*.

Cheshire Cat Talking, grinning cat in *Alice's Adventures in Wonderland*. The cat could vanish at will, and sometimes just his huge grin appeared.

Chingachgook Mohican chief and companion of Natty Bumppo in the *Leatherstocking Tales*.

Christian The pilgrim hero in John Bunyan's allegorical novel *The Pilgrim's Progress*.

Fletcher Christian Former friend of Captain William Bligh and the leader of the mutiny that ended Bligh's first journey to Tahiti.

Christopher Robin In A.A. Milne's *Winnie-the-Pooh* stories, Christopher Robin is the little boy who owns Pooh, Piglet, Eeyore, and the other toys/characters in the story. He is based on the writer's son, Christopher Robin Milne, and is the only human in the stories.

David Copperfield Title character of Charles Dickens's novel *David Copperfield*. The novel is semi-autobiographical. Like many of Dickens's stories, it reflects the hardships often faced by poor children.

Cowardly Lion One of Dorothy's companions as she searches for the Wizard of Oz. He hopes the wizard will give him courage.

Ichabod Crane In "The Legend of Sleepy Hollow," a schoolmaster who moves to Sleepy Hollow and tries to win a young woman who is loved by Brom Bones. Crane is scared away when Brom imitates the town's legendary Headless Horseman.

Bob Cratchit Father of Tiny Tim and employee of Ebenezer Scrooge in Charles Dickens's *A Christmas Carol*.

Robinson Crusoe Main character in Daniel Defoe's 1719 classic *Robinson Crusoe*, about a man who is castaway on an island and learns to survive.

D'Artagnan Charles de Baatz-Castelmore, Comte d'Artagnan, in real life was the captain of the musketeers for Louis XIV of France and died in battle. His life was fictionalized in a novel, and the fictionalized character was then adopted by Alexander Dumas for a series of novels in which D'Artagnan is the main character. The best known of these novels is *The Three Musketeers*.

Doctor Dolittle An animal-loving doctor who learns to talk to animals in a series of children's books by Hugh Lofting.

Dorothy Main character in L. Frank Baum's *The Wonderful Wizard of Oz*. She and her dog Toto are transported from Kansas to Oz by a tornado. She must find the wizard in order to return home. She is accompanied in her search by the Tin Woodman, Cowardly Lion, and Scarecrow.

Count Dracula Vampire in Bram Stoker's masterpiece *Dracula*. He uses his supernatural powers to move from Transylvania to England, to find more victims. He is, in time, destroyed by Jonathan Harker, who narrates the tale, and Dr. Van Helsing.

Eloi Beautiful, aristocratic people raised for food by the Morlocks in the H.G. Wells classic *The Time Machine.*

Fagin In Dickens's *Oliver Twist,* Fagin is the leader of a gang of thieves. He trains young boys in pick-pocketing and robbery.

Faust Legendary character who sells his soul to the devil in exchange for youth, love, and experience.

Huckleberry Finn In Mark Twain's novel *The Adventures of Huckleberry Finn,* young Huck escapes from his brutal, drunken father and heads down the Mississippi River with a runaway slave named Jim.

Huck Finn, Thomas Hart Benton, 1936

Phileas Fogg Wealthy, eccentric British hero of Jules Verne's adventure novel *Around the World in Eighty Days.*

Anne Frank German-Jewish girl who hid from the Nazis for two years in Amsterdam. She is both the hero and the author of *The Diary of a Young Girl,* written while she and her family were in hiding. She was eventually discovered and died in a concentration camp.

Frankenstein Dr. Victor Frankenstein is the doctor/scientist in Mary Shelley's novel *Frankenstein, or the Modern Prometheus.* He builds a creature from corpses and brings it to life. At first, the creature is innocent and only wishes friendship, but it is hideous and rejected by all who see it, so it takes revenge on Frankenstein for creating it.

Barbara Fritchie Hero of a poem by John Greenleaf Whittier, loosely based on one woman's defiance of the Southern army during the Civil War.

Gandalf Wizard in *The Hobbit* and *The Lord of the Rings* by J.R.R. Tolkien.

Gargantua A giant who was the hero of a series of novels by François Rabelais. The adventures of Gargantua and his son Pantegruel lampoon the follies of the day.

Gargantua's name gives us our adjective *gargantuan,* which describes things that are extremely large.

Gollum A character in J.R.R. Tolkien's tales of Middle-Earth. At the beginning of *The Hobbit,* Gollum possesses the One Ring, but loses it to Bilbo Baggins. Throughout *The Lord of the Rings,* he pursues Bilbo's nephew Frodo to get his precious ring back.

Sam Gribley Young boy who runs away from home and lives with a falcon and a weasel in the Catskill Mountains in the Jean Craighead George novel *My Side of the Mountain.*

The Grinch Hard-hearted Dr. Seuss character who tries to steal Christmas. Someone who tries to spoil the fun of others may be called a *grinch.*

Lemuel Gulliver Hero of Jonathan Swift's masterpiece *Gulliver's Travels.* From the tiny people of Lilliput to the giants of Brobdingnag to the intelligent horses of Houyhnhnmland, Gulliver keeps landing in situations that satirize the people and politics of Swift's era. Today, we use the term *Lilliputian* to denote something very small and a *yahoo* is an uncouth or rowdy person, from the race of brutish Yahoos in Swift's novel.

Hamlet Prince of Denmark and central character of Shakespeare's play *Hamlet.* Hamlet learns from his father's ghost that his death was not natural. Hamlet must determine whether his uncle murdered his father, whether his mother, now married to his uncle, was in on it, and if the woman he loves might also have been involved. He is called the "melancholy prince," because he wears black and mourns for his father.

Jim Hawkins Young boy who finds a treasure map in Robert Louis Stevenson's *Treasure Island.* While in pursuit of the treasure, Jim learns of a plot by Long John Silver and a group of pirates to mutiny and steal the treasure.

Uriah Heep One of the most famous characters in fiction, Heep is a detestable sneak who grows into an evil blackmailer in Charles Dickens's *David Copperfield.* Heep's horrid deeds are finally uncovered by Mr. Micawber.

Sherlock Holmes The most famous detective in all of fiction, the brilliant Holmes was the creation of Sir Arthur Conan Doyle. Holmes appeared in a series of short stories, generally in the company of his closest friend, Dr. John Watson, and often battling the evil Moriarity.

Captain Hook Leader of the pirates and enemy of Peter Pan in the story by J.M. Barrie. The "Hook" in his name refers to the hook that replaced his hand, which was eaten by a crocodile.

Humpty Dumpty Originally a character in a Mother Goose rhyme, Humpty Dumpty is an egg who falls off a wall, and "all the kings horses and all the kings men couldn't put Humpty together again." Humpty Dumpty argued with Alice in Lewis Carroll's

Through the Looking-Glass and has popped up in numerous songs and stories. The end of the rhyme was picked up by Robert Penn Warren for his novel *All the King's Men,* and Humpty serves as an image of the fall of all men in James Joyce's *Finnegan's Wake.*

Mr. Hyde Dangerous, evil man in Robert Louis Stevenson's *The Strange Case of Dr. Jekyll and Mr. Hyde.* Hyde is actually the evil side of the kind and respected Dr. Jekyll, who has developed drugs that separate the good and evil nature in a person.

Ingalls Family The central characters of the largely autobiographical *Little House* novels of Laura Ingalls Wilder, who wrote of the pioneer life she knew as a child.

Jane The love interest in the *Tarzan* novels by Edgar Rice Burroughs.

Dr. Jekyll The good doctor in Stevenson's *The Strange Case of Dr. Jekyll and Mr. Hyde.* Exploring the nature of good and evil, he develops drugs that allow him to separate the two. Over time, he begins to lose control over Mr. Hyde.

Julie Young Eskimo girl who runs away from home, gets lost, and is befriended by wolves in the Jean Craighead George novel *Julie of the Wolves.*

Juliet The female title character in Shakespeare's tragedy *Romeo and Juliet.* Juliet loved Romeo, and the two secretly married, but their families were bitter enemies.

Karana Young Indian girl who lived alone for 18 years on an island off the coast of California, in Scott O'Dell's classic novel *Island of the Blue Dolphins.*

Helen Keller Blind and deaf woman who is the central character of the play *The Miracle Worker,* which is based on her early life and the relationship with her teacher, Anne Sullivan. Helen went on to become a writer and advocate for the blind.

Lad The four-footed hero of Albert Payson Terhune's classic novel *Lad: A Dog.*

Lassie A beautiful, faithful collie that originally appeared in Eric Knight's *Lassie Come-Home.* Lassie went on to appear in other books, movies, and a TV series.

Simon Legree Evil overseer in Harriet Beecher Stowe's *Uncle Tom's Cabin.* He beats the slave Uncle Tom to death because Tom will not reveal the hiding place of two escaped female slaves. The name Simon Legree is used now to denote any brutal taskmaster.

Mary Lennox Young girl who is the central character in Frances Hodgson Burnett's *The Secret Garden.* Unhealthy and ill-tempered, Mary, who has been raised in India, returns to England when her parents die. In England, she discovers a long-abandoned garden. As she works to restore the garden, she finds she also improves herself and reforms her spoiled cousin.

Man Friday A young man rescued from cannibals by Robinson Crusoe. In gratitude, he becomes Crusoe's faithful attendant and sidekick. The name Man Friday is now often used to denote a particularly competent or resourceful servant or assistant.

Sam McGee Character in Robert W. Service's humorous poem "The Cremation of Sam McGee." While freezing to death, McGee, who has moved to Alaska from Tennessee, makes the narrator promise to cremate his remains. When the narrator finally finds a place to build the fire, McGee thaws out, happy to be warm at last.

Dan McGrew In Robert W. Service's poem "The Shooting of Dan McGrew," McGrew is a dangerous gambler during the time of the Alaska gold rush.

Milo Young boy who learns that life is not as boring as he thought in the classic tale of *The Phantom Tollbooth* by Norton Juster.

Walter Mitty Central character of James Thurber's short story "The Secret Life of Walter Mitty." Mitty is a quiet, hen-pecked daydreamer who imagines himself as a daring pilot, a brilliant surgeon, and other fabulous characters but is always brought back to reality, usually by his wife. His name has come to be the definition of the timid man who uses fantasy to escape an unpleasant reality.

Mole Character in Kenneth Grahame's classic tale *The Wind in the Willows*. A home-loving little creature, he adapts to the hustle and bustle of life on the river with a little help from Ratty.

Morlocks Evil, ape-like creatures that live underground and raise the beautiful people known as the Eloi for food in the H.G. Wells classic *The Time Machine*.

Mowgli An Indian boy raised by Mother Wolf with her cubs in Rudyard Kipling's *Jungle Books*.

Captain Nemo Inventor and captain of the *Nautilus*, a fantastic submarine. Nemo is the hero of Jules Verne's science fiction novel *Twenty Thousand Leagues Under the Sea*.

Scarlett O'Hara Strong-willed central character in Margaret Mitchell's *Gone With the Wind*. Scarlett is a survivor, and she does whatever is necessary to protect herself and her property.

Old Yeller A stray yellow dog adopted by fourteen-year-old Travis in the Fred Gipson classic novel *Old Yeller*. The story is set on a farm in Texas in the late 1800s.

Captain Nemo observes an octopus

Passepartout Phileas Fogg's resourceful French servant in Jules Verne's *Around the World in Eighty Days*.

Peter Pan Central character of J.M. Barrie's drama and later novel *Peter Pan*. Peter runs away to Never-Never-Land, where he will never have to grow up.

Sancho Panza   In Miguel de Cervantes's novel *Don Quixote*, Panza is the squire to the aging knight. He is famous for his proverbs.

Pinocchio   A puppet who becomes a boy in the children's story *The Adventures of Pinocchio* by Carlo Collodi. While Pinocchio is still made of wood, his nose gets longer if he tells a lie.

Pollyanna   Title character in the novel by Eleanor H. Porter. No matter what happens to her, Pollyanna tries to see the good in it. Her name has become a synonym for a relentlessly optimistic person who tries to make the best of every situation.

Harry Potter   Magician and hero of the *Harry Potter* novels by J.K. Rowling.

Hester Prynne   The heroine of Nathaniel Hawthorne's *The Scarlet Letter*.

Quasimodo   The tragic, deformed bell ringer who is the title character of Victor Hugo's *The Hunchback of Notre Dame*.

Don Quixote   Title character of the novel by Miguel de Cervantes. A man who imagines that he is a knight, Don Quixote sets off to right the world's wrongs. He rides off on Rocinante, a horse as old as he is, stopping to make the rustic Sancho Panza his squire. He battles windmills, thinking they are giants, and chases flocks of sheep, believing them to be armies. Our word *quixotic,* which means to have a romantic or unrealistic view of life, comes from his name.

Ransom   The hero of C.S. Lewis's *Space Trilogy: Out of the Silent Planet, Perelandra,* and *That Hideous Strength.*

Uncle Remus   The title character of Joel Chandler Harris's book *Uncle Remus, His Songs and His Sayings.* Uncle Remus is an aging African American servant who relates to a young white boy the folk tales and fables of the African Americans of the South. Harris created the character as a way of sharing the stories he had heard as a child.

Rikki-Tikki-Tavi   In the *Jungle Books* by Rudyard Kipling, Rikki-Tikki-Tavi is a pet mongoose that saves a family from the great cobras, Nag and Nagaina.

Rocinante   In Cervantes's *Don Quixote,* Rocinante is the aging horse who carries the old knight on his adventures. When John Steinbeck took a road trip with his dog, recorded in his book *Travels with Charley,* he named his camper van *Rocinante.*

Romeo   The male title character in Shakespeare's tragedy *Romeo and Juliet.* Romeo, a great swordsman of noble birth, loved Juliet. They married secretly because their families were bitter enemies. It seemed they would be happy, until Romeo is banished after a sword fight.

Tom Sawyer   The main character of Mark Twain's *The Adventures of Tom Sawyer,* as well as the three sequels. A clever and adventurous boy, he moves between the respectable world of his Aunt Polly and the footloose world of his friend Huckleberry Finn. Among their adventures, Tom witnesses a murder, runs away from home, and finds a treasure. By the last of the four novels, he has become a detective—the persona later borrowed for *The League of Extraordinary Gentlemen*.

Scarecrow One of Dorothy's companions in *The Wonderful Wizard of Oz*. He hopes the wizard will give him a brain.

Scheherazade The narrator of the tales in *The Arabian Nights*. She tells the tales to her husband, Sultan Schahriah, but leaves the ending for the next day. The Sultan has sworn that every woman he marries must die the day after the wedding, but he wants to hear the end of each story, so he spares Scheherazade's life. By the time she has told tales for 1001 nights, the Sultan has given up his plan.

Ebenezer Scrooge The grasping old miser in Charles Dickens's classic story *A Christmas Carol*. Scrooge is transformed after a series of ghosts show him his past, present, and possible future. Today, a person who is tight with money is often called a *scrooge*.

Anne Shirley Orphan girl who is raised by a kindly couple on Canada's Prince Edward Island, from L.M. Montgomery's *Anne of Green Gables* and its sequels.

Shylock Money lender in Shakespeare's *The Merchant of Venice*. When his daughter elopes, he hopes to destroy the man who made it possible by demanding a pound of flesh as repayment for a debt.

Long John Silver Pirate who hopes to steal a treasure from Jim Hawkins in Robert Louis Stevenson's *Treasure Island*.

Sinbad the Sailor In *The Arabian Nights,* an adventurer from Baghdad who gains fame and fortune during seven astonishing voyages.

Tarzan Hero of a series of popular novels by Edgar Rice Burroughs about a boy from an aristocratic English family who is born in Africa and, when his parents die soon after, is adopted and raised by a family of apes. In Burroughs's tales, Tarzan had adventures far greater, and in far more places, than have ever been shown in the movies or TV shows that feature Tarzan.

Becky Thatcher Tom Sawyer's sweetheart in Mark Twain's *The Adventures of Tom Sawyer*.

Three Musketeers Athos, Porthos, and Aramis—skilled swordsmen and among the most renowned fighters of their day. They are companions of D'Artagnan in the famous Alexander Dumas novel *The Three Musketeers*.

Tin Woodman One of Dorothy's companions as she searches for the Wizard of Oz. He hopes the wizard will give him a heart.

Tinker Bell Fairy and companion to the title character in J.M. Barrie's drama and novel *Peter Pan.*

Tiny Tim Small, crippled boy, the son of Bob Cratchit, in Dickens's *A Christmas Carol.*

Mr. Toad Character in Kenneth Grahame's classic tale *The Wind in the Willows.* A wealthy toad and owner of Toad Hall, he likes boats and fast cars.

Tweedledum and Tweedledee Names invented by John Byrom, who used them to satirize two almost-identical groups who constantly argued. The characters were later adopted by Lewis Carroll in *Through the Looking-Glass,* the sequel to *Alice's Adventures in Wonderland.*

Oliver Twist Young boy raised in a workhouse in Charles Dickens's novel *Oliver Twist.* As the story follows Oliver from poverty to danger to eventual rescue, it reveals the conditions of the poor in England's cities at that time.

Goody Two-Shoes Title character of a story by Oliver Goldsmith. Goody is a very poor child, and when she gets a pair of shoes, she is so excited, she tells everyone, "Look, two shoes," from which she gets her nickname. She grows up to be a wise and wealthy woman.

Uncle Tom An old African American slave in Harriet Beecher Stowe's novel *Uncle Tom's Cabin.*

Jean Valjean Hero of Victor Hugo's novel *Les Misérables.*

Rip Van Winkle Title character of a story by Washington Irving. Rip Van Winkle goes into the mountains, where he meets a group of dwarfs and, after drinking with them, falls asleep for twenty years. He returns home to find his wife dead, the United States independent from Britain, and his town completely changed.

Dr. John Watson Companion of Sherlock Holmes.

Winnie-the-Pooh Toy bear in a series of books by A. A. Milne.

Wizard of Oz Character from L. Frank Baum's *The Wonderful Wizard of Oz.* The wizard is a fraud, but he sends Dorothy and her friends on a mission that helps them find for themselves the things they are seeking.

White Fang Wolf-dog who is saved from a brutal owner and gradually domesticated in Jack London's novel, *White Fang,* which was a sequel to *The Call of the Wild.* White Fang dies defending his new family against an escaped convict.

White Rabbit Character in Lewis Carroll's *Alice's Adventures in Wonderland.* Alice follows the White Rabbit down the hole that leads to Wonderland. References to the White Rabbit exist in music, literature, and movies, and usually relate to something that leads a person into a dramatically altered reality.

Characters, Places, and Creatures from Mythology

Myths are founding stories of civilizations—the tales that unified families, tribes, and cities into a single society. Mythologies are peopled with gods, goddesses, imaginary creatures, mortals with supernatural powers, as well as normal humans. These characters influence not only our literature but our language as well.

Achilles A Greek warrior and king who is the hero of Homer's *The Iliad,* an epic poem about the Trojan War. As an infant, Achilles was dipped into the River Styx, which made him invulnerable—except for the heel by which his mother held him. Today, the tendon that is attached to the heel is called the *Achilles tendon*, and the phrase "Achilles heel" refers to someone's weakness.

Adonis A beautiful young man loved by the goddess Venus. He was killed by a wild boar, and the goddess turned his blood into the flower called *Adonis.* Today, people often say that an exceptionally good-looking young man is an *Adonis*.

Aeneas A Trojan warrior, a son of the goddess Venus. Aeneas is the hero of Virgil's epic poem *The Aeneid,* which tells of Aeneas's adventures on his way to Italy where he is considered the legendary ancestor of the Romans. Aeneas has become a symbol of devotion, because he carried his aged father to safety when Troy fell.

Agamemnon The king who led the Greeks into battle against the Trojans. He was wounded, but eventually won the war against Troy. When he returned home, he was murdered by his wife, Clytemnestra, and her lover.

Ajax Greek warrior, second only to Achilles among the heroes of the Trojan War.

Amazon A legendary race of warlike women. Amazons came to the aid of Troy during the Trojan War. Today, a very strong, large, or assertive woman is sometimes called an *Amazon.*

Andromeda An Ethiopian princess in Greek mythology who was rescued from a sea monster by her future husband, Perseus. When Andromeda died, she was placed among the stars, forming the constellation of the same name.

Apollo One of the most important Greek gods, Apollo was the ruler of music, archery, prophecy, and healing. He eventually became identified with the sun god, taking over the sun chariot and fiery horses of Helios (the sun), driving them across the sky each day. Apollo, who was considered the most beautiful of the gods, was later adopted into Roman mythology. The chariot and horses of Apollo became the symbol of NASA's Apollo missions to the moon.

Arachne A young Greek woman who challenged the goddess Athena to a weaving contest. Athena wove a tapestry depicting the gods as powerful, while Arachne created a tapestry that mocked the gods. Enraged, Athena tore Arachne's work to pieces and turned her into a spider. Today, the scientific name for spiders is *Arachnida,* from Arachne.

Ares The Greek god of war and one of the great gods of Olympus. He was known as Mars to the Romans.

Argo The ship in which Jason set out to find the Golden Fleece.

Argonauts The sailors and adventurers who joined Jason in his search for the Golden Fleece.

Ariadne The daughter of King Minos of Crete. She helped Theseus by giving him a sword to use against the Minotaur and a ball of thread that would help him escape the Labyrinth.

Artemis The Greek goddess of wild animals, the hunt, and vegetation. She was the twin sister of Apollo. The Romans knew her as the goddess Diana.

Asgard In Norse mythology, the home of the gods, reached by a rainbow bridge. It has many mansions, among them, Valhalla, where warriors who died in battle were rewarded.

Athena Greek goddess of war, wisdom, and the arts and sciences. She sprang, full-grown and in full armor, from the head of Zeus. She was the patron of Athens, which was named in gratitude for the goddess's gift of the olive tree. She was identified with the Roman goddess Minerva.

Atlantis A legendary island that was said to have existed in the Atlantic Ocean just west of the Straits of Gibraltar. The Greek philosopher Plato wrote about Atlantis, saying he had heard about it from the Egyptians.

Atlas One of the Titans who fought against Zeus and brother of Prometheus. Defeated in battle, Atlas was condemned to hold the heavens on his shoulders. He was later turned to stone when Prometheus showed him the head of Medusa, thus creating the Atlas Mountains in northwest Africa.

Aurora Roman goddess of the dawn. Identified with the Greek goddess Eos.

Avatar In Hinduism, the incarnation of a deity in human or animal form to counteract some particular evil in the world usually referring to appearances of the god Vishnu. The word is now used most commonly in computer role-playing games, where it is a lifelike graphic that represents a user.

Bacchus In Greek and Roman mythology, the god of wine and vegetation. Also called Dionysus. From this god's name, we get the word *bacchanalia,* a drunken feast or party.

Balder Scandinavian god of light, son of Odin and Frigga. He is the central figure of many Norse myths. He was killed with a branch of mistletoe.

Boreas The mythological being who acted as the north wind. Today, this name appears in words that refer to things that are northerly, from the Aurora Borealis to the boreal forests of Alaska.

Brahma In Hinduism, the creator of the universe.

Brunhild A beautiful Amazon-like princess in ancient Germanic heroic literature who falls in love with Siegfried, the only man who exceeds her in strength. When she learns that he has won her for someone else, she takes vengeance, which leads to Siegfried's death. In Norse tales, she has supernatural qualities and is the leader of the Valkyrie.

Callisto A nymph who was transformed into a bear by Jupiter. Placed in the heavens on her death, she became the constellation known as the Great Bear. *Callisto* is also the name given to one of the moons of the planet Jupiter.

Calypso The queen of the island of Ogygia. She kept the shipwrecked Odysseus on her island for seven years.

Cassandra The Trojan princess who was given the gift of foresight, although her prophetic statements were ignored. She predicted the destruction of Troy. The term *Cassandra* refers to someone who predicts doom or destruction.

Centaur Mythological creature who is half horse and half human.

Cerberus A three-headed dog with a mane of snakes that guards the entrance to Hades, letting the souls of the dead in but not out.

Ceres The Roman goddess of the growth of food plants. It is from her name that we get the word *cereal.*

Chaos In Greek mythology, the original confusion in which earth, sea, and air were mixed up together.

Charon In Greek mythology, the boatman who transports the souls of the dead over Styx and Acheron, the rivers of the underworld. It was traditional to put a coin in a corpse's mouth before burial, as payment to Charon.

Charybdis A sea monster that sucked in the seas three times a day. Charybdis was positioned on the opposite side of the Straits of Messina from the monster Scylla. Being caught between Scylla and Charybdis has come to refer to a situation in which danger lies on both sides.

Chimera In Greek mythology, a fire-breathing female monster with the head of a lion, body of a goat, and tail of a dragon. The word now refers to an illusion or imaginary thing.

Circe In Greek mythology, a sorceress, the daughter of the sun god Helios, who turned all of Odysseus's companions into pigs when they landed on her island. Odysseus escaped her spell by using an herb given to him by Hermes.

Cronos One of the Titans, father of many Greek gods, including Zeus, Hades, and Poseidon. He was overthrown by Zeus.

Cupid Roman god of love, identified with the Greek love god, Eros.

Cyclops (plural, Cyclopes) A gigantic creature in the form of a human, with one eye in the middle of its forehead. Cyclopes ate humans and helped the god Vulcan to forge thunderbolts for Zeus.

Daedalus A skilled Greek inventor who created the fabulous maze called the Labyrinth for king Minos of Crete. When the king imprisoned Daedalus and his son, Icarus, the inventor crafted wings of wax and feathers, and they escaped, though Icarus died during the escape.

Danaë Mother of the Greek hero Perseus.

Daphne Nymph who was loved by Apollo. To help her escape Apollo, her father, a river god, turned her into a laurel tree. The laurel tree became Apollo's favorite tree, and a laurel wreath is still a symbol of both poetry and victory.

Demeter Greek goddess of vegetation and mother of Persephone. Identified with the Roman goddess Ceres.

Diana Roman goddess of the moon and of hunting, known as a protector of women. She was sometimes identified with the Greek goddess Artemis. She is usually pictured as a huntress, with a bow and arrows. She became a symbol of strong, virtuous women. Many poems were written during the reign of England's Elizabeth I comparing the queen to Diana.

Dionysus Greek god of wine. See *Bacchus*.

dryad Female tree spirits in Greek mythology.

Echo A nymph who was condemned by the Roman goddess Juno to repeat what someone else had said. Ignored by Narcissus, whom she loved, she faded to nothing but a voice. Source of the word *echo,* the voice we sometimes hear coming back to us.

Elysian Fields Also called Elysium, this is the paradise of Greek mythology. The term *Elysian Fields* is still used to express something that offers the promise of happiness.

Erebus In Greek mythology, a place of darkness through which souls passed on their way to Hades.

Eros The Greek god of love. He was the youngest of all the gods. Parallels Cupid in Roman mythology.

Eurydice The wife of Orpheus, killed by a snake.

Fates Three goddesses who determine the course of human life; one spins out the thread of a person's life, one holds the thread and decides when it is long enough, and the third cuts the thread, ending the person's life.

faun A woodland creature in Roman mythology. It appears in human form, but with small horns, pointed ears, and sometimes a goat tail. Mr. Tumnus of *The Lion, The Witch and the Wardrobe* is a faun.

Freya Norse goddess of love, beauty, and the dead. She is remembered in our word *Friday*, which was originally Freya's day.

Frigga (also, Frigg) In Norse mythology, the supreme goddess, wife of Odin, and goddess of marriage.

fury One of a group of avenging spirits in Greek mythology.

Genius In Roman mythology, a guardian spirit that watched over a person from cradle to grave.

Golden Fleece The wool of a mythical winged ram. The ram was sacrificed to Zeus and the wool was given to King Aeetes. It later became the prize sought by Jason and the Argonauts.

Gorgons In Greek mythology, hideous female monsters with snakes for hair. Medusa was the most famous of the Gorgons. Whoever looked at her turned to stone. She was killed by Perseus.

Graces Three goddesses who increased enjoyment of life by encouraging refinement and gentleness.

Hades The god of the underworld in Greek mythology. Later, the word was given to the place Hades ruled.

harpies Monsters in Greek mythology that were half woman and half bird. They had sharp claws and tormented anyone they encountered. The word *harpy* is now used to describe an ill-tempered woman.

Hector Son of King Priam of Troy and the noblest of Troy's warriors in Homer's *Iliad*. He is killed by Achilles.

Helen of Troy A Greek beauty, wife of the Spartan King Menelaus, and daughter of the Greek god Zeus. She ran away with Paris, son of King Priam of Troy. Menelaus raised an army to win her back, sparking the Trojan War. After Troy's destruction, she returned home with Menelaus.

Hera Queen of the Greek gods and goddesses, wife of Zeus. She parallels Juno from Roman mythology.

Hercules A mighty Greek hero and son of Zeus. He showed his great strength and intelligence by accomplishing a series of seemingly impossible deeds known as the Twelve Labors of Hercules. Today, we use the word *Herculean* to describe huge tasks or efforts.

Hermes Greek god of dreams and protector of cattle and sheep. He was also a messenger of the gods, and is often identified with the Roman god Mercury.

Horus Egyptian sun god, often appearing as a falcon or as a falcon-headed man. Horus's eye was damaged in a battle with an enemy, but his mother healed it. The image of Horus's eye became a symbol of healing and later gave rise to the Rx symbol used by many pharmacies.

Icarus Son of Daedalus, he escaped the Labyrinth using the wings crafted by his father, but he ignored his father's warnings to not fly too high. The sun melted the wax of which the wings were made, and he fell to his death.

Janus In Roman mythology, the spirit of doorways, looking both forward and backward. Janus gives us the word *January.*

Jason Greek prince who led the Argonauts in pursuit of the Golden Fleece.

Juno Wife of the Roman god Jupiter and queen of heaven. She is identified with the Greek goddess Hera, and like Hera, is the protector of marriage.

Jupiter The king of the Roman gods and goddesses. He was the son of Saturn and father of Vulcan, the Muses, Apollo, and many of the heroes of Roman mythology. He is identified with the Greek god Zeus. The largest planet in the solar system is named for him.

Labyrinth Enclosed maze created by Daedalus for King Minos of Crete. People condemned to the Labyrinth became hopelessly lost and were eventually killed by the Minotaur that lived there. Theseus killed the Minotaur and escaped the Labyrinth, with the help of Ariadne.

Lethe A river in Hades, the water of which erases the memory of whoever drinks of it. *Lethe* has become a metaphor for that which helps people forget unpleasant memories.

Loki The god of strife and a trickster spirit of evil in Norse mythology.

Mars Roman god of war. From his name we get not only the name of the planet Mars, but also the root word for war and warrior—*martial.*

Medea Sorceress and princess who helped Jason obtain the Golden Fleece. She married Jason, but Jason later left her for the daughter of King Creon. Wild with revenge, Medea murdered King Creon, Jason's new wife, and her own children. She escaped to Asia, and the Greek historian Herodotus wrote that the people known as the Medes came from the region where she settled.

Medusa One of the Gorgons. She was killed by Perseus, but even when she was dead, looking at her turned people to stone. Perseus survived by looking at her reflection in his shield.

Memnon An Ethiopian prince, son of the goddess Aurora. He joined the Trojans in their fight against the Greeks and was killed by Achilles.

Mentor A friend of Odysseus. Minerva assumed the form of Mentor when she helped Telemachus search for his father. This is the origin of our word *mentor*.

Mercury The Roman god of science and commerce who acted as messenger for other gods. Equivalent of the Greek Hermes. He is most often pictured with wings on his feet and wearing a hat with wings.

Midas A king of Phyrigia, who was granted a wish by the god Bacchus. Midas asked that everything he touched be turned to gold. Today, a person who is very successful is often said to have the Midas touch.

Minerva Roman goddess of wisdom, equivalent to the Greek Athena. Like Athena, she was "born" full grown and wearing armor, springing from the head of Jupiter.

Minotaur A monster that was half bull and half man. King Minos of Crete kept it in the Labyrinth built by Daedalus and fed it on the bodies of captives. It was killed by Theseus, with the help of Minos' daughter, Ariadne.

Mnemosyne Greek goddess of memory and mother of the nine Muses. It is from her name that we get the word *mnemonic*—a device that helps us remember.

Morpheus Son of Hypnos (sleep), Morpheus is the Greek god of dreams and also a character in *The Matrix* trilogy of movies.

Muses Nine daughters of Zeus and Mnemosyne. They were the goddesses of arts and sciences. We refer to someone as a *muse* if they inspire another in the arts.

Narcissus A beautiful young man who was cruel to the loving Echo, and as a result, he was cursed to fall in love with someone he could not have—his own reflection in a pond. He pined away and finally died, still admiring his own image. The flower we call *narcissus* grew up where he died. Those that are afflicted with self love are said to be *narcissistic*.

Neptune Roman god of the sea, corresponding to the Greek Poseidon.

nymphs Beautiful female creatures that were minor divinities of nature. There were nymphs of trees, rivers, mountains, and other features of the natural world.

Odin The chief Norse god, called Woden by the Anglo-Saxons. He was the god of wisdom, poetry, war, and agriculture. It is from Woden that we get our word *Wednesday*.

Odysseus Greek king and hero of Homer's epic poem *The Odyssey*. After victory at Troy, Odysseus spends years wandering in his attempt to return to his faithful wife, Penelope. The Roman name for Odysseus was Ulysses. Odysseus/Ulysses is one of the most commonly portrayed characters in Western literature, and the source of the word *odyssey*—a long journey.

Oedipus Greek hero who guessed the riddle of the Sphinx and became king of Thebes. He had been abandoned as a child and rescued by a shepherd. He later fought with and killed the king of Thebes and married the queen, not knowing that these people were his father and mother. When the truth was learned, his mother killed herself and he blinded himself.

Olympus Mount Olympus is a real mountain in Greece, and it was once believed that the peak of the mountain was the home of the Greek gods and goddesses.

Orpheus One of the Argonauts. Son of Apollo, he was a musician of such skill that even inanimate objects were moved. When his wife Eurydice died, he charmed Pluto into releasing her from the underworld. When he broke his promise and looked back to see if Eurydice was following him, he lost her for good.

Pan The Greek god of nature. Part man, part goat, the emotion he was thought to produce in those who saw him gave us the word *panic*, which means literally "of Pan."

Pandora In Greek mythology, the first woman. She was given many gifts, including a box that she was told not to open. Curious, she lifted the lid, releasing all the known evils into the world. *Pandora's box* is a phrase that describes something that will lead to all kinds of problems.

Paris The son of King Priam of Troy. He was asked to judge who of three goddesses was the fairest, and he chose Venus, goddess of love, who helped him carry off Helen of Troy, which led to the Trojan War. Paris was not respected by his own people because he was a coward. He killed Achilles with a poisoned arrow and was then killed himself when the city fell.

Pegasus The winged horse of the Muses, born of sea foam and the blood of the beheaded Medusa.

Penelope Wife of Odysseus. She waited patiently during all the years of Odysseus's wandering. She is a symbol of faithfulness.

Persephone In Greek mythology, daughter of Zeus and Demeter; paralleled in Roman mythology by Prosperpine, daughter of Jupiter and Ceres. She was taken captive by the king of the underworld. Her mother, goddess of vegetation, mourned, causing all plants to die. Zeus demanded the return of Persephone. She had eaten six pomegranate seeds, however, making it possible for her to return to her mother only six months of the year. Persephone's death and rebirth are the source of the seasons.

Perseus Greek hero who killed the gorgon Medusa and saved Andromeda.

Pluto Roman god of the underworld, parallel to the Greek god Hades.

Poseidon Greek god of the sea; comparable to the Roman god Neptune.

Priam Legendary king of Troy and father of Paris and Hector.

Procrustes In Greek mythology, a robber who captured people and forced them to try his iron bed. He stretched those who were too short and cut short those who were too tall. He was eventually killed by Theseus. Today, the term *procrustean* describes a person who tries to force everything into a predetermined pattern.

Prometheus One of the Titans. Jupiter assigned him the job of forming humans from mud. Out of pity, Prometheus stole fire from heaven and gave it to humans. Jupiter punished him by chaining him to a mountain and having an eagle tear out his liver every day. (Because Prometheus was immortal, the liver always grew back.) Prometheus was finally rescued by Hercules. The word *Promethean* is used to describe a light-giver—a creative and bold person.

Proteus Neptune's herdsman, an old man famous for his power to change shapes at will. From this comes our word *protean,* which describes anything that can change shapes, adapt quickly, or display variety.

Psyche A beautiful young woman who married Cupid and in time was made immortal. Psyche became a symbol of the human soul.

Pygmalian A sculptor who created a statue of a perfect woman, then fell in love with it. The statue was brought to life by Venus. *Pygmalian is* the title of a play by George Bernard Shaw about a professor who teaches an uneducated woman how to behave in society—a story that was remade into the musical *My Fair Lady.*

Quetzalcoatl A deity of Mesoamerican mythology. The term literally means "feathered serpent." Most Mesoamerican civilizations, such as the Mayan, Aztec, Olmec, and Toltec, claim Quetzalcoatl as the founder of their cultures.

Saturn Roman god who was father of all the other Roman gods and goddesses. In addition to becoming the name of one of the planets, his name also became part of the weekend: Saturn's day, or *Saturday.*

satyr In Greek mythology, one of a race of half man/half goat creatures who lived in woodlands. Comparable to the Roman faun.

Scylla Monster with six heads who snatched sailors out of ships that came too close as they tried to steer clear of nearby Charybdis. Choosing between Scylla and Charybdis meant choosing between two bad options. In the real world, Scylla was a dangerous rock and Charybdis was a whirlpool that, together, posed a great danger to sailors along the coast of Sicily.

sirens Sea nymphs whose singing was so sweet that sailors would jump into the sea to try to join them. When Odysseus passed the island of the sirens, he had his men stop their ears with wax, so they could not hear the sirens, and then had himself tied to the mast. He was almost driven mad by the sweetness of their music. A *siren song* is anything that is seemingly sweet yet capable of luring someone in a potentially dangerous direction.

Sphinx A monster in Greek mythology, with the body of a lion and head of a woman. The Sphinx would stop people traveling to Thebes and demand that they answer a riddle. Those that failed to answer correctly would be killed. She killed herself in rage when Oedipus correctly guessed the answer.

Styx In Greek mythology, the main river of the underworld.

Tantalus In Greek myths, a king who revealed secrets belonging to the gods. As punishment, he was tied to a fruit tree and surrounded by water. When he reached up to eat, the branches moved out of reach; when he bent down to drink, the water vanished. Thus he was tormented by hunger and thirst with the things he wanted just out of reach. From his name, we get the word *tantalize*.

Telemachus The only son of Odysseus and Penelope. He went in search of his father and aided Odysseus to defeat the suitors who had tried to take over his kingdom.

Theseus A great hero of Greek mythology whose many adventures included killing the Minotaur, saving his father from Medea, and killing Procrustes.

Thor Norse god of thunder; in power and importance second only to Odin. He carried a great hammer, a belt of strength, and iron gloves.

Titans In Greek mythology, the children of Uranus who were overcome by Zeus and imprisoned in the underworld. Prometheus, Cronos, and Atlas were among the Titans who lost power.

Trojan horse A large wooden horse created by the Greeks. It was left outside the gates of Troy. The Trojans pulled it into their city, not realizing that Greek soldiers were hiding inside. The Greeks waited until nightfall and then let their army into the city, thus bringing about the destruction of Troy. Today, anything that looks harmless but that carries something damaging is called a *Trojan horse*.

Ulysses Roman name for Odysseus.

Valhalla In Norse mythology, one of the mansions of Asgard where warriors slain in battle are rewarded.

Valkyrie Warrior maidens in Norse mythology.

Venus Roman goddess of beauty and love. She helped Paris carry off Helen of Troy.

Vulcan The god of fire and metalwork in Roman mythology. He was a son of Jupiter and husband to Venus. His workshop was said to be under Mount Etna, his fire spilling out of the top of the mountain. It is from Vulcan that we get the word *volcano*.

Zeus In Greek mythology, the leader of the gods and goddesses. He is comparable to Jupiter in Roman mythology.

Characters and Creatures from Folklore

Folklore is a body of tales, fables, and legends that has been passed from generation to generation, usually by word of mouth.

Abominable Snowman Human-like monster supposed to inhabit the Himalayas at about the level of the snow line.

Arthur A legendary king of Britain and head of the knights of the Round Table. Thought to be based upon a historical figure, the story of King Arthur became the basis of an elaborate fantasy, including the magician Merlin, Arthur's magic sword Excalibur, the exploits of the other knights of the Round Table as they search for the Holy Grail, and the romance between Queen Guinevere and Sir Lancelot.

Beauty and the Beast Characters in a tale about a beautiful woman whose love turns a Beast back into a handsome prince.

Brer Rabbit Character from African American folktales of the South. Brer, or Brother, Rabbit was introduced to a wider audience by Joel Chandler Harris, who created the fictional character Uncle Remus to tell the tales. In the stories, clever Brer Rabbit continually outsmarts Brer Fox, Brer Wolf, and Brer Bear.

Paul Bunyan Giant lumberjack who was the hero of lumber camps across the United States. The giant Bunyan, along with his companion Babe the Blue Ox, created Puget Sound, the Grand Canyon, and the Black Hills with little effort. Bunyan's camp stove covered an acre, and his hotcake griddle was so large that it was greased by men using sides of bacon like skates.

Cinderella The central character of an ancient fairy tale, whose name means "little cinder girl." The story, probably of Eastern origin, was made popular when it was translated into French in the late 1600s. Poor Cinderella is abused by her elder sisters until she is rescued by her fairy godmother.

The Flying Dutchman In the 1600s, a Dutch captain was caught in a storm near the Cape of Good Hope. The captain vowed to make it around the Cape, despite the storm. He failed, but the phantom image of his ship sails forever around the Cape.

Febold Feboldson In regional tales of the Great Plains, particularly in Nebraska, Feboldson became the expression of the fight against drought, flood, blistering heat, terrible cold, dust, and mud. Feboldson, a Swedish farmer, fears that everyone will move West, and, left alone, he might die of loneliness. He comes up with a series of plans to convince people that there is gold in Nebraska.

Goldilocks A young girl who visits three bears, the tale of Goldilocks had its origin in a story published by Robert Southey in 1837. In the original tale, it was an old woman who visited the bears, who was replaced by a girl named Silverhair, then Goldilocks. It is possible, but not certain, that Southey based his story on an older tale.

Hansel and Gretel Characters in a German fairy tale recorded by the Brothers Grimm. It tells the adventures of two poor children as they encounter the Sand Man, The Dew Man, and the Crunch Witch.

John Henry Hero of an African American folk ballad, John Henry is at least in part based on a real person. He is a "steel-driving man," one of the workers hired by the railroad to hammer steel stakes into rock walls in order to make holes for the placement of dynamite. John Henry worked with a hammer in each hand. In the ballad, he challenges the new steam drill that threatens to replace him to a contest. He wins the contest but dies of exhaustion.

Henry Hudson British explorer for whom Hudson Bay and the Hudson River are named. The folktale associated with Hudson is that when he visited the Catskill Mountains, he encountered a group of gnomes. The tale says that Hudson's men were transformed by the liquor offered them by the gnomes, but that they returned to normal once back on their ship. The real Hudson was set adrift in a small boat when his crew mutinied in 1611, and he was never seen again. Rip Van Winkle sees the spirit of Henry Hudson playing with the gnomes before he falls into his 20-year slumber.

Tommy Knockers In folktales that came from Cornwall in England with the miners who moved to the United States, these are either the spirits of dead miners who help the living miners or spiteful spirits who cause miners problems. They are said to knock before a cave-in, but depending on whether they are viewed as good or bad, they knock in warning or they knock to cause the cave-in. It was traditional to leave a little bit of one's lunch for the Tommy Knockers, to stay on their good side.

Leprechaun A fairy in Irish folktales who takes the form of a tiny old man. The leprechaun is often pictured with cocked hat and leather apron. He possesses a hidden crock of gold, and if he is captured, he might reveal its hiding place. But usually the captor is tricked into glancing away, and the leprechaun vanishes.

Little Red Riding Hood Character in a fairy tale that appears in France, Sweden, and Germany, but probably originated in Italy. The Brothers Grimm added a happy ending to the tale.

Loch Ness Monster A prehistoric sea monster that many believe lives in the exceptionally deep lake (loch) near Ness in Scotland. Though many investigators have searched for the monster, the results have neither proved nor disproved its existence.

Menehunes The little people of the island of Kauai in Hawaii. While they are creatures of folktales, there is evidence that there were ancient people on the Hawaiian Islands. The Menehune Fishpond at Niumalu, built about 1,000 years ago, was formed by a 900-foot stone wall at a bend in the Huleia Stream. Folk tales say the wall, which is four feet high, was built in one night by the menehunes.

mermaid Creature from sailors' stories, half woman and half fish, which may have been inspired by a dugong, a sea-going mammal with a fish-like tail.

Pecos Bill Cowboy featured in tall tales of the American Southwest. He could ride any horse and even rode a tornado once. He was raised by coyotes, tamed a mountain lion, used a snake as a whip, and led the first cattle drive. His true love was Slue-foot Sue, who could ride almost as well as he could.

Phoenix A fabulous bird that has been identified with Egypt, India, and Arabia, which at the end of its life makes a nest of spices, flaps its wings to set the nest on fire, and then perishes in the flames, only to rise again from the ashes. The phoenix appears as a symbol of rebirth from China to Europe and is frequently mentioned in literature.

A depiction of a mermaid

Pied Piper of Hamelin A magician in a German folktale. In the story of the Pied Piper, the town of Hamelin was overrun by rats in 1284. A mysterious stranger in multi-colored (pied) clothes appeared and offered to chase the rats away. When the people of Hamelin refused to pay him for the service, he then lured away their children.

pixies Sprites or fairies in British folktales, especially in the west-English regions of Cornwall and Devon. Pictures of pixies (also called "piskeys") are still popular souvenirs for travelers to these regions.

Puck Also known as Robin Goodfellow. In British folktales, he ranges from being a slightly naughty fairy to being an evil goblin. Puck is a key figure in Shakespeare's *A Midsummer Night's Dream,* and it is his mischievous character in this play that gave rise to the term *puckish,* which means "impish."

Sasquatch The name comes from a Native American word that means "wild men." Also called Big Foot, the sasquatch is a large, hairy, human-like creature believed to exist in the northwestern United States and western Canada. It appears to be a North American version of the Abominable Snowman, or Yeti.

Puss in Boots A witty, clever cat that wins a fortune for his poor master. There are many sources for the tales, and the accomplished cat also appears in other stories.

Rapunzel Title character in a German fairy tale about a woman who is imprisoned by a witch in a high tower. The witch uses Rapunzel's long hair to climb up to the tower, and a prince who sees this tries the witch's call of "Rapunzel, Rapunzel, let down your long hair," discovering the fair maiden in the tower. Rapunzel is banished and the prince blinded before they finally reunite for the happy ending.

Robin Hood English hero of a 12th-century legend who stole from the wealthy in order to give to the poor.

Rumpelstiltskin A deformed dwarf in a German folktale. He helps a young woman spin straw into gold so that she can become queen, but the price is her first-born child.

Sleeping Beauty A young princess who is cursed to sleep until wakened by the kiss of a prince brave enough to make his way through the dark woods that surrounds her castle.

Snow White The title character in a fairy tale that exists in many places in Europe. The best-known is the German version collected by the Brothers Grimm. The plot is essentially the same in all forms of the story—jealous queen wants beautiful young princess dead—but the talking mirror and seven dwarfs do not appear in every version.

troll In Scandinavian folktales, mischievous dwarfs. They were skilled at working with metal, but had a bad habit of stealing things, including children.

unicorn A fantastic animal with the body and head of a horse, the beard of a goat, and a single horn in the middle of its forehead. In the Middle Ages, people believed that the unicorn could detect virtue in people.

vampire A criminal or heretic who returns from the grave in the shape of a large bat to suck the blood of the living. The original folktales of vampires are Slavonic.

werewolf From the Old English, *wer,* which means "man," a "man-wolf." A werewolf was a man who could turn into a wolf or who was turned into a wolf. In other parts of the world, similar stories revolve around people turning into tigers, hyenas, or leopards.

Yeti Tibetan name for the Abominable Snowman

A Guide to Literary Genres

Fiction

allegory A narrative in which the characters, settings, and actions represent abstract ideas, qualities, or situations beyond their literal function in the work. The general purpose of an allegory is to teach a moral lesson.

fable A short, often humorous, tale in which animals talk and behave as humans, intended to teach a lesson about human behavior. The lesson, or *moral,* is usually expressed at the end but may remain unstated. Aesop (Greece, c. 6th century B.C.) is probably the most famous fabulist.

fairy tale A type of folktale characterized by supernatural characters, such as spirits, talking animals, and magic. A fairy tale need not have a fairy as a character but will have the common element of magic. Jacob and Wilhelm Grimm collected oral accounts for their collection of fairy tales (Germany, 1812–1815), while Hans Christian Andersen wrote most of his own tales (Denmark, 1835).

fantasy A literary work that is set in an unreal world and is characterized by impossible characters or events. Fantasy is a very large category, encompassing such genres as animal fantasy and science fiction. *High fantasy* is a term given to epics that may create new worlds and races of beings, such as J. R. R. Tolkien's *The Lord of the Rings* (England, 1954–1955).

folktale A traditional story often passed orally from generation to generation before being written down. There are many kinds of folktales, including myths, legends, tall tales, fairy tales, and epics.

ghost story A narrative characterized by the presence or the suspected presence of supernatural elements, usually including a ghost, the spirit of one who has died. Ghost stories generally have a strong element of terror and suspense. Some authors, such as Vivian Vande Velde and Neal Shusterman, may include humor or romance.

historical fiction A novel or short story in which fictional characters react to specific historical events and sometimes interact with known historical figures. *Johnny Tremain* by Ester Forbes and *Sarah Bishop* by Scott O'Dell are two popular examples set during the American Revolution.

legend A traditional story derived from folk literature that may be based on real people or events but that has become exaggerated and romanticized over time. For example, stories about England's King Arthur and his knights of the Round Table are known as Arthurian legends. They cannot be proved historically, but they almost certainly accrued related tales and details as they were told and retold over centuries.

mystery A type of fiction in which there is a problem to be solved. A mystery may be in the form of a novel, short story, or play. Many popular mysteries center around the solution of a murder. Dame Agatha Christie was a prominent writer of mysteries such as *Murder on the Orient Express* (England, 1934).

myth A traditional narrative that usually expresses the beliefs of a people concerning origins or aspects of nature or history. A myth generally has less historical background than a legend.

novel A book-length fictional prose narrative, containing a plot, characters, setting, and theme. Shorter novels may be called *novellas* or *novelettes*.

parable A simple story expressing a moral or religious lesson. The best-known parables are those told by Jesus in the Bible, such as "The Prodigal Son."

parody A humorous imitation of a serious work of literature. A parody usually achieves its humorous effects by exaggerating obvious features or shortcomings of the original work. Terry Pratchett's *Discworld* novels are gentle parodies of high fantasy literature such as Tolkien's *Lord of the Rings.*

saga A prose form based upon Scandinavian and Icelandic narratives concerning the exploits of historical kings and warriors. The term has come to refer to any fictional or nonfictional tale of adventure, bravery, or heroism.

satire Writing, usually humorous, that employs wit to ridicule human foibles or institutional excesses. A satire may be in any number of specific literary forms.

science fiction A form of fantasy that explores the impact of science and technology on individuals and society. The science and technology in question may be real or imagined, and the setting is often in the near or far future. H. G. Wells's *The Time Machine* (England, 1895) is a popular example.

short story A fictional narrative that contains characters, plot, setting, and theme, but is often short enough to be read in one sitting. Many writers from around the world have written and experimented with the short story form. Langston Hughes' "Thank You, Ma'm" is an example.

tall tale A humorous narrative that uses realistic detail, a literal manner, and common speech to recount impossible happenings. The hero or heroine of a tall tale usually has superhuman abilities of some sort. Tall tales may derive from oral tradition or may be written deliberately. The American legends of the giant lumberjack Paul Bunyan are tall tales.

Nonfiction

autobiography An account of all or part of a person's life, written by that person.

biography The story of a person's life, in whole or in part, written by someone other than the subject.

diary A day-to-day record of events in a person's life. Also called a *journal,* a diary may include thoughts, impressions, and descriptions of events and is written for personal use rather than for publication. *Anne Frank: The Diary of a Young Girl* is a well-known example.

essay A short piece of nonfiction writing on any topic, with the purpose of communicating an idea or opinion. A *formal essay* is characterized by serious subject matter, impersonal tone, and logical construction. An *informal essay* may be in a light, conversational style and may include humor.

history A nonfiction account of real events from the past and the real people that lived them. A history is usually written chronologically and maintains an objective voice. *Reflections on the Civil War* by Bruce Catton is an example.

memoir Autobiographical writing that may be more concerned with personalities and events of public importance than with the author's private life.

speech A public talk given for some purpose. A written speech carries the implication that it is the exact transcription of the words that were delivered or are yet to be delivered by the speaker to a specific audience at a specific location. One of the most famous speeches in history is Abraham Lincoln's "Gettysburg Address."

Poetry

ballad A narrative song or poem. A *folk ballad* may be passed down, word of mouth, for generations before being written down. A *literary ballad* is written in a style to imitate a folk ballad but has a known author. "The Highwayman" by Alfred Noyes is a well-known example of a literary ballad.

concrete poetry A form of poetry in which the appearance of the words on the page suggests the subject of the poem. It is sometimes called *shaped poetry.*

epic A long narrative poem that celebrates the adventures of a hero or a band of adventurers. A *folk epic* has no certain authorship and arises usually through collective storytelling over centuries.

haiku A traditional Japanese verse form consisting of three lines of five, seven, and five syllables respectively. A haiku evokes a simple image, usually of nature, that arouses a distinct emotion or spiritual insight. Translations of haiku from the Japanese sometimes do not maintain the seventeen-syllable form; haikus written in English do, however.

limerick A poem, usually humorous, of five lines. The rhyme scheme is usually *aabba*, and the meter is usually rigid. A great many variations are possible, however. Edward Lear (England, 1812–1888) is credited with popularizing the form.

lyric A poem that expresses the speaker's personal thoughts and feelings. For example, the works of Emily Dickinson (United States, 1830–1886) are lyric poems. Many specific verse forms are considered lyric poetry. (The term *lyric* is also used generically to refer to the words set to music in popular songs.)

narrative poetry Any poem that tells a story. Various forms of narrative poetry exist, including the ballad and epic, as well as shorter forms that concentrate on single events.

nonsense verse Humorous poetry that is deliberately silly or absurd. Nonsense verse usually has a regular rhythm and rhyme scheme and may contain nonsense or made-up words.

nursery rhyme A simple, traditional song or poem for children. Nursery rhymes usually feature strong rhythms and rhymes and may include alliteration, onomatopoeia, and other sound devices. There is a great variety of such rhymes from a great variety of sources.

psalm A song of praise to God, such as those in the Biblical book of *Psalms,* attributed to David, king of Israel around 1000 B.C.

sonnet A lyric poem with a traditional form of fourteen lines and a formal structure of verses and couplets.

Drama

comedy A type of drama that is humorous and usually has a happy ending. *Classical* comedy may deal with serious subject matter, but the presence of the happy ending is enough to qualify it as comedic. The term *comedy* may be applied generically to other literary genres.

farce A type of comedic drama characterized by ridiculous situations and outlandish characters.

pantomime A story or idea presented through body movement and expression rather than words.

Readers Theatre A form of drama in which actors are seated and read aloud from scripts.

screenplay A play written to be filmed. As such, it contains all the elements of a play, plus directions for camera shots and angles. Because of film-editing techniques, a screenplay is usually divided into many more scenes than a play for the stage.

theatre of the absurd A type of drama based on the idea that life is meaningless and that searching for order only brings about confusion and conflict.

tragedy A play in which the main character, the *tragic hero,* a man or woman of high position or stature, suffers a downfall or death, often because of a weakness in character, known as a *tragic flaw.* In William Shakespeare's *Macbeth* (England, 1606), Macbeth's tragic flaw is his excessive ambition. (The term *tragedy* is often used generically to refer to any unfortunate event, usually concerning a death.)

A Glossary of Literary Terms

allegory a literary work in which characters, objects, and events stand for abstract qualities such as goodness, pleasure, or evil

alliteration the repetition of beginning consonant sounds

allusion a reference to an artistic; historical; or literary figure, work, or event

anecdote a short incident or story that illustrates a point; usually has an informal storyteller's tone

antagonist a character who opposes the hero or main character of the story

anti-hero a main character who displays traits opposite to the qualities usually associated with a traditional hero

appeal to emotion a persuasive technique that encourages others to act based on emotions rather than facts; see also *propaganda*

assonance the repetition of vowel sounds in a literary work, especially in a poem

author a person who creates any piece of literature

autobiography a nonfictional account of the author's life

biography a nonfictional account of someone's life

character a person or animal in a story

characterization the manner in which an author creates and develops a character using exposition, dialogue, and action

cliché a trite phrase that has become so overused that it has lost its meaning or value

climax the high point of a plot

colloquialism a local or regional expression

comedy a type of drama in which characters avoid disaster and enjoy a happy ending; a play that is humorous in nature

conflict the struggle between opposing forces; *external conflict* involves an outer force such as nature or another character, while *internal conflict* exists inside a person; for example, between a hero's sense of duty and desire for freedom

connotation the emotional associations surrounding a word

consonance a type of alliteration in which the repeated pattern of consonants is marked by changes in the intervening vowels, such as in the words *linger, longer,* and *languor*

couplet two consecutive lines of poetry that end in a rhyme

denotation the dictionary definition of a word

dialect the distinctive speech pattern of people from a certain group or region

dialogue conversation between characters in a literary work

drama a staged narrative portraying conflict between characters through action and dialogue

epilogue a short passage often designed to bring closure to a literary work

epitaph an inscription carved on a gravestone; the final statement spoken by a character before his or her death

essay a literary composition, usually dealing with its subject from a limited and often personal point of view

eulogy a formal expression of praise, usually about the dead

exposition information about the background of a story's plot that is directly conveyed or explained, usually by the narrator

fable a tale that demonstrates a moral or truth; frequently contains fantasy elements such as talking animals

fairy tale a story involving fairies, elves, giants, and other make-believe characters

falling action the events of a plot that follow the climax; also referred to as the *resolution*

fantasy fiction that contains characters, settings, and objects that could not exist, such as dragons or magic swords

fiction literature created from the imagination, not presented as fact, though it may be based on a true story or situation

figurative language language that includes figures of speech such as similies, metaphors, personification, and hyperbole

figure of speech an expression that conveys meaning or increases an effect, usually through figurative language

first-person point of view see *point of view*

flashback an interruption of the normal chronological order of a plot to narrate events that occured earlier

folktale a narrative, usually originating in an oral tradition, with a timeless and placeless setting and traditional plot elements and characters; may contain elements of fantasy as well

foreshadowing the use of hints or clues about what will happen later in a plot

free verse poetry based on the rhythms and pauses of natural speech rather than the constraints of rhyme

genre a distinctive type or category of literature such as science fiction or mystery

hero the main character in a story; often one who accomplishes exemplary deeds; also called the *protagonist*

hyperbole an overstatement or exaggeration used for both serious and comic effect

idiom an expression whose sense cannot be understood from the literal meaning of the words that form it; idioms are often peculiar to a group or locale

imagery vivid and striking descriptions of objects and details in a literary work

inference a reasonable conclusion drawn by the reader based on clues given in a literary work

internal rhyme rhyming of words or accented syllables within a line of poetry

interpretation an explanation of the meaning of a piece of literature, dependent in part on the perspective of the reader

irony a recognition of the difference between appearance and reality; *situational irony* occurs when events turn out differently from what is expected; *dramatic irony* occurs when the audience has important knowledge that a main character lacks

jargon specialized words and phrases used in an occupation, trade, or field of study

legend a traditional story or group of stories told about a particular person or place

memoir an autobiographical sketch—especially one that focuses less on the author's personal life or psychological development and more on the notable people and events the author has encountered or witnessed

metaphor a figure of speech that implies a similarity between two unlike things

meter the pattern of stressed and unstressed syllables in poetry; see also *ryhthm*

mood the overall atmosphere of a work

motivation the reasons or forces that cause characters to act as they do

myth a traditional story, often one that explains a belief or natural phenomenon

narrator a teller of a story; an *unreliable narrator* makes incorrect conclusions and biased assumptions; a *naïve narrator* does not fully understand the events he or she narrates

nonfiction a story of actual people and events sometimes told with the dramatic techniques of a novel

novel a fictional prose work of substantial length

onomatopoeia words that sound like their meaning; "pop," "squeak," "whiz" are examples

oral tradition body of legends, folktales, or poems passed down through oral story telling or songs

oxymoron a contradiction that makes sense on a deeper level; *jumbo shrimp* is a simple example

parable a story or short narrative designed to reveal some religious principle, moral lesson, or general truth

paradox a statement or situation that seems contradictory but may in fact be true

parody a humorous imitation of a serious piece of writing

personification a figure of speech in which human characteristics are given to nonhuman things

plot the events of a story that show the characters in action

poem a work written in verse

point of view the perspective from which a story is narrated: in *first-person point of view*, the narrator is a character in the story and uses the personal pronoun "I"; in *third-person limited point of view*, the narrator is outside the story but presents the story through the thoughts and feelings of one character; in *third-person omniscient point of view*, the narrator is outside the story, knows the thoughts and feelings of all characters, and can comment on any part of the story

prologue introductory section before a work of fiction or nonfiction

propaganda writing that is designed to sway the reader or viewer to hold certain views or to take certain actions

prose any literary material that is not written in a regular meter

protagonist the main character of a story; see *hero*

proverb a brief saying that is in general use and expresses a commonly held idea or belief; "a fool and his money are soon parted" is an example

pun a play on two words similar in sound but different in meaning. For example, Shakespeare, in *Romeo and Juliet*, puns upon Romeo's *vile death* (*vile=vial*, the vial of poison Romeo consumed)

refrain a repeated line or set of lines at the end of a stanza or section of a longer poem or song

repetition a technique in which words or phrases are repeated to stress a theme or to provide unity to a work

resolution the point at which the chief conflict or complication of a story is worked out

rhyme scheme the pattern of end rhymes in the lines of a poem; usually represented by pairs of letters. In the scheme *aabb*, for example, the last syllables of the first two lines rhyme as do the last syllables of the last two lines.

rhythm the pattern of sounds in speech or writing that is created by the careful arrangement of stressed and unstressed syllables; may create mood or emphasize ideas or themes

rising action the events leading up to the climax of a plot

saga a prose form based upon Scandinavian and Icelandic narratives concerning the adventures of historical kings and warriors

satire writing that uses humor or ridicule to point out human shortcomings

sensory details descriptive elements based on the five senses: taste, touch, smell, sight, and hearing

setting the time and place of the action of a story

short story a work of narrative fiction that is shorter than a novel; may contain description, dialogue, and commentary but typically relies on plot for its success

simile a comparison of one thing to another that uses *like* or *as*

soliloquy a monologue spoken by an actor at a point in the play when the character believes he or she is alone; frequently reveals a character's innermost thoughts, feelings, motives, or intentions; often provides necessary but otherwise unavailable information to the audience

sonnet a lyric poem of fourteen lines with rhymes arranged according to certain definite patterns

stanza a set of lines of verse; in formal verse, stanzas will form a set pattern

subtext a hidden meaning, often symbolic that must be inferred from the text

surprise ending an unexpected plot twist at the end of a story

symbol an object that stands for, or represents, an abstract concept, such as an eagle for freedom or a rose for love

tale a story about series of facts or events either told or written

tall tale an obviously untrue story with exaggerated situations and characters

theme the underlying meaning or message of a literary work

third-person point of view see *point of view*

title the name of a piece of writing

tone the author or narrator's attitude toward the subject of a work; the attitude might be *ironic, humorous, sarcastic, serious*, etc.

tragedy a dramatic form in which the hero, due to a tragic flaw, suffers a series of misfortunes leading to a final, devastating catastrophe

tragic flaw a flaw in the character of the hero of a tragedy that causes his or her downfall

voice an author or character's distinctive way of expressing himself or herself

Glossary of Grammar, Composition, and Thinking Terms

abstract noun word that names a quality, a condition, or an idea

action verb word that tells what action a subject is performing

active voice the voice a verb is in when the subject is performing the action

adjective word that modifies a noun or a pronoun

adjective clause subordinate clause that is used like an adjective to modify a noun or a pronoun

adjective phrase prepositional phrase that is used to modify a noun or a pronoun

adverb word that modifies a verb, an adjective, or another adverb

adverb clause subordinate clause that is used like an adverb to modify a verb, an adjective, or an adverb

adverb phrase prepositional phrase that is used like an adverb to modify a verb, an adjective, or an adverb

alliteration repetition of a consonant sound at the beginning of a series of words

allusion reference to persons or events in the past or in literature

analogies logical relationships between pairs of words

analyzing breaking down a whole into its parts to see how the parts fit together to form the whole

antecedent word or group of words that a pronoun replaces or refers to

antonym word that means the opposite of another word

appeal to fear propaganda technique that plays on fears in order to get people to reject or accept a particular idea

appositive noun or a pronoun that identifies or explains another noun or pronoun in a sentence

assonance repetition of a vowel sound within words

bandwagon appeal propaganda technique that appeals to the natural tendency to want to belong to a group

body one or more paragraphs comprised of details, facts, and examples that support the main idea

brainstorming prewriting technique of writing down everything that comes to mind about a subject

case form of a noun or a pronoun that indicates its use in a sentence. In English there are three cases: the *nominative case*, the *objective case*, and the *possessive case*.

cause and effect method of essay development in which details are grouped based on the relationship between an effect and its causes or on a cause and its effects

chronological order the order in which events occur

citation note that directs a reader to the original source

classification method of essay development in which details are grouped into categories

classifying (thinking) process of grouping items into classes, or categories

clause group of words that has a subject and a predicate and is used as part of a sentence

cliché overused expression that is no longer fresh or interesting to the reader

clustering a visual form of brainstorming used for developing supporting details

coherence logical and smooth flow of ideas connected with clear transitions

common noun names any person, place, or thing

comparative degree modification of an adjective or adverb used when two people, things, or actions are compared

comparison and contrast method of essay development in which the writer examines similarities and differences between two subjects

complement word that completes the meaning of an action verb

complete predicate all the words that tell what the subject is doing or that tell something about the subject

complete subject all the words used to identify the person, place, thing, or idea that a sentence is about

complex sentence sentence composed of one independent clause and one or more subordinate clauses

compound adjective adjective made up of more than one word

compound-complex sentence sentence composed of two or more independent clauses and one or more subordinate clauses

compound noun word made up of two smaller words that can be separated, hyphenated, or combined

compound sentence sentence composed of two or more independent clauses

compound subject two or more subjects in one sentence that have the same verb and are joined by a conjunction

compound verb two or more verbs that have the same subject and are joined by a conjunction

concluding sentence the ending to a paragraph that summarizes the major points, refers to the main idea, or adds an insight

conclusion paragraph that completes an essay and reinforces its main idea

conjunction word that joins together sentences, clauses, phrases, or other words

connotation the emotional meanings that are associated with a word (See *denotation*.)

consonance repetition of a consonant sound, usually in the middle or at the end of words

context clue clue to a word's meaning provided by the sentence or passage in which the word is used

coordinating conjunction single connecting word used to join words or groups of words

correlative conjunction pairs of conjunctions used to connect compound subjects, compound verbs, and compound sentences

dangling modifier phrase that has nothing to describe in a sentence

declarative sentence statement or expression of an opinion that ends with a period

demonstrative pronoun word that substitutes for a noun and points out a person or a thing

denotation the literal, dictionary meaning of a word. (See *connotation*.)

descriptive writing writing that creates a vivid picture of a person, an object, or a scene by appealing to the reader's senses

developmental order information that is organized so that one idea grows out of the preceding idea

dialect regional variation of a language distinguished by distinctive pronunciation and some differences in word meanings

dialogue conversation between two or more persons

direct object noun or a pronoun that receives the action of a verb

direct quotation passage, sentence, or words written or spoken exactly as a person wrote or said them

drafting stage of the writing process in which the writer puts ideas down on paper

editing stage of the writing process in which the writer corrects errors in grammar, usage, mechanics, and spelling

E-mail electronic mail

essential phrase or clause group of words essential to the meaning of a sentence and therefore not set off with commas

etymology a word's history from its earliest recorded use to its present use

evaluating making reasoned judgments about whether something is right or wrong, good or bad, valuable or trash

exclamatory sentence expression of strong feeling that ends with an exclamation point

expository writing writing that explains, informs, or directs through the use of facts and examples

fact statement that can be proved (See *opinion*.)

figurative language imaginative, nonliteral use of language

fluency a quality of good writing characterized by appropriate transitions, a variety of sentence types and lengths, and a logical flow of ideas

formal English conventional rules of grammar, usage, and mechanics

free verse verse without meter or a regular, patterned beat

freewriting prewriting technique of writing freely about ideas as they come to mind

generalizing the process of drawing conclusions based on facts and experiences

gerund verb form ending in *–ing* that is used as a noun

gerund phrase a gerund with its modifiers and complements working together as a noun

helping verb auxiliary verb that helps to make up a verb phrase

hyperbole use of exaggeration or overstatement

imagery use of concrete details to create a picture or appeal to senses other than sight

imperative mood verb form used to give a command or to make a request

imperative sentence a direction, a request, or a command that ends with either a period or an exclamation point

indefinite pronoun word that substitutes for a noun and refers to an unnamed person or thing

independent clause group of words that can stand alone as a sentence because it expresses a complete thought

indirect object noun or a pronoun that answers the question *to* or *from whom?* or *to* or *for what?* after an action verb

inferring making inferences; filling the gaps in knowledge based on what is already known

infinitive verb form that usually begins with *to* and is used as a noun, an adjective, or an adverb

inquiring prewriting technique in which the writer delves into a subject by answering questions such as *Who? What? Where? Why?* and *When?*

intensive pronoun word that adds emphasis to a noun or another pronoun in the sentence

interjection word that expresses strong feeling

interrogative pronoun word used to ask a question

interrogative sentence a question; a sentence that ends with a question mark

intransitive verb an action verb that does not have an object

introduction paragraph that introduces a subject, states or implies a purpose, and presents a main idea

inverted order condition when the subject follows the verb or part of the verb phrase

irregular verb verb that does not form its past and past participle by adding –ed or –d to the present

linking verb verb that links the subject of a sentence with another word that either renames or describes the subject

literary analysis interpretation of a work of literature supported by appropriate responses, details, quotations, and commentaries

loaded language the unfair use of emotion-laden words to sway the opinion of a listener or reader

metaphor figure of speech that compares by saying that one thing is another

misplaced modifier phrase or a clause that is placed too far away from the word it modifies, thus creating an unclear sentence

mood overall atmosphere or feeling created by a work of literature

narrative writing writing that tells a real or an imaginary story

nonessential phrase or clause group of words that is not essential to the meaning of a sentence and is therefore set off with commas

noun a word that names a person, a place, a thing, or an idea. A *common noun* names a general thing; a *proper noun* names a specific person, place, or thing and always begins with a capital letter; a *collective noun* names a group of people or things.

noun clause a subordinate clause that is used like a noun

objective complement a noun or an adjective that renames or describes the direct object

opinion belief or judgment that cannot be proved. (See *fact*.)

order of importance order of details in an essay in which supporting evidence is arranged from least to most or (most to least) important

outline ordering of information about a subject into main topics and subtopics

paraphrase restatement of an original work in one's own words

parenthetical citation source and page number (in parentheses) within a sentence in which the source of information must be credited

participial phrase participle with its modifiers and complements—all working together as an adjective

participle verb form that is used as an adjective

passive voice the voice of a verb when the action is being performed upon its subject

peer conference a meeting with one or more peer reviewers to share ideas and offer suggestions for the revision of a piece of writing

personal pronoun type of pronoun that can be categorized into one of three groups, depending on the speaker's position: *first person*, *second person*, and *third person*

personal writing writing that expresses the writer's personal point of view on a subject drawn from the writer's own experience

personification comparison in which human qualities are given to an animal, an object, or an idea

persuasive writing writing that states an opinion and uses facts, examples, and reasons to convince the reader to agree with the opinion

phrase group of related words that functions as a single part of speech and does not have a subject and a verb

phrase fragment an error in writing in which a phrase is written as if it were a complete sentence

point of view vantage point from which a writer tells a story or describes a subject

positive degree adjective or adverb used when no comparison is being made

possessive pronoun pronoun used to show ownership or possession

predicate adjective adjective that follows a linking verb and modifies the subject

predicate nominative noun or a pronoun that follows a linking verb and identifies, renames, or explains the subject

prefix one or more syllables placed in front of a root or base word to form a new word

preposition a word that shows the relationship between a noun or a pronoun and another word in the sentence

prepositional phrase a group of words that begins with a preposition, ends with a noun or a pronoun, and is used as an adjective or an adverb

prewriting invention stage in the writing process in which the writer generates ideas and plans for drafting based on the subject, occasion, audience, and purpose for writing

principal parts of a verb the *present*, the *past*, and the *past participle*. The principal parts help form the tenses of verbs.

pronoun word that takes the place of one or more nouns

proofreading carefully rereading and making corrections in grammar, usage, spelling, and mechanics in a piece of writing

propaganda effort to persuade by distorting and misrepresenting information or by disguising opinions as facts

protagonist the main character, or hero, of a story

publishing stage of a writer's process in which the writer may choose to share the work with an audience or make the work "public"

purpose reason for writing or for speaking

recalling thinking skill that involves remembering specific details or facts

reflexive pronoun pronoun formed by adding *–self* or *–selves* to a personal pronoun and is used to reflect back to another noun or pronoun

regular verb verb that forms its past and past participle by adding *-ed* to the present tense form

relative pronoun pronoun that relates an adjective clause to the modified noun or pronoun

repetition repeat of a word or phrase for poetic effect

research paper a composition based on information from books, magazines, and other sources

revising stage of a the writing process in which the writer rethinks what is written and reworks it to increase its clarity, fluency, and power

rhyme scheme regular pattern of rhyming in a poem

root part of a word that carries the basic meaning

run-on sentence two or more sentences that are erroneously written together as one sentence

sensory details details that appeal to one of the five senses: seeing, hearing, touching, tasting, and smelling

sentence fragment a group of words presented as a sentence but that does not express a complete thought

sequential order manner of ordering details of an essay based on time order or on a series of steps that follow logically one after the other

setting the time and place in which a story takes place

simile figure of speech comparing two unlike objects using the words *like* or *as*

simple predicate main word or phrase in the complete predicate

simple sentence sentence composed of one independent clause

simple subject main word in a complete subject

snob appeal propaganda technique often used in advertising in which the reader or viewer is urged to do, think, or buy something in order to become part of an elite, aristocratic group

spatial order order in which details in an essay are arranged based on their location

speech oral composition presented by a speaker to an audience

standard English conventions of usage accepted most widely by English-speaking people throughout the world

style visual or verbal expression that is distinctive to an artist or writer

subject word or group of words that names the person, place, thing, or idea a sentence is about

subordinate clause group of words that cannot stand alone because it does not express a complete thought

subordinating conjunction single connecting word used in a complex sentence to introduce an adverb clause

suffix one or more syllables placed after a root or base word to change the word's part of speech and possibly its meaning

summary information written in a condensed, concise form, touching only on the main ideas. (The related thinking process is called *summarizing*.)

superlative degree modification of an adjective or adverb used when more than two people, things, or actions are compared

supporting sentences specific details, facts, examples, or reasons that explain or prove a topic sentence

symbol object, an event, or a character that stands for a universal idea or quality

synonym word that has nearly the same meaning as another word

tense the form a verb takes to show time. The six tenses are the *present, past, future, present perfect, past perfect*, and *future perfect*

testimonial propaganda technique in which an endorsement of a product by a famous person implies that the use of the product will make the user more like the famous person

theme underlying idea, message, or meaning of a work of literature

thesis statement statement of the main idea or purpose of an essay

tone writer's attitude toward the subject and audience of a composition (may also be referred to as the *writer's voice*)

topic sentence statement of the main idea of the paragraph

transitions words and phrases that add fluency and increase understanding by connecting ideas

transitive verb action verb that passes the action from a doer to a receiver

understood subject unstated subject that is understood

unity combination or ordering of parts in a composition so that all the sentences or paragraphs work together as a whole to support one main idea

verb word that expresses action or state of being

verbal verb form used as some other part of speech

verb phrase main verb plus one or more helping verbs

voice particular quality of a writer's language; a writer's attitude toward his or her subject. (See *tone*.)

working thesis thesis statement used early in the planning and drafting stages of a composition or research paper

works cited page alphabetical listing of sources cited in a research paper

writing process recursive series of stages a writer proceeds through when developing ideas and discovering the best way to express them

Index

A

AABB pattern in comparison/
contrast, 267, 326
ABAB pattern in comparison/
contrast, 269, 326
abbreviations
  capitalization of, 132
  common, 144
  defined, 143
  in E-mail, 367
  with periods, 143–144
  state, 145
  without periods, 144
abstract nouns, 11
accent marks, 430
accuracy, checking for, 350
acronyms, 435
action verbs, 19, 22
  distinguishing from linking
    verbs, 22
active voice, 86–87
addresses
  abbreviations for, 144
  commas to separate items in,
    146–147
  for envelopes, 363
  inside, in business letter,
    358, 359
adjective(s), 25–28
  defined, 25
  demonstrative, 17
  different positions of, 25
  distinguishing between
    nouns and, 27
  modifying with adverbs, 31
  need for comma with, 26
  nouns as, 27
  participles as, 51
  possessive, 96
  predicate, 39
  proper, 27
  separating with commas,
    148–149, 211
adjective clauses, 60–63
  as fragment, 71
  misplaced, 63
  relative pronouns in
    beginning, 61–63
adjective phrases, 45–46

adverb(s), 29–31
  common, 29
  conjunctive, 169
  distinguishing from
    prepositions, 35
  in modifying adjectives and
    other adverbs, 31
  in modifying verbs, 30
adverb clauses, 63–64
  commas after, 150
  as fragment, 71
  subordinating conjunctions
    in beginning, 64
adverb phrases, 45, 46–48
agreement
  pronoun and antecedent,
    98–101
  gender, 99
  indefinite pronouns, 100–101
  number, 99
  subject and verb, 103–113
  collective nouns, 109–110
  compound subjects, 109
  contractions, 106–107
  indefinite pronouns, 111–112
  interrupting words, 107
  number, 103–104
  singular and plural
    subjects, 104
  singular nouns that have
    plural forms, 113
  subjects in inverted order, 108
  titles, 113
  verb phrases, 105–106
  words expressing amounts
    and times, 113
  you and *I* as subjects, 110–111
allegory, 517, 522
alliteration, 310, 317, 522
allusion, 522
American dialects, 417
amounts, words expressing,
    subject-verb agreement
    and, 113
analogies, 407–408
  types of, 408
analysis, 376
  literary, 313
anecdotes, 522
animals, capitalization of

names of, 133
antagonists, 522
antecedents, 13
  agreement with pronouns,
    98–101
  indefinite pronouns as, 100–101
  unclear or missing, 101
anti-hero, 522
antonyms, 406, 424
apostrophes
  in contractions, 165–166
  in dates, 167
  in plurals, 166
  to show possession, 163–164
appeal
  bandwagon, 378, 459
  to emotion, 522
  to fear, 379
  snob, 379
application, letters of, 362
appositive(s), 48
  commas to set off, 152–153
  gerunds as, 55
appositive phrases, 48–49
  as fragments, 70
argument
  developing, 282
  organizing, 282
articles, 26
  definite, 26
  indefinite, 26
art works
  capitalization of, 141
  italics for titles of, 155, 156
assonance, 310, 522
attachments in E-mail, 367
audience, in prewriting
  considering, 180, 262
  determining, 231
  identifying, 254, 280
authors, 461–480, 522
  questioning the, 394
autobiography, 519, 522
auxiliary verbs, 5–6
awards, capitalization of, 138

B

ballad, 519
bandwagon appeal, 378, 459

bias, identifying, 390–391
Biblical chapters and verses,
    colon in writing, 171
biography, 519, 522
blends, 435
block quotations, 161
block style, 357
body, drafting, 235, 341
    in business letter, 358, 359
    in informal letter, 354, 355
    in informative writing, 273
    in persuasive writing, 277
    in research report, 331
    in writing process, 186
books
    italics for titles, 155–156
    quotation marks for
        chapters, 157
    for young adults, 481–491
brainstorming, 182, 185, 209, 210,
    232, 253
brand names, capitalization of, 138
bridges, capitalization of, 138
bring/take, 77
buildings, capitalization of, 138
businesses, capitalization of
    names of, 135
business letters, 357–364
    block style of, 357
    colons after salutations in, 171
    forms of, 358–359
    modified block style of, 357
    parts of, 358
    types of, 360–362

C

capitalization
    of entry words in dictionary,
        428
    first words
        direct quotations, 159
        outlines, 132
        poetry, 131
        sentences, 131
    in letters, 131, 364
    pronoun *I*, 132
    proper adjectives, 27, 139
    proper nouns, 12, 132–138
        awards, 137
        brand names, 137
        bridges and buildings, 137

geographical names,
    133–134
Internet terms, 137
languages and specific
    school courses, 137
monuments and memorials,
    137
names of groups and
    businesses, 135
names of nationalities
    and races, 136
names of persons and
    animals, 133
names of planets, moons,
    stars, and constella-
    tions, 137
nouns of historical
    importance, 135
religions, religious
    references, 136–137
specific time periods and
    events, 136
vehicles, 137
titles, 140–141
    art works, 140–141
    with names of persons, 140
    showing family relation-
        ships, 140–141
    written works, 140–141
case
    nominative, 89, 90–92
    objective, 89, 93–95
    possessive, 89, 95–96
categories, grouping information
    into, 266
cause, 389
cause/effect
    in descriptive writing, 256
    identifying, 389–390
    in informative writing, 201
    in ordering evidence, 326
    in persuasive writing, 283
characterization, 522
characters, 522
    in drama, 317
    famous, from literature,
        492–501
    in fiction, 316, 318
    in folklore, 513–516
    in mythology, 502–512
    in plays, 307
    in short stories, 296, 299–300

checklists
    in editing, 191, 205, 239, 259,
        304, 351
    in revising, 189, 238, 247,
        258–259, 274–275, 289,
        303–304, 328–329, 350–351
    for conventions, 189, 227,
        47, 289
    for ideas, 189, 227, 238, 247,
        258, 274, 289, 303, 328, 350
    for organization, 189, 227, 238,
        247, 259, 274, 289, 303,
        329, 351
    for sentence fluency, 189, 227,
        238, 247, 259, 275, 289, 304,
        329, 351
    for voice, 189, 227, 238, 247,
        259, 275, 289, 304, 329, 351
    for word choice, 189, 227, 238,
        247, 259, 275, 289, 304,
        329, 351
chronological organization,
    185, 301
    arranging details in, 233
    in descriptive writing, 256
    in informative writing, 267
    in narrative writing, 201
    in ordering evidence, 326
    in personal writing, 243
    transitions for, 226, 244
clarity, checking for, 288
classics, 319
classification, 371–372
clauses
    adjective, 60–63
    adverb, 63–64, 150
    defined, 59
    as fragments, 70–71
    independent, 59
    noun, 65
clichés, 419, 522
climax, 522
    in short stories, 296
close reading, 402
closing
    in business letter, 358, 359
    in informal letter, 354, 355
clustering, 183, 185, 209, 210
coherence, 226, 273
    checking for, 274, 288
collective nouns, 12
    subject-verb agreement and,
        109–110
colloquialisms, 418, 522

colons
after salutations in business letters, 171
in Biblical chapters and verses, 171
to introduce list of items, 170
in writing hours and minutes, 171
comedy, 520, 522
commas
with addresses, 146–147
with adverb clauses, 64
in compound sentences, 149
with dates, 146–147
to enclose appositives, 152–153
to enclose direct address, 151
to enclose parenthetical expressions, 152
after introductory elements, 151
with introductory phrases, 48
in letters, 147, 363
need for, with adjectives, 26
to separate items in a series, 148
separating adjectives with, 148–149, 211
to set off nonessential elements, 153
to set off nonessential phrases, 49, 53, 62
common nouns, 12
companies, abbreviations for, 144
comparative degree, 115
comparison, 372, 388–389
comparison/contrast, 388–389
AABB pattern in, 267, 326
ABAB pattern in, 269, 326
in informative writing, 201, 267
in persuasive writing, 283
transitions for, 226, 285
comparison of adjectives and adverbs, 115–119
comparative degree, 115
double comparisons, 118
double negatives, 119
good or *well*, 119
irregular, 117
other or *else*, 118
positive degree, 115
regular, 115–117
superlative degree, 115
complaint, letters of, 361
complements, 39

subject, 39
complete subjects, 4
complex sentences, 67
compositions, 229–239
drafting, 234–237
editing, 239
parts of, 229–230
prewriting, 231–233
publishing, 239
revising, 237–238
compound direct objects, 40
compound indirect objects, 41
compound nouns, 11, 422, 443
hyphens with, 171
compound object of a preposition, 34
compound predicate adjectives, 43
compound predicate nominatives, 42
compound predicates, 8
compound sentences, 66
commas in, 149
semicolons in forming, 168
compound subjects, 8
subject-verb agreement and, 109
compound words, 435
concluding sentence, 219, 224
in personal narrative, 241
conclusions
drafting, 236
in informative writing, 273
in persuasive writing, 277
in research report, 331
in writing process, 186
drawing, 392–393
concrete nouns, 11
concrete poetry, 519
conferencing, 190
peer, 190
conflict, 522
in fiction
external, 316
internal, 316
in plays, 307
in short stories, 296, 307
conjunctions, 35–36
coordinating, 35–36, 168
correlative, 36
subordinating, 64, 213
conjunctive adverbs, semicolons with, 169
connections, making, while reading, 395

connotations, 419, 522
cons, 282
consonance, 310, 522
consonant, doubling, in adding suffixes, 448
constellations, capitalization of names of, 137
context clues, 420
contractions
apostrophes in, 165–166
distinguishing between possessive pronouns and, 96
subject-verb agreement and, 106
contrasting, 388–389. *See also* comparison/contrast
conventions, 205. *See also* editing
checklist for, 189, 227, 247, 289
in informative writing, 275
in personal writing, 239
coordinating conjunctions, 35–36, 168
in forming compound sentences, 66, 212
correlative conjunctions, 36
couplet, 522
creative writing, 290–311
details in, 232
of dramatic scenes, 305–311
forms of, 291
of poems, 309–311
purpose of, 291
of short stories, 291–304
word choice in, 311
critical reading, 380–399
analyzing cause and effect in, 389–390
asking questions in, 394
comparing and contrasting in, 388–389
creating meaning in, 381–382
identifying fact, opinion, and bias in, 390–391
identifying main ideas and details, 387–388
inferring in, 392–393
making connections in, 395
making mental pictures in, 395
monitoring understanding in, 396–397
before reading, 382–385
sequencing in, 386
strategies for after reading, 398
summarizing in, 395–396

synthesizing in, 396
using writing after, 399
critical thinking, 370–379
propaganda in, 378–379
thinking skills in, 371–377
critical writing, 399

D

dates
abbreviations in, 144
apostrophes in certain, 167
commas to separate items in, 146–147
days, abbreviations for, 144
declarative sentence, 9
period to end, 9, 143
definite articles, 26
definition(s)
as context clue, 420
in dictionary, 431
degrees of comparison, 115
demonstrative adjectives, 17
demonstrative pronouns, 16–17, 28
denotations, 419, 522
dependent clauses.
See Subordinate clauses
derived words, 427
description, in short stories, 296
descriptive writing, 249–259
common transitions in, 201
drafting in, 256–257
editing in, 259
elements of, 249
figurative language in, 252
organizational pattern for, 201
prewriting in, 252–255
publishing in, 259
revising in, 257–259
sensory words in, 250–251
specific details in, 250–251
voice in, 203
details
adding, in revising, 188
brainstorming, 182
defined, 197
identifying, 387–388
kinds of, 197
organizing, 185, 233, 254–255
sentence combining with specific, 211
specific, 250–251
supporting, 181, 232, 264–265

developmental order, 267
diacritical marks, 429
dialects, 417, 522
American, 417
ethnic, 417
regional, 417
dialogue, 523
defined, 160
in fiction, 316
in plays, 307–308
quotation marks for, 160
in short stories, 296
diary, 519
dictionaries, 424–435
alphabetic order of terms in, 426
defined, 424
entry words in, 427
guide words in, 426
information in entry, 426
in spelling, 437
structure of, 424–433
direct address
capitalization of titles used in, 140
commas to enclose, 151
directions
details in, 232
giving, 451–452
direct objects, 39–40
compound, 40
gerunds as, 55
noun clauses as, 65
pronouns used as, 93
relative pronouns as, 61
direct quotations
capital letters with, 159
punctuating, 159–160
quotation marks with, 158
divided words, hyphens with, 173
double comparisons, 118
double negatives, 119, 124
double passage, 410
drafting, 175, 185–187, 234–236
of body, 186, 235, 273, 303, 341
citing sources in, 342–349
composing title in, 342
of conclusion, 186, 236, 273, 303–304, 342
in creative writing, 302–303
defined, 185
in descriptive writing, 256–257
of essay answers, 414
in informative writing, 271–273

of introduction, 186, 234, 271, 302, 340–341
of literary essay, 327–328
of personal writing, 244–245
of persuasive language, 285
of research reports, 340–349
strategies for, 186
of title, 187, 236
transitions in, 285–286
drama, 523. *See also* plays
characters in, 317
guide to genres for, 520–521
plot in, 317
questions for finding meaning in, 319
setting in, 317
theme in, 317

E

editing, 175, 191–192, 239.
See also conventions
checklist for, 191, 205, 239, 259, 304
in creative writing, 304
in descriptive writing, 259
of essay answers, 415
in informative writing, 275
of literary essays, 329
in personal writing, 246
proofreading in, 191–192
of research reports, 351
effect, 389. *See also* cause/effect
E-mail, 365–369
abbreviations in, 366
attachments in, 367
emoticons in, 367
follow up in, 367
netiquette in, 368–369
responding to, 367–368
emoticons, 367
emotion, appeal to, 522
empty expressions, 217
end marks, 143
endnotes, 343–344
format of, 344
English
formal, 120
informal, 120
nonstandard, 120
nonstandard American, 418
standard, 120
Standard American, 417

tests of standard written,
410–411
entertaining speech, purpose of,
454
entertaining writing, 180
envelopes, 363
epic, 519
epilogue, 523
epitaph, 523
essays, 519, 523
literary, 312–329
essay tests, 411–415
drafting answer, 414
editing answer, 415
kinds of questions on, 412
prewriting answer, 413
revising answer, 415
writing effective answers,
412–415
ethnic dialects, 417
eulogy, 523
evaluation, 377
events
capitalization of specific, 136
listing, in chronological
order, 301
everyday speech, 451
evidence, gathering, 323–325
examples, as context clue, 420
exclamation point
after interjections, 37
to end an exclamatory
sentence, 9, 143
to end an imperative
sentence, 9, 143
with quotation marks, 159–160
exclamatory sentence, 9
exclamation point to end, 9, 143
exposition, 523
expository writing, 261.
See also informative writing
expressive writing, 180
external conflict, 316

F

fable, 517, 523
facts, 278–279, 372, 458
distinguishing from opinions,
372–373
identifying, 390–391
fairy tale, 517, 523
falling action, 523

family relationships, titles showing,
capitalization of, 140–141
fantasy, 517, 523
farce, 520
fear, appeal to, 379
fiction, 523
characters in, 316, 318
conflict in, 316
dialogue in, 316
guide to genres for, 517–518
historical, 517
plot in, 316, 318
point of view in, 316
questions for finding meaning
in, 318
science, 518
setting in, 316, 318
theme in, 316, 318
tone in, 316
figurative language, 252, 393
metaphors, 252
similes, 252
figures of speech, 317, 523
filler, 199
first-person narratives, 245
first-person point of view, 298–299,
524–525
flamewar, 369
flaming, 369
flashback, 523
focus points, 231
folklore, 513
characters and creatures
from, 513–516
folktales, 517, 523
follow up in E-mail, 367
footnotes, 343–344
format of, 344
foreign languages
italics for words and phrases
in, 156
words from, 433–434
foreshadowing, 523
formal English, 120
formal speaking, 452
occasions for, 452
fractions, hyphens with, 172
fragments, 3, 69–71
free verse, 523
freewriting, 177–178, 185, 315
future perfect progressive
tense, 85
future perfect tense, 79, 81

future progressive tense, 85
future tense, 79, 80

G

gender, in pronoun-antecedent
agreement, 99
generalizations, 374–375
revising, 375
genre, 523
guide to literary, 517–521
geographical names, capitalization
of, 133–134
gerund(s), 51, 55
distinguishing between
participles and, 55
gerund phrases, 55–56, 56
ghost story, 517
graphic organizers
for cause and effect, 390
for comparing and
contrasting, 389
for main ideas and details, 388
in note taking, 403, 404
for prewriting essay
answer, 413
for sequencing, 387
groups, capitalization of names
of, 135

H

haiku, 520
heading
in business letter, 358, 359
in informal letter, 354, 355
helping verbs, 5–6, 23
common, 23
hero, 523
historical fiction, 517
historical importance, capitalization of nouns of, 135
historical novels, 291
history, 519
homographs, 428
homonyms, 428
hyperbole, 523
hyphens
with compound nouns, 171
defined, 171
with divided words, 173
with fractions, 172
with numbers, 172

I

I, capitalization of, 132

ideas
  checklist for, 189, 227, 238, 247, 258, 274, 289, 303, 328, 350
  deleting unnecessary, 188
  developing, 197–199
  in developing theme, 323
  in informative writing, 269
  main, 181
  narrowing and focusing, 197
  for poem, 309
  for research reports, 332
  in writing process, 179, 197, 223

idiom, 523
imagery, 523
imperative sentence, 9
  exclamation point to end, 9, 143
  period to end, 9, 143
impression
  developing overall, 254
  main, 250
indefinite articles, 26
indefinite pronouns, 16, 28
  as antecedents, 100–101
  possessive of, 163
  subject-verb agreement and, 111–112
independent clauses, 59
  in complex sentences, 67
  in compound sentences, 66
  as simple sentence, 66

indirect objects, 39, 40–41
  compound, 41
  distinguishing between object of a preposition, 41
  gerunds as, 55
  noun clauses as, 65
  pronouns used as, 94
indirect quotations, 158
inferences, 374, 392–393, 523
infinitive(s), 51, 56–57
infinitive phrases, 56–57
  commas after, 150
  distinguishing between prepositional phrases and, 57
  as fragments, 70
informal English, 120
informal letters, 353–356
  form of, 355
  parts of, 354
informal outlines, 403, 404
  creating, 325–326

informal speaking, 451–452
information
  adding, in revising, 188
  criteria for validity of, 377
  gathering, 264–265, 333–334, 455
  organizing, 266–271, 455
informative speech, purpose of, 454

informative writing, 180, 261–275, 399
  body in, 273
  conclusion in, 261, 273
  details in, 232, 265
  drafting in, 271–273
  editing in, 275
  introduction in, 261, 271–272
  organizational patterns for, 201
  prewriting in, 262–271
  publishing in, 275
  revising in, 274–275
  structure of, 261
  supporting sentences in, 261
  transitions in, 201
  voice in, 203
initials, abbreviations for, 144
inquiring as strategy for exploring subject, 184
inside address, in business letter, 358, 359
intensive pronouns, 15
interest inventory, taking, in finding subjects, 177
interjections, 37
  commas after, 150
internal conflict, 316
internal rhyme, 524
Internet terms, capitalization of, 138
interpretation, 524
interrogative pronouns, 17, 28
  who versus *whom*, 98
interrogative sentence, 9
  question mark to end, 9, 143
interrupting words, subject-verb agreement and, 107
intransitive verbs, 20
introduction
  drafting, 186, 234, 340–341
  in informative writing, 271–272
  in persuasive writing, 277
  in research report, 331
introductory elements, commas after, 150

inverted order, 6, 7
inverted sentences, 6–7
invitations, 356
irony, 524
irregular comparison, 117
irregular verbs, 74–76
italics
  for foreign words and phrases, 156
  for letters, numbers, and words, 156
  for names of vehicles, 156
  for titles of longer works, 155–156

J

jargon, 419, 524
journal
  keeping in, finding subject, 178, 313
  spelling, 437
  two-column, 385, 388, 390

K

K-W-L chart, 385

L

language(s). *See also* foreign languages
  capitalization of names of, 138
  figurative, 252
  persuasive, 285
learning log, keeping in, finding subject, 178
learn/teach, 78
leave/let, 78–79
legend, 517, 524
let/leave, 78–79
letters (alphabetical)
  apostrophes with, 166
  forming plurals of, 444
  informal, 353–356
  italics for, 156
  of regret, 356
  of request, 360
  social, 356
  thank-you, 356
letters (correspondence)
  of application, 362
  business, 357–364

capitalization of parts of, 131
commas to set off parts of, 147
of complaint, 361
envelopes for, 363
informal, 353–356
invitations as, 356
of regret, 356
of request, 360
social, 356
thank-you, 356
limerick, 520
linking verbs, 21–22
distinguishing from action
verbs, 22
listening, 456–459
critically, 458–459
to enjoy and appreciate, 457
for information, 457–458
taking notes, 457–458
list of items, colon to introduce,
170
literary analysis, 313
developing skills of, 313
literary essay, 312–329
drafting, 327–328
editing, 329
prewriting, 320–326
publishing, 329
revising, 328–329
literary genres, 314, 517–521
characteristics of, 314
literary responses, synthesizing
personal responses and, 321
literary terms, 522–526
literary works, evaluating, 319
literature
characteristics of great, 320
famous characters from,
492–501
questions for evaluating, 320
responding to, 314–320
from literary knowledge,
316–317
from personal experience,
315–316
questions for finding
meaning, 318–320
loaded words, 379, 459
logical organization, 185
arranging categories in,
266–267
lyric, 520

M

magazines
italics for titles of, 155, 156
quotation marks for articles
in, 157
main ideas, 181
identifying, 387–388
main impression, 250
meaning, creating, in critical
reading, 381–382
media titles
italics for longer, 155–156
quotation marks for shorter,
157–158
memoir, 519, 524
memorials, capitalization of, 138
mental pictures, making, 395
metaphors, 252, 317, 393, 524
meter, in poetry, 311, 317, 524
misplaced adjective clauses, 63
misplaced modifiers, 46
mnemonic devices, 437
modified block style, 357
modifiers, 25. See also
adjective(s); adverb(s)
choosing specific, 208–209
misplaced, 46
monitoring, 396–397
months, abbreviations for, 144
monuments, capitalization of, 138
mood, 524
moons, capitalization of names
of, 137
motivation, 524
movies, italics for titles of, 155, 156
music titles, italics for longer, 155
mystery, 518
myths, 518, 524
characters, places, and
creatures from, 502–512

N

narrative poetry, 520
narrative writing
common transitions in, 201
organizational pattern for, 201
voice in, 203
narrators, 524
in short stories, 296
nationalities, capitalization of
names of, 136

Native American origins, words
with, 434
natural order of sentence, 6, 7
negatives, double, 119, 124
newspapers, italics for titles of,
155, 156
nominative case, 89, 90–92
nonessential elements, commas to
set off, 153
nonfiction, 524
guide to genres for, 519
nonsense verse, 520
nonstandard American English,
418
nonstandard English, 120
notes
organizing, 337–338
taking, 335–336, 403–405
on speech, 457–458
noun(s)
abstract, 11
choosing specific, 207
collective, 12
common, 12
compound, 11, 171, 422, 443
concrete, 11
defined, 11
of direct address, 151
distinguishing between
adjectives and, 27
proper, 12
use of, as adjectives, 27
noun clauses, 65
introductory words for, 65
novels, 314, 518, 524
number(s)
apostrophes with, 166
hyphens with, 172
italics for, 156
in pronoun-antecedent
agreement, 99
in subject-verb agreement,
103–104
numerals, forming plurals of, 444
nursery rhyme, 520

O

objective case, 89, 93–95
object of a preposition
compound, 34
distinguishing between
indirect objects and, 41

gerunds as, 55
noun clauses as, 65
pronouns used as, 94
relative pronouns as, 61
objects
direct, 39–40
indirect, 39, 40–41
observing, in developing subject,
181–182
occasion, considering, in prewriting, 180
onomatopoeia, 310, 317, 524
opinions, 278–279, 372, 458
distinguishing facts from,
372–373
identifying, 390–391
opinion words, 373
oral tradition, 524
order of importance, 185
arranging details in, 233
in informative writing,
201, 256, 267
in ordering evidence, 326
in persuasive writing, 201, 283
transitions for, 226, 285
organization
basic structure in, 200–203
cause/effect, 201, 256, 283,
326, 389–390
checklist for, 189, 227, 238, 247,
258, 274, 289, 303, 329, 351
chronological, 185, 201, 226,
233, 243, 244, 256, 267, 301
comparison/contrast, 201, 226,
267, 269, 283, 285, 326,
388–389
in descriptive writing, 256
developmental order, 267
in effective compositions, 237
in informative writing, 269
logical, 185
of notes, 337–338
order of importance, 185, 201,
267, 283
sequential order, 233, 256, 267
spatial, 185, 201, 226, 233,
254–255, 255, 267
other or *else*, 118
outcomes
predicting, 393
in short stories, 296
outlines, 338–339
capitalization in, 132
creating informal, 325–326

informal, 403, 404
making, 270–271, 283
periods in, 146
oxymoron, 524

P

pantomime, 521
parable, 518, 524
paragraphs
coherence of, 226
concluding sentence in, 219,
224, 241
defined, 219
strategies for developing,
225–226
structure of, 219–221
supporting sentences in, 219,
223–224, 241
topic sentence in, 219, 221–222,
241
unity of, 226
varied structures in, 221
parenthetical citations, 342–343
formats of, 343
parenthetical expressions
commas to enclose, 152
common, 152
parody, 518, 524
participial phrases, 53–54
commas after, 150
as fragments, 70
misplaced, 54
participles, 51–52
distinguishing between
gerunds and, 55
distinguishing between
verbs and, 52–53
past, 52
present, 52
parts of speech labels,
in dictionary, 431
passages, quotation marks for,
160–161
passive voice, 86–87
past participles, 52, 73
past perfect progressive tense, 85
past perfect tense, 79, 81
past progressive tense, 85
past tense, 79, 80
peer conferencing, 190
periods
with abbreviations, 143–144

to end a declarative sentence,
9, 143
to end an imperative sentence,
9, 143
in outlines, 146
with quotation marks, 159
personal experiences, responding
to literature from, 315–316
personalized editing checklist,
191, 205
personal narratives, 241–242
chronological order of, 243
drafting, 244–245
editing, 246–247
prewriting, 243
revising, 246–247
structure of, 241
personal pronouns, 14
cases of, 89–98
as direct objects, 93
first-person, 14
gender of, 99
as indirect objects, 94
nominative case of, 89, 90–92
objective case of, 89, 93–95
as objects of prepositions, 94
possessive case of, 89, 95–96,
163
as predicate nominatives,
91–92
second-person, 14
as subjects, 90–91
third-person, 14
personal responses, synthesizing
literary responses and, 321
personal response statement, 315
personal titles
abbreviations for, 144
capitalization of, 140
personal writing, 241–247, 399
checklist for good writing in,
247
drafting in, 244–245
editing in, 246
personal narratives in, 241–242
prewriting in, 243
revising in, 246
personification, 524
persons, capitalization of names
of, 133
persuasive speech, purpose of,
454
persuasive writing, 180, 277–289
body in, 277

common transitions in, 201
conclusion in, 277
details in, 232
developing argument in, 282
drafting in, 285–288
editing in, 288–289
facts and opinions in, 278–279
introduction in, 277
organizational patterns in, 201, 283
organizing argument in, 283
prewriting in, 280–284
revising in, 288–289
structure of, 277–278
voice in, 203
writing outline, 283–284

phrases
adjective, 45–46
adverb, 45, 46–48
appositive, 48–49
defined, 45
as fragments, 69–70
gerund, 55–56, 56
infinitive, 56–57, 150
participial, 53–54, 150
prepositional, 34–35, 45–48, 150
verb, 5–6, 23
plagiarism, 340, 342
planets, capitalization of names of, 137
plays, 314. *See also* drama
italics for titles of, 155, 156
writing scenes for, 305–308
characters in, 307
conflict in, 307
dialogue in, 307–308
props in, 308
sentence fluency in, 308
setting in, 307
stage directions in, 305, 308
plot, 524
in drama, 317
in fiction, 316, 318
in short story, 297–298

plurals, 440–444
agreement of verb and, 104
apostrophes in certain, 166
for compound words, 443
for nouns ending in *f* or *fe*, 443
for nouns ending in *o*, 442
for nouns ending in *y*, 441
for numerals, letters, symbols, and words as words, 444
for regular nouns, 440–441

poetry, 291, 309, 314, 524
capitalization of first words of, 131
figures of speech in, 317
finding idea for, 309
guide to genres for, 519–520
italics for longer, 155
meter in, 311, 317
questions for finding meaning in, 319
quotation marks for short, 157
rhyme in, 311, 317
rhythm in, 311
shape of, 317
sound devices in, 310, 317
speaker in, 317
theme in, 317
word choice in, 311
writing, 309–311
point of view, 298–299, 524–525
in fiction, 316
first-person, 298–299
third-person, 298–299
voice and, 299
positive degree, 115
possession
apostrophes to show, 163
relative pronouns to show, 61
possessive adjectives, 96
possessive case, 89, 95–96
possessive pronouns, 14
apostrophes and, 164
distinguishing between contractions and, 96

predicate(s), 3–8
complete, 5
compound, 8
defined, 3
simple, 5
predicate adjectives, 39, 43
compound, 43
predicate nominatives, 39, 42
compound, 42
gerunds as, 55
noun clauses as, 65
pronouns used as, 91–92
predictions, 383
checking, 398
prefixes, 421, 445
prepositional phrases, 34–35, 45–48
commas after, 150
distinguishing between infinitive phrases and, 57

as fragments, 69
prepositions, 33–35
common, 33
defined, 33
distinguishing between adverbs and, 35
pre-reading, using writing in, 385
present participles, 52, 73
present perfect progressive tense, 85
present perfect tense, 79, 80
present progressive tense, 85
present tense, 79, 80
prewriting, 175, 176–185, 231–233
arranging details in logical order, 233
brainstorming in, 182, 185, 209, 210, 232
building plot in, 297–298
choosing subject in, 231, 243, 252, 262, 280, 321, 332
clustering in, 183, 185, 209, 210
considering purpose, question, and audience in, 180
creating informal outline in, 325–326
in creative writing, 297–301
defined, 178
determining point of view, 298–299
developing subject, 181–184, 253–255
developing theme in, 322–323
developing thesis in, 281–282, 322–323, 336–337
developing thesis statement, 281–282
developing voice in, 180
essay answers, 413
finding subject in, 176–177
gathering evidence in, 323–325
gathering information in, 333–334
identifying audience, 280
in descriptive writing, 252–255
in informative writing, 262–271
limiting subject in, 231, 243, 263–264, 321–322, 333
listing supporting details in, 232
of literary essay, 320–326
note taking in, 335–336
occasion in, 180
organizing details in, 185
organizing notes in, 337–338

outlining in, 338–339
in personal writing, 243
in persuasive writing, 280–284
research reports, 332–340
synthesizing personal and
 literary responses, 321
prior knowledge, using, 383
problem/solution, 375
progressive verb forms, 85–86
prologue, 525
pronouns, 12–17
 agreement with antecedents,
 98–101
 antecedents for, 13, 98–101
 apostrophes with, 164
 defined, 12
 demonstrative, 16–17, 28
 indefinite, 16, 28
 intensive, 15
 interrogative, 17, 28
 personal, 14
 possessive, 14
 reflexive, 15
 relative, 61–63
pronunciation of entry word in
 dictionary, 428–429
proofreading, 191–192
 symbols for, 192
propaganda, 378–389, 525
proper adjectives, 27
 capitalization of, 27, 139
proper nouns, 12
 awards, 137
 brand names, 137
 bridges and buildings, 137
 capitalization, 12, 132–138
 geographical names, 133–134
 Internet terms, 137
 languages and specific school
 courses, 137
 monuments and memorials,
 137
 names of groups and
 businesses, 135
 names of nationalities and
 names of persons and
 animals, 133
 names of planets, moons,
 stars, and constellations, 137
 nouns of historical
 importance, 135
 races, 136
 religions, religious references,
 136–137

specific time periods and
 events, 136
 vehicles, 137
props, 308
pros, 282
prose, 525
protagonist, 525
proverb, 525
psalm, 520
publishing, 176, 193–195, 239
 in creative writing, 304
 defined, 193
 in descriptive writing, 259
 in informative writing, 275
 literary essays, 329
 outside school, 193
 of research reports, 351
 in school, 193
 standard manuscript form
 and, 193–195
pun, 525
purposes
 adjusting reading rate to,
 401–402
 considering, in prewriting, 180
 determining, 231
 for giving speech, 453–454
 setting, for reading, 383

Q

question(s)
 audience profile, 180
 in exploring subject, 184
 while reading, 394
question marks
 to end a interrogative
 sentence, 9, 143
 with quotation marks, 159–160
quotation(s)
 block, 161
 direct, 158–160
 indirect, 158
 with a quotation, 161
quotation marks
 capital letters with, 159
 with direct quotations, 158
 punctuating direct quotations,
 159–160
 in quoting passages, 160–161
 with titles, 157–158
 in writing dialogue, 160

R

races, capitalization of names
 of, 136
radio series, italics for longer, 155
rambling sentences, 216
readers
 conferencing guidelines for,
 190
 sources of responses to
 literature, 314–315
Readers Theatre, 521
reading. *See also* critical reading
 close, 402
 of textbook, 402
 for young adults, 481–490
reading rate, adjusting, to purpose,
 401–402
reading tests, 409–410
recalling, 371
reflecting, 398
reflexive pronouns, 15
refrain, 525
regional dialects, 417
regret, letters of, 356
regular comparison, 115–117
regular verbs, 73
relative pronouns, 61–63
 functions of, 61–63
 misplaced, 63
religion/religious references,
 capitalization of, 136–137
repetition, 217, 310, 525
request, letters of, 360
rereading, 398
research, in finding subject, 177
research reports, 330–351
 body of, 331
 citing sources in, 342–349
 composing title, 342
 conclusion in, 331
 drafting, 340–349
 editing of, 351
 introduction in, 331
 prewriting, 332–340
 publishing, 351
 revising, 350–351
 sentence fluency in, 349
 structure of, 331
 works cited page in, 331
resolution, 525
 in short stories, 296
revising, 175, 188–190, 237–238

adding details and information in, 188

checking for accuracy in, 350

checking for adequate development, 246, 350

checklist in, 189, 238, 247, 258–259, 274–275, 289, 303–304, 328–329, 350–351

clarity in, 288

coherence in, 190, 288

in creative writing, 303–304

defined, 188

deleting unnecessary words or ideas in, 188

in descriptive writing, 257–259

essay answers, 415

generalizations, 375

getting second opinion in, 350

in informative writing, 274–275

literary essays, 328–329

in personal writing, 246

rearranging, 188

of research reports, 350–351

strategies for, 189

substituting words and sentences, 188

time out for reflecting in, 258

unity in, 288

revision-in-context, 411

rhyme, 310, 311

rhyme scheme, 311, 317, 525

rhythm, 311, 525

rising action, 525

root words, 421

run-on sentences, 71

S

saga, 518, 525

salutation

in business letter, 358, 359

in informal letter, 354, 355

satire, 518, 525

scanning, 401

school courses, capitalization of names of, 138

schwa, 429

science fiction, 291, 518

screenplay, 521

second opinion, getting, 350

semicolons

with compound sentences, 168

with conjunctive adverbs, 169

in forming compound sentences, 66

in a series, 170

with transitional words, 169

senses

appealing to, 209–210

using, in learning to spell, 438

sensory details, 525

sensory diagram, 253

sensory words, 250–251

sentence(s)

capitalization of first words of, 131

complex, 67

compound, 66

concluding, 219, 224, 241

creating variety in, 213–215

declarative, 9

defined, 3

exclamatory, 9

imperative, 9

interrogative, 9

inverted order, 6, 7

natural order, 6, 7

predicate of, 3–8

rambling, 216

run-on, 71

simple, 66

subject of, 3–8

supporting, 219, 223–224, 241

topic, 219, 221–222, 241

varying beginnings of, 214–215

varying construction of, 215

varying length of, 214

writing concise, 216–217

sentence combining, 211–215

by coordinating, 212

with specific details, 211

by subordinating, 213

sentence-completion tests, 408–409

sentence-correction questions, 411

sentence fluency, 204–205

checklist for, 189, 227, 238, 247, 259, 275, 289, 304, 329, 351

in descriptive writing, 258

in plays, 308

in research reports, 349

varying sentence beginnings in, 205

varying sentence patterns in, 205

varying sentence types in, 205

in writing process, 204–205, 216

sentence fragments, 3, 69–71

clause, 70–71

phrase, 69–70

sequencing, 386

sequential order

in descriptive writing, 256

in informative writing, 267

arranging details in, 233

series, separating items in

with commas, 148

with semicolons, 170

setting, 525

in drama, 317

in fiction, 316, 318

in plays, 307

in short stories, 296, 300–301

shape of poem, 317

shortened forms of words, 435

short stories, 291–304, 314, 518, 525

building plot in, 297–298

characters in, 299–300

defined, 291

determining point of view, 298–299

drafting, 302–303

editing, 304

elements of, 296

listing events in chronological order, 301

prewriting, 297–301

publishing, 304

revising, 303–304

setting in, 300–301

structure of, 296

voice in, 299

signature

in business letter, 358, 359

in informal letter, 354, 355

similes, 252, 317, 393, 525

simple sentences, 66

simple subjects, 4

singular nouns that have plural forms, subject-verb agreement and, 113

singular subject, agreement of verb, 104

six traits of writing, 197–205

skimming, 383, 401

slang, 418

snob appeal, 379

social letters, 356

soliloquy, 525

sonnet, 520, 526
sound devices, 310, 317
   alliteration, 310, 317
   assonance, 310
   consonance, 310
   onomatopoeia, 310, 317
   repetition, 310
   rhyme, 310
sources, citing, 342–349
spamming, 369
spatial organization
   arranging details in, 233
   in descriptive writing, 201,
     254–255
   in informative writing, 267
   in organizing details, 185,
     254–255
   transitions for, 226, 255
speaker, in poetry, 317
speaker tags, 158
   commas to separate direct
     quotations from, 159
speaking skills
   developing, 451–452
   everyday, 451
   formal, 452
   giving directions, 451–452
   informal, 451–452
speech, 519
   choosing and limiting subject,
     453
   delivering, 456
   gathering and organizing
     information for, 455
   practicing, 455
   preparation of, 453–455
   purpose of, 453–454
   taking notes on, 457–458
spelling
   of entry word in dictionary, 427
   list of words to master, 449
spelling journal, 437
spelling patterns, 438–440
   for plurals, 440–444
   prefixes, 445
   suffixes, 445–448
   words ending in -cede, -ceed,
     or -sede, 441
   words with ie and ei, 439
spelling strategies, 436–449
   learning, 437–438
   senses in, 438
SQ3R, 402
stage directions, in plays, 308

Standard American English, 417
standard English, 120
standardized tests, 405–411
   analogies in, 407–408
   double passage in, 410
   reading in, 409–410
   revision-in-context in, 411
   sentence-completion in,
     408–409
   sentence-correction questions
     in, 411
   strategies for taking, 405
   tests of standard written
     English in, 410–411
   vocabulary tests in, 406
standard manuscript form, 193–195
standard written English, tests of,
   410–411
stanza, 526
stars, capitalization of names of,
   137
state-of-being verbs, 21
storyboards, 387
study skills, 401–405
subject complements, 39
subjects (grammatical), 3–8
   complete, 4
   compound, 8
   defined, 3
   gerunds as, 55
   in inverted order, subject-verb
     agreement and, 108
   noun clauses as, 65
   position of, in sentence, 6
   pronouns used as, 90–91
   relative pronouns as, 61
   simple, 4
   understood, 4
   you and *I* as and subject-verb
     agreement, 110–111
subjects (of composition)
   choosing, 179, 243, 253, 280,
     321, 332, 453
   developing, 253–255
   finding, 176–177
   focusing, 263–264
   limiting, 179, 243, 321–322,
     332, 453
subordinate clauses, 60–65
   in complex sentences, 67
subordinating conjunctions, 64
   sentence combining by, 213
subtext, 526
subtopics, 338

suffixes, 422, 445–448
summarizing, 335, 376–377,
   395–396, 403, 404
   techniques for, 396
superlative degree, 115
superscript, 343
supporting details, 181, 338
supporting points, 338
supporting sentences, 219, 223–224
   in personal narrative, 241
surprise ending, 526
syllables, of entry words in dictionary, 428
symbols, 526
   apostrophes with, 166
   plurals of, 444
symphonies, italics for, 155
synonyms, 406, 422
   as context clue, 420
   in dictionary, 432
synthesizing, 396
   personal and literary
     responses, 321
   techniques for, 396

T

take/bring, 77
tale, 526
tall tales, 518, 526
teach/learn, 78
television series, italics for titles
   of, 155, 156
tenses, verb, 79–86
testimonial, 378, 459
test-taking, 405–415
   essay tests, 411–415
   standardized tests, 405–411
textbook, reading, 402
thank-you letters, 356
that, which, 63
theatre of the absurd, 521
theme, 526
in drama, 317
   in fiction, 16, 318
   in poetry, 317
   in short stories, 296
thesaurus, 422
thesis
   developing, 322–323, 336–337
   working, 336–337
thesis statement
   developing, 281–282, 326

refining, 341
thinking skills, 371–377
third-person narratives, 245
third-person point of view,
    298–299, 525
time
    abbreviations for, 144
    colon in writing hours and
        minutes, 171
    subject-verb agreement and,
        113
timed writing, 415
timelines, 387
time order. *See* chronological
    organization
time periods, capitalization of
    specific, 136
tired words, 419
titles of art works
    capitalization of, 141
    italics of, 156
titles of written works, 526
    capitalization of, 141
    drafting, 187
    italics for longer, 155–156
    quotation marks for shorter,
        157–158
    subject-verb agreement and,
        113, 236
titles showing family relationships,
    capitalization of, 140–141
titles used in direct address,
    capitalization of, 140
tone in fiction, 316
topic sentence, 219, 221–222
    in personal narrative, 241
tragedy, 521, 526
tragic flaw, 526
transitional words, semicolons
    with, 169
transitions, 244–245
    for comparison/contrast, 286
    for order of importance, 285
transitive verbs, 20
triggering events, in short stories,
    296
two-column journal, 385, 388, 390

U

underlining. *See* italics
understanding, monitoring,
    396–397

understood subjects, 4
unity, 226, 273
    checking for, 274, 288
usage, 120–129
    a, an, 121
    at, 123
    accept, except, 121
    advice, advise, 121
    affect, effect, 121
    ain't, 121
    all ready, already, 121
    all together, altogether, 122
    among, between, 122
    amount, number, 122
    anywhere, everywhere,
        nowhere, somewhere, 122
    bad, badly, 123
    bring, take, 77, 123
    can, may, 123
    doesn't, don't, 123
    double negative, 124
    etc., 124
    fewer, less, 124
    good, well, 119, 124
    have, of, 125
    hear, here, 125
    hole, whole, 125
    in, into, 125
    its, it's, 125
    knew, new, 125
    learn, teach, 78, 126
    leave, let, 78–79, 126
    lie, lay, 126
    like, as, 126
    a lot, 122
    rise, raise, 127
    shall, will, 127
    sit, set, 127
    than, then, 127
    that, which, who, 127
    their, there, they're, 128
    theirs, there's, 128
    them, those, 128
    this here, that there, 128
    threw, through, 128
    to, too, two, 129
    when, where, 129
    where, 129
    which, that, 63
    a while, awhile, 123
    who, whom, 98, 129
    whose, who's, 129
    your, you're, 129

V

vehicles
    capitalization of, 138
    italics for names of, 156
Venn diagram, 389
verb(s), 5, 19–23
    action, 19, 22
    choosing specific, 208
    defined, 19
    distinguishing between
        action and linking, 22
    distinguishing between
        participles and, 52–53
    helping, 5–6, 23
    intransitive, 20
    irregular, 74–76
    linking, 21–22
    principal parts of, 73
    progressive forms of, 85–86
    regular, 73
    state-of-being, 21
    transitive, 20
    use of adverbs to modify, 30
    voice of, 86–87
verbals, 51
verb conjugations, 82–84
verb phrases, 5–6, 23
    interrupted, 6
    subject-verb agreement
        and, 105–106
verb tenses, 79–86
    future, 79, 80
    future perfect, 79, 81
    past, 79, 80
    past perfect, 79, 81
    present, 79, 80
    present perfect, 79, 80
    progressive forms, 85–86
vivid words, choosing, 207–210
vocabulary development, 416–435
    antonyms in, 424
    clichés in, 419
    compound nouns in, 423
    connotations in, 419
    denotations in, 419
    determining word meaning in,
        420–424
    dictionary skills in, 424–435
    jargon in, 419
    learning new, 383
    prefixes in, 421
    root words in, 421
    suffixes in, 422

synonyms in, 423
tired words and, 419
varieties of English in, 417–418
vocabulary tests, 406
voice, 526
checklist for, 189, 227, 238, 247,
259, 275, 289, 304, 329, 351
in creative writing, 299
defined, 180, 203
focusing on, in writing, 181, 203
in personal writing, 244
in persuasive writing, 281
voice of verbs
active, 86–87
passive, 86–87

W

which, that, 63
who, whom, 98
word origins
in dictionary, 432–433
foreign languages, 433–434
Native American, 434
unusual, 434–435
words
checklist for choice of, 189,
227, 238, 247, 259, 289, 304,
329, 351
connotation of, 419
in creative writing, 311
deleting unnecessary, 188
denotation of, 419
derived, 427
determining meaning of,
420–424
loaded, 379, 459
opinion, 279, 373
in personal writing, 246
root, 421
sensory, 250–251
specific, 204, 207
substituting, 188
tired, 419
vivid, 207–210
words as words
apostrophes with, 166
forming plurals of, 444
italics for, 156
working thesis, 336–337
works cited page, 331, 345–349
works-consulted page, 346

writer, conferencing guidelines
for, 190
writing
critical, 399
informational, 399
personal, 399
timed, 415
traits of
conventions, 189, 205, 227,
239, 247, 275
ideas, 179, 181, 188, 189,
197–199, 223, 227, 238,
247, 269, 274, 289
organization, 185, 189, 200–
203, 227, 237, 238, 247,
256, 269, 274, 289
sentence fluency, 189,
204–205, 227, 238, 247,
258, 275, 289
voice, 181, 189, 203, 227,
238, 244, 247, 275, 289
word choice, 189, 204, 227,
236, 238, 246, 247,
275, 289
writing process
defined, 175
drafting in, 175, 185–187
editing in, 176, 191–192
prewriting in, 175, 176–185
publishing in, 176, 193–195
revising in, 175, 188–190
writing style
concise sentences in, 216–217
defined, 207
sentence combining in,
211–213
sentence variety in, 213–216
vivid words in, 207–210
written communication, 352–369
business letters as, 357–364
capitalization in, 364
commas in, 363
E-mail as, 365–369
envelopes in, 363
informal letters as, 353–356
purpose of, 353
written works, titles of
capitalization of, 141
italics for, 155–156
quotation marks with, 157–158

Acknowledgments

TEXT CREDITS

"Thank You, Ma'm" by Langston Hughes from *The Langston Hughes Reader*. Copyright © 1958 by Langston Hughes. Renewed © 1986 by George Houston Bass. Reprinted by permission of Harold Ober Associates Incorporated.

from *The American Heritage Student Dictionary*. Copyright © 1998 by Houghton Mifflin Company. Reproduced by permission.

Excerpt from ""Stopping by Woods on a Snowy Evening" by Robert Frost, from *The Poetry of Robert Frost*, edited by Edward Connery Lathem. Copyright 1942, 1951, 1955, 1958, 1962 by Robert Frost, copyright © 1967, 1970 by Lesley Frost Ballantine, copyright 1923, 1930, 1939, © 1969 by Henry Holt & Company. Reprinted by permission of Henry Holt & Company, Inc.

Every reasonable effort has been made to properly acknowledge ownership of all material used. Any omissions or mistakes are unintentional and, if brought to the publisher's attention, will be corrected in future editions.

PHOTO CREDITS

Every reasonable effort has been made to properly acknowledge ownership of all material used. Any omissions or mistakes are unintentional and, if brought to the publisher's attention, will be corrected in future editions.

Page 7: Louie Psihoyos/Science Fiction/Getty Images; Page 8: Lester Lefkowitz/Taxi/Getty Images; Page 13: Philip J. Brittan/Photographer's Choice/Getty Images; Page 15: Abe Gurvin/Stock Illustration RF/Getty Images; Page 16: Vance Vasu/Stock Illustration Source/Getty Images; Page 22: George Doyle/Stockbyte Platinum/Getty Images; Page 27: David Deas/DK Stock/Getty Images; Page 28: Susan Farrington/Photodisc Green/Getty Images; Page 34: Stephen Chemin/Getty Images News/Getty Images; Page 37: Jeff Gross/Getty Images Sport/Getty Images; Page 41: Stockdisc/Stockdisc Premium/Getty Images; Page 43: Robert Warren/Stone/Getty Images; Page 47: Alan Abramowitz/Stone/Getty Images; Page 49: Winold Reiss. American Writer. Pastel, 1925. The Granger Collection, New York; Page 54: Panoramic Images/Getty Images; Page 57: Jill Enfield/Photonica/Getty Images; Page 62: John Drysdale/Hulton Archive/Getty Images; Page 64: Nina Frenkel/Photodisc Red/Getty Images; Page 67: G. Brad Lewis/Science Fiction/Getty Images; Page 77: AFP/Getty Images; Page 79: David Hallett/Getty Images News/Getty Images; Page 81: Fiona Hawthorne/Photodisc Green/Getty Images; Page 84: Hansel and Gretel 20th Century Block Print. © Stapleton Collection/Corbis; Page 87: Henri Matisse (1869–1954) © Vase with Irises. 1912. Oil on cavas. Roman Beniaminson. Hermitage, St. Petersburg, Russia/Bildarchiv Preussischer Kulturbesitz / Art Resouce, NY; Page 91: Jakubaszek/Getty Images Entertainment/Getty Images; Page 93: McMillan/Photodisc Green/Getty Images; Page 95: Yellow Dog Productions/Riser/Getty Images; Page 97: DAJ/Getty Images; Page 105: Joe Raedle/Reportage/Getty Images; Page 108: Eastcott Momatiuk/Stone/Getty Images; Page 110: Photodisc/Photodisc Blue/Getty Images; Page 112: Matthew King/Reportage/Getty Images; Page 134: Astromujoff/Riser/Getty Images; Page 137: Jan Cossiers/The Bridgeman Art Library/Getty Images; Page 140: Dennis M. Ochsner/Photodisc Green/Getty Images; Page 145: Jasper Johns (b. 1930) © VAGA, NY. Map. 1961. Oil on canvas. Digital Image © The Museum of Modern Art/Liscensed by SCALA/Art Resources, NY; Page 147: William Michael Harnett (1848–1892). Still life with letter to Denis Gale, 1879. Art Resource, NY; Page 151: Tay Rees/The Image Bank/Getty Images; Page 158: © Brooklyn Museum/Corbis; Page 167: Stephen Stickler/Stone/Getty Images; Page 171: Tatjana Krizmanic/Photodisc Green/Getty Images; Page 172: © Ron Sachs/CNP/Corbis; Page 176: Alberto Ruggieri/Illustration Works/Getty Images; Page 179: Digital Vision/Getty Images; Page 184: © Richard T. Nowitz/CORBIS; Page 187: Ty Downing/Workbook Stock/Getty Images; Page 190: Photodisc/Photodisc Blue/Getty Images; Page 194: White Packert/Photonica/Getty Images; Page 195: Howard Sokol/Stone/Getty Images; Page 199: Gabriela Hasbun/Taxi/

Getty Images; Page 200: © Gary W. Carter/
CORBIS; Page 208: Ted Humble-Smith/
Photonica/Getty Images; Page 211: Tim Boyle/
Getty Images News/Getty Images; Page 212:
Cousteau Society/The Image Bank/Getty
Images; Page 215: © Bettmann/CORBIS;
Page 214: Identikal/Photodisc Red/Getty Images;
Page 220: Glowimages/Getty Images; Page 222:
David Tipling/Stone/Getty Images; Page 223:
Pony Express: Stamp, 1940. The Granger
Collection, New York; Page 229: Susan LeVan/
Photodisc Green/Getty Images; Page 235:
Lisa Berkshire/Illustration Works/Getty Images;
Page 236: Robert Daly/Riser/Getty Images;
Page 242: © Hulton-Deutsch Collection/CORBIS;
Page 251: Gail Shumway/Taxi/Getty Images;
Page 257: Yann Layma/The Image Bank/Getty
Images; Page 255: AP Images/Robert Spencer
(02040103894); Page 265: © Lester V. Bergman/
CORBIS; Page 268: Bettmann/CORBIS;
Page 273: © Bettmann/CORBIS; Page 278:
© Bill Stormont/CORBIS; Page 284: Photodisc
Blue/Getty Images; Page 293: William H.
Johnson (1901–1970) © Jim. 1930. Oil on canvas
Smithsonian American Art Museum, Washington
DC / Art Resource, NY; Page 298:
© David C./CORBIS; Page 301: © Steve Terrill/
CORBIS; Page 306: Juliet (oil on canvas),
Waterhouse, John William (1849-1917)/Private
Collection, by courtesy of Julian Hartnoll/The
Bridgeman Art Library; Page 317: Corbis; Page
322: © Blue Lantern Studio/Corbis; Page 325:
William H. Johnson (1901–1970) © Minnie. 1930.
Oil on canvas. Smithsonian American Art
Museum, Washington, DC / Art Resource, NY;
Page 337: Hulton Archive/Getty Images;
Page 348: Hulton Archive/Getty Images;
Page 341: © Joseph Sohm; ChromoSohm Inc./
CORBIS; Page 354: Henriette Browne (1829–
1901). A girl writing. French, 19th century. Victoria
& Albert Museum, London/Art Resource, NY;
Page 359: Steve Cole/Photodisc Green/Getty
Images; Page 366: Frank Renlie/Illustration
Works/Getty Images; Page 373: Jennifer Knaack/
Photodisc Green/Getty Images; Page 384:
© PictureNet/CORBIS; Page 387: © The Art
Archive/Corbis; Page 391: © Images.com/Corbis;
Page 403: © Gianni Dagli Orti/CORBIS;
Page 406: © Images.com/Corbis; Page 408:
© Ralph A. Clevenger/CORBIS; Page 420:

© Bob Krist/CORBIS; Page 423: © Fine Art
Photographic Library/CORBIS; Page 431:
© Images.com/Corbis; Page 433: © Images.com/
Corbis; Page 441: © Reuters/CORBIS;
Page 454: © Heiko Wolfraum/dpa/Corbis;
Page 457: Peter Hamlin/Photodisc Red/Getty
Images; Page 466: Hulton Archive/Getty Images;
Page 469: Time & Life Pictures / Getty Images;
Page 476: Getty Images Entertainment/Getty
Images; Page 479: Hulton Archive/Getty Images;
Page 492: John Tenniel (1820-1914). Illustration
from Lewis Carroll's "Alice in Wonderland."
Snark/Art Resource, NY; Page 495: Thomas
Hart Benton (1889-1975) © VAGA, NY. Huck
Finn. 1936, Lithograph. Art Resource, NY;
Page 498: © Bettmann/CORBIS; Page 515:
© Blue Lantern Studio/CORBIS